THE *Chef's*
COMPANION

A Culinary Dictionary

THE *Chef's* COMPANION

THIRD EDITION

Elizabeth Riely

Illustrations by
David Miller

WILEY

JOHN WILEY & SONS, INC.

For my Mother and Father

P R E F A C E

The changes in three editions of *The Chef's Companion* mark the transitions in the American culinary scene at large. The main difference in this third edition is the Chinese entries: they have been entirely overhauled. Most are now in Pinyin, the system of romanization that China officially adopted in 1979. The older system, Wade-Giles, remains correct but outmoded.

In 1980, Mandarin Chinese became the official national language throughout China. The various regional dialects are still spoken locally, but more and more Chinese people all over the country understand and use Mandarin. New emigration policies have allowed mainland Chinese to come to the United States, and indeed they are, more than ever before, perhaps altering the Cantonese character of many Chinese restaurants here. We know their dishes by their Cantonese names, but many of them are enjoyed on the mainland as well. Looking forward rather than back, this edition gives the main entries of Chinese dishes in Mandarin (with a few exceptions) rather than Cantonese. Numerous cross-references serve as signposts to save readers from confusion and guide them on their way.

Wine entries in this new edition reflect the huge growth of that industry outside Europe—in Australia, New Zealand, South Africa, Chile, Argentina, Canada, and the United States. The dictionary now includes many more grape varieties, as well as regions, styles, and winemaking terms, but no specific vineyards; such detailed information changes too rapidly for inclusion here. Thus readers will find full entries on Shiraz and Riesling, Vin Santo and Viognier, *vendange tardive* and Meritage, but nothing on Château Cheval Blanc or Stag's Leap.

Political events and new immigration have brought to our markets an explosion of vegetables and fruits previously unknown here, often from exotic cultures and corners of the world. Simultaneously, the revival of old varieties, so-called heirloom plants, and new hybrids have needed recording in the shifting geography of the edible landscape. In addition, many entries have sharper detail and updated information. Others concern controversial new or threatening issues, such as genetic modification (GM) and bovine spongiform encephalopathy (BSE, also known as mad cow disease). Familiar foodstuffs taken for granted in the first two editions are now included with fully commensurate entries.

Readers who need more information should look at the updated bibliography. I hope they will let me know of any errors, which are mine alone.

A C K N O W L E D G M E N T S

I wish to thank those people who have so generously helped me with this third edition of *The Chef's Companion*. Their names belong beside those whom I have acknowledged in previous editions. Scott McKay and Sheryl Avruch gave important technical assistance. Sari Abul Jabein of Casablanca and Zaki Royan of Helmand, both restaurants in Cambridge, Massachusetts, aided me in the pronunciation of Middle Eastern and Afghan dishes. The Robert Family of Maison Robert in Boston have given freely of their time and experience *pour la cuisine française*.

Alvaro Ribeiro and John Alexander dispensed cheer along with specific information on Portuguese and American terms. Laxmi Rao once more shared her knowledge of Indian cooking. Members of the Culinary Historians of Boston continue to sharpen my awareness of food past and present; Dr. Wilfred Arnold's talk on absinthe was particularly illuminating. I have relied on Alice Arndt for graciously replying to all my questions on spices and cooking in Afghanistan, and on Nancy Stutzman for her help on nutrition and public health. Lynn Kay and Sarah Boardman have provided detailed answers to my queries as well as friendship at every turn. Florence Trefethen bore more than her share of responsibilities for the *Radcliffe Culinary Times*, allowing me to finish this revision on schedule.

I would like to thank the authors of two recent books that have been an immense help to me. Alan Davidson's *The Oxford Companion to Food* is magnificent and masterly in its scope and execution. Elizabeth Schneider's *Vegetables from Amaranth to Zucchini: The Essential Reference* is a cornucopia of information on unfamiliar produce.

Over many years, John Riely has supplied me with excellent books that have proved to be invaluable resources. Suzanne Cohen's insight and outlook have genuinely influenced this book, indeed all my work. Warm thanks go to Michael Loo for sharing his understanding, both textual and culinary, of Chinese cooking in the United States and Asia. Ying Bai, with the assistance of Eileen Lee, contributed her scholarly expertise in Chinese language with accuracy, skill, and good humor. Nicholas A. Anagnostis's close reading of the text, extensive knowledge of food and wine, and keen curiosity have added precision and depth to this edition.

Michael A. Choate of the Lescher Agency has encouraged me with his wise counsel and his belief in my abilities; Susan Lescher has again provided her understanding and knowledge of publishing. My gratitude also goes to those at John Wiley & Sons for their high standards throughout: to Pamela Chirls, culinary editor at the outset, for her enthusiasm for a third edition; to Susan Wyler, culinary editor, for improving the dictionary with her broad experience and discerning judgment; to Amy Handy, copy editor, who thought about the meaning as well as the correctness of entries; to Carlye Lay, designer, for her clear and elegant design; and to Monique A. Calello, managing editor, for listening to me as she expertly brought the book to publication.

To my sister, Emily Klarberg, and her husband, Richard Klarberg, I give particular and hearty thanks. They fielded all my questions and gave unqualified support at a crucial time. My sons, Christopher and Andrew Riely, have helped me more than they can know, especially as the deadline approached, with their patience and good sense. Lastly, I wish to pay homage to my father and the memory of my mother, who always nourished my interest in food and gastronomy and to whom this book is dedicated.

P R O N U N C I A T I O N   G U I D E

Vowels

A

a   = short a as in "apple"
ah   = a as in "fava"
ay   = long a as in "bake"
ar   = ar as in "carve"
aahr   = ar as in "garni"
anh   = nasal an as in "blanc" (also amh)

E

e or eh = short e as in "set"
ee   = long e as in "leek"
eu   = eu as in "feu"
enh   = nasal en as in "entrée" (first e; also emh)

I

i   = short i as in "mix"
ī   = long i as in "knife"
inh   = nasal in as in "vin" (also imh)
ee   = i as in "bistro"

O

o   = short o as in "hot"
ō   = long o as in "rosemary"
oh   = o as in "pomme"
onh   = nasal on as in "fond" (also omh)
eu   = ö as in "Möhre"
ow   = ao as in "bacalao"

U

u or uh	=	short u as in "butter"
oo	=	long u as in "tuna"
ü	=	French u as in "tu" or German ü as in "Küche"
unh	=	nasal un as in "aucun" (also umh)

Consonants

g	=	hard g as in "gumbo"
j	=	hard j as in "juniper"
jh	=	soft j as in "julienne"
kh	=	gutteral ch as in "challah" or "Kuchen"
s	=	s as in "salad"
z	=	s as in "risotto"
ts	=	z or zz as in "pizza"

Rhythm and Stress

Syllables in uppercase show emphasis. A double dash (—) in some Turkish words denotes an extra moment's pause.

This pronunciation guide aims for clarity and simplicity, using a minimum of diacritical marks. Some sounds foreign to English are difficult to render in phonetic transcription—for example, the French r as in "croissant"; the German ch as in "Küche"; and the Vietnamese ng as in "gung." Some words sound just as they look and so have no transcription.

Readers should note that the phonetic guide tells how to say the term in the original language, not in common Americanized pronunciation (see sauter, dim sum, Spätzle).

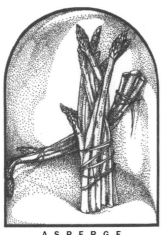

A S P E R G E

Aal [ahl]   German for eel.

abadejo [ah-bah-DAY-hō]   Spanish for fresh cod.

abaissage [a-bes-sajh]   Rolling out pastry dough, in French.

abalone [a-bah-LŌ-nee]   A MOLLUSK whose large adductor muscle connecting its single shell is edible; used widely in Japanese and Chinese cooking, either fresh, dried, or canned; found throughout the Pacific Ocean, off the coast of California, and in the English Channel, where it is called ormer.

abatis [a-ba-tee]   French for external poultry trimmings, such as wing tips, necks, and feet; sometimes used interchangeably with ABATS for giblets.

abats [a-bah]   French for poultry giblets and meat offal; internal organs or variety meats, such as hearts, liver, sweetbreads, and gizzards; sometimes used interchangeably with ABATIS.

abbacchio [ah-BAH-kyō]   Italian for a very young suckling lamb.

abgusht [ahb-GOOSHT]   Stew in Persian cooking, usually of lamb and vegetables.

abricot [a-bree-kō]   French for apricot.

1

absinthe [ab-sinht]   A bitter green liqueur, very popular in France in the late nineteenth and early twentieth centuries, made from WORMWOOD, anise, and other herbs. Typically, it was diluted with water and poured over a sugar cube on a slotted spoon into a glass, turning an opalescent yellow, shown in the paintings of Toulouse-Lautrec and others. Its toxic powers, from the chemical thujone, caused it to be outlawed in many countries. PASTIS, containing no thujone, is related.

abura [ah-boo-rah]   Japanese for oil; *aburage* means deep-fried tofu.

acaçá [ah-ka-SAH]   A Brazilian porridge, similar to PIRÃO, of coconut milk and rice flour, which is molded, cooled, and sliced, to be served with sauces and stews; sometimes steamed in banana leaves.

acarajé   See AKKRA.

acciuga [ah-CHOO-gah]   Italian for anchovy.

accra de morue [AH-krah deu mor-ü]   Salt cod fritters from the French Caribbean eaten as an hors d'oeuvre; related to another fritter, AKKRA.

aceite [ah-CHAY-tay]   Spanish for oil, often but not necessarily olive oil.

aceituna [ah-chay-TOO-nah]   Spanish for olive.

acetic acid   The acid in vinegar that comes from a second fermentation of wine, beer, or cider.

aceto [ah-CHAY-tō]   Italian for VINEGAR; see also BALSAMIC VINEGAR.

aceto-dolce [ah-CHAY-tō-DŌL-chay]   A sweet-and-sour mixture of vegetables and fruits used in Italy as an ANTIPASTO.

achar [ah-CHAHR]   Pickle in Indian cuisine; also a special curry that is piquant with blended pickle spices.

achiote [ah-CHYŌ-tay]   ANNATTO seeds used in Latin American cooking, primarily to impart a yellow or orange color; often sold in a paste that combines annatto with garlic, cumin, Mexican oregano, and citrus juice.

acidophilus milk   Milk slightly soured with the *Lactobacillus acidophilus* bacterium, which converts the lactose in milk to lactic acid, making it both easy to digest and healthful.

acidulated water   Water to which a small amount of lemon juice or vinegar has been added; used to prevent fruits and vegetables from discoloring and to blanch certain foods, such as SWEETBREADS.

ackee   The pod of a tropical fruit that bursts open when ripe to expose the yellow flesh and black seeds; eaten for breakfast with salt fish in Jamaica.

adega [ah-DAY-gah] A Portuguese wine cellar or storage space, usually above ground, like a French *chai* as opposed to *cave*.

adobo [ah-DŌ-bō] Spanish for marinade; the word extends to the method of preparing meat or seafood in a marinade and to the dish itself; the Mexican version is hot with chilies, the Philippine pungent with vinegar.

adrak [ah-DRAHK] Fresh ginger, in Indian cuisine.

adzuki See AZUKI.

aemono [ī-mō-nō] Japanese for salad or dressed foods; a Japanese version of salade COMPOSÉE with a tofu- or miso-based dressing.

agar-agar [AH-gar-AH-gar] An Asian seaweed used by commercial food processors as a gelatin substitute in soups, sauces, jellies, and ice cream; it has a remarkable capacity for absorbing liquids—far greater than that of GELATIN or ISINGLASS.

age [ah-gay] Japanese for deep-fried.

aging A method of improving and maturing the flavor of a food, such as game, cheese, or wine, by allowing controlled chemical changes to take place over time.

agiter [a-jhee-tay] To stir, in French.

aglio [AH-lyō] Italian for garlic.

agneau [a-nyō] French for lamb.

agnello [ah-NYEL-lō] Italian for lamb.

agnolotti [ah-nyō-LOHT-tee] Stuffed squares of pasta, such as ravioli, with a meat filling, in Italian cooking.

agrio [ah-GREE-ō] Spanish for sour.

agrumes [a-grüm] French for citrus.

aguacate [ah-gwah-KAH-tay] Spanish for avocado.

aguardiente [ah-gwar-DYEN-tay] A very strong Spanish liqueur, similar to Italian *grappa* or French MARC.

aiglefin [AY-gluh-FINH] French for haddock.

aigre [AY-gruh] French for sour, tart, sharp, bitter.

aiguillette [ay-gwee-yet] In French cuisine, a thin strip of poultry cut lengthwise from the breast; a strip of meat cut lengthwise with the grain.

ail [ī] French for garlic.

aïoli [ī-yō-lee]   A garlic mayonnaise from French Provence, thick and strongly flavored, usually served with salt cod and poached vegetables, BOURRIDE, and other traditional dishes; also spelled *ailloli*.

airelle rouge [ay-rel roojh]   French for cranberry.

aji [ah-jee]   Japanese for horse mackerel.

ají [ah-HEE]   Spanish-American for hot chili pepper; also refers to a dish in which hot peppers are a major ingredient, as *ají de gallina*.

ajilimójili [ah-HEE-lee-MŌ-hee-lee]   Puerto Rican pepper and garlic sauce served with pork and other meats.

ajo [AH-hō]   Spanish for garlic; *ajo e ojo* is an Italian dialect name for a pasta sauce of garlic sautéed in olive oil.

ajouter [a-jhoo-tay]   To add an ingredient, in French.

ajowan [ah-joh-WAHN]   A plant, originally from southern India, whose small seeds have a pungent thymelike flavor with undertones of caraway and cumin, to which it is closely related. Ajowan is used both whole and crushed in Indian and Ethiopian cooking, where it gives flavor and aids in digestion. The plant, also spelled *ajwain*, is sometimes called *omam* or bishop's weed.

akkra [AHK-rah]   Caribbean dried pea or bean fritters, found with variations on several islands, descended from a Nigerian snack. Brazilian *acarajé*, black-eyed pea fritters served with a spicy shrimp sauce, is closely related.

akvavit [ahk-vah-VEET]   A colorless Swedish liquor, aqua vitae or "water of life," distilled from grain or potatoes and flavored variously, often with caraway; served very cold and drunk neat, often with beer, before or after the meal.

à la [ah lah]   In the style of, the full phrase being *à la mode de*; this term designates a specific garnish. Often the *à la* is assumed rather than stated, so that a dish such as *Sole à la bonne femme*, for instance, is usually contracted to *Sole bonne femme*. The same holds true for the Italian *alla*.

alaria [ah-LAHR-yah]   Seaweed similar to WAKAME; mild in flavor, thick and crunchy in texture, usually dried and presoaked before it is cooked in soups.

albacore   See TUNA.

Albariño [al-bah-REE-nyō]   A white wine grape variety, widely grown in Galicia, in northwestern Spain, and in Portugal, where it is known as Alvarinho, for VINHO VERDE; fresh, fruity, with high acidity and considerable promise.

albigeoise, à l' [ah l'al-bee-jhwahz]   In the style of Albi in southern France, that is, garnished with tomatoes, ham, and potato croquettes.

albóndigas [ahl-BOHN-dee-gahs]   Spicy Spanish or Mexican meatballs made of pork, beef, etc.; also a dumpling.

Albuféra [al-BÜ-fayr-ah]   In classic French cuisine, a SUPRÊME sauce with meat glaze and pimento butter, named after the lagoon near Valencia in Spain. The garnish *à l'Albuféra* consists of poultry stuffed with rice, TRUFFLES, and FOIE GRAS, served with elaborate tartlets, named for one of Napoléon's generals. The name also designates a small pastry topped with chopped almonds.

albumen [al-BYOO-men]   The protein portion of egg white, comprising its greater part, which coagulates with heat; also found in milk, animal blood, plants, and seeds.

alcachofa [ahl-kah-CHŌ-fah]   Spanish for artichoke.

alcohol   See FERMENTATION.

al dente   See DENTE, AL.

ale   English beer made from unroasted barley malt and hops, quickly top-fermented, and drunk fresh; usually stronger and more bitter than beer; varies in color from light to dark.

Aleppo pepper [al-LEP-pō]   A dark red hot chili pepper variety, not available in the West, named for the city of Aleppo in northern Syria, whose cuisine is celebrated in that region. The pepper is used fresh in dishes such as MUHAM-MARA, also used dried and powdered.

algérienne, à l' [ah l'al-jhayr-yen]   Garnished with tomatoes braised in oil and sweet-potato croquettes, in French cuisine.

alicot [al-ee-kō]   A dish of duck or goose wings and giblets braised with cèpes and chestnuts, from southwestern France.

Aligoté [al-ee-gō-tay]   A white wine grape variety planted in Burgundy, producing crisp, acidic whites best drunk young.

alioli [ahl-YŌ-lee]   Spanish for AÏOLI.

alla [ahl-lah]   Italian for in the style of; see À LA.

allemande [al-leh-mahnd]   Veal VELOUTÉ reduced with white wine and mush-room essence, flavored with lemon juice, and bound with egg yolks. *Sauce allemande*, which means "German sauce," is a basic classic sauce in French cuisine.

allspice   A spice from the berries of the Jamaica pepper tree, dried and ground, which tastes like a combination of cloves, nutmeg, and cinnamon with hints of pepper (hence its name). Allspice, sometimes called Jamaica pepper, is used in a wide range of sweet and savory cooking.

allumette [al-lü-met]   A "matchstick" strip of puff pastry with either a sweet or savory filling or garnish. The term, from French cuisine, also applies to potatoes peeled and cut into matchstick-size strips.

almeja [ahl-MAY-hah]   Spanish for clam.

almendra [ahl-MEN-drah]   Spanish for almond; in Portuguese, *amêndoa*.

almond   The kernel of the tree native to the eastern Mediterranean and cultivated for its nut in temperate climates since prehistoric times, now especially Spain, Italy, California, China, and Australia. The sweet almond, nutritionally important in medieval times in jellied BLANCMANGE, is used in both savory and sweet dishes, especially for snacks, desserts, and confections such as MARZIPAN, NOUGAT, and MACAROONS. The distinctive bitter almond flavors liqueurs, drinks, and almond extract, but only after cooking removes its toxic prussic acid.

almondine   A misnomer often used incorrectly for AMANDINE.

almond paste   See MARZIPAN.

almuerzo [ahl-MWAYR-thō, ahl-MWAYR-sō]   Spanish for lunch.

aloo [AH-loo]   Potato in Indian cuisine; also spelled *alu*.

alose [a-lōz]   French for shad.

aloyau [al-wah-yō]   French for sirloin.

Alsace [al-sas]   A province in northeastern France along the Rhine, whose German and French cuisine reflects its political history; famous for its FOIE GRAS, CHARCUTERIE, ducks, wine, and many other specialties.

alsacienne, à l' [ah l'al-sas-syen]   Garnished with sauerkraut and potatoes, ham, or sausages, or with other Alsatian specialties in French cuisine.

Altenburger [AHL-ten-boor-ger]   A soft, uncooked German cheese made from goats' milk or goats' and cows' milk mixed; it has a delicate white mold on the exterior and a creamy, smooth, flavorful interior.

Alto Adige [AHL-tō AH-dee-jay]   A valley in northeastern Tirolean Italy around Bolzano, which exports a large quantity of good wines, both red and white, across the border to Austria.

alum [AL-um]   A colorless crystalline salt used to keep the crisp texture of fruits and vegetables, especially in pickles; an ingredient in BAKING POWDER.

am [ahm]   Mango in Indian cuisine. Dried green mango powder is *amchoor*, for use as a souring agent like TAMARIND or lemon juice, especially in vegetarian dishes.

amai [ah-mī]   Japanese for sweet.

amalgamer [a-mal-ga-may]   To mix, blend, or combine ingredients, in French.

amandine [a-manh-deen]   French for garnished with almonds; often misspelled almondine.

amaranth [a-mah-ranth]   A New World plant that has been rediscovered for its nutritious, high-protein seeds, eaten as cereal and ground into flour, and leaves, eaten fresh or cooked. Amaranth is much used in the cooking of tropical Asia, West Africa, and the Caribbean. There is some confusion over this plant and its various names: the leaves of some species are all green, others splotched with red or purple. Among its names are CALLALOO, Chinese spinach, Joseph's coat, *quelite*, *bledo blanco*, and *chauli*.

amardine [ah-mar-DEEN]   Middle Eastern dried apricot paste, in sheet form.

amaretto [ah-mah-RET-tō]   Italian for MACAROON, made from sweet and bitter almonds, also the liqueur, *Amaretto de Saronno*, made from apricot kernels.

ambrosia   Food of the gods that, in Greek mythology, they ate with nectar; a Southern fruit dessert, often citrus, topped with grated coconut.

amêijoas na cataplana [ah-may-JHŌ-ahs nah kah-tah-PLAH-nah]   A Portuguese stew of cockles with CHOURIÇO, tomatoes, garlic, and peppers, from the Algarve.

amêndoin [ah-men-DŌ-in]   Peanut, a staple in Brazilian cooking, from *amêndoa*, the Portuguese word for almond.

américaine, à l' [ah l'a-mayr-ee-ken]   In French cuisine, garnished with sliced lobster tail and truffles; also, a dish of lobster sautéed with olive oil and tomato in the style of Provence; often confused with ARMORICAINE.

amiral, à l' [ah l'a-mee-ral]   A classic French fish garnish of mussels, oysters, crayfish, and mushrooms in sauce NORMANDE, enriched with crayfish butter.

amontillado [ah-mon-tee-YAH-dō]   A Spanish SHERRY, literally in the MONTILLA style, usually somewhat darker and older than a FINO; the term is sometimes loosely used to mean a medium sherry.

amoroso [ah-mor-Ō-sō]   A kind of OLOROSO sherry, sweetened and darkened.

amuse-gueule [a-müz-geul]   French slang for cocktail appetizer, "taste tickler"; *amuse-bouche* is more polite.

anadama   An American yeast bread made with cornmeal and molasses; despite apocryphal stories as to the origin of the name, it remains obscure.

anago [ah-nah-gō]   Japanese for conger eel.

Anaheim chili   See GÜERO.

ananas [a-na-na, a-na-NAS]   French and German for pineapple.

ancho [AHN-chō]   A deep red chili pepper, actually a dried POBLANO; fairly mild in heat but with depth of flavor that adds to many Mexican sauces and is essential to MOLE poblano.

anchois [anh-shwah]   French for anchovy.

anchovy   A small silvery fish, sometimes broiled or fried fresh like a SARDINE with which it is often confused, but most often salted, filleted, and canned, or pounded to a paste; sometimes used in WHITEBAIT. See also NUOC MAM and GARUM.

ancienne, à l' [ah l'anh-syen]   In French cuisine, various preparations, often fricasséed and garnished in the old-fashioned style; usually a mixture such as cocks' combs and truffles; there are classic recipes for braised beef rump and chicken *à l'ancienne*.

andalouse, à l' [ah l'anh-da-looz]   In French cuisine, garnished with tomatoes, sweet red peppers, eggplant, and sometimes rice pilaf and CHIPOLATA sausages or ham.

andouille [ANH-DOO-yuh]   A spicy French sausage made from pork CHITTER-LINGS and TRIPE, smoked, sliced, and served cold as an hors d'oeuvre; an integral part of CAJUN cuisine.

andouillette [anh-doo-yet]   A French sausage similar to ANDOUILLE but made from the small intestine rather than the large; the many varieties are sold poached, then grilled before serving hot with strong mustard.

angel food cake   A sponge cake made with stiffly beaten egg whites but no yolks, producing a light and airy texture and white color.

angel hair   See CAPELLI D'ANGELO.

angelica   An herb of the parsley family whose roots, stems, leaves, and seeds are used for medicinal and culinary purposes. Its aroma flavors several liqueurs and confections and often imparts a green color. Its thick, hollow stems are often candied or crystallized for Italian cheesecakes and dessert decorations. In tart fruit compotes, angelica's sweetness reduces the amount of sugar needed.

angels on horseback   Oysters wrapped in bacon, skewered, grilled, and served on buttered toast fingers; a favorite hors d'oeuvre or SAVORY in England.

anglaise, à l' [ah l'anh-glez]   In French cuisine, English style—that is, plainly boiled or roasted, or coated with an egg-and-bread-crumb batter and deep-fried.

angler   See MONKFISH.

angostura bitters   See BITTERS.

anguille [anh-gwee]   French for eel; *anguila* in Spanish; *anguilla* in Italian.

animelles [a-nee-mel]   The French culinary term for testicles of animals, especially rams; *animelles* are less popular in Europe today than formerly but still common in the Middle East. In Italy, *animelle* means SWEETBREADS.

anise [A-nis]   A plant native to the eastern Mediterranean, esteemed by the ancient Greeks and Romans, whose leaves and especially seeds taste of licorice; it flavors alcoholic drinks such as ouzo, arak, pastis, sambuca, and anisette, in addition to many cheeses, pastries, and confections. Also called aniseed and sweet cumin, anise is related to dill, caraway, cumin, and FENNEL and often confused with the latter; it is no relation to Asian STAR ANISE.

anitra [AH-nee-trah]   Italian for duck; wild duck, *anitra selvatica*; *anatra*, drake.

Anjou [anh-jhoo]   A northwest central region of France, around Angers and Saumur, known for its wines, both still and sparkling, and for excellent poultry, fish from the Loire, and produce, especially pears. Curnonsky, the great gastronome, came from Anjou and praised its cuisine and wine in his writings.

Anna, pommes   See POMMES ANNA.

annatto [a-NAT-tō]   A red dye from the seeds of a tropical Latin American tree, used to color cheese, butter, and confectionery; in the Caribbean, Mexico, and Philippines, it is also used for its delicate flavor and aroma; also called ACHIOTE, *bija*, *roucou*, and lipstick tree.

antipasto   In Italian, literally "before the pasta," an antipasto is an appetizer or starter; antipasti, like *hors d'oeuvres variés*, exist in great variety and profusion.

ants climbing a tree   See MĂ YĬ SHÀNG SHÙ.

anversoise, à l' [ah l'anh-vayr-swahz]   In the style of Anvers (now Antwerp), that is, garnished with HOPS in cream.

aonegi [ah-ō-nay-gee]   Japanese green onion.

apéritif [a-payr-ee-teef]   A drink, usually alcoholic, taken before the meal to stimulate the appetite.

Apfel   German for apple; *Apfelstrudel* is thin STRUDEL dough filled with apples, white raisins, and spices—a very popular dessert in Germany and Austria.

aphrodisiac   A food or drink that arouses the sexual appetite, generally psychologically rather than biologically.

apio   See ARRACACHA.

aporeado de tasajo [ah-por-ay-AH-dō day tah-SAH-hō]   A Cuban salt-dried beef hash in a spicy vegetable sauce.

appareil [a-paarh-ray]   French for a mixture of ingredients ready for use in a preparation, such as *appareil à biscuit*.

Appellation Contrôlée [a-pel-a-syonh conh-trō-lay]   Two words found on French wine labels, designating a particular wine by its place of origin, grape variety, or district tradition. This control, used for the best French wines, was established in 1935 to guarantee that the wine is what its label claims it to be, and it is strictly enforced by French law. Similar attempts have been made to certify cheese, both by type and by origin. Sometimes abbreviated A.C. or A.O.C.

Appellation d'Origine [a-pel-a-syonh d'ohr-ee-jheen]   The name of a wine, giving its geographic location, whether a château, vineyard, town, river valley, or general region; strictly regulated by French law.

Appenzell [AP-pen-tsel]   A Swiss whole-milk cows' cheese made in large wheels, cured, and washed in a brine with white wine and spices, which impart their flavor; the cheese is pale straw-colored with some holes and a yellow-brown rind. Similar to EMMENTAL, it is firm, buttery, yet piquant.

apple   The fruit of the tree native to the Caucasus as a small sour crabapple and improved since the Stone Age into some six thousand known varieties today. The archetypal apple is the stuff of legend, from the Garden of Eden to American apple pie. Whether for eating out of hand or for cooking, to choose a particular variety, qualities to consider are sweet or tart flavor; juicy or firm texture; skin coloration; how it holds its shape in cooking; whether the cut flesh darkens quickly; time of ripening; keeping ability; and versatility. New and Old World varieties differ, but in the United States popular ones are Braeburn, Cortland, Empire, Fuji, Gala, Golden Delicious, Granny Smith, Honeycrisp, Jonagold, McIntosh, Macoun, Pink Lady, Red Delicious, Stayman Winesap, and Suncrisp. Today there is a movement to revive or at least preserve older heirloom varieties.

apple butter A preserve of chopped apples cooked slowly for a long time, usually with sugar, cider, and spices, until reduced to a thick, dark spread.

applejack Brandy distilled from fermented cider; CALVADOS is one type that is double-distilled.

apple pandowdy See PANDOWDY.

apple schnitz Dried apple slices, much used in Pennsylvania German cooking for such dishes as apple pie and *Schnitz un Gnepp* (apple and smoked ham stew with dumplings).

apricot The stone fruit of the tree native to China, brought to the West by Arab silk traders, and grown in temperate regions for its blush-to-amber color and intense flavor, tangier than that of its cousin the PEACH. The name apricot comes from its habit of ripening early: precocious. Most of California's large crop is dried or turned into jam for confectionery and pastries such as SACHER-TORTE and glazes, but savory Middle Eastern dishes often pair apricot with meat. The kernel, heated to destroy its prussic acid, is used commercially as a flavoring, like bitter almond, for AMARETTO and other fare.

aquavit See AKVAVIT.

Arabian coffee Coffee ground to a powder, spiced with cardamom, cloves, or even saffron, and drunk without sugar or milk; in Arab countries, the ceremony of its preparation and service is symbolic of hospitality.

arabic See GUM ARABIC.

arabica [ah-RAH-bee-kah] A species of coffee tree whose beans give the delicate, complex, subtle flavors of the best quality of coffee, with low caffeine. It is grown at high altitudes in semitropical climates, usually near the equator, giving low yields, unlike ROBUSTA, the other main species. See also COFFEE.

arachide [a-ra-sheed] French for peanut.

aragosta [ah-rah-GOS-tah] Italian for lobster.

arak [AR-ak] A Middle Eastern liqueur made from various plants; strong and anise-flavored.

arame [ah-rah-may]   Asian seaweed, strong in flavor; usually dried, reconstituted, cooked, and seasoned with lemon juice or soy sauce, for salads.

arància [ah-RAHN-chyah]   Italian for orange; *arancini*, "little oranges," are rice croquettes flavored with saffron and butter and wrapped around savory fillings before frying.

Arborio rice [ar-BOR-yō]   A short, fat-grained starchy Italian rice variety used for cooking RISOTTO; grown in Lombardy and Piedmont and available in the United States.

Arbroath smokies [AR-brōth]   In Scottish cooking, small haddock that are gutted, salted, and smoked but not split until broiling before serving.

archiduc, à l' [ah l'aahr-shee-dük]   In French cooking, seasoned with paprika and blended with cream.

ardennaise, à l' [ah l'aahr-den-nez]   In the style of Ardennes, that is, with juniper berries, small game birds, and pork.

arenque [ah-REN-kay]   Spanish for herring.

Argenteuil [aahr-jhenh-toy]   Garnished with asparagus; named for the town near Paris where the best asparagus used to be grown.

arhar dal   See DAL.

aringa [ah-REEN-gah]   Italian for herring.

arista [ah-REES-tah]   Italian for roast loin of pork.

arlésienne, à l' [ah l'aahr-lay-zyen]   Garnished with eggplant and tomato, cooked in oil with fried onion rings; there are other French garnishes by this name, and all contain tomatoes.

Armagnac [aahr-ma-nyak]   A famous brandy from Gascony, in southwestern France, which can be compared to COGNAC; it is dry, smooth, dark, and aromatic.

armoricaine, à l' [ah l'aahr-mohr-ee-ken]   In French cuisine, lobster in the Breton style, some say after the ancient Roman name for Brittany and often confused with AMÉRICAINE; the sliced lobster is sautéed in olive oil with tomato, tarragon, and Cognac.

aromatic   A plant, such as an herb or spice, that gives off a pleasing scent and is used to flavor food or drink.

arrabbiata [ah-rah-BYAH-tah]   A spicy Italian sauce of tomatoes and hot chili peppers; *arrabiata* means "enraged."

arracacha [ahr-ah-KAH-chah]   A knobby tropical tuber from Latin America similar to celeriac and carrot in flavor and used similarly in purées and soups; the Spanish name is *apio*.

arrack   See ARAK.

arroser [a-rōz-ay]   To baste or moisten, in French cooking.

arrowhead   The corm, or bulbous root, of a marsh plant with arrow-shaped leaves, tasting like potato crossed with Jerusalem artichoke though more bitter. Steamed or braised in regional Chinese and Asian cooking, it has become popular in France in recent years.

arrowroot   A powdered flour from the root of a tropical plant of the same name, used as a thickener; in cooking it remains clear when mixed with other foods, rather than turning cloudy, but is more sensitive to heat than wheat flour or cornstarch. Light and easily digested, it is often in the diet of invalids.

arroz [ah-RŌTH, ah-RŌS]   Spanish for rice; when cooked and combined with other foods it makes dishes such as *arroz con pollo*, rice with chicken; *arroz a la milanesa*, not the Italian RISOTTO, but a Cuban-style dish made with long-grain rice cooked with onion and various seasonings.

arsella [ar-ZEL-lah]   Italian for mussel.

artichaut [aahr-tee-shō]   French for artichoke, both the globe artichoke, a favorite French vegetable, and the JERUSALEM ARTICHOKE.

artichoke   A vegetable in the thistle family, related to cardoon, actually the artichoke flower. Relished in ancient Rome, artichoke is favored in contemporary Mediterranean cooking. In large specimens the base of the outer leaves and the heart, after removal of the fuzzy choke, are considered choice. The large Green Globe is the variety grown in California and marketed in the United States, but others, often with purple tips and smaller chokes, are becoming more popular in the United States. The central shoots of the plant grow the largest terminal flowers, with smaller ones around the sides. Artichoke is eaten raw or more often boiled or braised and served with sauce; sometimes only the heart, or *fond*, is used as a receptacle for other food.

arugula [ah-ROO-guh-lah]   American term for rocket, a salad herb with peppery, piquant flavor, eaten raw or barely wilted; the Italian name is *rucola*, the French *roquette*.

asado [ah-SAH-dō]   Spanish for roasted or broiled.

asafetida [a-sah-FEH-ti-dah]   A spice derived from the resinous gum of a giant fennel; in cooking it imparts an interesting onion flavor, but uncooked it is offensively rank. Asafetida, favored by the ancient Romans, is used today in the cooking of southern India, especially vegetarian dishes and pickles, and in Afghanistan for drying meat. Other names are devil's dung, stinking gum, and food of the gods.

asam manis [ah-sahm mah-nis]   Indonesian for sweet and sour.

asciutta   See under PASTA.

ash [ahsh]   Persian for soup thickened with grain.

Asiago d'Allevo [ah-SYAH-gō d'ah-LAY-vō]   A scalded-curd cheese usually made from skimmed evening and whole morning cows' milk and aged up to two years; the large wheels have a thin brownish rind and a smooth pale paste with holes. Other Asiago cheeses from Vicenza, Italy, are used mainly as table cheeses.

Asian pear   A fruit distantly related to the familiar common pear; the variety available in the United States looks like a round, firm apple with a yellow, brownish, or green skin; although delicate in flavor, it holds its crisp, firm texture well in cooking.

asparagus   The young shoots of a plant in the lily family whose tips, lightly cooked or occasionally raw, make a vegetable favored since ancient times. Green asparagus, sometimes purple-tipped, is preferred in the United States, Britain, Italy, and parts of France. Blanched white asparagus, grown in darkness to avoid developing chlorophyll, is preferred in Germany, Belgium, Spain, the Netherlands, the other parts of France, and China, its seasonal celebration reaching cult worship. Argenteuil is the town outside Paris where choice asparagus were once grown and in French cuisine designates the vegetable's presence in a dish.

aspartame [AS-par-taym]   An artificial sweetener, much sweeter than sugar; not suitable for cooking or use with acids.

asperge [as-payrjh]   French for asparagus.

aspic   A clear jelly made from meat or vegetable stock and gelatin, strained, cleared, and chilled; used to dress savory foods of all kinds by covering them in a mold or surrounding them, chopped into cubes, as a garnish. Aspic, based on fruit juice and gelatin, is also used for sweet dishes.

assaisonner [a-sez-onh-nay]   To season, in French; *assaisonnement* means seasoning, condiment, or dressing.

Assam [AH-sahm]   A tea, from the province in northern India of the same name, which is strong and pungent in character and often blended with milder teas.

Asti Spumanti [AHS-tee spoo-MAHN-tee]   A sweet sparkling white wine from the town of Asti in the Piedmont region of northern Italy.

Asturias [ah-stoo-REE-ahs]   A strong, sharp-flavored cheese from northern Spain.

asure [ah-SHOO-ray]   "Noah's pudding," in Turkish cuisine, made of hulled wheat, chickpeas, nuts, and dried fruit, of religious significance to Muslims.

ataïf [ah-TAY-if]   Arab pancakes, either sweet with nuts and syrup or savory with cheese; the filling is put on half of the round, folded in two, and deep-fried.

atemoya [a-teh-MOY-ah]   A fruit cross between the CHERIMOYA and sugar apple that looks like a strange, melting artichoke; the creamy smooth flesh is sweet, rich, and custardlike, with dark flat seeds.

athénienne, à l' [ah l'a-tay-nyen]   In French cuisine, garnished with onion, eggplant, tomato, and sweet red pepper fried in olive oil.

atole [ah-TŌ-lay]   In Mexican cooking, a thin gruel drink varying widely but usually made from cornmeal; it can be flavored with sugar and fruit, chocolate, or dried chilies.

atr [AH-tahr]   Arabic for sugar syrup, often scented with orange- or rosewater, used in desserts and pastries.

attereau [a-tay-rō]   In French, a metal skewer on which sweet or savory food is threaded, coated with bread crumbs, and deep-fried.

aubergine [ō-bayr-jheen]   French for eggplant, also the word for eggplant in many places but not North America.

Auflauf [OWF-lowf]   German for SOUFFLÉ.

Aufschnitt [OWF-shnit]   A variety of thinly sliced cold meats and sausages sold in German delicatessens; cold cuts.

aurore, à l' [ah l'ohr-ohr]   In French cuisine, BÉCHAMEL sauce colored pink with a small amount of tomato purée; "dawn" implies a rosy hue.

aushak [aw-SHAK]   In Afghan cooking, a large dumpling or ravioli stuffed with chopped leeks or flat-leaf chives and served with a yogurt and ground meat sauce sprinkled with mint.

Auslese [OWS-lay-zeh]   A superior German wine made from particularly ripe and fine grapes specially picked at harvest and pressed separately from the other grapes, making a sweeter and more expensive wine. See also TROCKEN-BEERENAUSLESE.

Auster [OW-stayr]   German for oyster.

Auvergne [Ō-VAYR-nyeh]   A mountainous region in central France known for its relatively simple, straightforward, robust cooking; the Auvergne is renowned for its fine cheeses, CHARCUTERIE, vegetables and fruits, nuts, wild mushrooms, lamb, and freshwater fish.

aveline [av-leen]   French for HAZELNUT or filbert.

avgolemono [av-gō-LEH-mō-nō]   A Greek soup made from egg yolks and lemon juice, combined with chicken stock and rice, that is very popular in the Balkans; also a sauce made from egg yolks and lemon juice.

avocado   The fruit of a tree native to Mexico with smooth green-gold flesh and buttery-nutty texture; the size of the pear-shaped or oval fruit can also vary greatly, can its oil content and skin texture. Most of the American crop is grown in California, especially the familiar Hass with creamy flesh and dark pebbly skin; Florida avocados are fruitier and leaner. The name avocado comes from the Aztec word *ahuacatl*, meaning testicle; *aguacate* is the Spanish word, *avocat* ("lawyer") the French; alligator pear is another descriptive name in English.

ayam [ah-yam]   Indonesian for chicken; *soto ayam*, chicken soup, which can be a main course served with rice, delicate or very spicy; *kelia ayam*, a chicken curry from Sumatra; *ayam panggang bumbu besengek*, roasted and grilled chicken in coconut sauce.

azafran [ah-thah-FRAHN]   Spanish for saffron.

azeite [ah-ZAY-tay]   Portuguese for olive.

azúcar [ah-THOO-kar, ah-SOO-kar]   Spanish for sugar.

azuki [ah-zoo-kee]   A dried bean, russet with a white line at the eye, used widely in Japan and prized for its sweet flavor; azuki flour is used in confections and puddings in Japan and China. Also spelled adzuki.

BACCHUS

B

baba A yeast cake, sometimes with currants, that is baked in a special cylindrical mold and soaked with syrup and dark rum or kirsch; supposedly named by Stanislaus I. Lesczyinski, king of Poland, when he steeped a KUGELHOPF in rum and named it after Ali Baba in *The Arabian Nights' Entertainment.*

baba ghanoush [BAH-bah gah-NOOSH] A Middle Eastern purée of eggplant with TAHINI, lemon juice, olive oil, and garlic; spelled variously.

bā bǎo [bah bow] "Eight-treasure," in Chinese cooking, a common description for dishes with eight ingredients; *bā bǎo fàn* is a glutinous rice pudding with eight different candied fruits and nuts, the penultimate course of a banquet; the Cantonese is *bot boh.*

babka [BAHB-kah] A Polish cake, savory or sweet, related to BABA.

bacalao a la vizcaina [bah-kah-LOW ah lah veeth-KĪ-nah] Salt cod pieces soaked, fried in oil with onions, garlic, tomatoes, and red peppers, then layered and baked; originally from the Spanish Basque region but popular in Cuba.

bacalhau [bah-kah-LOW] Portuguese for salt cod; the Spanish spelling is *bacalao.*

Bacchus The Roman god of wine; Dionysus in Greek mythology.

backen [BAHK-en]   To bake, in German.

Backhün, Backhändl [BAHK-hün, -HEN-del]   Chicken rolled in bread crumbs, then fried; a German dish.

Backobst [BAHK-ōbst]   German for dried fruit.

Backpflaume [BAHK-pflow-meh]   German for prune.

bacon   Side or belly of pork that has been boned, dried, and preserved with salts and possibly sugar and other seasonings, also usually trimmed of rind, smoked, and sliced thin. Small pieces of blanched bacon (see LARDON) are often browned and used for braising, the fat for frying, the meat for flavoring and garnishing the finished dish. See also PANCETTA.

badaam [bah-DAHM]   Almond in Indian cooking; the Turkish is *badem*.

Baden [BAH-den]   A province in southwest Germany containing the Schwarz-wald (Black Forest) and many vineyards, producing mostly white wines.

bagel   Traditionally, an unsweetened yeast bread, eggless, shaped like a dough-nut, cooked first in boiling water, then baked. Traditional bagels are often eaten with lox and cream cheese; there are now many untraditional types of bagels.

bagna cauda [BAH-nyah KOW-dah]   An Italian dipping sauce, literally "hot bath," of garlic and anchovies in olive oil and butter or sometimes cream, served warm with raw vegetables on festive occasions. In Piedmont dialect, *bagna caôda*.

baguette [ba-get]   A long cylindrical loaf of French white bread, literally a "stick."

bái cài [bī tsī]   Chinese cabbage, literally "white cabbage," with thick white stems and long, narrow dark green leaves. Large or "baby" size, this is one of the many popular cabbages in the Chinese kitchen. The Cantonese term is *bok choy*.

baigan [BĪ-gahn]   Eggplant in Indian cooking.

bai horapa [BĪ hor-rah-pah]   Thai for BASIL, the variety familiar in the United States and Europe, used in Thailand as a vegetable and flavoring for curries; *bai horapa mangluk*, lemon basil, with paler leaves, for soups and salads; *bai horapa grapao*, another variety with reddish-purple, narrower leaves, cooked in meat and fish dishes.

bain-marie [binh-ma-ree]   French for a container of warm water over which a smaller pot or pots rest, to provide slow, even, indirect heat and protect the contents from overheating; a hot-water bath used on the stove or in the oven. A double boiler is a type of *bain-marie*.

bā jiǎo [ba jow]   Chinese star anise, literally, "eight points"; this seed from the magnolia family flavors marinades and slowly cooked dishes. Although anise-flavored, it is no relation to FENNEL.

bake   To cook food by surrounding it with hot, dry air in an oven or on hot stones in a dry metal pan.

bake blind   To bake a pastry shell unfilled; the dough is pricked with the tines of a fork, fitted with grease-proof paper, filled with dried beans, rice, or pie weights to hold it down, and partially baked.

baked Alaska   Ice cream set on sponge cake, the whole masked with meringue, and quickly browned in a hot oven; the air bubbles insulate the ice cream from the heat.

bakers' cheese   Pasteurized skimmed-milk cows' cheese used by bakers in the United States; it is similar to cottage cheese but smoother, softer, and more sour.

baking powder   A leavening agent for bread and pastry; when moistened, it produces carbon dioxide to aerate and lighten dough. There are many types, each combining alkaline and acidic material. In double-acting baking powder, the chemical action occurs twice, first when moistened and second when heated.

baking soda   Bicarbonate of soda; a leavening agent similar to baking powder but used with an acid such as sour milk.

baklava [BAHK-lah-vah]   A Middle Eastern sweet pastry made of extremely thin sheets of PHYLLO dough layered with chopped nuts and honey syrup, baked with butter and oil, and cut into diamonds.

balachan, blachan [BLAH-kan]   A Malaysian condiment of fermented shrimp or other seafood with chilies; salty and pungent, it is an acquired taste; spelled variously.

baldo [BAL-dō]   A short-grain Italian rice variety similar to ARBORIO RICE; grown in Piedmont and used for RISOTTO.

ballotine, ballottine [bal-ō-teen]   In French cuisine, a large piece of meat, often poultry or occasionally fish, which is boned, possibly stuffed, rolled or shaped, braised or roasted, and served hot or cold. *Ballotine* is often confused with GALANTINE, which is poached and served cold with its own jelly; also known as *dodine*.

baloney   See MORTADELLA.

balouza [bah-LOO-zah]   A Middle Eastern pudding made of cornstarch, flavored with orange- or rosewater and textured with chopped nuts.

balsamella [bal-zah-MEL-lah]   Italian for BÉCHAMEL sauce.

balsamic vinegar   A very fine, expensive type of Italian vinegar, *aceto balsamico tradizionale*, made in Modena, aged in a series of special wooden casks for a dark, mellow, subtle flavor, to be used with discretion. Industrial balsamic, with added caramel for color and flavor, is now widely available and affordable for more general uses.

balsam pear   See BITTER MELON.

balut [bah-loot]   A fertilized duck egg nearly ready to hatch; considered a great delicacy to Filipinos and some Malaysians, but an acquired taste to others.

bamboo   A tropical treelike grass whose young shoots are eaten raw, freshly boiled, and pickled; some American markets carry them fresh, although they are available canned.

ba mee [bah mee]   Thai for egg noodles.

bamia [BAH-myah]   Arabic for OKRA; the Turkish word is *bamya*, the Greek *bamies*.

bami goreng   See under NASI.

banana   The banana tree is really an oversized herb, its familiar fruit a berry; overlapping leaves form a false trunk through which the true stem grows. The weight of the upturned fruit fingers, as many as 20 in a hand, as many as 15 hands in a bunch, can bring the whole tree crashing down. The hybrid reproduces by sending up new shoots on its extensive underground rhizome. This Asian native, a staple since before the cultivation of rice, is grown in many varieties unknown in the United States. Small lady's fingers, Blue Java, mahogany red bananas, Canary from the Canary islands, round lemon bananas from Banana Island in the Nile, and the perfumed Lakatan from the Philippines are but a few of its many sizes and colors; Cavendish is what we see commonly. Whether green, yellow, or brown-black, PLANTAIN is the banana variety that needs to be cooked, as a savory starchy vegetable or sweet fragrant fruit. Banana bud is eaten in Southeast Asia. There and in Latin America, banana leaves are used to wrap food for baking or steaming.

Banbury cake   A cake from Oxfordshire, England, of oval flaky pastry filled with currants, lemon peel, and spices.

banger   British slang for a sausage that is filled with ground pork and bread crumbs.

banh [bahn]   Vietnamese for dough or cake.

banh can [bahn kang]   "Silver dollar cakes," from a batter of rice and yellow mung bean, filled with scallions and dried and fresh shrimp; from Vietnam.

banh cuon [bahn koon]   Vietnamese rolled dumplings with shallots, cucumber, bean sprouts, and mint.

banh hoi thit nuong [bahn hoy tit noong]   Marinated grilled pork strips with noodle cakes, a classic Vietnamese dish.

banh trang [bahn trang]   Rice paper, in Vietnamese cuisine, made of cooked rice processed into paper-thin rounds and dried; it is moistened and chewed as a flatbread, or filled and fried as a crisp snack.

banh xeo [bahn SAY-ō]   Happy cakes; Vietnamese pancakes made of rice flour, with various fillings.

banku [BAHN-koo]   Cornmeal dumpling, like SADZA; from Ghana.

banlay [bahn-lī]   Cambodian for vegetables.

bannock [BAN-nuk]   A traditional Scottish cake of barley, wheat, or oatmeal; large and round, varying widely according to region.

Banyuls [ba-nyül]   A sweet fortified dessert wine, sometimes very fine, usually red but also white or rosé; made primarily from the Grenache grape in the town of Banyuls in Roussillon, in the eastern French Pyrenees.

bào [bow]   Chinese for abalone.

baobab [BAY-ō-bab]   A central African tree with a very thick trunk; its fruit, called monkey bread, is eaten fresh and made into a refreshing, healthful drink, while its edible leaves are dried and powdered.

báo bǐng [bow bing]   In Chinese cooking, Mandarin pancakes, used to accompany Peking duck, moo shoo pork, and other stir-fry dishes. The dough is made of wheat flour and boiling water brushed with sesame oil and fried in a wok; the pancakes are then steamed before serving.

bào yú [bow yü]   Chinese for ABALONE, highly prized. The best (and dearest) comes from Japan, eaten fresh, dried, or canned; the Cantonese is *bau yue*.

bap   A small round loaf of soft white bread, eaten in Scotland and parts of England for breakfast.

bap [bahp]   Korean for cooked rice, a medium-length grain of sticky rice.

bar [baahr]   French for sea bass.

baraquille [baahr-a-keel]   French for a triangular stuffed pastry hors d'oeuvre.

barbabiètola [bar-bah-BYAY-tō-lah]   Italian for beet root; the tops are *biètola*.

barbacoa [BAR-bah-kō-ah]   Spanish for meat cooked in a barbecue pit; also, by extension, the word often means breakfast.

Barbaresco [bar-bah-RES-kō]   A renowned red wine from the Italian Piedmont; produced from the NEBBIOLO grape.

barbecue, barbeque   A method of cooking marinated food on a grill or spit over a slow and smoky hardwood, charcoal, or briquette fire; the name also extends to marinades and social gatherings at such cookouts. The word has sometimes (mistakenly) come to mean a grill, or grilled food, cooked over high direct open heat.

Barbera [bar-BEHR-ah]   A red grape variety, productive and popular in northern Italy, especially Piedmont, producing dark, astringent, fruity wines that can be outstanding.

barberry   A shrub whose berries are pickled or ripened and made into various preserves, syrup, and wine; red in color, high in acid; also called Oregon grapes.

barbue [baahr-bü]   French for BRILL.

bard   To tie extra fat, usually bacon, around fish, poultry, or meat to baste it while cooking. The barding fat is usually removed before serving.

Bardolino [bar-dō-LEE-nō]   A popular red wine made in northern Italy; fruity, light, best drunk young.

barfi [BAHR-fee]   An Indian fudgelike sweet made with nuts and often decorated with edible silver leaf; also spelled *burfi*.

barigoule, à la [ah lah baahr-ee-gool]   In French cuisine, artichokes braised in olive oil and wine with mushrooms, onions, garlic, perhaps other vegetables, ham, or bacon, served with a reduction of the cooking broth; from Provence. The name probably comes from a wild mushroom of the agaric family.

Bar-le-Duc [baahr-leu-dük]   A red currant preserve whose name comes from the town in the French Lorraine where it is made.

barley   An ancient hardy grain grown in most climates, common in soups, but today a staple only in the Middle East. In the modern world barley is used mostly for animal feed and for malt for brewing beer and distilling whiskey;

only a small proportion is used for soup, cereal, and bread. It is processed into hulled barley (whole-grain), Scotch barley (husked and coarsely ground), barley grits, pearl barley (bran removed, grains steamed and polished), and barley sugar candy.

Barolo [bah-RŌ-lō]   An Italian red wine from Piedmont, south of Turin, made from the NEBBIOLO grape; deep, full-bodied, and slow-maturing, it is an exceptional wine best drunk after 10 to 15 years of aging.

baron   In England, a double sirloin of beef roasted for ceremonial occasions; in France, the saddle and two legs of lamb or mutton.

barquette [baahr-ket]   In French cuisine, a boat-shaped pastry shell filled and baked as an hors d'oeuvre or sweet; the name sometimes applies to vegetable cases for stuffing, such as zucchini.

Barsac [baahr-sak]   A wine commune in the SAUTERNES district of Bordeaux, which produces a white dessert wine that is sweet and fruity.

basbousa [baz-BOO-zah]   A Middle Eastern baked pudding made with semolina, yogurt, and nuts.

basil [BA-zel, BAY-zel]   An aromatic, pungent herb from the mint family, used extensively in Mediterranean, Indian, Southeast Asian, and North African cooking; its name comes from the Greek word meaning royal, and its associations are often religious or erotic. Among many varieties of the warm-weather annual are sweet basil (the basis of PESTO sauce), holy basil (considered sacred by Hindus and has a clove or licorice fragrance), opal basil (spicy in scent), hairy basil, purple basil, lemon basil, and others. See also BAI HORAPA.

basilico [bah-ZEE-lee-kō]   Italian for BASIL.

basmati rice [baz-MAH-tee]   A high-quality, long-grain rice with an aromatic, nutty flavor that grows in the Himalayan foothills; excellent for PULAO, pilaf, and BIRYANI dishes as well as plain steamed rice.

basquaise, à la [ah lah bas-kez]   With tomatoes, peppers, Bayonne ham, cèpes, or rice characteristic of Basque cooking.

bass   A name for many fish, not necessarily related, some of which have separate entries under their individual names.

baste   To moisten during cooking by spooning liquid over food, in order to prevent toughness.

bastilla [bs-TEE-yah]   Pigeon pie, the traditional dish of Morocco. The best-known version, from Fez, is comprised of a large pie of squab or chicken on the bottom, in an egg, lemon, and onion sauce with almonds, all enclosed in thin layers of WARQA pastry covered with cinnamon and sugar; one of the glories of Moroccan cuisine. Also spelled *bisteeya, bstilla,* and *pastilla.*

bâtard [ba-taahr]   A long loaf of French bread, thicker than a BAGUETTE but shorter.

bâtarde [ba-taahrd]   A French sauce of white ROUX with water, bound with egg yolks, with butter and lemon juice added; called "bastard" for its indirect relationship to other classic sauces.

batata [bah-TAH-tah]   Spanish and Portuguese for sweet potato.

batinjan [BAHT-in-jahn]   Arabic for eggplant; often spelled *badhinjan.*

bâton, bâtonnet [ba-tonh, ba-tonh-nay]   French for shaped like a "stick"; vegetables such as potatoes cut in this manner are generally larger than ALLUMETTES or JULIENNE.

batter   A liquid mixture of flour and milk or water before it is spooned, poured, or dipped for cooking; it can be thick or thin, but when no longer liquid it becomes DOUGH.

batter bread   See SPOON BREAD.

batterie de cuisine [ba-tay-ree deu kwee-zeen]   French for kitchen utensils.

battuto [bah-TOOT-tō]   In Italian cooking, a base for soups and stews consisting of diced onion, garlic, celery, herbs, *pancetto,* cooked in olive oil or pork fat, to which the rest is added; after the *battuto* is cooked it becomes a *soffrito.* When added to a dish without cooking, it is a *battuto crudo.* See also the Spanish SOFRITO.

baudroie [bō-dwah]   French for monkfish.

Bauernsuppe [BOW-ayrn-ZOOP-eh]   In German cooking, a peasant soup of vegetables, legumes, and bacon; the adjective *bauern* means peasant or country-style.

Baumkuchen [BOWM-koo-khen]   A traditional German Christmas cake, baked in many layers to resemble the rings of a tree trunk, and iced with barklike chocolate.

bau yue   See BÀO YÚ.

Bavarian cream   A cold custard pudding, often molded into peaks, made from gelatin, eggs, whipped cream, and various sweet flavorings.

bavarois [ba-vaahr-wah]   In French cuisine, BAVARIAN CREAM, but not to be confused with the *bavaroise* drink of sweetened tea enriched with egg yolks and milk and perhaps flavored with citrus.

bavette [ba-vet]   French for tip of sirloin; flank steak.

bay   An herb from the laurel family whose dried leaves are an ingredient of the BOUQUET GARNI and whose leaves and berries have many medicinal uses; symbolic of intellectual achievement or victory.

bayerisch [BĪ-rish]   Bavarian, of the southern region of Germany around Munich; also spelled *bayrisch*.

Bayonne [bō-yohn]   A fine cured ham named for the town in the French Pyrenees where it is made.

bay poum [bī puhm]   Cambodian molded fried rice with pork, chicken, and onions.

beach plum   A small round purple plum that grows on a wild shrub in the sandy acidic soil of the northeastern Atlantic coast of the United States; usually too astringent for eating raw, its pectin makes excellent jellies, jams, and savory sauces.

bean   A loose term for the edible and nutritious seed or pod of a legume eaten fresh (the seed, pod, sprout, or young shoots) or dried; these are generally grouped into the fava or broad bean, the kidney or common green bean, and the lima, also the pea; many of these have separate entries.

bean curd   See TOFU.

bean sprout   The germinated seed pod of a leguminous plant whose nutritional value is between that of a seed and a vegetable; bean sprouts are eaten fresh or lightly cooked and are appreciated for their crisp texture.

bean threads   See FĔN SĪ.

béarnaise [bayr-nez]   A sauce of the warm emulsion type in classic French cuisine; wine vinegar is reduced with shallots and tarragon, then cooled; egg yolks and butter are beaten in and the mixture is strained and finished with chopped tarragon and perhaps chervil. One of the classic sauces, it is served primarily with grilled meat, fowl, and eggs.

Beaufort [bō-fohr]   A whole-milk cows' cheese from the French Savoy; similar to GRUYÈRE and available year-round.

Beauharnais, à la [ah lah bō-aahr-nay]   A classical French garnish for TOUR-NEDOS made of stuffed mushrooms, artichoke hearts, château potatoes, and Beauharnais sauce (BÉARNAISE with puréed tarragon).

Beaujolais [bō-jhō-lay]   A popular red wine from the region of the same name in southern Burgundy, made from the Gamay grape; pleasant, fruity, light, best served cool and drunk young. Beaujolais Nouveau, new wine bottled immediately after fermentation, is very light and pleasant, its success a marketing phenomenon. Beaujolais-Villages designates wine of higher quality; Beaujolais Cru, from one of ten villages, better still.

Beaumes-de-Venise [BŌM-deu-VEH-NĒZ]   A village in the Vaucluse of the southern Rhône valley of France known for its dry red and especially sweet Muscat wines. The best of the latter, tasting of honey and apricots, makes an excellent dessert wine.

Beaune [bōn]   Wine from Burgundy, on the southern slope of Côte d'Or, mostly red and of very good quality. The city of Beaune is the center of its wine trade. See also CÔTE D'OR and HOSPICES DE BEAUNE.

bécasse [bay-kas]   French for woodcock; the Italian word is *beccaccia*.

bec fin [bek finh]   A French slang term for a connoisseur of fine food.

béchamel [bay-sha-mel]   In French cuisine, a basic white sauce of milk stirred into a roux and thickened; one of the "mother" sauces of classic cuisine.

bêche de mer   French for sea cucumber. See also HĂI SHĒN.

bee balm   An herb in the mint family used in salads, teas (Oswego tea) and other drinks, and vegetable and meat dishes, especially pork; also called wild bergamot or horse mint.

beef   The bovine family, developed for meat, milk, and other products, also for draft (heaving loads), descended from wild cattle of Eurasia that were domesticated about 5000 years ago. The term "beef" refers especially to meat from domesticated adult cattle, including cows, bulls, and steer. Most beef for the table comes from steer, that is, bulls castrated young and grown to 1½ to 2 years of age, also from young heifers and bullocks, retired dairy cows, and oxen. Oxen are mature steer bred as draft animals, but the term "ox" applies to secondary cuts of meat, as opposed to primary beef: oxtail and beefsteak. Dairy cows are bred for milk and, except for dual-purpose breeds, tend to be leaner. French cuts differ from British and American; some have separate entries. See also VEAL.

beefalo   A cross between bison (American buffalo) and beef (cattle), with a predominance of beef; flavorful, lean, and lower in cholesterol than beef.

beef Stroganoff   Strips of beef sautéed with chopped onions and mushrooms, thickened with sour cream; perhaps named after the Russian diplomat Count Paul Stroganov.

beef Wellington   Fillet topped with DUXELLES, wrapped in puff pastry, and baked.

beer   Any beverage made by the action of yeast on an infusion of malted cereal, brewed, flavored with hops, and fermented.

Beerenauslese [BAYR-en-ows-lay-zeh]   A celebrated German wine made from overripe berries selected individually from specially chosen bunches of grapes; a sweet, fruity, intense wine of extraordinary flavor and expense.

beet   A family of plants that includes the common beet (beetroot in Britain), Swiss chard (bred for its leafy greens), sugar beet (the main source of sugar in Europe), and others. The Chioggia variety, newly available in the United States, has a striped red and white root bulb; colors range from white, yellow, rose, or crimson to black; sizes from tiny to huge; shapes from round to tapered.

Beetensuppe [BAY-ten-ZOOP-eh]   German for BORSCHT.

beggar's chicken   See FÙ GÙI JĪ.

beid [bīd]   Arabic for egg dishes; *beid bi lamoun*, AVGOLEMONO.

beignet [beh-nyay]   French for food dipped in batter and fried in deep fat. Also a yeast fritter, common to New Orleans, deep-fried and dredged in sugar or occasionally savory.

Běi jīng kǎo yā [bay jing kow yah]   Peking duck: an elaborate and famous dish made from specially reared ducks. The skin of the bird is inflated with air to dry the skin, then smeared with a honey mixture and hung for a long time to dry again; it is then roasted until crisp, the skin removed to be served separately, and the meat shredded; skin and meat are served together with sliced scallions and cucumbers all rolled up in pancakes spread with soybean sauce and eaten with the fingers.

beijos de anjo [BAY-jhōs day AHN-jhō]   "Angel's kisses," rich eggy little cakes in syrup, popular in Brazil.

Beilagen [BĪ-lah-gen]   German for accompanying dishes, such as vegetables or salad.

belegtes Brot [beh-LAYG-tes brōt]   German for sandwich, usually open-faced.

Belgian endive   A specially cultivated chicory, whose leaves are cut off and the plant shielded from the light, so that new pale yellow leaves grow back in their characteristic cigar shape. Slightly bitter and crisp, it is used fresh in salads or braised in various preparations. This curious new vegetable was discovered in the nineteenth century near Brussels, where it is grown today during fall and winter; also called witloof and Belgian chicory. A new variety bred in California, a cross with its cousin RADICCHIO di Treviso, has red leaves and the cigar shape; its name is Red Belgian or California endive.

bell pepper   See PEPPER (SWEET BELL).

Belon oyster [beu-lonh]   A choice oyster, slightly metallic in flavor, from the river of the same name in Brittany; now cultivated in Canada and the United States.

Bel Paese [bel pah-AY-say]   A semisoft, mild, uncooked Italian cheese made from whole cows' milk; it is produced on a large scale and is very popular.

beluga   See CAVIAR.

Bénédictine   A liqueur made since 1510 by the monks of that order in Fécamp, Normandy, based on COGNAC and flavored with many herbs and plants; B & B is a drier combination of Bénédictine and brandy.

benne seeds [BEN-nee]   Sesame seeds, brought from Africa with the slave trade and used especially in the African-American cooking of South Carolina, often to symbolize happiness.

bento box   A black lacquered box with compartments used to serve meals, especially lunch, in Japan; it is the Japanese version of the lunch box commonly sold to commuters at railroad stations.

berbere [BUHR-buhr-ray]   An Ethiopian hot mixture of herbs and spices used in northeastern Africa; it includes basil, cardamom, chilies, cloves, coriander, cumin, fenugreek, garlic, ginger, mint, and onion.

Bercy [bayr-see]   A classic French fish sauce of white wine and fish FUMET reduced with shallots and finished with butter and parsley; also made with meat glaze and beef marrow for grilled meat.

bergamot   A bitter, pear-shaped orange whose skin is used for its essential oil in EARL GREY TEA and perfume-making; also the name of a pear and a type of mint, for their association with the city of Bergamo in Italy.

Bergkäse [BAYRG-kay-zeh]   A hard yellow cheese from the Bavarian Alps; this is really a generic name for various cooked pressed cheeses from the region.

Berliner Weisse [bayr-LIN-er VĪ-seh]   A pale, tart German ale made from wheat and low in alcohol; often drunk with a dash of raspberry syrup for refreshment.

Bernkastel [BAYRN-kast-el]   A town in the Mosel region of Germany with some of the region's best vineyards, all estate-bottled wines.

besan [BAY-sahn]   Chickpea flour in Indian cooking.

betingan   See BATINJAN.

betterave [bet-rav]   French for beet root.

beurre blanc [beuhr blanhk]   A French sauce of white wine and shallots reduced, thickened with butter, and served warm with seafood, poultry, or vegetables.

beurre Chivry [beuhr shee-vree]   A French compound butter flavored with parsley, tarragon, chives, and shallots.

beurre manié [beuhr ma-nyay]   In French cooking, flour and butter, usually in equal proportion, kneaded into a paste to thicken sauces and gravies; the flour can be browned or not.

beurre noir [beuhr nwaahr]   A French sauce of butter cooked until brown, often flavored with chopped parsley, capers, and vinegar; served with fish or brains.

bhajia [BAH-jah]   In Indian cuisine, vegetables stir-fried and highly spiced.

bharta [BAHR-tah]   Indian roasted and mashed vegetable dishes.

bhendi [BAYN-dee]   In Indian cooking, okra.

bhuna [BOO-nah]   A style of Indian curry made from roasting meat or vegetables with spices in very little oil and water, giving a rich flavor.

bialy [bee-AH-lee]   A wheat roll topped with onion flakes, in the Jewish-American tradition; named after the city of Bialystok in Poland.

biber [bee-BAYR]   Turkish for sweet peppers.

bibimbap [bee-BEEM-bahp]   A Korean dish, a mixture of rice and stir-fried beef strips, GOCHU JANG, bean sprouts, scallions, seaweed, sesame seeds, and a fried egg, all cooked together in a TUKBAEGE clay pot; made in many variations.

bicarbonate of soda   See BAKING SODA.

bicchiere [bee-KYAYR-ay]   In Italian, a measuring glass roughly equivalent to one cup.

bien cuit [byinh kwee]   French for well done, as for steak.

Bierwurst [BEER-voorst]   A fat German sausage of pork, pork fat, and beef, dark reddish brown in color.

biètola [BYAY-tō-lah]   Italian for Swiss chard.

bigarade [bee-ga-rad]   A Seville or bitter orange; in French cuisine, a classic brown sauce for roast wild duck or game made of caramelized sugar, lemon and orange juices, stock, and DEMI-GLACE, with blanched zest.

bigos [BEE-gosh] A Polish hunter's stew of sauerkraut with sausages, bacon, mushrooms, red wine, and meat (usually venison).

bilberry A small berry similar to the blueberry but usually smaller and tarter, with the same silvery cast; used for pies, jams, and the like; native to Europe, especially northern Europe.

Billy Bi [BEE-lee BEE] French mussel soup with cream and white wine, originally created for a customer at Maxim's without the mussels themselves, but now often served with them.

bind To hold together by means of a LIAISON.

Bingen [BING-en] A wine town in Hessia, Germany, overlooking the Rhine and Nahe Rivers, producing excellent white wines.

bird's nest See YÈN WŌ.

bird's nest fryer A hinged double wire basket for deep-frying straw-potato nests to be filled with other food, such as peas.

birmuelos [beer-MWAY-lōs] Deep-fried little cakes, sometimes shaped like doughnuts, made with MATZO meal during Passover; either savory with potato or sweet with honey; also spelled *bemuelos*; Sephardic in origin.

Birne [BEER-neh] German for pear.

biryani [beer-YAH-nee] In Indian cooking, a substantial, elaborate, and spicy rice dish showing the Muslim-Mughal influence on the PULAO of the north, but richer, layered with meat or fish and vegetables.

Bischofsbrot [BEE-shofs-brōt] An Austrian cake containing dried fruit and chocolate drops.

biscuit A small flat cake, usually round and unsweetened, originally double-baked (see ZWIEBACK), hence its name; the term now covers a wide variety of small cakes and breads. In Britain it means cookie.

biscuit de Savoie [bees-kwee deu sa-vwah] A sponge cake from the French Savoy, often baked in a BRIOCHE parisienne mold and served with fruit.

biscuits à la cuillère [bees-kwee ah lah kwee-yayr] French ladyfingers; so named because before, the invention of the pastry bag, they were shaped by dropping the dough from a spoon (*cuillière*).

biscuit tortoni See TORTONI.

bishop A mulled wine drink, often made with port or Champagne, flavored with orange and lemon, cinnamon, clove, and other spices; a traditional drink in England and northern Europe.

Biskote [bees-KŌ-teh]   German for ladyfinger.

Bismarck herring   Herring marinated in vinegar, filleted and split, seasoned with onion, and eaten with sour cream.

bisque   A thick puréed soup, often made from shellfish, with the shells flambéed and pulverized for maximum flavor, then strained through a sieve. Bisque, which originally meant a poultry or game soup, is sometimes used loosely to mean a creamy purée. Bisque can also mean an ice cream with crushed macaroons or nuts.

bistec de palomilla [bees-TEK day pal-ō-MEE-yah]   Steak first pounded thin, marinated, and fried in oil, then topped with chopped fried onions and parsley; very popular in Cuba.

bisteeya   See BASTILLA.

bistro [bee-strō]   Originally a small informal French restaurant, often family owned; now a popular casual French restaurant, specializing in dishes such as steak frites. Bistros became popular in Paris during World War II; the name's derivation from the shouts of Russian soldiers demanding quick service is apocryphal. Also spelled *bistrot*.

bitter almond   See ALMOND.

bitter melon   A gourd vegetable, quite sour in flavor, with a ridged rind resembling a furrowed cucumber, used in Malaysian and Asian cooking. Also called balsam pear.

bitter orange   See SEVILLE ORANGE.

bitters   A liquid, usually alcoholic, steeped with aromatic herbs and roots and used as a tonic or flavoring for alcoholic drinks.

Bitto   A cows' milk cheese from Sondrio in Italy, which is aged from two months to three years and used as a table or grating cheese; it is popular in Italy sprinkled on top of POLENTA with butter.

bivalve   A MOLLUSK with two hinged shells, such as a clam, mussel, or oyster.

bizcocho boracho [beeth-KŌ-chōth bor-AH-chōth]   A Spanish sponge cupcake sugared, splashed with wine, and sprinkled with cinnamon, "tipsy cake."

black bass   A freshwater fish of several varieties, both smallmouth and largemouth, with firm, lean meat; suitable for most kinds of cooking.

black bean   A common bean variety, black, shiny, and sweet; this dried bean is a staple food in Central and South America, especially in rice dishes, stews, FRIJOLES refritos and in the southern United States, as in black bean soup.

blackberry   The dark purple-black berry of the genus *Rubus*, closely related to RASPBERRY and many others in this thorny family. A blackberry, unlike the conical raspberry, retains its central hull when picked. Blackberries, which grow profusely in the wild, are often called brambles.

black butter   See BEURRE NOIR.

black-eyed pea   A white pea with a black eye, brought to the southern United States from Africa in the seventeenth century with the slave trade; a favorite bean in African-American cooking, either fresh or dried, and an essential ingredient in dishes such as HOPPIN' JOHN; also called cowpea. See also DÒU SHÌ.

Black Forest   See SCHWARZWALD.

black pepper   See PEPPER (BLACK).

black pudding   See BLOOD PUDDING.

black sea bass   A small mid-Atlantic warm-weather fish; its lean, delicate white flesh is suitable for most cooking methods and is widely used in Chinese cuisine.

blackstrap   Dark, heavy, strong MOLASSES originally made in the West Indies and considered low quality, but nutritious and flavorful for certain uses.

blakhan   In Indonesian cooking, a salty and pungent shrimp paste, related to the Philippine BALACHAN and other Asian fermented fish condiments, such as NUOC MAM.

blanc [blanhk]   French for "white"; also cooking stock or COURT BOUILLON in which certain foods, such as artichokes, are cooked *au blanc* to retain their color; it usually includes a little flour mixed with water; lemon juice and butter or oil are sometimes included.

Blanc de Blancs [BLANHK deu BLANHK]   A white wine made from white grapes, especially sparkling wine; in Champagne this means that it is made from the Chardonnay grape only. Blanc de Noirs means sparkling white wine made from black grapes, the juice separated from the skins to exclude their color; in Champagne this means sparkling white wine made from the Pinot Noir and/or Pinot Meunier grape only.

Blanc Fumé   See SAUVIGNON BLANC.

blanch   To immerse vegetables, fruit, or meat in boiling water briefly, then plunge them into cold water to stop the cooking; this technique is used to firm or soften flesh, to set color, to peel skin, or to remove raw flavor.

blancmange [bluh-manhjh]   A medieval or older jellied mixture originally made of pulverized almonds and veal stock, spiced and sweetened; blancmange has changed over the centuries into a kind of sweet white pudding or custard.

blanquette [blanh-ket]   A French stew of veal, chicken, or lamb braised in stock, thickened with egg yolks and cream, and garnished with mushrooms and small white onions; the sauce is always white.

Blaufränkisch [BLOW-frenk-ish]   An Austrian wine variety that constitutes an important part of Burgenland red wines; called *Kékfrankos* in Hungary, *Lemberger* in Germany; also grown in Washington State.

blé [blay]   French for wheat.

blending   Mixing wines of different qualities or origins to produce a better wine or to give consistency; usually an honorable practice but sometimes unscrupulous.

blette [blet]   French for Swiss chard.

bleu   In French, very rare, as for steak; rarer than À POINT.

bleu, au   A French method of preparing trout or other fish whereby the fish is killed immediately before being plunged into a boiling court bouillon with vinegar, which turns the skin bluish and curls the body of the fish.

Bleu d'Auvergne [BLEU d'ō-VAYR-nyeh]   A whole-milk cows' cheese made in several areas in the French Auvergne; it is a soft, unpressed blue cheese with a distinctive flavor.

blind Huhn [blint HOON]   A German casserole of beans, vegetables, dried apples, and bacon.

blini [BLEE-nee]   A Russian yeast-raised pancake, usually of buckwheat flour, often served with sour cream and caviar.

blintz   A pancake, of eastern European and Jewish tradition, cooked on one side, filled with cottage or similar cheese, and topped with apple or another fruit, then folded over and fried.

bloater   In English cooking, inshore herring that are lightly salted and smoked, then gutted only just before serving.

Blockwurst [BLOHK-voorst]   A German sausage of beef and pork, similar to salami.

blond de veau [BLONH deu VŌ]   In French cuisine, white veal stock; *blond de volaille* means clear chicken stock.

blondir [blonh-deer]   In French, to cook lightly in fat.

blood orange   One of several varieties of the sweet orange with crimson flesh and juice; the skin may be flecked or blushed with red or purple, and the flavor can be like raspberry, as in the Moro variety.

blood pudding   A cooked cereal sausage colored black and flavored with blood and diced pork fat from fresh-killed pig.

blueberry   A shrub of the genus *Vaccinium* that grows in high- and low-bush varieties; those we find at market—large, pale, sweetly bland—are usually crossbred. The cranberry is kin but the huckleberry, though similar, is not. Blueberries taste best picked off the bush on a summer day, but frozen wild berries, increasingly available, do well cooked without thawing; blueberry raisins are a new-old idea adapted from the Native Americans.

blue cheese   Cheese injected with a mold such as *Penicillium roqueforti* (from ROQUEFORT, the oldest cheese of the genre), which gives the cheese its characteristic flavor and blue-green veining; there are many varieties, some of which are individually noted. Bleu cheese is incorrect.

blue crab   A variety of crab found on the Chesapeake Bay, eastern Atlantic, and Gulf coastlines, best appreciated in the form of SOFT-SHELL CRAB, "busters," that are harvested and cooked virtually whole, when they have just formed a new shell.

bluefish   A voracious fish found off the North American East Coast and in the Mediterranean; its oily and flavorful flesh should be eaten very fresh and takes well to assertive seasonings and accompaniments; best for baking, broiling, and smoking.

Blue Point   A species of oyster found off the coast of Long Island, usually served raw.

Blumenkohl [BLOO-men-kōl]   German for cauliflower.

blush wine   A red wine vinified with the skins and stems in contact with the juice for a short time, like traditional rosé, imparting a pinkish color. Blush wine can range from dry to sweetish, pale pink to light red, but is usually insipid, to be served lightly chilled with light food. The fashion for blush wine, mainly American, appears to be passing, especially as vintners recognize that Zinfandel, the variety most subjected to this treatment, can bring heftier prices when vinified as a full-blooded red.

Blutwurst [BLOOT-voorst]   German for BLOOD PUDDING.

bo bohng [bah buhng]   A Vietnamese dish of rice noodles with sautéed beef and onions, cucumbers, bean sprouts, herbs, and greens.

bocadito [bō-kah-DEE-tō]   Spanish for "little mouthful," a tiny sandwich served as an appetizer.

Bock [bohk]   A strong Bavarian beer, usually dark.

bodega [bō-DAY-gah]   A Spanish wine cellar or store.

boeuf à la bourguignonne   See BOURGUIGNONNE, À LA.

bogavante [bō-gah-VAHN-tah]   Spanish for large-clawed lobster.

Bohne [BŌ-neh]   German for bean.

boil   To cook in liquid at or above the boiling point (100° Celsius, 212° Fahrenheit), when liquid bubbles and evaporates into steam; a rolling boil is a vigorous boil.

boiled dinner   See NEW ENGLAND BOILED DINNER.

bok choy   See BÁI CÀI.

bola [BŌ-lah]   Portuguese for dough, pie, cake, or dumpling; *bolo* means a meatball.

Boletus [bō-LEE-tus]   A genus of wild mushroom of which the bolete, cèpe, or porcino, as it is variously known, is best known and most prized; with a thick fleshy cap and stem, the cèpe grows in chestnut and oak woods from June to November and is eaten fresh and dried; not to be confused with other species.

boliche mechado [bō-LEE-chay meh-CHAH-dō]   Cuban beef pot roast stuffed with ham and braised in a marinade flavored with SEVILLE ORANGE juice.

bollito [bōl-LEE-tō]   Italian for boiled; refers especially to mixed boiled meats.

bologna   See MORTADELLA.

bolognese, alla   See RAGÙ ALLA BOLOGNESE.

Bombay duck   An Indian fish (*bombil*) that is dried and used to flavor curry dishes.

bombe [bomhb]   In French cuisine, ice cream that is layered and packed into a special mold, originally shaped like a bomb.

bonbon [BONH-bonh]   French for candy, sweet.

bo nhung dam [boh nyung yam]   The Vietnamese version of Mongolian hot pot: sliced beef poached in flavored broth, then rolled up in a lettuce leaf with onion and ginger, served with NUOC MAM dipping sauce.

boniato [bō-NYAH-tō]   A sweet potato with white rather than orange flesh, much used in Caribbean cooking, and sometimes confusingly called a "Florida yam"; *boniatillo* is a rich dessert of the puréed root dusted with cinnamon.

bonito [bō-NEE-tō]   A small member of the TUNA family; often used in Japanese cooking, dried, salted, or flaked.

bonne femme, à la [ah lah bon fam]   "In the style of the good woman or wife," in a simple home style, often accompanied by small onions and mushrooms, in a white wine sauce flavored with lemon juice.

boquerón [bō-kayr-ŌN]   Spanish for anchovy or whitebait.

borage [BOR-aj]   An herb, Mediterranean in origin, with cucumberlike taste used to flavor vegetables and drinks (PIMM'S CUP NO. 1); its flowers are made into fritters, its young leaves used in salads, and its mature leaves cooked like spinach and finely chopped; the flowers are also crystallized, the leaves dried.

Bordeaux wine   Wine from the region around the city of Bordeaux on the Garonne River, in western France. North of the city, the Dordogne River joins the Garonne, forming the broad estuary called the Gironde. It gives its name to the *département* comprising the whole Bordeaux region and its wine, both the general category and its important APPELLATION CONTRÔLÉE, regulating some of the very finest French wines. Most are made from Cabernet Sauvignon and/or Merlot grapes. West of the Gironde, the region or district of the Médoc produces red wines in communes or villages such as St. Estèphe, Pauillac, St. Julien, and Margaux. To the south, the region of Graves produces white wine, both dry and somewhat sweet, and red. Sauternes, farther south, is known for its sweet and complex white wines affected by NOBLE ROT. To the east of the Gironde and Dordogne are the communes of Pomerol and St. Emilion, among others. Between the Garonne and Dordogne, Entre-Deux-Mers produces white wines. Many of the regions, communes, and grape varieties of Bordeaux (but not specific vineyards) have separate entries. Claret is the British word for red Bordeaux wine.

bordelaise, à la [ah lah bohr-de-lez]   In French cuisine, garnished with a reduction sauce of red or white wine with bone marrow and chopped parsley; with cèpes added; with MIREPOIX; or a garnish of artichokes and potatoes.

börek [BEU-rek]   In Turkish cuisine, a very thin pastry filled with savory or sweet stuffing, folded or rolled up, and fried or baked.

borlotto bean [bor-LOHT-tō]   A common bean variety, eaten fresh or dried; tan splotched with red, the legume is especially popular in Italy where it is cooked to a creamy purée or added to soups; also called shellbean.

borracha, salsa [bor-RAH-chah]   A Mexican sauce, literally "drunken sauce," made with pasilla chilies, orange juice, onion, and tequila.

borscht, borsch   A Polish and Russian soup based on fresh beets (which impart their vibrant color), meat broth, and winter vegetables, and often flavored with the fermented drink KVASS; the soup varies widely but is always served with sour cream; traditional for Christmas Eve, without meat.

Boston baked beans   Navy beans flavored with molasses and salt pork and baked in an earthenware pot; originally prepared on Saturday and cooked in a communal oven to allow Puritan housewives to observe the Sabbath—hence Boston's nickname of Bean Town.

Boston brown bread   A traditional accompaniment to Boston baked beans, this rye bread is flavored with molasses and often contains whole wheat and cornmeal; the dark sweet bread is steamed, usually in coffee cans.

Boston cream pie   A traditional dessert, first made at the Parker House hotel in Boston, of white cake layered with custard and topped with chocolate icing.

bot boh   See BĀ BǍO.

bot gao [bo gow]   Vietnamese for rice flour, a staple made from ground white rice. See also GLUTINOUS RICE.

botifarra [bō-tee-FAHR-rah]   Spanish for BLOOD PUDDING.

Botrytis cinerea   See NOBLE ROT.

bottarga [bō-TAHR-gah]   Italian for botargo, roe of tuna or gray mullet dried, pressed, and salted, similar to *tarama* (see TARAMOSALATA); eaten with toast, egg, or pasta in Italian and Mediterranean cooking; the French word is *boutargue*.

bottom round   See ROUND.

bouchée [boo-shay]   A small puff-pastry savory, in French literally a "mouthful," filled variously.

boucher [boo-shay]   French for butcher.

bouchon [boo-shonh]   French for cork.

boudin noir [boo-dinh nwaahr]   French for BLOOD PUDDING.

bouillabaisse [boo-yah-bes]   This famous specialty from Marseilles, originally a hearty fisherman's stew, is made from a wide variety of native fish and shellfish and flavored with saffron; the exact recipe is hotly disputed.

bouillir [boo-yeer]   In French, to boil.

bouillon [boo-yonh]   In French cooking, stock or broth that forms the basis of soups and sauces; it can be made from vegetables, poultry, or meat boiled in water, depending on its use, and need not contain gelatin.

boulage [boo-lajh]   In French cooking, shaping the dough in baking.

boulanger [boo-lanh-jhay]   French for baker; *boulangerie* means bakery.

boulangère, à la [ah lah boo-lanh-jhayr]   In French cuisine, garnished with braised onion and potato, originally cooked in the baker's oven.

boule-de-neige [BOOL-deu-NEJH]   A French dessert pastry, resembling "snow-balls," of round cakes dipped in whipped cream; made in individual servings.

bouquet [boo-kay]   In French, the aroma of wine, which gives it much of its character and charm.

bouquet garni [boo-kay gaahr-nee]   In French cooking, a bunch of herbs tied together in a small bundle for flavoring a dish as it cooks and removed before serving; it usually includes parsley, thyme, and bay leaf, among other herbs.

bouquetière, à la [ah lah BOO-keh-TYAYR]   In French cuisine, "in the style of the flower girl"; meat garnished with vegetables that are arranged in bouquets.

bourbon   American whiskey distilled from a mash that is at least 51 percent corn; sour mash bourbon contains some old mash to help start fermentation; named for Bourbon County, Kentucky.

bourekia   Greek version of BÖREK, phyllo bundles with a savory filling served as part of the MEZZE or appetizer plate; sometimes called *borekakia*, which may be sweet.

bourgeoise, à la [ah lah boor-jhwahz]   Braised meat garnished with carrots, onions, and diced bacon.

Bourgogne [BOOR-GŌ-nyeh]   French for Burgundy.

bourguignonne, à la [ah lah boor-gee-nyon]   In French cuisine, in the style of Burgundy; often beef braised in a red wine sauce garnished with mushrooms, small onions, and diced bacon, sometimes shortened to boeuf bourguignon.

bourride [boo-reed]   A fish stew from Provence, similar to BOUILLABAISSE, served on a croûte, and flavored with AÏOLI.

bo vien [boh veen]   Vietnamese beef meatball soup.

bovine spongiform encephalopathy   "Mad cow disease," often shortened to BSE; a brain-wasting cattle disease that is a new variant of Creuzfeldt-Jacob disease, fatal to humans; the disease comes from feed containing infected pulverized waste from slaughterhouses and over time can be passed to humans eating beef thus contaminated.

boysenberry A hybrid cultivar of the blackberry that tastes like a raspberry, developed early in the twentieth century and named after an American, Rudolf Boysen.

bo xao ot [boh sow EU] In Vietnamese cooking, marinated sliced beef stir-fried with bell peppers.

braciola [brah-CHYŌ-lah] Italian for cutlet or chop.

braewat [bray-WAHT] Moroccan small pastry triangle parcels filled variously, baked, and served warm; savory or sweet.

Brägenwurst [BRAY-gen-voorst] German smoked sausage of pig's brains, oats, flour, and onions; long and thin.

brains Usually from a calf or lamb, brains should first be blanched in ACIDU-LATED WATER, then poached in a court bouillon or fried in butter; often served with BEURRE NOIR or NOISETTE.

braise To cook in a small amount of flavored liquid in a tightly covered pan over low heat.

bramble See BLACKBERRY.

bran The thin brown outer covering of the wheat grain, which is removed during the refining of white flour; although bran is not absorbed into the body during digestion, its fiber, usually eaten in baked goods and breakfast cereal, is beneficial.

brandade [branh-dad] A salt-cod dish from Provence in which cod is pounded with olive oil, milk, garlic, and often potatoes into a thick, flavorful purée and served with croûtes. The name derives from the Provençal word for stirred. See also MORUE.

brandy A spirit distilled from wine; types of brandy have separate entries.

brasato [brah-ZAH-tō] Italian for braised.

brasserie [brah-sayr-ee] An informal French restaurant open long hours, serving a variety of fare and featuring beer on tap; its origin is Alsatian.

Braten [BRAH-ten] In German, a cut of meat roasted in the oven or braised on the stove.

Brathering [BRAHT-hayr-ing] German for herring that is grilled or floured and fried, then pickled in a boiled vinegar marinade; usually served cold.

Bratwurst [BRAHT-voorst]   A German sausage of spiced pork, fried or grilled; very popular.

Braunschweiger [BROWN-shvīg-er]   German liver sausage.

brawn   See HEAD CHEESE.

Brazil nut   The nut of a tall tree indigenous to the Amazon and growing mostly in the wild. The woody pod, looking something like a coconut, contains up to twenty seeds whose segments fit together in their husks; the nut is white, creamy, and high in fat. The tree grows only in Brazil and, curiously, almost all of the nuts are exported.

bread   Flour mixed with water or other liquid and often a LEAVENING to form a dough or batter, then cooked; humans have been making this staple food since the Stone Age, especially in Europe and western Asia. Today bread usually means milled wheat (for its high GLUTEN content) mixed with yeast, eggs, baking powder, or baking soda (causing the elastic dough to rise), salt, and water or milk, possibly other grains and additions such as nuts or spices, then shaped and baked in an oven. Individual breads, grains, flours, and leavenings have separate entries.

breadfruit   The fruit of a tree native to the Pacific; large, round, and starchy, it is eaten boiled or baked; sometimes confused with its blander-tasting relative, JACKFRUIT.

bread pudding   A simple homey dessert of stale bread baked with milk, egg, sugar, and flavorings.

bread sauce   An English sauce of milk cooked with onions and cloves and thickened with bread crumbs; served with poultry and game.

bream   Several different species of fish, including the excellent Mediterranean GILTHEAD and the American PORGY.

bresaola [bres-ah-Ō-lah]   Dried salt beef sliced very thin from the fillet, served as an antipasto; a specialty of northern Lombardy in Italy.

Bresse [bres]   A region in southern Burgundy famous for its excellent chickens and for its factory-made blue cheese, Bleu de Bresse, devised in 1950; it is creamy, milder, and less salty than Roquefort.

Bretagne [BREH-TAN-yuh]   Brittany, the province in northwest France noted for its fresh- and saltwater fish and shellfish, cider, and many other foods.

bretonne, à la [ah lah breh-TON]   In French cooking, garnished with fresh white haricot beans.

brewer's yeast   See YEAST.

brick   A scalded-curd, surface-ripened whole-milk cows' cheese first made in Wisconsin; it is shaped in bricks and also weighted with bricks during pressing, hence its name; the taste and texture is between that of CHEDDAR and LIEDERKRANZ.

brider   [bree-day]   To truss, in French.

Brie   [bree]   A soft-ripened uncooked cows' milk cheese from the region of the same name east of Paris; made in large flat discs, this cheese, with its white, surface-ripened rind and smooth buttery interior, is made similarly to CAMEMBERT and is renowned for its fine aroma and taste.

brik   [breek]   A Tunisian type of pastry, in very thin sheets like phyllo, a variation on the Moroccan BRAEWAT; stuffed, deep-fried, and served at once.

brill   A member of the FLOUNDER family.

Brillat-Savarin   [bree-ya-sa-va-rinh]   A raw cow's milk triple-crème cheese, similar to Brie, from Normandy, with a buttery paste and bloomy rind, named for the great gastronome and author of *The Physiology of Taste*; the cheese made today is not the original extraordinary one of the same name, now sadly lost.

brinjal   [BRIN-jawl]   In Indian cooking, eggplant.

brio   [PREE-oo]   Thai for sour.

brioche   [bree-ŌSH]   A French cake or pastry made from a rich yeast dough containing butter and eggs, often baked in a characteristic fluted mold with a smaller knob on top (*brioche parisienne*), as well as in various other shapes and sizes.

brisket   A cut of beef from the lower forequarter, between the foreshank and short plate; usually braised or cured for CORNED BEEF.

brisling   The sprat, a small fish similar to the HERRING.

Brittany   See BRETAGNE.

broa   [BRŌ-ah]   Spanish for cornbread.

broad bean   See FAVA.

broccoflower   See CAULIFLOWER.

broccoli   A member of the CABBAGE family whose dark green clustered buds and shoots are highly nutritious; some of the many types have separate entries.

Broccolini A new member of the broccoli family, actually a trademarked cross between broccoli and Chinese kale; the long sideshoot stalks with small flowerheads are sweet, slightly pungent, and crunchy; though expensive, there is no waste or trimming for the cook.

broccoli rabe A cousin of broccoli cultivated for its branches and leaves as well as flowerets and especially for its bitter, assertive flavor; it is best eaten not raw, but sautéed, braised, or steamed and served with strongly flavored foods, especially Mediterranean. Also called *broccoli raab*, *broccoletti*, and *rapini*.

broccoli romanesco See CAULIFLOWER.

broche, à la [ah lah BRŌSH] French for spit-roasted.

brochet [brō-shay] French for pike.

brochette [brō-shet] French for a skewer for grilling pieces of food.

brodo [BRŌ-dō] Italian for broth or bouillon; *brodo ristretto* means consommé.

broil To cook under or over direct intense heat.

bronzino [brohn-ZEE-nō] Italian for sea bass.

Bröschen [BREUS-shen] German for sweetbreads.

Brot [brōt] German for bread.

broth See BOUILLON and STOCK.

brou [broo] A French liqueur made from walnut husks.

brouillé [broo-yay] French for scrambled.

Brouilly [broo-yee] A wine-producing district in BEAUJOLAIS with one of the best wines of that type.

brown To cook by high heat, causing the surface of the food to turn dark and imparting a richer, cooked flavor; browning affects the outside of the food only, leaving the inside moist; it can be achieved by sautéing, frying, grilling, or broiling; see also CARAMEL.

brown betty An American pudding made of sliced fruit thickened with bread crumbs, sweetened, and baked; usually made with apples.

brown sauce See ESPAGNOLE.

brown sugar Refined sugar with a thin coating of MOLASSES; not to be confused with raw, unrefined sugar.

brûlé [brü-lay] French for burned or flamed, as in CRÈME BRÛLÉE.

Brunello [broo-NEL-lō] A Tuscan red wine grape variety, a type of Sangiovese, which is full-bodied, powerful, and long-lived.

brunoise [brün-wahz] In French cuisine, a mixture of carrots, onion, and celery cut into very fine dice and cooked slowly in butter for soups, sauces, and the like; BÂTONNETS cut across into cubes make *brunoise*.

Brunswick stew A southern U.S. stew originally made with squirrel or whatever game was available, but now mostly made with chicken and a variety of vegetables.

bruschetta [broos-KET-tah] Bread slices toasted, rubbed with garlic, and dribbled with new green olive oil; a specialty of Rome.

Brussels sprouts Midget member of the cabbage family, growing on tall stalks, whose origin is hazy; a mainstay of the British winter table, Brussels sprouts await their rediscovery in the United States, although a new garnet variety is appealing.

brut [broot] Bone-dry Champagne, usually the best; drier than "extra dry." The term can also mean raw or crude.

bruxelloise, à la [ah lah brük-sel-wahz] In French cuisine, garnished with Brussels sprouts, braised endives, and château potatoes and served with a Madeira sauce.

BSE See BOVINE SPONGIFORM ENCEPHALOPATHY.

bstilla See BASTILLA; also spelled *b'stilla*.

Bual [boo-WAL] A type of MADEIRA, golden in color and quite sweet, now usually drunk as a dessert wine; the name comes from the particular grape variety.

bubble and squeak In Britain, fried cabbage and mashed potatoes.

bûche de Noël [BÜSH deu NŌ-EL] Literally "Yule log"; the traditional French gâteau for Christmas, made of génoise and buttercream and decorated to look like a log.

buckwheat flour Not a true cereal, buckwheat flour is made from dry fruit seeds of the plant; most popular in Russia (see BLINI), buckwheat is made into pancakes and special breads (sometimes mixed with wheat) but mostly used for fodder; also called saracen wheat or saracen corn.

Buddha rice See COM CHAY.

Buddha's delight See LUÓ HÀN ZHĀI.

budín [boo-DEEN] Spanish for pudding; the Italian word is *budino*.

bue [BOO-ay]   Italian for beef; the Spanish word is *buey*.

buffalo fish   A freshwater American fish with sweet, white, lean flesh; a type of sucker, the buffalo is similar to CARP and versatile in cooking.

bülbül yuvası [BUHL-buhl YOO-vah—seu]   "Bird's nest," a Turkish pastry made of paper-thin dough filled with pistachios, coiled, baked, and served in syrup.

bulghur   Cracked wheat, hulled and parboiled, originally Persian; this nutty-textured cereal is ground in different grades for various dishes such as TAB-BOULEH, KIBBEH, and PILAU; also spelled bulgur and burghul.

bulgogi [BOOL-gō-gee]   Korean barbecue of marinated beef, or, less commonly, chicken or squid, cooked over a wood fire or, more recently, a gas grill.

bulgur   See BULGHUR.

bullabesa [BOO-yah-BAY-sah]   A fish stew of Catalonia; a cousin of BOUILLA-BAISSE.

bumbu [bum-boo]   An Indonesian sauce, usually a spicy peanut sauce, as for SATÉ.

bun bo hue [buhn boh hway]   A popular Vietnamese soup with beef, pork, lemongrass, shrimp paste, and noodles.

bundi [BOON-dee]   An Indian sweet; BESAN batter is poured through a sieve and deep-fried, sometimes then pressed into a ball, and served in a hot syrup.

Bündnerfleisch [BÜNT-ner-flīsh]   Swiss cured, dried beef sliced very thin.

buñuelo [boo-NWAY-lō]   Spanish for a yeasty doughnut, similar to a CHURRO but lighter; in Mexico, a popular flat fritter sprinkled with cinnamon sugar or drizzled with caramel sauce.

burdock   A large plant whose very long, thin, tapered root is used sliced or shredded and cooked; much favored in Japan, where it is known as *gobō*.

Burgenland [BOOR-gen-lahnt]   A province and wine region in eastern Austria well known for its sweet wines, also good reds and whites.

burghul   See BULGHUR.

burgoo [BUR-goo]   A thick stew, originally an oatmeal porridge for sailors, later containing many different meats and vegetables and thickened with okra; associated with the southern United States and Kentucky.

Burgos [BOOR-gōs]   A fresh ewes' milk cheese, from the Spanish province of the same name; mild, soft, and pleasant, often served for dessert; the rindless discs weigh approximately three pounds.

Burgundy wine   Wine from the province of Burgundy, southeast of Paris, from Auxerre south to Lyons, with a great diversity of red and white wines. Geographically the region includes Chablis, the Côte d'Or, Côte Chalonnaise, and Mâconnais of southern Burgundy; Beaujolais, made from the Gamay grape, is usually considered separately. The best red Burgundies, concentrated in the Côte d'Or (comprising the Côte de Nuits and Côte de Beaune), are made from the Pinot Noir grape. The best whites, dry and complex, are made from Chardonnay. Total vineyard area is limited compared to that of Bordeaux, with individual vineyards small and often jointly owned; accordingly, the supply of Burgundy wines is low, the price high. Many of Burgundy's wine regions, communes, and grape varieties (but not specific vineyards) have separate entries.

burnet   An herb whose leaves, which taste like cucumber, are used to flavor salads, cool drinks, vinegar, and sauces.

burrida [boor-REE-dah]   A fish stew from Genoa, a cousin of BOURRIDE.

burrito [boor-REE-tō]   A TACO of wheat rather than maize (TORTILLA), folded to enclose a savory filling such as shredded meat, refried beans, and grated cheese; from Mexican cuisine.

burro [BOO-rō]   Italian for butter.

Busserl [BOO-sehrl]   Small round sweet pastries, literally "kiss" in German.

butaniku   Japanese for pork.

butifarra [boo-tee-FAR-rah]   A Spanish sausage of pork with white wine and spices.

butter   The fatty portion of rich milk, usually cows', churned to a creamy emulsion of butterfat (80 percent), releasing the watery buttermilk (18 percent) and milk solids (2 percent). For the ideal consistency, butter is cooled for smooth texture. Ripening with a lactic culture or light salting preserves it by discouraging undesirable bacteria. With a burning point of 250°F, lower than that for other fats, butter should be heated with care. At 212°F its water droplets sizzle; hotter, the solid whey proteins and salts turn from white to brown to black. For clarified butter, this froth is skimmed off and the liquid poured off the dark sediment below; covered and chilled, clarified butter keeps well and has a higher burning point, useful for cooking and for sauces. Butter is about 60 percent saturated fat, with some 800 calories in a quarter-pound stick, but its performance in the kitchen and taste at table are irreplaceable.

butter bean   See LIMA BEAN.

buttercream   A mixture of butter, sugar, and egg yolks or custard made into an emulsion, flavored in a wide variety of ways, and used to ice or garnish dessert pastries and cakes.

butterfly   To cut open but not quite through and spread apart (as with butterfly wings), especially for a piece of meat or shrimp.

buttermilk   Originally the low-fat by-product from cream churned to make butter, containing milk casein, with a slightly sour flavor. Now it is usually skim milk with culture added, imparting a tangy taste but heated to stop fermentation. Buttermilk is easily digested and often used with baking soda for breads and pastries.

Byrrh [beerh]   A French apéritif wine, red, dry, and slightly bitter, from the Pyrenees.

CHÈVRE

C

cabbage   The common vegetable of the genus *Brassica*, whose green, white, or red leaves form a head on a central stalk; other cabbages such as kale and Brussels sprouts are closely related. Highly nutritious, cabbage is eaten raw, as in coleslaw, cooked, and pickled in dishes such as sauerkraut and kimchee. Its unpleasant smell in cooking comes from sulfuric compounds.

Cabernet [ka-bayr-nay]   A red wine grape variety from which most of the French Bordeaux red wines and many of the world's Bordeaux-style wines are made. Of the two types of Cabernet grape, Cabernet Sauvignon is characteristically powerful and assertive, its dark tannic flavors growing spicy, fragrant, fruity, and complex with long, slow maturing; it is often blended with Merlot, Cabernet Franc, or Petite Syrah. Besides its importance in Bordeaux, especially the Médoc, Cabernet Sauvignon is grown in southern France, also Tuscany, Spain, Portugal, and Eastern Europe, especially Bulgaria. In the New World, it has had remarkable success in California, Australia, and New Zealand, now also Chile, Argentina, and South Africa. Cabernet Franc, the other type of Cabernet grape that shares the "black currant" fruit, is more productive and often used for blending; in France, besides Bordeaux, it is grown widely in the Loire for red and rosé wines.

Cabernet Rosé d'Anjou [ka-bayr-nay rō-zay d'anh-jhoo]   A rosé wine, of the Cabernet Franc grape, from the Loire Valley of France.

cabillaud [ka-bee-yō]   French for fresh cod; see also MORUE.

cabinet   See KABINETT.

cabra [KAH-brah]   Spanish for goat.

Cabrales [kah-BRAH-lays]   A blue-veined cheese from northern Spain; usually made from goats' milk but sometimes from cows' and sheep's milk mixed; earthy, pungent, salty in flavor; sometimes called *Picón*.

cabrito [kah-BREE-tō]   Spanish for kid.

cacao [kah-KOW]   A tree from whose seeds, fermented, roasted, and ground, come CHOCOLATE and COCOA; native to South America, it now grows in many tropical countries around the globe.

cacciagione [ka-chah-JŌ-nay]   Italian for game.

cacciatora [ka-chah-TOR-ah]   Italian for hunter's style: in a sauce of mushrooms, onions, tomatoes, and herbs with wine.

cacık [JAH-jeuk]   A Turkish dish of sliced cucumbers in yogurt with garlic, mint, dill, and perhaps olive oil.

Caciocavallo [KA-chō-kah-VAHL-lō]   A whole-milk cows' cheese, spindle-shaped and tied with string, from southern Italy; made by the spun-curd method. Table cheeses are aged for two months, grating cheeses up to twelve, and their flavor ranges from delicate and sweet to more pungent with age; this pale straw-colored cheese is used for eating and cooking and is sometimes smoked.

cactus pads   See NOPALES.

cactus pear   See PRICKLY PEAR.

Caen, à la mode de [KANH, ah I'ah MŌD deu]   A classic French preparation for TRIPE in which blanched squares of tripe are slowly braised with onions, carrots, leeks, blanched ox feet, herbs, garlic, brandy, and white wine. It is cooked for twelve hours in a hermetically sealed MARMITE.

Caerphilly [kayr-FIL-lee]   A cows' milk cheese, mild, crumbly, moist, and slightly sour; the traditional lunch of the Welsh coal miners, it is now mostly made in western England rather than Wales.

Caesar salad   Romaine lettuce with croûtons, coddled eggs, and grated Parmesan cheese in vinaigrette flavored with garlic and Worcestershire sauce; originally created in 1924 by Caesar Cardini in Tijuana. Updated versions eliminate the egg but include ingredients such as grilled shrimp or sliced chicken breast with Parmesan.

café [ka-fay]   French for coffee, coffeehouse, or informal restaurant; *un café*, small black cup of coffee; *café au lait*, large coffee with hot milk; *café crème*, small coffee with cream or cold milk; *café brûlot*, coffee with flamed brandy; *faux café*, decaffeinated coffee; *café glacé*, iced coffee; *café en grains*, coffee beans; *café complet*, continental breakfast.

caffè [kah-FAY]   Italian for coffee, or coffeehouse; *caffè espresso*, strong black coffee in a small cup, made with a special machine that forces steam through coffee grounds; *caffè macchiato*, espresso "stained" with a little cold milk; *caffè corretto*, espresso with grappa or brandy; *caffè ristretto*, extra strong espresso; *caffè lungo*, less strong espresso in a larger cup; *cappuccino*, lungo with hot milk whisked in and perhaps grated chocolate on top (named for the color of a Capuchin friar's habit); *caffè con latte*, lungo with more than a dash of cold milk; *caffè e latte* (*caffelatte*), half coffee, half hot milk. In Italy, espresso is never drunk with the meal, only after dessert, and never ever with lemon zest; cappuccino is drunk at breakfast, never at lunch or dinner.

Cahors [ka-OHR]   A dark, tannic red wine from the city of the same name in Toulouse, France, made from the MALBEC grape; very dark red and, when well made, distinctively rich and plummy, slow maturing, long lasting.

caille [kī]   French for quail.

Cajun   Originally, this term pertained to the French Canadian settlers in Louisiana, a corruption of Acadia (from the colony of Acadia in southeastern Canada). Cajun cooking combines French methods with rural southern ingredients and a strong African influence; it is often confused with CREOLE. Typically, many dishes use a dark ROUX and pork fat and begin with sauté of green peppers, celery, and onions. Other common seasonings are garlic, chili peppers, black pepper, mustard, and FILÉ POWDER for thickening. GUMBO and JAMBALAYA are typical dishes of this unique cuisine.

cake   A baked or fried mixture usually made of flour, fat, eggs, sugar, liquid, and leavening; it can be fried on a griddle but more often is baked in an oven, the batter shaped in a mold. Many specific cakes have separate entries.

cake comb   See PASTRY COMB.

calabacita [KAHL-ah-bah-SEE-tah]   Spanish for zucchini.

calabash   See PASSION FRUIT.

calabaza [kal-ah-BAH-sah]   A large hard-skinned winter squash with orange flesh, native to the Americas and much used in South and Latin American cooking; similar to pumpkin, Hubbard, and butternut squashes, which can be substituted for it.

calamari [kal-ah-MAHR-ee]   Italian for squid.

Caldaro [kal-DAHR-ō]   A town in the Italian Tirol that produces a number of light and pleasant red and white wines.

caldeirada [kahl-dayr-AH-dah]   A Portuguese fish stew similar to BOUILLA-BAISSE, but thicker, often including squid and shellfish.

calderada [kahl-dayr-AH-dah]   A thick fish stew from Spanish Galicia similar to BOUILLABAISSE.

caldereta [kahl-dayr-AY-tah]   A Spanish meat or fish stew, whose name derives from the cauldron in which it is cooked.

caldo [KAL-dō]   Italian for hot; in Spanish and Portuguese, *caldo* means broth.

caldo verte [kal-dō VAYR-tay]   Potato and kale or cabbage soup, widely popular in Portuguese cooking.

caliente [kahl-YEN-tay]   Spanish for hot.

Californian chili   See GÜERO.

callaloo [KAL-lah-loo]   In Caribbean cooking, the leafy green tops of the TARO plant, cooked into a spicy vegetable stew with okra, eggplant, tomatoes, onions, garlic, chilies, herbs, salt pork or other meat, coconut milk, and sometimes crab; a popular and variable native dish related to CREOLE crab GUMBO; also spelled calalou and callilu. The same word, callaloo, is also used for AMARANTH, confusingly.

calmar [kal-maahr]   French for squid.

calsones [kal-SŌ-nays]   Sephardic pasta, like cheese ravioli.

Calvados [KAL-vah-dōs]   Apple brandy, twice distilled, from the department of the same name in Normandy.

calzone [kal-ZŌ-nay]   A turnover made of pizza dough, literally "pant leg," stuffed with various savory fillings, usually in individual portions; originally from Naples and now popular in the United States.

camarón [kah-mah-RŌN]   Spanish for shrimp.

Cambridge sauce   A mayonnaiselike sauce of hard-boiled egg yolks, anchovies, capers, herbs, mustard, vinegar, and oil, finished with chopped parsley.

Camembert [ka-memh-bayr]   A cows' milk cheese, soft and creamy with a white mold rind; from the town of the same name in Normandy; neither cooked nor pressed, this rich cheese in four-inch rounds is very popular and famous and, at its best—farmhouse cheese from unpasteurized milk—superb.

camote [kah-MŌ-tay]   Spanish for sweet potato.

campagnola [kahm-pah-NYŌ-lah]   Italian for country style, usually with onions and tomatoes.

Campari [kahm-PAHR-ee]   An Italian apéritif, brilliant red and bitter, often mixed with soda or in cocktails.

canapé [ka-na-pay]   A small piece of bread spread or garnished with savory food and served as an hors d'oeuvre, originally French.

canard sauvage [ka-naahr sō-vajh]   French for wild duck.

Canary melon   See WINTER MELON.

caneton [ka-neh-tonh]   French for duckling.

cangrejo [kahn-GRAY-hō]   Spanish for crab.

canh bap su [kan bop shoo]   Cabbage roll soup in pork or chicken stock, from Vietnam.

canh chua ca [kan tchyoo kah]   Sweet and sour fish soup, hot with chilies, sour with tamarind, from Vietnam.

canja [KAHN-jhah]   Clear chicken soup with rice, very popular in Brazil.

canneberge [kan-bayrjh]   French for cranberry.

cannèlla [kah-NEL-lah]   Italian for cinnamon; the French word is *cannelle*.

cannellini [kan-nel-LEE-nee]   Italian for white kidney beans.

cannelloni [kan-nel-LŌ-nee]   Italian pasta squares usually boiled, stuffed, rolled, and baked in a sauce.

cannoli [kan-NŌ-lee]   Italian pastry tubes or horns filled with ricotta cheese, chocolate, and candied citron.

Cannonau [kah-NŌ-now]   A Sicilian grape variety, the equivalent of Spanish Garnacha and French Grenache Noir.

canola oil   Rapeseed oil, neutral in flavor and with a high burning point; low in saturated fats but with poly- and monosaturated fats; also called *colza*.

Cantal [kanh-tal]   A cows' milk cheese from the French AUVERGNE, uncooked, pressed, and cured for three months; similar to CHEDDAR, this ancient cheese, known by the Romans, is cylindrical in shape with a nutty, full flavor.

Cantaloupe The true Cantaloupe, named for the town of Cantelupo near Rome, is a small, round, segmented melon with aromatic and flavorful orange flesh; what Americans call cantaloupe is a MUSKMELON.

Cantenac [kanh-teh-nak] A town in the MÉDOC region of France that produces several excellent clarets.

capeado [kah-pay-AH-dō] In Spanish cooking, dipped in batter and fried.

Cape gooseberry A small golden or orange berry from South America, named for the Cape of Good Hope in South Africa, in a fragile husklike covering similar to that of its cousin the TOMATILLO; the colorful flesh is dense, sweet, tart, and slightly bitter; the husk lends itself to decoration; also called ground cherry.

capelli d'angelo [kah-PEL-lee D'AHN-jeh-lō] Angel hair pasta; the thinnest pasta, almost too fine to cut by hand.

caper The bud or young fruit of a climbing plant, native to Africa and the Mediterranean, which is pickled to make a condiment; nasturtium buds or seeds are sometimes substituted.

capitolade [ka-pee-tō-lad] In French cuisine, cooked chicken or other food, chopped and served in a sauce; a kind of chicken hash.

capitone [kah-pee-TŌ-nay] Italian for large conger eel.

capon A castrated male chicken, whose flesh is well fattened, gaining up to ten pounds in as many months. Capon is prepared like chicken, although its flesh has a distinctive taste of its own.

caponata [kah-pō-NAH-tah] A Sicilian sweet-and-sour vegetable salad of fried eggplant, onions, olives, anchovies, capers, and tomatoes.

cappelletti [kap-pel-LET-tee] Small squares of pasta stuffed and shaped like little hats, hence their name; very similar to TORTELLINI.

cappone [ka-PŌ-nay] Italian for capon.

cappuccino [ka-poo-CHEE-nō] See CAFFÈ.

capretto [kah-PRET-tō] Italian for kid.

Capsicum See CHILI.

carambola [kar-ahm-BŌ-lah] Star fruit, native to Malaysia and pale yellow when ripe, with five pointed ridges around the central core. It comes in sweet or sour varieties and is star-shaped when sliced across.

caramel Sugar dissolved and cooked to a rich dark brown color and burnished flavor, for use in savory and especially sweet dishes; caramelized sugar is used in candy, desserts, stocks, and sauces.

caraway   An herb in the parsley family whose pungent seeds are used in making cheese, bread, and pastry, and whose milder leaves are used in cooking; a staple seasoning in German and Hungarian cuisine. The seeds look like CUMIN seeds and are often confused with them, but taste very different.

carbonada [kar-bō-NAH-dah]   A beef stew from Argentina combining apples, pears, tomatoes, onions, and potatoes; *carbonada criolla*, a stew of beef, yellow winter squash, corn, and peaches, sometimes served in a squash shell.

carbonara, alla [ahl-lah kar-bō-NAHR-ah]   An Italian spaghetti sauce of bacon sautéed in olive oil, eggs, Parmesan cheese, and sometimes (especially in the United States) cream, poured over very hot pasta to barely curdle the eggs.

carbonnade à la flammande [kaahr-bō-nad ah lah fla-manhd]   A Belgian beef stew from Flanders flavored with bacon, onions, and a little brown sugar, and simmered in beer. The term *carbonnade* originally referred to meat cooked over charcoal.

carciofo [kar-CHŌ-fō]   Italian for artichoke.

cardamom   A spice of the ginger family whose pungent seeds are dried and used in Asian, Indian, Middle Eastern, and Scandinavian cooking. A papery cardamom pod encloses up to 20 tiny seeds that, whole or crushed, give aroma and warmth to a range of dishes, savory and sweet, hot or cold, often with other spices. Also spelled cardamon and cardamum.

cardinal, à la [ah lah kaahr-dee-nal]   A French fish garnish of BÉCHAMEL sauce flavored with truffle essence, lobster butter and slices, and cayenne pepper; cardinal sometimes refers to a brilliant red dessert sauce of puréed raspberries, strained and sweetened.

cardoon [kahr-DOON]   A member of the thistle family, often wild, whose thick stalks are cooked much like artichoke, to which it is closely related; traditionally eaten by Italians and North Africans but little known in the United States.

cari [ka-ree]   French for curry.

ca-ri ga [ka-ree ga]   A classic Vietnamese chicken stew with curry and coconut milk.

Carignan [kaahr-ee-nyahnh]   A red wine grape variety grown prolifically in the south of France but producing mostly unexceptional wine; also grown in California and Chile.

carmine   A red dye used for food coloring, obtained from the female cochineal insect.

Carnaroli [kar-nah-RŌ-lee]   An Italian short-grain rice variety similar to Arborio and suitable for RISOTTO.

carne [KAR-nay]   Italian and Spanish for meat.

carne de res [KAR-nay day RAYS]   Spanish for beef.

carnero [kar-NAYR-ō]   Spanish for lamb or mutton.

carob   An evergreen tree whose pods are eaten both fresh and dried; high in sugar and protein, carob is used for confectionery (often as a chocolate substitute) and in pharmaceuticals and animal feed. Carob may be the biblical locusts —a mistranslation of locust bean—that St. John ate in the dessert.

carp   A freshwater fish found in Asian, European, and American waters that, unless farmed, tends to live in muddy water. Mild flavored but bony, it is cooked and used in many ways, including GEFILTE FISH.

carpaccio [kar-PAH-chō]   Very thin slices of beef fillet served with mustardy mayonnaise, created by Arrigo Cipriani, of Harry's Bar in Venice, in 1961. The term is now used loosely for raw beef dressed with olive oil, lemon juice, and truffles or Parmesan, or perhaps capers and onions.

carrageen, carragheen [KAAHR-a-geen]   Commonly known as "Irish moss," really a seaweed that grows wild along the north Atlantic shore; the red plant is eaten fresh or dried, when it is bleached almost white; used in sweet and savory dishes and as an excellent source of gelatin.

carré d'agneau [kaahr-ay d'a-nyō]   French for loin or rack of lamb; *carré*, literally "square," can also mean best end of neck, sometimes of veal or pork as well as lamb or mutton.

carrot   A vegetable of the parsley family whose tapered root is common and familiar, but whose broader range of colors—white, yellow, pink, maroon—is exotic though not necessarily new; baby and round carrots are increasingly available, but peeled mini carrots may be large old ones prepared for the hurried consumer.

carrottes à la Vichy [ka-roht ah lah vee-shee]   Sliced carrots cooked, if possible, in Vichy mineral water, with butter, a little sugar, and salt until glazed, and garnished with chopped parsley.

carte [kaahrt]   French for menu; *carte des vins*, wine list; *à la carte*, menu items individually priced.

casaba [kah-SAH-bah]   A large winter melon or MUSKMELON with yellow ribbed skin and very pale flesh.

Casablanca [kah-sah-BLAHN-kah]   A valley in Chile along the cool coast producing very good white wines and occasional reds.

casalinga [kah-zah-LEENG-ah]   Italian for homemade.

cascabel [kahs-kah-BEL]   A small, round, dried chili pepper with a smooth reddish-brown skin, about one inch across and fairly hot; its name (literally, "rattlesnake") refers to its rattle.

cashew [ka-SHOO]   A kidney-shaped nut of an Amazonian tree much favored in South American, Indian, and Asian cooking; the nut is attached to an applelike false fruit; wine, vinegar, and liqueur are made from the cashew apple.

casing   The intestinal membrane that is cleaned and stuffed with sausage forcemeat; a synthetic tubing used similarly.

cassareep [KAS-ah-reep]   Cassava juice reduced, sweetened, and spiced, used as a seasoning in Guianan cooking.

cassata [kah-SAH-tah]   An Italian dessert of ice cream molded in layers of contrasting colors with candied fruits soaked in liqueur; also a rich chocolate dessert from Sicily combining layers of sponge cake and ricotta with candied fruits.

cassava [kah-SAH-vah]   The "bread" of the MANIOC plant, the name used in the Orinoco and Caribbean region; see also YUCA and TAPIOCA.

cassia [KASH-ah, KASS-ee-ah]   A relative of cinnamon often confused with it as a cheap substitute when sold ground, as in the United States; cassia is reddish brown, cinnamon a lighter tan. Originally from Burma, today cassia is grown widely there and in southern China, where it has been known for millennia; the bark is used rolled or ground into powder. The leaves are used whole to flavor stews, the clovelike buds to flavor fruit compotes and drinks.

cassis [ka-sees]   French for black currant; a liqueur made from black currants is called *crème de cassis* and it is used alone or mixed to make apéritifs such as KIR—white wine colored with a few drops of cassis—or Kir royale, made with CHAMPAGNE.

cassoulet [ka-soo-lay]   A French stew of dried haricot beans baked with various meats (usually pork and mutton), preserved goose or duck, onions, and so on, with a distinctive bread-crumb crust, in an earthenware pot; from the LANGUEDOC region.

castagna [kah-STAH-nyah]   Italian for chestnut.

caster sugar   British for superfine (granulated) sugar; also spelled castor sugar.

catalane, à la [ah lah ka-ta-lan]   In French cooking, garnished with sautéed eggplant and rice pilaf, and sometimes also with tomatoes.

catfish   A fresh- and saltwater fish with a slick, scaleless skin, sharp, poisonous spines, and "whiskers" (hence its name); the catfish is very popular in the southern United States where it is increasingly farmed; cooked in various ways, especially deep-fried, usually pan-dressed, steaked, or filleted.

caudle [KAW-duhl]   A hot, spiced drink, often including wine or ale, with a cereal base; a favorite cold-weather beverage in England and Scotland, originally for the sick.

caul   The thin, fatty membrane, like netted lace, from a pig's or sheep's intestines; used to contain and cover pâtés, roasts, and the like; the fat melts away during cooking.

cauliflower   A member of the genus *Brassica*, related to cabbage and mustard, whose flower head is usually white and large, looking like a pale broccoli, its cousin; actually there are pale green and purple, even yellow and orange, varieties, also small or miniature cauliflower. Cauliflower needs to be blanched (covered from the sun) while growing to keep its white color; this explains its expense compared to that of broccoli. Romanesco cauliflower (sometimes broccoli Romanesco or Roman broccoli) has spiky turreted points; it is a traditional variety from the region near Rome with refined, nutty flavor. Broccoflower is a cauliflower with light green color, not a broccoli-cauliflower cross. American cooks tend to disregard the cauliflower, unlike the French, who bestow it with the name du Barry, after Louis XV's mistress.

causa a la limeña [KOW-sah ah lah lee-MAY-nyah]   In South American cooking, a large potato cake filled with vegetables, meat, or seafood; cut in wedges for serving and garnished generously.

causa azulada [KOW-sah ah-soo-LAH-dah]   In South American cooking, a large potato cake made with blue potatoes, giving a striking color, filled with Swiss chard, peppers, and olives.

Cavaillon   See WINTER MELON.

cave [kav]   French for wine cellar.

caviar   Sturgeon roe, ranging in color from pearl gray to light brown, from the Caspian Sea and rivers leading to it. *Malossol* caviar means "lightly salted" in Russian, regardless of the type of sturgeon, and so is considered fresh. The largest caviar is *beluga*, with gray eggs; *sevruga*, with darker smaller eggs, also has fine flavor and is in greater supply; *oscietr* (often spelled *osetra*) is gold-brown; *pausnaya* is pressed caviar from roe damaged or too small for higher grades, but can be delicious; sterlet caviar is the legendary "gold" caviar of the tsars, now extremely rare. Pasteurizing makes caviar less perishable. Substitutes for true caviar are lumpfish, whitefish, and salmon roe. See also BOTTARGA and TARAMOSALATA. Good-quality caviar is now produced in the American Northwest.

cavolfiore [kah-vōl-FYOR-ay]   Italian for cauliflower.

cavolo [KAH-vō-lō]   Italian for cabbage.

cayenne   A red chili pepper, long, thin, and tapered, 4 to 12 inches long; pungent and hot in flavor, eaten fresh or dried, often in Creole and Cajun dishes. Prepared ground cayenne pepper is made from dried hot red chili peppers that do not necessarily contain this particular pepper. The pepper is named for the Cayenne River in French Guiana.

cazuela [kah-THWAY-lah, kah-SWAY-lah]   Spanish for earthenware casserole.

cebiche [say-VEE-shay]   See SEVICHE.

cebolla [thay-BŌ-lah, say-BŌ-lah]   Spanish for onion.

Cebreto [thay-BRAY-tō]   A blue-veined Spanish cheese with a creamy texture and yellow rind.

ceci [CHAY-chee]   Italian for chickpeas, garbanzo beans.

celeriac [seh-LER-ee-ak]   Celery root, a variety of celery cultivated for its fat, knobby root rather than its stalks; best when peeled and shredded for salads, hors d'oeuvres, and RÉMOULADE; also delicious puréed in soups and braised in casseroles.

cellophane noodles   See FĔN SĪ.

cena [CHAY-nah, THAY-nah]   Italian and Spanish for supper.

cèpe [sep]   French for porcino or bolete mushroom.

cerdo [THAYR-dō, SAYR-dō]   Spanish for pork.

cerfeuil [sayr-foy]   French for chervil.

cerise [sayr-eez]   French for cherry.

çerkez tavuğu [chayr-KES tah-woo]   "Circassian chicken," poached chicken pieces in a rich spicy sauce of crushed walnuts and oil tinted red with paprika, usually served at room temperature; a classical Turkish dish popular throughout the Middle East that, because of the legendary beauty of Circassian women, supposedly evokes the splendor of the Turkish harem.

cervelas [sayr-vel-ah]   A French sausage of pork meat and fat (and formerly brains), flavored with garlic; also called *saucisson de Paris*; some nouvelle cuisine seafood sausages are called *cervelas*.

cervelles [sayr-vel]   French for brains.

cerveza [thayr-VAY-thah, sayr-VAY-sah]   Spanish for beer.

cèrvo [CHAYR-vō]   Italian for venison.

cetriòlo [chay-tree-Ō-lō]   Italian for cucumber.

cévenole, à la [ah lah say-ve-nōl]   With wild mushrooms and chestnuts, characteristic of the mountainous Cévennes region of the French Languedoc.

cha [chya]   Vietnamese for rolls; *cha ram*, shrimp rolls in rice wrappers deep-fried; *cha gio*, pork and crab spring rolls sold widely as a snack and also served with NUOC MAM dipping sauce.

cha [chah]   Cambodian for stir-fried.

Chabichou [sha-bee-shoo]   A goats' milk cheese from Poitou, France, small and conical or cylindrical in shape, soft and mild in flavor; also called Chabi.

Chablis [sha-blee]   A small town and its environs in Burgundy, southeast of Paris, producing a well-known white wine of the same name from the CHARDONNAY grape; pale-colored, dry, clean, flinty, sometimes aged in oak; it can vary widely in quality, from ordinary Chablis best drunk young to premier cru for aging; in other countries, the term Chablis has little meaning.

cha don   See CHÁ YÈ DÀN.

chafing dish   A metal pan or dish heated from below with a flame, hot coals, or electricity, for warming or cooking food; from the French word *chauffer*, to heat.

chai [chī]   Tea in India, especially the northern states; also *chah*, or *chaha*, and, in the south, *chaya. Chai* or *masala chai* often means tea with milk and sugar and a mixture of spices such as cardamom, cloves, cinnamon, ginger, and black pepper.

chai [shay]   French for wine storage space above ground, as opposed to a cellar or *cave*.

chai tom [chae tohm]   A Vietnamese dish of chopped shrimp with pork and scallions pressed around sugarcane skewers, steamed, grilled, and eaten with lettuce and mint, and served with NUOC MAM dipping sauce.

chakchouka   See SHAKSHOUKA.

challah [KHAH-lah]   Traditional Jewish Sabbath bread, made with yeast, oil, water, egg yolks, and honey, and baked in a braided loaf; for holidays it is often baked in a braided knot or spiral with raisins.

chalupa [chah-LOO-pah]   In Mexican cooking, a boat-shaped corn TORTILLA fried crisp and stuffed variously.

Chambolle-Musigny [chamh-bōl-mü-zee-nyee]   A village in the CÔTE D'OR of Burgundy that produces delicate, aromatic, and excellent red wines.

chambrer [shamh-bray]   In French, to bring wines up from the cellar to allow them to rise to room temperature before serving.

Champagne [SHAMH-PAN-yeh]   Sparkling white wine from the French region of Champagne, northeast of Paris, by law strictly delineated; made by the "classic" or "traditional" method of fermentation in the bottle. Properly speaking, only such wine should be called Champagne, although the term is used loosely (especially in the United States) for sparkling white wine made by this or another method.

champagne grapes   Very small red grapes clustered in large bunches; sweet in flavor but best used for garnishes; developed in California.

champignon [shamh-pee-nyon]   French for mushroom.

chanfana [shahn-FAH-nah]   In Portuguese cooking, a robust lamb or kid stew with red wine.

channa [CHAN-nah]   Chickpea, in Indian cooking.

chanterelle [shanh-teu-rel]   French name for a wild mushroom, common also to the United States, that is yellow and trumpet-shaped with a ruffled edge. Before being used in cooking, chanterelles are sautéed first to disgorge their liquid and then drained.

Chantilly [shanh-tee-yee]   French sauce of whipped cream, sweetened and sometimes flavored with vanilla or liqueur; also hollandaise or mayonnaise with whipped cream folded in at the last minute; a kind of MOUSSELINE.

chǎo [chow]   Stir-frying, in Chinese cooking; the Cantonese is *chau*, also *chow*.

chǎo fàn [chow fan]   Chinese fried rice with scrambled eggs and various bits of savory foods, leftover cold white rice, and seasonings such as soy sauce; the Cantonese is *chau fan*.

chǎo lóng xiā [chow lohng zhyah]   Lobster Cantonese, a celebrated Chinese dish of lobster chunks in scrambled eggs topped with a pungent sauce of black beans and scallions, and pork.

chap   The lower cheek or jaw of a pig.

chapati [chah-PAH-tee]   An Indian whole-wheat flatbread cooked on a griddle, then turned over (or out on coals) to puff up; *roti* is another name; also spelled *chappati* or *chapatti*.

chapelure [sha-peh-lür]   French for brown bread crumbs.

chapon [sha-ponh]   French for a heel of bread rubbed with garlic and olive oil; can be either rubbed along the rim of the salad bowl to impart its flavor or added to the salad itself; not necessarily removed before serving. *Chapon* also means CAPON.

chaptalization   A method of adding sugar to grape juice before fermentation, especially in bad years in cooler climates, to enable wine to reach minimum alcoholic content; a process not necessarily but often abused. Named for Chaptal, a French chemist (and Napoléon's Minister of Agriculture).

char   A member of the trout and salmon family; the Arctic char is particularly good for eating; sometimes spelled charr.

charcuterie [shaahr-kü-tayr-ree]   In French cuisine, the art of making cured and prepared meats, especially PORK; the meat specialties, such as sausages, ham, rillettes, galantines, and pâtés, made in a French butcher's shop.

charcutière [shaahr-kü-tyayr]   In French cooking, sauce ROBERT with julienne of gherkins added just before serving; served primarily with grilled pork chops and other meats.

chard   See SWISS CHARD.

Chardonnay [shaahr-don-nay]   A white wine grape variety that it easy to grow, with a remarkable adaptability; in France it is the grape from which white Burgundy and Champagne (Blanc de Blancs) are made, as well as wine from the Loire and Languedoc-Roussillon. Italy produces Chardonnay, as do other parts of Europe. In the New World, especially California and Australia, it has been spectacularly successful, with fermentation and aging in oak; also grown widely and successfully in New Zealand, Chile, and Argentina.

Charentais [shaahr-enh-tay]   A sweet and succulent variety of French melon, a true CANTALOUPE, with yellow-green ribbed skin and orange flesh.

charlotte [shaahr-loht]   A classic French or English dessert in a pail-shaped mold, large or sometimes small. The first type is an apple purée in a mold lined with buttered bread and served hot, named for Queen Charlotte, consort of George III of England. *Charlotte russe* is the second type of dessert, a BAVAR-

IAN CREAM in a ladyfinger-lined mold, created by Carême for Czar Alexander I. A *charlotte royale* replaces the ladyfingers with sponge cake cut into many thin layers sandwiched with jam; in a further elaboration, *charlotte royale à l'ancienne*, thin rolled layers of jelly roll line a shallow mold filled with Bavarian cream.

charmoula See SHARMOULA.

Charolais [shaahr-ō-lay] A French breed of white or cream-colored cattle fed on grass rather than grain (as in the United States), producing the lean but flavorful beef favored in France; often used for crossbreeding. Also a chèvre cheese from the Charolais region of Burgundy.

charoset See HAROSET.

char siu See CHĀ SHĀO.

Chartreuse [shaahr-treuz] A liqueur made by Carthusian monks, originally in Grenoble but now largely in Voiron, France, and Tarragona, Spain; the liqueur comes in two types, yellow and green, the latter being higher proof.

chā shāo [chah show] Barbecued pork, in Chinese cooking, a versatile dish of sliced marinated loin served alone or with many other foods, hot or cold; the Cantonese is *char siu* [chah syoo]. *Chā shāo bāo* are pork buns, a popular Chinese dim sum of barbecued pork in oyster sauce wrapped in yeast dough and steamed; the Cantonese name is *char siu bau*.

Chassagne-Montrachet [SHAS-SAN-yeh-MONH-RA-SHAY] A commune in the southern Côte d'Or in Burgundy, which produces outstanding white wines and very good reds.

Chasselas [shas-seu-lah] French name for a white grape variety, producing a light and fruity wine; although it does not make the best wines, it is valued for its hardiness and productivity and cultivated extensively, especially in Switzerland, where it is called Fendant.

chasseur [shas-seur] A classic French sauce of sliced sautéed mushrooms and shallots reduced with white wine, enriched with DEMI-GLACE and butter, and finished with chopped parsley; *chasseur* is the French word for hunter.

châtaigne [CHA-TA-nyuh] French for chestnut, the tree and the nut; in the kitchen, the term usually means a wild chestnut as opposed to a cultivated MARRON.

château-bottled Wine bottled where it was produced by the vineyard owner, especially in Bordeaux; this term ensures authenticity, if not quality, from the better vineyards; a statement such as *"Mise en bouteilles au Domaine"* or ". . . *par le Propriétaire"* should be on the main wine label.

chateaubriand, châteaubriant [sha-tō-bree-anh]   In French cooking, beef cut from the middle of the fillet, grilled, and garnished with château potatoes and béarnaise sauce; chateaubriand sauce is a reduction of white wine, shallots, herbs, and mushrooms, with demi-glace and butter added. Also a triple-crème cheese from Normandy.

Châteauneuf-du-Pape [sha-tō-neuf-dü-pap]   A village in the Rhône Valley near Avignon, site of the French pope's summer home in the fourteenth century, and a region of vineyards producing mostly red wine, and a small portion of whites; the reds can be outstandingly powerful, dark, long-lived wines.

chatni [CHAHT-nee]   Chutney; in Indian cooking the word means "pulverized"; a condiment, originally created to accompany Indian curries, of fruit and spices cooked with vinegar and sugar as a preservative; much loved by the English and anglicized into chutney.

chau   See CHĂŌ.

chaud-froid [shō-fwah]   French for poultry, game, or meat that is cooked but served cold, usually covered with aspic or a special sauce and highly garnished.

chaurice [shō-REES]   A highly spiced CAJUN sausage, related to CHORIZO.

chausson aux pommes [shō-sonh ō pohm]   French for apple turnover.

Chavignol [sha-vee-nyōl]   A small, soft French goats' milk cheese from Sancerre.

chá yè dàn [chah yeh dahn]   Tea eggs, a Chinese snack of eggs hard-cooked, the shells cracked, then simmered in black tea and savory flavorings; the Cantonese term is *cha don.*

chayote [chī-Ō-tay]   A vegetable of the melon and gourd family, with a prickly ribbed skin and pear shape; native to Mexico and the Antilles, it is often used in Spanish and Caribbean cooking and is prepared in a wide variety of ways; also called custard marrow, *mirliton,* and *christophine.*

cheddar   A whole-milk cows' cheese, originally from Somerset, England, in which the curd is scalded, pressed, and aged; this style is made in factories the world over, while true farmhouse Cheddar, made with unpasteurized milk, wrapped in cloth, and matured for six months to two years, is one of the great cheeses. The technique called cheddaring is a combination of milling and turning the curd.

cheese   Milk in solid and less perishable form, essentially a nutritious convenience food. The basic method for making cheese is the same for all milk: rennet (from the lining of a calf's or kid's stomach, or from a vegetable source) is introduced to warm milk, causing the solids to coagulate into a mass of curds. With time, perhaps also heat and pressure, the molded curd releases the watery whey, retaining in the solid curd most of the nutrients, to be eaten fresh or aged in infinite variations. This fermentation process, related to making bread, beer, and wine, protects the cheese from spoiling. Cave paintings in the Saharan desert from at least 5000 B.C. show milking and what is probably cheese making; a Sumerian bas relief of 3500 B.C. depicts in detail the entire process. Cheese can be made from the milk of cows, goats, sheep, and water buffalo; also from the milk of reindeer, yak, llama, camel, mare, donkey, elk, caribou, and doubtless other mammals. Many individual cheeses have separate entries.

chef de cuisine   French for the chef who directs the cooking team, directly under the executive chef.

chef de partie   French for section chef, such as *saucier* or PÂTISSIER.

chelo [CHAY-lō]   In Persian cooking, plain rice, as opposed to POLO; the Afghan word is *chelau*.

chemiser [sheu-mee-say]   In French, to coat a mold with aspic, ice cream, or some other lining; *en chemise*, literally "in a shirt," means any food in a coating, such as potatoes in their jackets or ice cream covered with a thin brittle layer of chocolate.

Chenin Blanc [cheu-ninh blanhk]   A white grape variety, made into some of the great sweet wines of the Loire (where it is called Pineau de la Loire), also into many dry or sparkling Loire wines; its acidity makes it important in hot climate countries such as South Africa and California.

chenna   See PANEER.

cherimoya [chay-ri-MOY-ah]   A tropical South American tree of the custard apple family with large green-skinned fruit; after peeling the smooth or scaly skin, the interior pulp is eaten raw and unsweetened; its taste is somewhere between that of the pineapple and the strawberry.

cherry   A tree of the prune family, originally from western Asia but grown around the Mediterranean since ancient times; the small, stoned fruit, usually dark red but sometimes blushed yellow or deep purple, falls into sweet and sour categories, with many varieties of each, some of which have separate entries.

Cherry Heering   The Danish fruit liqueur distilled from cherries, including a high proportion of stones.

cherrystone clam   A middle-sized hard-shell northeastern American clam. See also QUAHOG.

chervil   An herb of the parsley family, one of the French *fines herbes*, originating in Russia and the Middle East and known from ancient times; its delicate flavor, slightly aniselike, is lost in stewing and drying, so it is best used fresh.

Cheshire   An English cows' milk cheese, cooked, hard-pressed, and aged, made in red (with ANNATTO), white (uncolored), and blue; a venerable cheese that cannot be made elsewhere because of the special salty Cheshire pastureland; called Chester in continental Europe.

Chester   See CHESHIRE.

chestnut   A name loosely given to a number of different nut trees native to several continents, but usually meaning the sweet chestnut or Spanish chestnut. Because of its comparatively high starch content, it has long been a staple food in rural Europe, especially in times of famine or war; conversely, it can be a food of luxury, as with *marrons glacés*. Chestnuts can be used variously in the kitchen: boiled, steamed, roasted, grilled, mashed, dried, or ground into flour. See also CHÂTAIGNE and MARRON.

cheveux d'ange [she-veu d'anjh]   French for angel hair pasta, the thinnest vermicelli. See also CAPELLI D'ANGELO.

chèvre [SHEV-ruh]   French for goat; by extension, goats' milk cheese that, properly speaking, is soft and fresh, uncooked and unpressed; specific chèvre cheeses have separate entries.

chevreuil [shev-roy]   French for venison; roebuck.

Chevrotin [shev-rō-tinh]   A French cheese of goats' milk, or occasionally a mixture of goats' and cows' milk, from Savoy; the cheese is uncooked, pressed, and shaped in a small disc.

Chianti [kee-AHN-tee]   A red Italian table wine, ranging from pleasant to exceptional; very popular abroad as well as in its native Tuscany; Chianti Classico is particularly distinguished; Chianti bottles, or *fiaschi*, are shipped in their familiar woven-straw coverings.

Chiaretto [kyah-RET-tō]   An Italian rosé wine produced near Lake Garda; light, fresh, and agreeable; Chiarello is virtually the same wine.

Chiboust, crème [krem shee-boo] A dessert sauce of CRÈME PÂTISSIÈRE lightened with ITALIAN MERINGUE; named for the nineteenth-century French chef who also created gâteau SAINT-HONORÉ, which it adorns; today, crème CHANTILLY is often used instead because it is simpler to make.

chicharrones [chee-chah-RŌ-nays] Spanish for pork cracklings.

chicken Common domestic fowl, *Gallus domesticus*, bred for meat and eggs, also feathers, developed from the wild jungle fowl of Southeast Asia and India; the general term is poultry. Since World War II, battery-rearing methods have made chicken plentiful, cheap, and bland. Market chickens, of mixed breed, are classified by age and weight: a fryer or broiler chicken weighs 3½ to 4½ pounds; a roaster weighs 5 to 7 pounds; a stewing hen, often labeled simply fowl, is an older, spent breeder, best for soup. A capon is a rooster castrated young, fed and fattened to 8 to 10 pounds. A Cornish hen, a cross of a white Plymouth Rock hen and a Cornish cock, weighs about 1½ pounds. A very young poussin, or squab chicken (not to be confused with a pigeon squab), weighs about 1 pound. See also FREE-RANGE.

chicken-fried steak Steak dipped in batter and fried crisp like chicken; an African-American specialty.

chicken of the woods A wild fungus, colored golden to tan, that grows on trees in clusters, sometimes large, looking like coral or sponge; best young, sautéed or braised to serve with chicken, since its lemony flavor goes well with poultry; also called sulfur shelf and chicken mushroom; no relation to HEN OF THE WOODS.

chicken paprikash See PAPRIKÁS CSIRKE.

chicken steak A cut of beef from the CHUCK, in small individual portions with a characteristic white streak down the center.

chicken Tetrazzini Strips of cooked chicken and spaghetti in a cream sauce flavored with sherry and Parmesan, gratiné; named for the Italian coloratura soprano Luisa Tetrazzini.

chickpea A round beige legume, often dried, used extensively in Mediterranean, Middle Eastern, Indian, and Mexican cooking; an important ingredient in COUSCOUS, HUMMUS, and many soups and stews. The Spanish word is *garbanzo*, the Italian *cece* (plural *ceci*).

chicory A group of related plants—including BELGIAN ENDIVE, RADICCHIO, ESCAROLE, wild chicory (the roots of the latter are roasted and used to flavor coffee), and a bitter green often called curly endive or frisée, which is cooked or used in salads.

chiffonnade [shee-fohn-nad]   In French cuisine, leaf vegetables sliced into very thin strips, particularly lettuce and SORREL shredded and sautéed in butter.

chilaquiles [chee-lah-KEE-lays]   In Mexican cooking, leftover tortillas layered with beans, ham, chicken, tomato sauce, and cheese and baked.

chili   The fruit of the pepper plant, from the genus *Capsicum*, ranging in its many varieties from mild to fiery hot, along with other flavor components; the chili's pungency is concentrated in the capsaicin in the white rib tissue and attached seeds, which should be handled with care or even plastic disposable gloves. In general, smaller peppers are hotter than larger ones, and as they ripen from green to yellow to red, their flavor changes and gains heat. The fire can be measured in Scoville Heat Units, a scientific method devised in 1912, which allots 0 for a bell pepper, 4,000 to 10,000 for a jalapeño, and 300,000 for the hottest habanero. With repeated consumption, the chili eater gains tolerance, also a seeming addiction. Originating in South America, chili peppers are used in many cuisines the world over, with regional preferences. In common usage the word *chili* implies hot peppers, no botanical relation to black pepper, an error first made by Columbus, who thought the chilies he found in the West Indies were the black pepper of the Indies. The plural of the Spanish word *chile* is *chiles*; the English spelling is either chili (American) or chilli (more often British), with the plural chilies or chillies; but even so, the spelling remains a source of much confusion. Some individual chili peppers have separate entries.

chili con carne   A Mexican-American dish of beef highly seasoned with chili peppers and other spices and herbs; there are many variations, the subject of considerable controversy.

chilindrón, a la   See under POLLO.

chili powder   Dried crushed chili peppers with other dried spices and herbs, including onion, garlic, cumin, cloves, coriander, and oregano.

chimichanga   A deep-fried BURRITO.

chimichurri   A popular Argentine meat sauce of olive oil, vinegar, chopped parsley, onion, and spices.

chinchin   Round sweet dough balls, deep-fried, served at celebrations; from West Africa.

chin-chin   A toast, originally Chinese but now international; the pronunciation depends on where it is given.

Chincoteague [CHINK-uh-tig]   A type of oyster from the Chesapeake Bay region, closely related to the BLUE POINT.

chine   The backbone of an animal; also a butcher's term meaning to separate the backbone from the ribs of a roast to make carving easier.

Chinese anise   See BĀ JIǍO.

Chinese beans   "Yard-long" beans, also called asparagus beans or long beans; bright green in color when cooked and milder in flavor than ordinary green beans.

Chinese black beans   See DÒU SHÌ.

Chinese cabbage   See BÁI CÀI.

Chinese gooseberry   See KIWI.

Chinese pancakes   See BÁO BǏNG.

Chinese parsley   See CORIANDER.

Chinese sausages   Sausages usually of pork meat and fat, spiced, slightly sweet, and dried, reddish in color. Another type, brown pork liver or duck liver sausages, is available in Chinese groceries in the United States.

chinois [shee-nwah]   French for a fine-mesh conical sieve shaped like a coolie hat—hence its name.

chinook   See SALMON.

chipolata [chee-pō-LAH-tah]   A small Spanish sausage flavored with chives; in classic French cuisine the term designates a garnish of the sausages with braised chestnuts, diced pork, and glazed onions and carrots.

chipotle [chi-PŌT-lay]   A dull brown chili pepper, actually a smoked and dried jalapeño, with wrinkled skin; often canned in adobo sauce, this chili is very hot and has a distinctive smoky flavor.

chiqueter [sheek-tay]   To flute the edges of pastry with the fingertips, in French.

chitterlings, chitlins   The small intestines of pigs, scrubbed clean, boiled, and served with hot sauce; popular in African-American and southern U.S. cooking.

chive   An herb of the onion family, whose tall thin leaves delicately flavor savory foods.

chlodnik [KHLOD-nik]   In Polish cooking, a cold summer soup of beet greens and roots, cucumbers, and onions, flavored with herbs, vinegar, and KVASS, and garnished with sour cream; a warm-weather variety of BORSCHT.

choclo [CHŌ-klō]   Sweet corn, in South America.

chocolate   Product of the CACAO tree beans after they have been fermented, roasted, shelled to remove the nib (cotyledon), and ground to a paste to remove the chocolate liquor. The cooled chocolate liquor is pressed to produce un-sweetened chocolate. Pressing out more COCOA butter and grinding the residue makes cocoa powder. After refining (see CONCH) for high-quality chocolate, the various types are unsweetened chocolate (baking or bitter chocolate), containing only chocolate liquor and cocoa butter (50 to 58 percent in the United States); bittersweet chocolate (35 percent chocolate liquor), with a small amount of sugar added; semisweet chocolate, with slightly more sugar; sweet chocolate; milk chocolate, with milk solids (at least 12 percent and 10 percent chocolate liquor) to soften the chocolate flavor. Other flavorings can be added, but the more fat added other than cocoa butter, the cheaper the grade. Couverture is profes-sional-quality chocolate for coating, highly glossy, with at least 32 percent cocoa butter. WHITE CHOCOLATE is a mixture of cocoa butter, milk solids, and sugar, with no chocolate solids, so strictly speaking, is not chocolate at all.

cholent [KHŌ-lent]   Brisket with potatoes, lima beans, and pearl barley, slowly cooked overnight to be ready for the Jewish Sabbath.

chongos [CHONG-ōs]   A Spanish custard flavored with lemon and cinnamon.

chop   To cut in smaller pieces with quick blows of a knife or cleaver; a thin piece or slice of meat, such as pork or lamb, usually with a rib.

chop suey   A Chinese stir-fry of leftovers with bean sprouts and noodles, a dish often considered to be American in origin and highly derivative, but probably originating in Toisan, near Canton, where it is called *tsap seui*.

chorek [SHŌ-rek]   Sweet yeast bun, eaten for tea or toasted for breakfast in the Middle East.

chorizo [chor-EE-sō]   A spicy sausage used in Spanish and Latin cooking, made of pork meat and fat and flavored with garlic and spices; the Spanish is smoked and dried, the Mexican uses fresh pork. The Portuguese version is *chouriço*, of which *linguiça* is one type.

Choron [shohr-onh]   In classic French cuisine, BÉARNAISE sauce colored pink with a little tomato purée.

chou [shoo]   French for cabbage; *chou farci* means stuffed cabbage.

chouchi [choo-chee]   A Cambodian fish dish with coconut milk, chilies, garlic, lemongrass, and peanuts.

choucroute [shoo-kroot]   French for SAUERKRAUT; choucroute garnie à l'AL-SACIENNE is a favorite French dish: sauerkraut with a variety of sausages, smoked pork chops, knuckles of ham, and potatoes, all cooked together.

chou-fleur [shoo fleur]   French for cauliflower.

chouriço   See CHORIZO.

choux de Bruxelles [shoo deu brüks-el]   French for Brussels sprouts.

choux pastry   See PÂTE À CHOUX.

chow   See CHĂŌ.

chow-chow   A Chinese-American vegetable pickle flavored with mustard; the original Chinese condiment consisted of orange peel in a thick syrup, flavored with ginger and other spices.

chowder   A thick soup, made from various foodstuffs; the word comes from the French *chaudière*, the iron cauldron in which it was cooked, which, in turn, derives from the Latin word for "warm." Today, chowder is usually made of seafood or perhaps vegetables, with a milk base.

christophine   See CHAYOTE.

chuck   A cut of beef from the forequarter, between the neck and shoulder, usually best for stewing or braising.

chud [choot]   Thai for clear soup.

chuleta [choo-LAY-tah]   Spanish for chop.

chum   See SALMON.

chūn juăn [tswin juan]   Spring roll; a thin, round pastry wrapper made from flour and water, stuffed with various fillings, such as shrimp, pork, and black mushrooms, wrapped up, and deep-fried to a golden brown. This authentic Chinese food is served at the spring festival to celebrate the Chinese New Year, and its elegant appearance is said "to resemble a bar of gold"; not to be confused with DÀN JUĂN.

chuno   See under PAPA.

chupe [CHOO-pay]   Chowder, usually of seafood, in South American cooking.

churrasco [shoor-RAHS-kō]   Barbecued or charcoal-grilled meat, exported from Brazil to Portugal; restaurants that serve it are called *churrasqueirias*.

churro [CHOOR-rō]   Spanish for a finger or loop of dough, similar to BUÑUELO, fried in hot olive oil for breakfast or a MERIENDA.

chutney   See CHATNI.

ciboulette [see-boo-let]   French for chives.

cicely, sweet cicely   A fragrant hardy herb of the parsley family little used today, whose anise-flavored leaves and seeds contribute to salads and BOU-QUETS GARNIS; its natural sweetness reduces the need for sugar with tart fruits; also called Spanish chervil and anise root.

cider   Apple juice, or occasionally another fruit juice, either fermented or not. In the United States, sweet cider is unfermented, while hard cider is slightly alcoholic; in Europe, fermented cider can range widely in alcoholic content and quality and is often sparkling. Cider can also be made into apple brandy or vinegar and is often used in cooking in any of its many forms.

cigala [thee-GAH-lah]   Spanish for saltwater CRAYFISH, a small lobster; the British call it a Dublin Bay prawn, the French *langoustine*, the Italian *scampo*.

cilantro [see-LAHN-trō]   Spanish for fresh CORIANDER leaf.

cilièga [chee-LYAY-gah]   Italian for cherry.

Cincho [theen-CHŌ]   A ewes' milk cheese, from Spain; hard and pungent, similar to VILLALÓN.

cinnamon   A spice from the dried bark of an evergreen tree indigenous to Sri Lanka and used since the Egyptians (third millennium B.C.); cinnamon was one of the most desirable Eastern spices from ancient to medieval times, but is now mainly relegated to flavoring desserts, at least in the West. Cinnamon is often confused with its close relative CASSIA, especially in powdered form.

cioccolata [chōk-kō-LAH-tah]   Italian for chocolate.

cioppino [chō-PEE-nō]   A fisherman's stew of fish and shellfish, often made with tomatoes; originally the *ciuppin* of Genoa, by way of San Francisco, where it is a favorite.

cipolla [chee-PŌL-lah]   Italian for onion.

cipollina [chee-pō-LEE-nah]   Italian for small onion; the plural is *cipolline*. Those sold in farmers' and specialty markets are small and flat, with a full, mellow, complex flavor.

Circassian chicken   See ÇERKEZ TAVUĞU.

cisco [SIS-kō]   A North American lake WHITEFISH, usually smoked.

ciseler [see-zeh-lay]   In French, to cut into julienne strips or shred as for a CHIFFONNADE; to score a whole fish to hasten cooking.

citron   A fruit of the citrus family, resembling a large, lumpy lemon; cultivated for its thick rind, which is candied or pressed; its oil is used in making liqueurs, perfume, and medicine.

citron [see-tronh]   French for lemon; *citron vert* means lime.

civet [see-vay]   A French stew of furred game, cooked with red wine, onions, mushrooms, and LARDONS, traditionally thickened with the animal's blood.

civette [see-vet]   French for chives.

clabber   Buttermilk—soured, thickened milk that has not yet separated.

clafouti [kla-foo-tee]   A French pudding-cake from Limousin made of small fruit, such as cherries or plums, with a thick egg batter poured over and baked.

clam   A bivalve MOLLUSK with hinged shell, in many varieties and with some confusion between them, generally divided into hard-shell (see QUAHOG), which are eaten raw or cooked, and soft-shell, usually eaten cooked; the term does not include more specific varieties such as oyster and mussel, and is used more in the United States than elsewhere. Some clam varieties have separate entries.

Clamart, à la [ah lah kla-maahr]   In French cuisine, garnished with peas.

clambake   See NEW ENGLAND CLAMBAKE.

clapshot   In Scotland, a dish of mashed potatoes and turnips or rutabegas: "tatties 'n' neeps."

claret   The British term for red BORDEAUX WINE.

clarified butter   Butter that has been heated to separate the butterfat, thus allowing easy removal of the solids; butter so treated has a higher burning point and clearer color but less flavor; also called drawn butter.

clarify   To remove all impurities from stock or jelly (usually with egg white) or from fat.

classed or classified growth   Wine, especially from the French Bordeaux, that has been officially ranked, usually by the Classification of 1855 for Médoc. At that time, the best vineyards and estates were ranked Cru Classé ("Classed Growth"), including the five official Growths—Premier Cru (First Growth) through Cinquième Cru (Fifth Growth)—and various lower rankings, such as Cru Exceptionnel, Cru Bourgeois Supérieur, and Cru Bourgeois. (These latter were often fine wines and not "inferior" at all in the usual sense.) Since only Médoc and Sauternes were included in the 1855 Classification, many excellent wines were omitted altogether.

clementine   A hybrid citrus produced by crossing the orange with the tangerine; small, sweet, and usually seedless.

clos [klō]   A specific vineyard, usually one of distinction, such as Clos de Vougeot of the Côte d'Or in Burgundy.

clotted cream   Cream skimmed from scalded milk and slowly warmed until it thickens; a specialty of Devonshire, England.

cloud ear   See YÚN ĚR.

clou de girofle   [KLOO deu JHEE-RŌF-leh]   Clove; *clouté* means studded.

clove   The pungent dried bud of an East Indian evergreen tree known since ancient times and a desirable commodity in the medieval spice trade; the name derives from the Latin word for nail, *clavus*.

club steak   A cut of beef from the LOIN between the T-bone and rib section; tender and flavorful, it is the same as a STRIP LOIN unboned.

cobbler   A deep-dish fruit pie with a thick top crust of biscuit dough that looks like cobblestones.

cobnut   A type of HAZELNUT.

cocada   [kō-KAH-dah]   Spanish for coconut custard.

cochineal   See CARMINE.

cochino   [kō-CHEE-nō]   Spanish for pig; a suckling pig is *cochinillo*.

cochon   [kō-shonh]   French for pig; the culinary term, like that in English, is *porc*.

cocido   [kō-THEE-dō, kō-SEE-dō]   Spanish for stew; also means cooked, as opposed to fresh; *cozido* is an elaborate Brazilian stew.

cock-a-leekie   A Scottish soup made from chicken broth, leeks, and sometimes prunes and pieces of chicken.

cocoa   The remaining nibs in chocolate manufacture after the chocolate butter is liquefied; the pods of the CACAO tree are fermented, roasted, and ground until the chocolate butter is liquefied, leaving the nibs, which are then powdered to make cocoa. Cocoa is thus much lower in fat than chocolate. See also CHOCO-LATE.

coconut   The fruit of various palm trees, with a hard outer husk, fibrous shell with three penetrable "eyes" through which new shoots emerge, a lining of crisp meat, and sweet juice or water (but not milk) inside. Truly the tree of life in seashore tropics where it grows, every part of the coconut tree is used: the nut for drink, food, and oil; the shell for vessels; the palms for thatch; the sap boiled down for palm sugar or fermented for alcoholic drinks and vinegar; the trunks for hearts of palm, matting, and firewood. Coconut milk, basic to Southeast Asian and Indian cooking, is made by pouring boiling water over the grated white coconut meat and squeezing the liquid out through a cloth; coconut cream is made with a smaller proportion of water. This extraction can be repeated, each yielding milk with less fat. Coconut oil is high in saturated fat, making it less prone to rancidity in the ambient temperature of the tropics. The spelling cocoanut is incorrect.

cocotte [kō-KOT]   French for casserole; a cooking pot with a closely fitted lid for slow braising or stewing.

cod   A fish with great historic importance for its economic value in centuries past and an essential part of the triangle that supported the slave trade. Cod meat is lean, firm, white, and mild, with a large flake, suitable fresh for diverse cooking methods and with many flavors. Salted, smoked, or dried, it can be preserved for long periods; as *morue*, BRANDADE, *bacalao*, *bacalhau*, LUTEFISK, and finnan haddie, it is often preferred to fresh cod. Haddock, hake, and pollock are members of the cod family.

coda di bue [KŌ-dah dee BOO-ay]   Italian for oxtail.

codorniz [kō-DOR-neeth]   Spanish for quail.

coeur à la crème [KEUR ah lah KREM]   A cream-cheese dessert from provincial France in which cream and cream cheese are combined and molded in a heart-shaped form that allows the whey to drain off, then turned out and garnished with strawberries or other berries.

coffee   A small tree, originally from Arabia, probably Ethiopia, whose fruit or beans are ripened (six to eight months), cured (hulled and dried by the older sun-drying or newer wet method), roasted, and ground before they are brewed into the familiar beverage. Caffeine in coffee is a stimulant to the nervous system, causing wakefulness, which has been both desired and avoided since ancient times. Of the two types of coffee, arabica [ah-RAH-bee-kah] is grown at high altitudes and has an aromatic, complex, rich subtle flavor. Robusta, grown at lower altitudes, is hardier, less refined and complex, cheaper to produce, and has a higher caffeine content. Instant coffee is often, but not necessarily, of inferior quality. Coffee can be decaffeinated by chemical solvents, soaking or steaming, or carbon dioxide.

Cognac [kō-nyak]   Brandy, blended and aged, from the French town of the same name in the Charentes district north of Bordeaux. Different grades are designated by systems such as V.S.O.P. ("very special old pale") and three stars, but these are not regulated.

coing [kwinh]   French for quince.

Cointreau [kwonh-trō]   A colorless orange-flavored French liqueur, formerly called Triple Sec White CURAÇAO.

col [kōl]   Spanish for cabbage.

Colbert, à la [ah lah kōl-bayr]   In classic French cuisine, fish dipped in egg, coated with bread crumbs, and fried; Colbert butter is a chicken or meat glaze made of butter, chopped parsley, and perhaps tarragon.

Colby   An American variety of Cheddar cheese; a washed-curd cheese, originally from Colby, Wisconsin.

colcannon   An Irish peasant dish of cabbage, potatoes, leeks, and milk, traditionally eaten at Halloween with a "treasure," such as a ring, coin, thimble, or button, hidden within.

colère, en [enh kō-layr]   In French cooking, fish, usually whiting, cooked with its tail in its mouth, giving it a so-called "angry" look; often dipped in egg, coated with bread crumbs, deep-fried, and served *à la française*, with a tomato sauce.

coliflor [kō-lee-flor]   Spanish for cauliflower.

colin [kō-linh]   French for hake.

collage [kō-lahjh]   French for FINING.

collard, collard greens   A type of kale, or cabbage, whose leaves do not form a head; highly nutritious and able to withstand very hot and very cold temperatures; it is a favorite country vegetable in the southern United States but needs long, slow cooking.

collé [kō-lay]   In French, with gelatin added.

collop   A slice of meat; an old British term that has been used variously but now usually means a SCALLOP of meat or fish.

Colombard [kō-lohm-baahr]   A white wine grape variety distilled for Armagnac and Cognac, now also being vinified as a table wine in southwestern France; its fresh, fruity crispness makes it popular in California.

colza   See CANOLA OIL.

comal [kō-MAL]   A Mexican cast-iron griddle or earthenware plate for making tortillas.

com chay [kōhm chī]   "Buddha rice," cooked with coconut milk, ginger, and soy sauce; a Vietnamese vegetarian dish served on holidays.

comida [kō-MEE-dah]   Spanish for meal, usually meaning lunch.

comino [kō-MEE-nō]   Spanish for cumin.

commis [komh-mee]   French for apprentice.

commune [komh-mün]   French for a township or village and its surrounding land; frequently used to describe wine-producing regions.

composé(e) [komh-pō-zay]   French for compound; for salad, a substantial salad that is arranged or composed in its serving dish or plate, rather than tossed.

compote [komh-PŌT]   In French, a dish of fresh or dried fruit stewed slowly in syrup to keep its shape, often flavored with liqueur and spices and served cold.

compound butter   Butter combined with other seasonings such as herbs, shallots, and wine.

concasser [konh-kas-say]   In French cooking, to pound in a mortar or chop roughly; often applied to tomatoes that have been peeled, seeded, and chopped for sauce; *concassé* is the adjective.

conch [konk, konch]   A gastropod mollusk [konk] usually eaten in chowder or salad, mostly in Florida and the Caribbean. Conch is also the name of the curved trough, resembling the shell, in which refined chocolate particles are churned with cocoa butter to a smooth liquid; this process, essential to high-quality melting chocolate, is called conching [KONCH-ing].

conchiglia [kon-KEE-lyah]   Italian for shellfish; pasta in the shape of a conch shell.

concombre [KONH-KOMH-bruh]   French for cucumber.

Condé [konh-day]   In French cuisine, with rice; also a pastry strip covered with almond icing and many other sweet or savory dishes, often with rice.

condensed milk   Milk with its water content reduced by slightly more than half, sterilized, homogenized, and canned; sweetened condensed milk has sugar added as a preservative and may not be sterilized; both types taste sweeter than fresh milk.

condiment   A relish, pickle, or seasoning, highly aromatic, that accompanies food at the table and stimulates the appetite.

conejo [kon-AY-hō]   Spanish for rabbit.

confectioners' sugar   Powdered white sugar, crushed, not crystallized like superfine sugar, useful for its ability to dissolve quickly; a small amount of cornstarch is added to prevent caking; the British term is icing sugar.

confectionery   The art of sugar working or candy making.

confiserie [konh-fee-seh-ree]   French for confectionery, confectioner's shop; *confiseur* means confectioner.

confit [konh-fee]   Pork, goose, duck, or other meat, cooked and preserved in its own fat; a specialty of Gascony in southwestern France; also fruits and vegetables cooked and preserved in a brandy or liquor syrup. The term is now also used to connote a vegetable stewed in fat.

confiture [konh-fee-tür]   French for preserve, jam.

cōng [tzohng]   Chinese for scallion; *yáng cōng* (literally, "occidental scallion") means onion.

congee [KON-jee]   See ZHŌU.

congrí oriental [kon-gree or-yen-tal]   A popular dish of red beans and rice from eastern Cuba, where the red bean rather than black predominates.

cōng yóu bǐng [tzohng yō bing]   In Chinese cooking, scallion pancakes, traditionally for breakfast, usually eaten with soybean milk or Chinese porridge or for snacks; wheat dough rounds are spread with chopped scallion greens and sesame oil, rolled up, coiled, flattened, and fried.

coniglio [kō-NEE-lyō]   Italian for rabbit.

consommé [konh-somh-may]   French for clear broth; meat, chicken, game, or fish stock flavored with vegetables, strained, reduced, and usually clarified.

convection oven   A special oven, often used in professional kitchens, in which a fan circulates the air and cooks the food more evenly and faster than in a regular oven, often at lower heat. A convection oven can be gas, electric, or combined with microwave.

coo coo   A ball of steamed cornmeal and okra, sliced and served with CALLA-LOO, from Barbados.

cookie   A small cake made of sweetened dough, rolled and sliced or dropped from a spoon and baked on a flat sheet; some cookies have separate entries.

copeaux en chocolat [kō-pō enh shō-kō-la]   French for chocolate shavings.

coq au vin [kōk ō vinh]   In French cooking, a dish of chicken cut up, sautéed, and braised with onions, mushrooms, and LARDONS of bacon in red wine.

coquillage [kō-kee-yajh]   French for shellfish.

coquille de [kō-kee deu]   French for served in a scallop shell.

coquille Saint-Jacques [kō-kee sinh-jhak]   French for scallop; the apostle St. James wore the shell as his emblem; also the name of a creamy scallop dish.

coral   Lobster roe, which turns red when cooked; used for sauces and butters.

coratèlla [kor-ah-TEL-lah]   Italian for organ meats.

çorba [CHOR-bah]   Turkish for soup; the Persian is *shourba.*

cordero [kor-DAYR-ō]   Spanish for lamb; a suckling or milk-fed lamb is *cordero lechazo* or *lechal.*

Cordon Bleu   The "blue ribbon" awarded to outstanding women chefs, a tradition going back to a story, perhaps apocryphal, of Madame de Pompadour and Louis XV. The name also designates a dish of chicken or veal scallops cooked with cheese and ham, which came from the Cordon Bleu cooking school in Paris in the early twentieth century.

coriander   An annual herb of the parsley family whose leaves, seeds, and roots are much used in the cooking of the Mediterranean and Far East, where it originated, especially Asia (but not Japan), India, the Caribbean, and Mexico. Designated by the Spanish word *cilantro,* meaning its leaves, the fresh herb has been reintroduced and accepted in the United States and Europe in the last few decades. The distinctive flavor can be an acquired taste, also an example of cultural prejudice or fashion in food; the derivation from the Greek word for bedbug, whose smell it is said to resemble, is now also in question. Besides cilantro, coriander, always used fresh, is called Chinese parsley in the West; the Chinese Mandarin name for the leaves is *xiāng cài,* the Cantonese *yim sai* ("fragrant vegetable"). Coriander seed, ripened and dried, has a wholly different flavor, citrusy and aromatic. The roots are much used in Indian and Thai stews and curries.

corn   A New World grain from Central America, upon which the pre-Columbian cultures were founded; still the main food crop on the North American continent (in the United States indirectly, through livestock and dairy feed). Columbus brought corn, or maize, to the Old World, where it has slowly gained acceptance. Corn, of which there are countless varieties, cannot sow itself and is therefore unknown in the wild. In Europe, corn is the generic name for whatever grain is dominant in a particular area. See also POLENTA.

corned beef   Salted and spiced BRISKET of beef, the traditional ingredient of New England boiled dinner. "Corned" means granulated; hence, corning means to preserve with salt.

cornet [kohr-NAY]   In French, a horn-shaped puff pastry stuffed with sweetened whipped cream; a slice of meat, such as ham, rolled into a cone and often filled, for a garnish or hors d'oeuvre.

cornflour   The British term for CORNSTARCH.

cornichon [kor-nee-shohn]   French for a little gherkin or pickle used to garnish pâtés and smoked meat or fish.

Cornish hen   See CHICKEN.

Cornish pasty [PAS-tee, *not* PAYS-tee]   A pastry turnover enclosing a meat and potato filling; originally from Cornwall.

cornmeal   Dried kernels from yellow or white (and occasionally blue) corn, ground in various textures; of the methods for grinding it, stone-ground (or water-ground) cornmeal is the old-fashioned way, which retains the nutritious germ of the corn but requires refrigeration unless it is used quickly; industrial steel-ground cornmeal, where the germ and hull have been removed, has an indefinite shelf life. Because cornmeal has a low-gluten content, for baking it is usually combined with wheat or another high-gluten flour. Sometimes, especially in Britain, cornmeal is called Indian meal. See also POLENTA.

corn pone   Cornmeal dough shaped into ovals and deep-fried or baked; a southern U.S. bread served with butter and sometimes POT LIQUOR; the word *pone* is of American Indian origin.

corn salad   See LAMB'S LETTUCE.

cornstarch   Very fine white flour milled from the corn endosperm; used as a translucent thickening agent, first mixed with a cold liquid to avoid lumps, for sauces and sometimes for baking; used extensively in Chinese cooking; sometimes called corn flour. The British term for cornstarch is cornflour.

Corton [kohr-tonh]   Excellent red and white wines from the village of Aloxe-Corton in the Côte de Beaune region of Burgundy.

corvina [kor-VEE-nah]   Spanish for bass.

cos   Romaine lettuce.

coscetto [kō-SHET-tō]   Italian for leg of lamb.

coscia [KŌ-shah]   Italian for thigh, as of chicken; leg, as of lamb.

cosciotto, coscetto [kō-SHOT-tō, kō-SHET-tō]   Italian for leg of lamb; haunch.

costata [kō-STAH-tah]   Italian for rib or chop.

costoletta, cotoletta [kō-stō-LET-tah, kō-tō-LET-tah]   Italian for chop or cutlet; *costilla* is Spanish for chop or cutlet.

côte [kōt]   French for rib or chop.

cotechino [kō-teh-KEE-nō]   In Italian cooking, a large fresh sausage made with pork meat and rind and seasoned with nutmeg and cloves; sometimes delicate, sometimes very spicy.

Côte d'Or [kōt d'ohr]   A narrow strip of hillside along the Saône River valley in Burgundy, southeast of Paris, comprising the Côte de Dijon in the uppermost part, the Côte de Nuits in the middle, and the Côte de Beaune in the southernmost part; in the latter two most of the greatest French wines are produced, hence the meaning of its name, "golden slope."

côtelette [kōt-let]   French for cutlet.

Côte Rôtie [kōt rō-tee]   A famous red wine from steep slopes overlooking the Rhône River in France.

Côtes de Provence [kōt deu prō-venhs]   Red, white, and rosé wines produced on the southern coast of France between Nice and Marseilles; light, pleasant, fairly inexpensive, and popular.

Côtes du Rhône [kōt dü rōn]   Pleasant but undistinguished wines, mostly red, from the Rhône Valley between Vienne and Avignon in France; the finer wines of the region are sold under more specific appellations.

cotriade [kō-tree-ad]   A fish soup from Brittany.

cottage cheese   A fresh lumpy cheese made from skimmed pasteurized cows' milk in which the curds are washed; its taste is bland and slightly acid, lending itself to various flavorings; also used in salads and cheesecake and with fruit; it is high in protein but low in fat.

cotto [KOHT-tō]   Italian for cooked.

coulibiac [koo-lee-byak]   A hot pastry pie, adapted from the Russian *kulibyaka*, filled with layers of salmon or fish, rice or kasha, herbs, mushrooms, and onion; oval in shape, large or small in size.

coulis [koo-lee]   An old French culinary term of some confusion; originally the strained juices from cooked meat, then a purée of chicken, game, or fish; now it usually means a BISQUE, thick sauce, or purée, such as tomato or raspberry.

Coulommiers [koo-lohm-myay]   A whole-milk cows' cheese from Brie, east of Paris, usually eaten fresh but sometimes molded and aged like BRIE; shaped in wheels smaller than Brie, with a white rind flora; the interior is creamy white and increasingly flavorful with age.

country captain   Braised chicken with onion, garlic, green bell pepper, tomatoes, herbs, currants, and curry powder, topped with almonds, served with rice; the original dish is a west Bengal Anglo-Indian dish.

country-style spareribs   A cut of pork, the backbones from the shoulder end of pork loin, meatier and more expensive than regular breast SPARERIBS.

courge [koorjh]   French for marrow, squash.

courgette [koor-JHET]   British for zucchini.

couronne, en [enh koor-on]   French for in the shape of a crown; in a ring.

court bouillon [koor boo-yonh]   In French cuisine, flavored, acidulated stock for cooking food, primarily fish, but also vegetables and meat.

couscous [koos-koos]   The quintessential dish of Morocco, Algeria, and Tunisia prepared variously but usually consisting of SEMOLINA pasta steamed on top of a special two-part pot over meat and vegetable TAJINS cooked below, served all together with a hot sauce. Also the name for the tiny rounds of semolina pasta that go into it; Israeli couscous rounds are larger. The special pot is called a *couscoussière*.

couverture [koo-vayr-tür]   High-grade CHOCOLATE used especially for coating and ornamental work; it is semisweet and high in cocoa butter, giving it a glossy surface.

cozido   See COCIDO.

cozza [KOT-zah]   Italian for mussel.

crab   A large and varied family of ten-legged crustaceans, the front pair clawed, with delicate white meat; all true crabs are edible, and some of them have separate entries; the she-crab is the female, including her roe.

crabapple   The small, sour, hard fruit of the wild crabapple tree, from which the apple is cultivated; its tartness lends itself to jellies and jams to accompany savory meat and poultry dishes. It can be spelled as two words.

crackling   The crisp brown skin of pork or sometimes poultry with all its fat rendered; sometimes baked into breads.

cranberry   The fruit of a low creeping vine that grows in the sandy, acid soil of New England's coastal bogs, now cultivated also in Wisconsin, the Pacific Northwest, and northern Europe. The acid in the small crimson berry makes it suitable for both savory and sweet dishes, especially the jellies, preserves, chutneys, and pastries of autumn and the Thanksgiving table; cranberries also make a refreshing drink and dried raisinlike berries.

cranberry bean   A type of legume, eaten fresh or dried, that is tan streaked with red; also called shellbean or, in Italian, *borlotto*.

Cranshaw   See WINTER MELON.

crapaudine, à la [ah lah kra-pō-deen]   Poultry, especially small birds, trussed to look like toad (*crapaud* in French).

crayfish   A crustacean with many species, usually freshwater, varying widely in size but most often smaller than a lobster; these "dainties of the first order," as Audubon called them, are prized delicacies in many cuisines but largely ignored in the United States, except for the CREOLE and CAJUN cooking of Louisiana. The freshwater crayfish is sometimes called crawfish or (in French) *écrevisse*; the saltwater crayfish is also called crawfish, rock or spiny lobster, *langouste*, *langoustine* (in French), Dublin Bay prawn (in Britain), Norway lobster, and *scampo* (in Italy). There is considerable confusion among these terms.

cream   The fatty part of milk, which rises to the surface unless homogenized. Single cream is 45 percent butterfat, measured by the percentage of dry matter rather than volume; double cream is 60 percent butterfat; triple cream is 75 percent. In cheesemaking, additional cream must sometimes be added to the milk to bring it up to the degree of butterfat required.

cream cheese   Fresh unripened whole-milk cows' cheese, with a high fat content (varying with different types); in the United States this cheese is usually factory made, with stabilizers added to keep the whey from draining further, but there are many versions throughout the world.

cream puff pastry   See PÂTE À CHOUX.

Crécy, à la [ah lah kray-see]   With carrots; from the town of the same name, where the finest French carrots were grown.

crema [KRAY-mah]   Spanish for custard, cream.

crémant [kray-manh]   French wine term for a lightly sparkling wine.

crème à l'anglaise [krem ah l'anh-glez]   French for custard.

crème brûlée [krem brü-lay]   French for a rich custard topped with a brittle layer of sugar (usually brown sugar), caramelized under the broiler just before serving.

crème Chantilly   See CHANTILLY.

crème Chiboust   See CHIBOUST.

crème fraîche [krem fresh]   French for heavy cream with a lactic culture introduced; the culture acts as a preservative and gives a characteristic tangy flavor; see also FLEURETTE.

crème pâtissière [krem pa-tee-syayr]   French for pastry cream—a custard of eggs, flour, milk, and sugar used to fill cream puffs, line tarts underneath fruit, and garnish various pastries.

crème pralinée [krem pra-lee-nay]   CRÈME PÂTISSIÈRE flavored with powdered PRALINE; used to fill PARIS-BREST and other French pastries.

crème renversée [krem renh-vayr-say]   A French custard baked in a caramel-lined mold, chilled, and inverted for serving.

cremini [kre-MEE-nee]   A strain of the familiar cultivated white mushroom with darker color, fuller flavor, and earthier texture. Cremini is the same brown mushroom common in the United States before the 1920s, recently reintroduced, that fully mature becomes a PORTOBELLO MUSHROOM; the name and its derivation are unclear but have caused confusion.

Creole   In Louisiana, food cooked in the Creole style usually begins with sautéed tomatoes, onions, celery, and sweet peppers, and often includes rice; it combines the many local influences—French, Spanish, African, and Indian—in a unique way; see also CAJUN. In classic French cuisine, *à la créole* designates a dish garnished with rice and containing sweet peppers, onion, and tomatoes cooked in oil.

crêpe [krep]   A pancake made thin, light, and surprisingly strong from the eggy batter; invariably stuffed, spread, or served with moist mixtures, either savory or sweet.

crêpes Suzette [krep sü-zet]   Crêpes heated in a chafing dish at table with a sauce of orange juice and zest, butter, and orange-flavored liqueur, and flambéed.

crépinette [kray-pee-net]   A small French sausage wrapped in CAUL rather than casing, usually made of pork, and occasionally truffled; *crépine* is pig's caul.

Crescenza   See STRACCHINO.

crespella [kres-PEL-lah]   An Italian crêpe, usually stuffed or stacked with filling between the layers.

cress   A general name for various peppery small-leaved plants, especially watercress and other members of the mustard family, nasturtium, and garden cress; these are usually harvested very young, sometimes as sprouts, and used in salads, soups, and other savory dishes; in Asia especially they are valued as healthful tonics.

crevette [kreh-vet]   French for shrimp.

crisp   British for potato chip; food fried or dried to make the texture brittle; a baked American dessert, often apple, with sweet crumbly topping.

croaker   A large family of fish, sometimes called drum, found mostly in temperate western Atlantic waters; it is named for the noise it makes during spawning season; croaker is excellent in various culinary preparations but should not be eaten raw.

croissant [kwah-sanh]   A light yeast-dough pastry layered like puff pastry, rolled into a "crescent" shape, sometimes stuffed, and baked; an indispensable part of the traditional French breakfast.

croquembouche [krōk-emh-boosh]   French bite-size cream puffs, literally "crack-in-the-mouth," piled high into a pyramid and cemented together with sugar glaze or caramel; other pastries and fruits arranged in an ornamented pile.

croque monsieur [krōk muh-syeu]   The French version of a grilled ham and cheese sandwich, often cooked in a special device; a *croque madame* is a cheese and chicken and fried egg sandwich.

croqueta [krō-KAY-tah]   Spanish for croquette.

croquette [krō-ket]   Chopped meat or vegetables bound with a white sauce, coated with bread crumbs, and fried into a crisp, brown cylindrical shape; originally French.

cròsta, crostata, crostatina [KRŌ-stah, krō-STAH-tah, krō-stah-TEE-nah]   Italian for crust, pie, tart.

crostacei [krō-STAH-chay]   Italian for shellfish.

crostino [krō-STEE-nō]   Italian croûton or croûte; a small piece of toast brushed with oil and spread with a savory topping.

Crottin de Chavignol [krō-tinh deu sha-vee-nyōl]   A French goats' milk cheese from Berry; semihard to hard, shaped in very small discs; aging brings out its goaty flavor, an acquired taste that is favored by connoisseurs; *crottin* literally means "dung."

croustade [kroo-stad]   French for hollowed bread or pastry that serves as a base for a savory purée or ragoût.

croûte [kroot]   French for crust, shell, or piece of bread or dough used in various savory preparations; *en croûte* means encased in pastry.

croûton [kroo-tonh]   French for a small piece of bread or dough used for garnish; sautéed bread cubes.

crown roast A loin of pork or two loins of lamb from the rib section, tied into a crown, trimmed, and roasted; the ends of the rib bones are often decorated with paper frills, the center filled with a vegetable or starch stuffing.

cru [krü] French for growth; that is, a specific vineyard and its wine; a vineyard of superior quality. See also CLASSED GROWTH.

crudités [krü-dee-tay] Raw food, usually vegetables, eaten before a meal to assuage hunger and stimulate appetite.

crudo [KROO-dō] Italian and Spanish for raw, fresh.

crumble A British dessert of juicy raw fruit topped with crumbly pastry and baked.

crustacean A class of arthropods, mostly water-dwelling, with a hard shell; it includes all members of the lobster, shrimp, crayfish, and crab families.

cruzado [kroo-SAH-dō] "Cross-breed" soup of beef, chicken, or fish and vegetables in broth, in many variations, from Venezuela.

cú [tsoo] Chinese for vinegar.

cua rang muoi [kooah rang mooee] A Vietnamese dish of crabs fried with garlic and onion; sometimes called "salt and pepper crab."

cuaresmeño [kwah-res-MAY-nyō] A green chili pepper sometimes confused with the JALAPEÑO, but actually darker, rounder, hotter, and less flavorful.

cube To cut food into cubes about ½ inch across; larger than DICE or MIREPOIX.

cubeb [KYOO-beb] The berry of a pepper plant native to Indonesia, especially Java, used in that cuisine; the dried brown peppercorns taste more like allspice than pepper; once popular in Europe with the spice trade, but now unknown; also called tailed pepper.

cu cai hu [koo kaee hoo] Preserved cabbage in Vietnamese cooking.

cucumber A long, thin gourd native to India and cultivated over millennia for its crisp, juicy flesh that is especially refreshing in hot climates. Younger varieties, with thin skins, immature seeds, and mildly sweet flavor are preferable to the common fat, seedy, bitter ones in thick, waxy skins; the miniature gherkin cucumber is pickled or eaten fresh; the excellent English or hothouse cucumber, often labeled seedless, grows up to 2 feet in length.

cuillère [kwee-yayr] French for spoon.

cuisse [kwees] French for drumstick; *cuisseau* means leg, usually of veal.

cuissot [kwee-sō]   French for haunch of venison or boar.

culotte [kü-loht]   French for rump of beef.

Cumberland sauce   Red currant jelly dissolved with port and flavored with shallots, orange zest, and mustard—a traditional British accompaniment to ham, venison, and other game.

cumin [KUH-min, KOO-min, KYOO-min]   A pungent spice made from the dried and ground seeds of the cumin plant; a relative of parsley, cumin is used in Mexican, North African, Middle Eastern, and Asian cooking, especially curries. The seeds look like those of CARAWAY, and European languages often confuse the two spices despite their different tastes.

cuore [KWOHR-ay]   Italian for heart.

Curaçao [kyoor-a-SOW]   A liqueur made from the dried zest of the green sour orange found on the island of Curaçao in the Dutch Antilles; Cointreau is another brand of triple sec.

curd   The solid residue of coagulated milk that separates from liquid whey after acidification in the cheesemaking process.

cure   To age a food product, such as cheese, wine, fish, or meat, in order to preserve it by methods such as drying, salting, or smoking.

curly endive   See CHICORY.

currant   A small berry, juicy, tart, and high in pectin, used in savory and sweet cooking, especially in northern Europe. Of its three colors, red, black, and white, the red is most common; black (CASSIS) is larger in size and muskier in flavor than the translucent red; and white (actually colorless) is milder and least common, a variety of the red currant. Since the bush is host to white pine blister rot, its cultivation and sale are limited in some states. The currant raisin is a dried small black grape named for the city of Corinthe, no relation.

curry   A mixture of spices widely used in Indian cooking for thousands of years, originally as a preservative. Ground on a special stone, the particular spices vary according to individual taste, a specific dish, or regional preferences (those of the south tend to be hotter). The MASALA, or spice mixture, can be either wet (in which case it is ground with vinegar, coconut milk, or water and must be used immediately) or dry (in which case it is ground to a powder that can be kept for a while). The many spices (most have separate entries) include cardamom, chilies, cinnamon, clove, coriander, cumin, fennel seed, fenugreek, garlic, mace, nutmeg, onion, poppy seeds, saffron, sesame seeds, tamarind, and turmeric. The term curry can also mean a stew flavored with curry spices. See also GARAM.

curry leaf   An Asian plant whose leaves, fresh and dried, are widely used in the cooking of the western coastal and southern India; perhaps it gave its name to the spice blend we think of as curry powder.

custard   A milk and egg mixture cooked gently (below boiling to avoid curdling) on the stove or in the oven until thickened.

custard apple   A general term for various tropical fruits, including the CHERIMOYA and PAPAW.

custard marrow   See CHAYOTE.

cut in   To mix particles of fat, such as butter or lard, throughout flour with two knives or a pastry blender.

cutlet   A thin scallop of meat, usually a slice from the leg and preferably from one muscle.

cuvée [kü-vay]   French for a particular blend, lot, or batch of wine.

cygne [SEE-nyuh]   French for swan, made from PÂTE À CHOUX and filled with crème CHANTILLY.

cymling   See PATTYPAN.

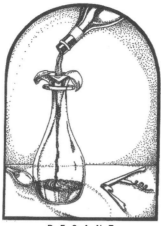

DECANT

D

dab See FLOUNDER.

dacquoise [da-KWAHZ] A French pastry made of MERINGUE combined with finely ground nuts, baked in discs, and filled with flavored whipped cream or buttercream and often fresh berries. Also, a white wine sauce in the style of Dax, in southwestern France, with onions, grapes, and ham.

daging [dah-ging] Indonesian and Malaysian for beef; *semur daging* is slices of cooked beef in gingered soy sauce.

daikon [dī-kon] A large mild white or sometimes black radish used extensively in Japanese cooking, in either raw or cooked form, for salads, stir-fries, and garnishes.

daiquirí A cocktail of white rum and lime juice, named for the town in eastern Cuba; Hemingway's favorite drink.

daizu [dī-zoo] Dried soybeans.

dak jim [tahk chim] A Korean chicken stew marinated and simmered with seasonings and vegetables.

dal In Indian cooking, the word refers to legumes of all sorts; *arhal dal* designates lentils.

dalchini [dahl-CHEE-nee] Cinnamon or cassia, in Indian cooking.

dam bay [dahm bī] Cambodian for cooked rice.

Dampfnudeln [DAHMPF-noo-deln] German yeast dumplings sweetened and served with fruit.

dàn [dahn] Chinese for egg.

Danablu [DAH-nah-bleu] A Danish blue cheese of whole raw cows' milk, made in the ROQUEFORT style.

dandelion The familiar weed whose young toothed leaves, *dents de léon*, contribute a pleasant bitterness to salads, braises, and sautés; wild dandelions should be picked in early spring before the plant has blossomed, its characteristic crown distinguishing it from the long, separate leaves of cultivated dandelion. Some types of chicory, tasting similar but unrelated, are marketed as "dandelion chicory," causing confusion. See also PISSENLIT.

dàn huā tāng [dahn whah tahng] Egg drop soup in Chinese-American restaurants, literally "egg flower soup": chicken stock into which beaten eggs are whisked to form silky strands that resemble flower petals, garnished with sliced scallions; Western versions often contain more elaborate ingredients.

Danish pastry A yeast pastry filled with nuts, fruit, custard, or cheese, and iced; originally from Denmark, but much traveled since.

dàn jiǎo [dahn jyow] Egg dumplings, traditionally for the Chinese New Year celebration for their supposed resemblance to gold coins; the dumplings have a pungent meat filling and a garnish of seasoned spinach; more often found in homes than restaurants; the Cantonese is *dan gau*.

dàn juǎn [dahn juan] Chinese for egg roll; a square crêpelike wrapper made from an egg, flour, and water batter, usually stuffed with pork, cabbage, or other vegetables, rolled up, and deep-fried or steamed, or sometimes shredded for garnishing. The egg roll, very popular in Cantonese-American cooking, is thicker and less elegant than CHŪN JUǍN (spring roll) and should not be confused with it.

Daõ [dow] Red and white table wines produced in the Daõ River valley in the town of Viseu in Portugal; they are full-bodied, deep in color, and made from the same grape varieties as PORT.

dariole [daahr-yōl] French for a cylindrical mold, usually small; also a cake baked in such a mold.

Darjeeling A variety of TEA from the Indian province of the same name.

darne [daahrn]   French for fish steak; a thick cross section of fish.

dasheen   See TARO.

dashi [dah-shee]   Japanese fish stock made of dried bonito and seaweed; used extensively in Japanese cooking.

date   The date palm and its fruit, a staple since prehistoric times in its native North Africa and Arabia, an ideal convenience food for desert nomads; today, arid areas of California and Arizona also produce dates. The many varieties fall into three categories: soft fruit with high moisture content, relatively less sugar, and mild flavor (Khadrawy and Halawy); semisoft with low moisture, higher sugar content, but aromatic flavor (Deglet Noor and Medjool, and to a lesser extent in the West, the Zahidi); and dry varieties, hard and high in sugar, rarely imported into the United States.

dàttero [DAT-tayr-ō]   Italian for date.

daube, en [enh dōb]   In French cooking, meat, usually beef, slowly braised in red wine and seasonings; stew; a *daubière* is a tight-lidded casserole for cooking *daubes*, originally with indentations in the lid for charcoal.

dau fu   See DÒU FÙ.

Daumont, à la [ah lah dō-monh]   In French cooking, a large fish garnished with quenelles, roe, mushrooms, and crayfish, served with NANTUA SAUCE.

dauphine, à la [ah lah dō-feen]   In French cooking, potato purée mixed with *pâte à choux* and deep-fried in balls or baked in piped shapes.

dauphinoise [dō-feen-waz]   In French cooking, in the style of Dauphiné; potatoes *à la dauphinoise* are sliced and baked with milk, egg yolk, nutmeg, Gruyère, and garlic.

daurade [dō-rad]   French for gilthead bream, considered superior to *dorade*, which is red sea bream.

dau sah bau   See *dòu shā bāo* under DÒU SHĀ.

débourbage [day-boor-bajh]   French for clearing the sediment from newly pressed grape juice, especially white, by allowing it to settle for 24 hours before starting fermentation; this technique must be closely controlled.

debrecziner [deh-breh-zeen-er]   A Hungarian sausage similar to a Frankfurter but spicier and coarser in texture.

decant   To transfer wine from bottle to carafe or decanter, in order to remove sediment before serving; decanting is practiced primarily with old red wines, whose bottles are held against the light of a candle to show sediment as it first appears.

découper [day-koo-pay]   In French, to cut up, to carve.

dee la   Thai for sesame seeds.

deep-fry   To cook food immersed in a large amount of hot fat, thus sealing the outside while keeping the inside moist.

déglacer [day-gla-say]   In French, to deglaze by dissolving—with wine, stock, or other liquid—the sediment left in the pan after meat, poultry, or fish has been cooked in a small amount of fat.

dégorger [day-gohr-jhay]   In French, to soak a food, such as sweetbreads, in cold water in order to cleanse it; also an important final step in making Champagne, whereby the sediment is removed from the bottle before the DOSAGE and final cork are added.

dégraisser [day-gres-say]   In French, to remove grease from the surface of liquid, by skimming, or from a large piece of meat, by scraping or cutting.

dégustation [day-gü-sta-syonh]   French for tasting or sampling.

Deidesheim [DĪ-des-hīm]   A town in the German Palatinate producing excellent white wines, mostly Rieslings, with full body, fine bouquet, and varying sweetness.

Delicata squash   A small oblong winter squash with thin skin striped yellow and green and sweet yellow flesh; developed in the late nineteenth century and recently revived.

Delmonico   A boneless cut of beef from the rib section, roasted or cut into steaks; also called Spencer steak; named for the nineteenth-century New York restaurant.

Demeltorte [DAY-mel-tor-teh]   A pastry filled with candied fruit, from Demel's Café in Vienna.

demerara sugar [deh-meh-RAHR-ah]   Partially refined raw cane sugar, naturally light brown in color from molasses, less moist than MUSCOVADO SUGAR; named for the river in British Guiana.

demi, demie [deu-mee]   French for half.

demi-deuil, à la [ah lah deu-mee-doy]   In French cooking, poultry and other pale-colored foods garnished with truffles to resemble "half-mourning"; with poultry, the truffle slices are slipped between the skin and breast meat.

demi-feuilletage   See ROGNURES.

demi-glace [deu-mee-glas]   In French cuisine, brown sauce reduced by half—nearly to a glaze—with veal stock.

demijohn   A large, narrow-necked wine bottle or jug of varying size, sometimes in a wicker or straw jacket; from the French Dame Jeanne.

demi-sec [deu-mee-sek]   A French term for Champagne and sparkling white wines denoting them as sweet, even though the literal meaning is "half-dry"; this is the sweetest category of Champagne.

demi-sel [deu-mee-sel]   Soft, fresh, whole-milk cows' cheese from Normandy, in a small square.

Demi-Suisse   See PETIT-SUISSE.

dendê [DEN-day]   Cooking oil from the *dendê* palm tree, originally West African, that gives Brazilian cooking its distinctive character; orange in color, nutty in flavor, highly saturated, and hard to digest, it should be used in tiny amounts as an accent; other fats are often substituted outside Brazil.

dénerver [day-nayr-vay]   In French, to remove gristle, tendons, membrane, and so on from meat.

denjang [DEN-jahng]   Korean for soybean paste, a staple seasoning.

Denominazione Controllata [day-nō-mee-na-TSYŌ-nay con-trō-LAH-tah]   The Italian equivalent of APPELLATION CONTRÔLÉE; recently implemented.

dente, al [al DEN-tay]   In Italian, literally, "to the bite"; refers to pasta or vegetables cooked only until firm and crunchy, not soft and overdone.

dépecer [day-peh-say]   In French, to cut up, to carve.

deposit   See SEDIMENT.

dépouiller [day-poo-yay]   In French, to skim the fat or scum from the surface of a sauce or stock.

Derby or Derbyshire [DAR-bee-shur]   An English cows' milk cheese, uncooked and hard, pale and mild, made in large flat rounds by a method similar to that of CHEDDAR; SAGE DERBY is flavored and colored with the herb.

desayuno [day-sī-YOO-nō]   Spanish for breakfast.

deshebrar [day-sheh-BRAR]   In Spanish, to shred.

désosser [day-sohs-say]   In French, to bone.

détrempe [day-tremhp]   In French, a dough of flour and water in which a layer of butter is encased in making PÂTE FEUILLETÉE.

devils on horseback   A British savory of prunes seasoned with chutney or per-haps hot sauce, wrapped in bacon, grilled, and served on toast points; like AN-GELS ON HORSEBACK, today it may be served as an appetizer.

Devonshire cream   See CLOTTED CREAM.

dhania [DUH-nyah]   Coriander in Indian cuisine.

dhansak [DAHN-sahk]   A substantial Indian Parsi dish of meat or chicken, veg-etables, lentils, and blended and dry MASALA, served at festival meals with rice and accompaniments.

diable, à la [ah lah DYA-bleh]   In French cooking, deviled; food, usually meat or poultry, spiced with mustard, vinegar, or hot seasoning, coated with bread crumbs, and grilled; *sauce diable* is DEMI-GLACE with white wine or vinegar and cayenne pepper; the Italian is *diavolo*.

diablotins [dya-blō-tinh]   In French, cheese-flavored croûtes or choux for gar-nishing soup.

diǎn xīn [dee-en sheen]   Mandarin for DÍM SUM.

dice   Small squares of food, technically smaller than a cube, therefore ¼- to ⅛-inch square.

dicke Bohnen mit Rauchfleisch [DI-keh BŌ-nen mit ROWKH-flīsh]   A West-phalian dish of broad beans with bacon and smoked pork belly.

dieppoise, à la [ah lah dyep-pwaz]   In French cuisine, saltwater fish, especially sole, garnished with mussels and crayfish in a white-wine reduction sauce.

diffa [DEE-fah]   A Moroccan banquet, where abundance is the hallmark of hos-pitality: very many dishes (but actually no waste).

digestif [dee-jhes-teef]   A drink, usually alcoholic, taken to help the digestion and therefore most often postprandial; the Italian word is *digestivo*.

Dijon [dee-jhonh]   The capital of Burgundy; Dijon mustard has a white-wine base; *à la dijonnaise* means with a mustard-flavored sauce.

dill   An herb whose leaves and seeds flavor food, especially in Scandinavia, Germany, central and eastern Europe, Persia, and Turkey; elsewhere the herb is little used other than for pickling cucumbers. Fresh leaves have a penetrat-ing, aromatic flavor and should be used with discretion; dried leaves have lit-tle flavor at all. Fish, especially GRAVLAX and crayfish, cucumbers, and sour cream are accompanied by dill in Scandinavia. In Russia and Ukraine, dill adorns borscht. Dill seeds, very similar to caraway, often flavor potato salads, carrots, and other vegetable dishes.

dím sum   In Chinese cooking, small dishes, such as various dumplings, fried shrimp balls, spareribs, or fried spring rolls, eaten for snacks during the day; served in restaurants specializing in these dishes, which are from Canton; the Mandarin is *diǎn xīn* [dee-en sheen]; the term means "close to the heart."

dinde [dinhd]   French for turkey hen; *dindon* is a cock, *dindonneau* a young turkey.

Dionysus   See BACCHUS.

dip   Thai for raw, half-cooked.

diplomat pudding   In British cooking, a molded dessert of ladyfingers soaked with candied fruit in liqueur or brandy and layered alternately with custard. Diplomat sauce is sauce NORMANDE with lobster butter, garnished with diced lobster and truffles.

dirty rice   A rice and beans dish from the southern United States, with chicken gizzards and livers that, along with garlic, onions, and peppers, give the rice its "dirty" appearance.

disossato [dee-sohs-SAH-tō]   Italian for boned.

djaj [djaj]   Arabic for chicken; in Moroccan cooking, one classic chicken TAJIN is *djaj emshmel*, with preserved lemons, olives, onions, and spices; another is *djaj masquid bil beid*, chicken with eggs, lemons, and olives.

Dobostorte [DŌ-bōsh-tor-teh]   Thin layers of sponge cake spread with chocolate cream, stacked, and glazed with hot caramel; created by the Austrian pâtissier Josef Dobos.

dodine   See BALLOTINE.

doigts de Fatma [DWAH de FAHT-mah]   "The fingers of Fatima," Mohammed's daughter; a Tunisian appetizer of meat, cheese, and so on, wrapped in MAL-SOUKA.

dolce [DŌL-chay]   Italian for sweet; the plural, *i dolci*, means desserts.

Dolcelatte [DŌL-che-LAH-tay]   An Italian mild blue-veined cheese, literally "sweet milk," a younger, milder, sweeter type of GORGONZOLA.

Dolcetto [dōl-CHET-tō]   A grape variety, grown in Piedmont, used in Italian red wines; early ripening, with purple juice; dry, fruity, fresh, and charming, best drunk young; very popular now.

dolmasi [dōl-MAH-see]   In Turkish cooking, stuffed leaves or other vegetables; usually a blanched grape leaf filled with rice and ground lamb and braised in stock, oil, and lemon juice; the Persian is *dolmeh*, the Greek *dolmathes*.

domaine [dō-men]   A French vineyard comprising a single property, whether or not it is contiguous; in Bordeaux and Provence, the word means château; the German word is *Domaene*.

domates [dō-MAH-tays]   Turkish for tomatoes.

Dom Perignon [domh payr-ee-nyonh]   A Benedictine monk, cellar master at the Abbey of Hautvilliers, whom tradition credits with the invention of the process for making Champagne; now the brand name of the best wine produced by Moët et Chandon.

dom yam gung [tohm yam guhng]   In Thai cooking, a very popular dish of shrimp in broth with chilies, lemongrass, lime juice, and citrus leaves.

donburi [don-boo-ree]   In Japanese cooking, a porcelain footed bowl with lid and, by extension, the food that goes in it; this is hot boiled rice with a topping of meat, fish, vegetables, eggs, condiments, and garnishes, often leftovers, and a last-minute addition of DASHI. *Donburi* has become a fast food lunch or snack, a convenience food usually bought at a chain restaurant.

döner kebab [deu-NAYR keh-BAHB]   See KEBAB.

dong [dohng]   To pickle, in Thai; *pak dong* means pickled vegetables.

dōng gū [dohng goo]   Chinese dried black mushrooms, eaten fresh but preferably dried and soaked in boiling water for their intense, smoky, distinctive flavor; the Cantonese is *dong gwoo*.

dōng guā tāng [dohng gwah tahng]   In Chinese cooking, winter melon soup, made with chicken broth, ham, and black mushrooms; the ingredients are steamed in the hollowed melon and then served in it. The winter melon resembles a watermelon splotched with white "snow" on the skin and white flesh inside, but the soup is savory. This classic festival soup, from southern China, is enjoyed throughout the country.

doo-boo   Korean for tofu.

Doppelbock [DOHP-pel-BOHK]   Extra strong German BOCK beer.

dorade [dō-rad]   French for red sea bream; see also DAURADE.

dorage [dō-rajh]   See DORURE.

dorato [dor-RAH-tō]   In Italian cooking, dipped in egg batter and fried to a golden color.

dorée [dō-ray]   French for JOHN DORY or Saint-Pierre.

Doria [dor-yah]   In classic French cuisine, a garnish for fish of cucumbers that are shaped into small ovals and simmered in butter.

Dorsch   German for cod.

dorure [dor-ür]   In French cooking, egg wash for "gilding" pastry, made by beating together egg or egg yolk and a little water and brushing a thin layer on the surface of the pastry to color during baking.

dosa [DŌ-sah]   An Indian pancake of rice flour and ground lentils, sometimes eaten with chutney and spicy potatoes, when it is *dosa masala*, from southern India.

dosage [dō-zajh]   French for sugar syrup added to bottled wine after the *dégorgement* (during the Champagne process), the amount of which determines the degree of sweetness of the finished wine.

dòu [dō]   Chinese for bean.

double boiler   See BAIN-MARIE.

Double Gloucester   A cows' milk cheese with a rich, mellow flavor, dense, almost waxy texture, and deep yellow color from ANNATTO, made in large flat rounds; so named because this English cheese, made from the whole milk of two milkings of the Gloucester cow, is twice as large as Single Gloucester.

dòu fù [dō foo]   Bean curd, the Chinese version of TOFU, usually made from coagulated soybean milk and an important source of protein in the Chinese diet. Chinese *dòu fù* is drier than Japanese tofu, and that found in the United States is generally softer and moister than in China. The soybean and its curd are made into many products: soybean milk; fermented bean curd (*fù rǔ*), comparable to a Chinese cheese; molded bean curd (*chòu dòu fù*), fermented in brine and eaten with pickled vegetables, a favorite snack and an acquired taste due to its stink; and dried bean curd (*dòu fù gān*); also soy sauce, sweet bean paste, hoisin sauce, and hot bean paste. It is also processed into sheets, sticks, noodles, and skins. The Cantonese is *dau fu* [dow foo].

dough   Flour or meal mixed with water, milk, or other liquid, for making bread or pastry.

dòu jiāng [dō jung]   Soy milk in Mandarin, a breakfast food and milk substitute in China; also called *dòu zhī*. The Cantonese is *dow ji*.

Douro Valley [DOOR-ō]   River valley in Portugal where PORT is made.

dòu shā [dō shah]   Red bean paste in Chinese cooking, made from azuki beans mashed and sweetened, probably also flavored, into a paste; used for pastry fillings such as *dòu shā bāo*, buns with red bean filling, a sweet pastry eaten for tea, dessert, or as part of a dim sum offering; the Cantonese name is *dau sah bau* [dow sah bow].

dòu shì [dō sheuh]   Fermented black beans, a Chinese condiment made from salted, fermented beans and used in delicate savory sauces; the Cantonese term is *dow see.*

doux, douce [doo, doos]   Sweet; as a wine term it implies sweetening by an agent rather than by nature.

Dover sole   See SOLE.

dovi [DOR-vee]   Peanuts in the cuisine of Zimbabwe; *huku ne dovi,* a chicken and peanut stew, with onions, tomatoes, and mushrooms; *nhopi dovi,* puréed pumpkin with peanut sauce, either hot or cold, sweet or savory.

dow ji   See DÒU JIĀNG.

dragée [dra-jhay]   French for sugar-coated almond; sugarplum.

dragoncello [drag-on-CHEL-lō]   Italian for tarragon.

Drambuie [drahm-BOO-ee]   A Scottish liqueur made from Scotch malt whisky flavored with heather honey.

drawn   Refers to a whole fish scaled and gutted but with head and fins left on; also, a bird with its gut removed.

drawn butter   See CLARIFIED BUTTER.

dredge   To coat food with a dry ingredient such as flour, cornmeal, or bread crumbs, shaking off the excess.

drum   See CROAKER.

dry   Wine term meaning not sweet.

dua [yoo-ah]   Vietnamese for coconut; *nuoc cot dua* is unsweetened coconut milk.

Dubarry, à la [ah lah dü-baahr-ee]   In French cuisine, garnished with cauliflower shaped into balls, coated with Mornay sauce, and glazed with château potatoes.

Dublin Bay prawn   British term for saltwater CRAYFISH; the French *langoustine,* the Italian *scampo,* the Norway lobster.

Dubonnet [dü-bohn-nay]   A popular French apéritif made of sweet fortified red wine, quinine, and herbs, drunk neat, with ice or soda, or mixed in cocktails; there is another type, less known, that is drier and pale golden.

duchesse, à la [ah lah dü-shes]   In French cuisine, potatoes boiled and puréed with eggs and butter and often piped as a garnish or border. A *duchesse* is a small cream puff stuffed with savory purée, coated with a CHAUD-FROID sauce, and served as an hors d'oeuvre.

duck   Web-footed water fowl, wild or domesticated, whose flavorful meat is relished at table; strictly speaking, ducks over 6 months old are mature birds, but most ducks sold in the United States are young, so the terms are used loosely. Those commonly available fresh and frozen are Long Island ducks, about 5 pounds, descended from the Peking duck, a type of mallard; the Muscovy duck (another species), a big large-breasted bird often used for crossbreeding; and Moulard, another specialty breed increasingly available. In Britain, Aylesbury and Norfolk are favorite breeds, in France, Nantes and Rouen. Domesticated ducks have a lot of fat under the skin, but proper cooking renders it while moistening the meat; wild ducks need moister methods for braising leaner birds.

duck sauce   See SUÀN MÉI JIÀNG.

duff   See PLUM DUFF.

Dugléré [dü-glay-ray]   Sole poached and served in a sauce of tomatoes, shallots, herbs, and white wine reduced and finished with cream; named for the famous eighteenth-century French chef Dugléré.

düğün çorbası [dun CHOR-bah—seu]   "Wedding soup," a Turkish dish of mutton soup with beaten egg yolks, lemon, and paprika.

dukkah [DOO-kah]   In Egyptian cooking, a dry mixture of crushed nuts and spices, such as hazelnuts with coriander, cumin, and sesame seeds, eaten with bread dipped in olive oil, for breakfast or a snack.

dulce [DOOL-thay, DOOL-say]   Spanish for sweet.

dulse   A coarse but edible seaweed from the North Atlantic, especially around Britain, used mostly for its gelatin.

dumpling   A round lump of dough steamed on top of a savory soup or stew, or stuffed and baked with a sweet fruit filling; the variety is infinite.

Dundee cake [dun-DEE]   A rich fruit cake topped with almonds, from Scotland.

Dungeness crab   Pacific rock crab, very popular, weighing up to four pounds.

dunkeles Bier [DOON-keh-les BEER]   German for dark beer.

Dunlop   A Scottish cows' milk cheese, similar to CHEDDAR but moister, softer, and blander.

dünsten [DÜN-sten]   In Germany, to steam, to stew.

durazno [doo-RAHTH-nō, doo-RAHS-nō]   Spanish for peach.

durian [DOOR-yan]   The fruit of a Malaysian tree with prickly rind and edible pulp and seeds; its highly offensive smell keeps most Westerners from tasting its flesh, considered exquisite by its advocates.

Dürkheim [DÜRK-hīm]   A town in the Rhine valley producing a very large amount of red and white wine, mostly unremarkable.

durra   See SORGHUM.

durum wheat [DOOR-um]   The hardest species of WHEAT, usually made into SEMOLINA flour.

dust   Finely broken tea leaves, inferior in grade, yielding a quick, strong brew.

Dutch oven   A large, heavy cast-iron or metal kettle with a close-fitting lid, used for cooking stews, pot roasts, and the like; originally, coals could be put on top to heat food from above as well as from below.

duxelles [dük-zel]   In French cooking, finely chopped mushrooms and shallots slowly cooked in butter to form a thick, dark paste that is used for seasoning sauces, as a spread for toast, and in other preparations; often said to be the invention of La Varenne, who worked for the Marquis d'Uxelles, but the story is probably apocryphal since he gives no such recipe in his books.

ÉCREVISSE

E

Earl Grey tea   A Chinese black TEA flavored with oil of BERGAMOT, especially popular as an afternoon tea.

eau de vie [ō deu vie]   French for fruit brandy, literally "water of life," often called *alcool blanc* ("white alcohol"); colorless *eau de vie* retains its clarity because it is aged in crockery rather than wood, unlike most brandies. Alsace, Germany, and Switzerland produce many *eaux de vie*, flavored with a wide variety of fruits; KIRSCHWASSER (cherry) and Poire Williams (pear) are among the best known.

ebi [eb-ee]   Japanese for shrimp; in Indonesia, dried shrimp, used as a side dish or garnish.

Eccles cake [EK-kuhls]   A small traditional cake, originally from Lancashire, England, of puff pastry filled with currants and sprinkled with sugar.

échalote [ay-shal-loht]   French for shallot.

échaudé [ay-shō-day]   French for pastry whose dough is first poached in water, then baked in the oven.

éclair [ay-klayr]   Choux pastry piped into finger shapes and filled with flavored cream; originally French.

écrevisse [AY-kreh-VEES]   French for freshwater crayfish.

Edam [EE-dum]   A round yellow Dutch cheese from the town of the same name, made of partly skimmed cows' milk and ripened for three months to a year; the finished cheese is coated with linseed oil and, if for export, covered with red wax.

edamame [ay-dah-mah-may]   In Japanese, fresh soybeans in the pod.

Edelfäule [AY-dehl-FOY-leh]   German for NOBLE ROT.

eel   A snakelike fish that migrates from the ocean to tidelands and rivers in spring; eel tastes best taken from fast-moving rather than brackish water and killed soon before eating. A rich and fatty fish, eel is excellent smoked, stewed, jellied, baked, and grilled; its shape may account for its unpopularity in the United States, but until the eighteenth century it was considered a delicacy in England and still is in many countries.

Eger [AY-ger]   A town in Hungary that produces two famous red wines, Egri Bikavér ("bull's blood") and Egri Kadarka; both are full-bodied, deep in color, and slow-maturing.

egg   Bird's gift to mankind, a perfectly designed and packaged unit of food, complex and potent in its simplicity, a metaphor for life. An eggshell is made of hard but porous calcium carbonate, enclosing a thin membrane, a small air pocket at one end, a transparent egg white surrounding a yellow yolk anchored by two white threads called chalazae. An egg is a powerhouse of nutrition, the watery white mostly protein, the dense, rich yolk containing fat, cholesterol, proteins, vitamins, and minerals, as well as lecithin. Although the yolk of one large egg contains 213 milligrams of cholesterol and 4½ grams of fat, a third of it saturated, recent studies suggest that moderate consumption of eggs has little effect on blood cholesterol levels. Fertile eggs, despite popular belief, have no nutritional advantage. The hen's breed determines the color of the shell; the type of feed determines the color of the yolk. Fresher eggs are cohesive and, shelled, stand higher in a dish. Eggs are sold in six sizes; most standard recipes use large. Besides the familiar chicken eggs, duck and quail are available, and occasionally those of other birds. See also SALMONELLA.

eggah   See IJJA.

egg-and-bread-crumb   To dip food into beaten egg and then into bread crumbs before frying to give it a crisp coating that keeps the food inside moist.

egg drop soup   See DÀN HUĀ TĀNG.

egg foo young   See FÚ RÓNG DÀN.

eggnog   A nutritious milk punch made of milk, beaten eggs, sugar, spices (such as nutmeg), and usually some kind of liquor.

eggplant   A member of the nightshade family, native to Asia, cultivated in many forms and colors besides the deep purple that gives it the name aubergine outside North America; the name eggplant comes from the small white oval variety first grown in the United States as an ornamental. The familiar large purple type can be hard and bitter, but salting the flesh disgorges some juices and keeps it from soaking up so much oil in cooking. Many newer specimens now available do not need this. Asian eggplants tend to be long, slender, and thin-skinned, with soft, unseedy, mild or sweet flesh; there are also small round shapes from Asia and Europe. Coloring ranges from near black to purple, lilac, pink, white, cream, green, orange, and red. The method of choosing a "female" eggplant by its rounded bottom has no botanical basis. Some eggplant dishes have separate entries.

egg roll   See DÀN JUǍN.

égrappage   [ay-grap-pajh]   French term for the process of removing stems from grapes before pressing, thus reducing the TANNIN content of the wine.

egushi   [ay-GOO-shee]   An African word for pumpkin or sesame seeds.

Ei, Eier   [Ī, Ī-er]   German for egg, eggs.

86   Restaurant kitchen slang for being out of an item on the menu.

eingelegt   [ĪN-ge-laygt]   German for pickled, marinated, preserved.

eingemacht   [ĪN-geh-mahkt]   German for pickled, preserved, bottled, canned; also preserves, jam, pickles.

Eintopf   [ĪN-tohpf]   German for "one-dish" stew or meal containing various meats and vegetables and possibly even fish.

Eis   [īs]   German for ice, ice cream.

Eisbein   [ĪS-bin]   German for pickled pork hocks, usually accompanied by mashed potatoes and sauerkraut.

Eiswein   [ĪS-vin]   German for wine made from very ripe grapes caught by an early hard frost and only partially frozen because of their high sugar content, thus concentrating the wine's sweetness; such late-harvest wines are rare.

ekmek   [ek-mek]   Turkish for bread.

elaichi   [ay-LĪ-chee]   CARDAMOM in Indian cooking.

elder   A shrub whose cream-colored flowers are delicious in fruit compotes and fritters, and whose deep purple berries contribute to fruit soups, jellies, homemade wines, and the liqueur SAMBUCA.

elote [ay-LŌ-tay]   Fresh corn in Mexican cooking.

Eltville   A town in the Rheingau region of Germany producing many consistently good white wines.

émincé [ay-minh-say]   In French, thinly sliced cooked meat, usually left over, covered with sauce and reheated.

Emmental, Emmentaler [EM-men-tahl]   A whole-milk cows' cheese from German-speaking Switzerland; the cheese is cooked, pressed, and shaped into large wheels with a hard, light brown rind and golden interior with large holes; its taste is mellow, rich, and nutty, excellent for eating or cooking, the quintessential Swiss cheese; incorrectly spelled Emmenthal or Emmenthaler.

empanada, empanadilla [em-pah-NAH-dah, em-pah-nah-DEE-yah]   A pie or tart with various savory fillings, originally from Galicia in Spain; *empanar* means to coat with bread crumbs.

empandita [em-pahn-DEE-tah]   A Spanish pastry turnover whose shape—square, round, triangular, or rectangular—indicates the specific type of filling, such as meat, seafood, or vegetable.

emshmel   With preserved lemons and olives, a Moroccan term.

emulsion   A stable liquid mixture in which one liquid is suspended in tiny globules throughout another, as with egg yolks in oil or butter for mayonnaise or hollandaise sauce.

enchilada [en-chee-LAH-dah]   In Mexican cooking, a tortilla, fried and filled variously, often with meat, chilies, or cheese.

endive [EN-dīv, enh-deev]   See CHICORY and BELGIAN ENDIVE.

enokitake [eh-nō-kee-tah-kay]   A Japanese wild and cultivated mushroom with long, thin stems and tiny caps, either white or tan; the stems should be trimmed before using these mushrooms fresh in salads or cooked in soup, stir-fried, or in TEMPURA dishes; mild in flavor, they are available fresh or canned; also called *enoki* and *enokidake*.

enrollada [en-rō-YAH-dah]   Spanish for rolled.

ensalada [en-thah-LAH-dah, en-sah-LAH-dah]   Spanish for salad.

Ente [EN-tay]   German for duck.

Entrammes   See PORT-SALUT.

entrecôte [ENH-treh-KŌT]   In French, a steak cut from between the ribs.

entrecuisse [ENH-treh-KWEES]   French for thigh or second joint of poultry and game birds, as opposed to drumstick (*cuisse*).

Entre-Deux-Mers [ENH-treh-DEU-MAYR]   A region "between two rivers," the Dordogne and Garonne, in Bordeaux, that produces a large quantity of wine; those using the name Entre-Deux-Mers are dry white wines, some of them exceptional.

entrée [enh-tray]   In the United States, this word today usually means the main course, but in France it retains its original meaning of first course.

entremeses [en-treh-MAY-ses]   Spanish for appetizers, hors d'oeuvres.

entremets [ENH-treh-MAY]   In French, literally "between courses," this vague term can denote side dishes, such as vegetables and salads, or desserts served after the cheese course.

entremettier [ENH-treh-MET-TYAY]   French for vegetable cook.

Enzian [ENT-zyan]   A German liqueur, *eau-de-vie de gentian*, made from the flower.

épaule [ay-pōl]   French for shoulder.

epazote [ay-pah-ZŌ-tay]   A wild perennial herb with strong flavor that can be an acquired taste; used in Latin American cooking, especially for tea and in bean dishes to reduce flatulence; also called stink weed.

éperlan [ay-payr-lanh]   French for smelt.

épice [ay-pees]   French for spice.

Epicurus   A Greek philosopher who espoused the pursuit of pleasure, often interpreted as indulgence in luxury and sensual pleasure; an epicure, with regard to food, can mean either a gastronome or a voluptuary.

épigramme [ay-pee-gram]   In French cooking, a preparation of lamb in which a cutlet or chop and a slice of breast are dipped in egg and bread crumbs and fried or grilled.

épinard [ay-pee-naahr]   French for spinach.

éplucher [ay-plü-shay]   To peel, in French; *épluchoir* is a paring knife.

Époisses [ay-pwahs]   A French raw or pasteurized cows' milk cheese from Burgundy, with a red-orange skin washed in white wine or marc, pungent odor, and creamy, runny, rich interior; the small discs are ripened one to three months and packed in a round, thin wooden box.

éponger [ay-ponh-jhay]   In French, to drain vegetables cooked in water or oil on towels.

Erbsen [AYRB-sen]   German for peas, usually dried and split.

Erdapfel [AYRD-ap-fel]   German for potato, especially in southern Germany and Austria. See also KARTOFFEL.

Erdbeere [AYRD-bayr-eh]   German for strawberry.

escabeche [eth-kah-BAY-chay, es-kah-BAY-shay]   Spanish and Portuguese for cooked fish, sometimes poultry, marinated in vinegar or wine (which pickles it) and other seasonings; served cold in the earthenware container in which it was pickled; often confused with *cebiche*.

escalibada [eth-KAH-lee-BAH-dah]   Spanish for mixed vegetables—sweet peppers, eggplants, tomatoes, and onions—grilled over charcoal; from Catalan.

escalope [es-ka-lōp]   French for scallop of meat or fish; a thin slice possibly flattened by pounding.

escargot [es-kaahr-gō]   French for snail.

escarole [es-kaahr-ōl]   A type of chicory with broader, less delicate leaves and a more bitter taste than lettuce; excellent for winter salads.

eshkeneh Shirazi   Persian yogurt soup with onions, walnuts, and fenugreek, from the city of Shiraz.

espadon [es-pa-donh]   French for swordfish.

espagnole [es-pa-nyōl]   A basic brown sauce that serves as the basis for many others in classic cuisine; made from brown roux, brown stock, browned MIREPOIX, tomato purée, and herbs cooked together slowly, skimmed, and strained.

espresso [es-PRES-sō]   Strong Italian coffee made with a special machine that forces steam through the coffee grounds; see also CAFFÈ.

essence   A concentrated substance, usually volatile, extracted by distillation, infusion, or other means, such as fish essence, coffee essence, vanilla extract; see also EXTRACT.

estate-bottled   See CHÂTEAU-BOTTLED.

estilo de, estilo al [eth-TEE-lō deu]   Spanish for in the style of, À LA.

estofado [eth-tō-FAH-dō, es-tō-FAH-dō]   Spanish for stew.

estouffade [es-too-fad]   In French, a dish cooked by the ÉTOUFFER method; also a brown stock used to dilute sauces and moisten braised dishes.

estragon [es-tra-gonh]   French for tarragon.

estufa   See MADEIRA.

étamine [ay-ta-meen]   In French, a cloth for straining stocks, sauces, and the like; see also TAMIS.

étouffer, étuver [ay-too-fay]   A French method of cooking food slowly in a tightly closed pan with little or no liquid; *estouffade* refers to the dish itself.

evaporated milk   Milk with its water content reduced by half and sterilized; this causes it to taste caramelized, but no sugar is actually added.

extract   Concentrated stock, juice, or solution produced by boiling and clarification (as for vegetables, fish, poultry, game, and meat, when the extract may be reduced to a jelly or *glace*) or by distillation (as for fruits, seeds, or leaves, such as vanilla, almond, rosewater, and peppermint essence). Fish extract is usually called FUMET.

eye of round   See ROUND.

FENNEL

F

fabada asturiana [fah-BAH-dah ah-thtoo-RYAH-nah]   A hearty Spanish peasant stew of dried fava or white beans cooked slowly with salt pork, ham, sausages, and onions.

fagara [fah-GAH-rah]   The berry of a Chinese prickly ash tree, also known as Szechwan peppercorn but not related to pepper; the dried berry is reddish brown, aromatic, and tingly, an essential part of Chinese five-spice powder and other Chinese seasonings.

fagioli [fah-JŌ-lee]   Italian for beans, usually white haricot or kidney beans; *fagiolini* are green string beans.

faisan [fay-sanh]   French for pheasant; the Spanish term *faisán* sometimes includes other game birds.

faisinjan   See FESENJAN.

falafel, felafel [fah-LAH-fuhl]   Dried FAVA beans or CHICKPEAS minced, spiced, shaped into balls, and deep-fried; this Egyptian dish is eaten throughout the Middle East with slight variations; also called *ta'amia*.

falooda [fah-LOO-dah]   Refreshing sweet drink made from tapioca or other starches, with AGAR-AGAR and SHARBAT; served with curry or for dessert in Indian cuisine.

fàn [fahn]   Chinese for rice; *bài fàn* is plain rice, *chǎo fàn*, fried rice, and *zhōu fàn*, *congee* rice (see ZHŌU).

fannings   Tea made from broken leaves, yielding a quick, strong brew.

farce [faahrs]   French for stuffing, forcemeat; *farci* means a stuffed dish, such as cabbage, breast of veal, or flank steak stuffed and braised.

farcito [fahr-SEE-tō]   Italian for stuffed.

farfalle [fahr-FAL-lay]   "Butterfly-" or bow-tie-shaped pasta.

farfel [FAHR-fel]   In Jewish cooking, egg dough grated, dried, and cooked in soup as a garnish.

farina [fah-REE-nah]   Italian for flour; farina is also a grade of wheat finer than SEMOLINA.

farinaceous   Made of flour or meal; from cereal grains, starchy.

farmer cheese   Cheese made from whole or partly skimmed cows' milk, similar to COTTAGE CHEESE.

farofa [fah-RŌ-fah]   A mixture of DENDÊ, onion, MANIOC meal, and chili peppers, all browned in a pan and used for stuffings and side dishes in Brazilian cuisine.

Fasnacht, Fastnacht [FAHS-nahkt, FAHST-nahkt]   A potato doughnut deep-fried in pork fat; the diamond-shaped yeast pastry, Pennsylvania German in origin, is traditionally eaten on Shrove Tuesday (*Fastnacht* in German), to use up the fat before Lent.

fasulye [fah-SOO-lyah]   Turkish for beans; *fasulye pilaki*, dried white beans stewed with onions.

fat   Fatty acids, similar to oil, but solid at room temperature, unlike most oils. Fats are stored in animals and plants for energy. They can be heated to high temperature without breaking down. For giving flavor, texture, richness, and succulence to food, they are highly important, their uses in cooking manifold. Of the different types of fat, saturated fat, usually from animals, raises cholesterol levels and is implicated in cancer and heart disease; butter, lard, suet, vegetable shortening, and margarine, also coconut and palm oil, are common types of saturated fats and have separate entries. See also OIL.

fatta [FAH-tah]   An Egyptian soup of leftover sacrificial lamb, ritually eaten 70 days after Ramadan as part of a feast; lamb soup with rice and herbs is poured over toasted bread.

fatto in casa [FAHT-tō een KAH-zah]   Italian for homemade.

fattoush [fah-TOOSH]   A Syrian salad, like PANZANELLA, of PITA or other Middle Eastern flatbread toasted and soaked with chopped cucumber, tomatoes, onions, herbs, lemon juice, and olive oil.

fava [FAH-vah]   Broad or faba bean, of Mediterranean origin; important as a nutritional component of the diet and as a rotation crop; fava beans can be eaten raw, cooked fresh, or dried, and though esteemed for their distinct flavor in the Mediterranean are largely ignored in the United States.

fegato [FAY-gah-tō]   Italian for liver; *fegatelli* means pork liver; *fegatini*, chicken livers.

feijoa [fay-YŌ-ah]   A fruit native to South America and now grown commercially in New Zealand; deep green with a white pulp, it is eaten fresh in salads or made into preserves.

feijoada [fay-JHWAH-dah]   A robust Brazilian dish halfway between a soup and a stew, made of pork trimmings (jowl, trotters, tail, ears), sausage, beef (dried, salted, and tongue), black beans, rice, and MANIOC meal, seasoned with peppers and garnished with oranges; *feijão* [fay-JHOW] is the Portuguese word for beans.

Feingebäck [FIN-geh-bek]   German for pastry.

fencen yuk   See FĚN ZHĒNG NIÚ RÒU.

fennel   A vegetable, herb, and spice in many varieties whose bulb, stems, leaves, and seeds are edible; anise-flavored, it is esteemed in Mediterranean countries where it originated; Italians call the bulb *finocchio*, the English refer to it as Florence fennel; it is no relation to Chinese anise (see BĀ JIĂO). Fennel is refreshing raw, but gains mellow subtlety and nutty flavor when sautéed or grilled. American markets often mislabel it as ANISE.

fenouil [feh-NOO-ee]   French for fennel; *au fenouil* means grilled over dried wild fennel stalks.

fēn sī [fen seu]   Cellophane or translucent noodles made from mung beans, softened in a liquid before being used in Chinese cuisine.

fenugreek   A leguminous plant from western Asia whose slightly bitter leaves are consumed fresh in salads and whose celery-flavored seeds are eaten by people and cattle; usually added to curries, fenugreek is eaten mostly in India (where it is called *methi*), the Near East, North Africa, and East Africa; in the United States it is used as the main flavoring in imitation maple syrup.

fěn zhēng niú ròu [fen zhuhng nyō rō]   Chinese steamed beef with five-spice rice powder; the Cantonese is *fencen yuk* [fen-zen yōk].

fermentation   A chemical process in making bread, cheese, wine, beer, and other foods, in which yeast, mold, or bacteria act upon sugar and bring about a transformation.

fermière, à la [ah lah fayr-myayr]   In French cooking, in the style of the farmer's wife; with mixed vegetables.

ferri, ai [ī FAYR-ree]   Italian for grilled over an open fire; also *ferri alla griglia*.

fesenjan [FES-in-jahn]   A classic Persian dish of duck or chicken pieces braised in a rich dark sauce of ground walnuts and pomegranate juice.

feta [FEH-tah]   A goats' or ewes' milk cheese originally from Greece, pressed, then cured in brine or its own salted whey; crumbly, salty, white, and rindless, it is often used in salads and cooking. Generic feta is increasingly made with cows' milk or a mixture of cows' and goats' milk, especially by large commercial producers outside Greece; commonly made in France, Israel, Rumania, Bulgaria, and the United States, with considerable distinctions in flavor and pungency.

fetta [FET-tah]   Italian for slice, fillet.

fettucine [fet-too-CHEE-nay]   Long, flat thin strips or "ribbons" of egg pasta; this is the Roman and southern Italian name for TAGLIATELLE, almost the same, but slightly narrower and thicker.

feuilletage [FOY-eh-TAJH]   French for puff pastry, PÂTE FEUILLETÉE.

fiambre [FYAHM-bray]   Spanish and Portuguese for cooked cold food.

fiasco [FYAHS-kō]   Italian for a flask or wine bottle, thin and round-bottomed, with a woven straw covering for strength and support; the plural is *fiaschi*; Chianti has the most familiar *fiasco*.

fico [FEE-kō]   Italian for fig.

fiddlehead   The young shoot of certain ferns, such as ostrich, harvested in spring as they unfurl, at which time the tips resemble violin heads, thus the name; foragers should be wary as certain fern varieties, bracken among them, are carcinogenic.

fig   An orchard tree native to western Asia, whose fruit has been valued since prehistoric times for its high sugar content, fine flavor, and voluptuous shape; its inverted form encloses multiple fruits within its structure. Of the types available in the United States today, the Smyrna fig (called Calimyrna in California) is pale gold and large; the Black Mission fig, brought to California by padres in the eighteenth century, is deep purple with red interior, gaining an intensely dark flavor when dried; the Kadota, often canned, is light green; Adriatic and Genoa are other varieties showing a Mediterranean pedigree. Highly nutritious, figs are excellent fresh and dried, in savory and sweet dishes, in bland or spicy treatments—or simply on their own.

fila   [FEE-lah]   Arabic for phyllo.

filbert   A cultivated HAZELNUT, so called because the nuts ripen around St. Philbert's Day, August 22.

filé powder   [FEE-lay]   Dried ground sassafras leaves used to thicken GUMBO in Creole cooking; added at table, not before, and (properly) instead of OKRA.

filet   [fee-lay]   French for fillet; a boneless cut or slice of meat, poultry, or fish, especially beef TENDERLOIN; filet mignon, a small, boneless, tender slice of beef from the thick end of the tenderloin.

filfil mihshi   [FIL-fil MEE-shee]   A Tunisian dish of sweet peppers stuffed with ground lamb, onions, eggs, and seasonings, then lightly battered and fried in oil.

filo   See PHYLLO.

financière, à la   [ah lah fee-nanh-syayr]   In French cuisine, "banker's style," that is, expensive: meat or poultry garnished with cocks' combs and kidneys, sweetbreads, mushrooms, olives, and truffles; sometimes these ingredients are encased in VOL-AU-VENT pastry.

fines herbes   [feen ayrb]   A mixture of chopped herbs such as parsley, chervil, tarragon, and chives used to flavor omelets, salads, chops, and so on; occasionally the term means chopped parsley alone.

fining   The process of clarifying wine by adding various substances and removing sediment.

finnan haddie   Smoked haddock; originally from the Scottish town of Findon, hence the name.

fino   [FEE-nō]   Pale, light, dry sherry, generally used as an apéritif and considered by some the best type of sherry.

finocchio   [fee-NŌK-kyō]   Italian for fennel.

Fior di Latte [fyor dee LAHT-tay]   A cows' milk cheese of the spun-curd type, similar to MOZZARELLA; originally from southern Italy.

fiorentina, bistecca alla [bee-STEK-kah ah-lah fyor-en-TEE-nah]   In Italian cooking, a T-bone steak charcoal-grilled in the Florentine style—rare and plain but moistened after grilling with a few drops of olive oil.

fiori di zucca [fyor-ee dee TZOOK-kah]   Italian for squash blossoms, often sautéed or dipped in batter and fried.

Fior Sardo [fyor SAR-dō]   A whole, raw ewes' milk cheese—the original Sardinian PECORINO and still produced in Sardinia; this Italian cheese is good for the table when young and excellent for grating when mature.

firm-ball stage   Sugar syrup that has reached a temperature of 243°F (117°C) and that forms a firm ball between the fingers when immersed in cold water.

firni [FEER-nee]   An Indian dessert pudding of ground rice cooked in milk, usually with cardamom and nuts.

first-growth wine   See CLASSED GROWTH.

five-spice powder   See WǓ XIĀNG FĚN.

flageolet [fla-jhō-lay]   French for a small pale green bean, fresh or dried, similar to the HARICOT or kidney bean.

flamande, à la [ah lah fla-manhd]   In French cuisine, "Flemish-style," garnished with braised cabbage, carrots, turnips, sliced pork belly, sausage, and potatoes.

flambé [flamh-bay]   The French word for flamed; used to describe food that is ignited with a small amount of heated liquor poured over it, the burning alcohol enveloping the dish in flames.

flameado [flah-may-AH-dō]   Spanish for flambé.

flan   Spanish caramel cream custard, a very popular dessert. Also, a bottomless ring mold, set on a sheet, usually filled with pastry, perhaps custard, and baked, either sweet or savory.

flank   A cut of beef from the lower hindquarter that, well trimmed, is true LONDON BROIL.

flanken   A cut of beef from the chuck end of the short ribs, a traditional Jewish dish, boiled and served with horseradish.

flatbread   Thin bread, leavened or unleavened, from many cultures around the world; types include CHAPATI, CRÊPE, CRESPELLA, FLATBRØD, FOCACCIA, LAVASH, MATZO, NAAN, PANCAKE, PARATHA, PITA, PIZZA, and TORTILLA.

flatbrød [FLAT-breud] "Flatbread," very thin and crisp, traditionally made in Norway of rye, barley, and wheat flours.

flatfish Any saltwater fish with both eyes on one side of the head; this includes sole, flounder, turbot, halibut, and plaice.

Fleisch [flīsh] German for meat.

Fleischkäse [FLĪSH-kay-zeh] German for meat loaf.

flétan [flay-tanh] French for halibut.

fleurette [fleur-et] French sweet cream that has not been cultured with lactic acid to make CRÈME FRAÎCHE.

fleuron [fleur-onh] French for a small ornament, such as a crescent, cut from flaky pastry to garnish hot food.

floating island See ÎLE FLOTTANTE.

flor In Spanish, literally "flower"; the name for the yeast that naturally forms after fermentation on Spanish FINO and AMONTILLADO sherries and on those of other countries by inoculation, and which greatly improves the wine.

Florence fennel See FENNEL.

florentine, à la [ah lah flohr-enh-teen] In French cuisine, "Florentine-style," with spinach; a garnish, especially for eggs and fish, of a bed of spinach; the whole dish is often masked with MORNAY sauce. Also a confection of butter, sugar, honey, cream, candied orange zest, and almonds cooked to the soft-ball stage; mounds are baked and coated on the bottom with chocolate. The term is not used in the same way in Italy.

flounder A flatfish member of the SOLE family in many varieties, including plaice, brill, halibut, sanddab, turbot, and so-called gray, lemon, rock, and petrale sole. The flounder's shape is rounder than that of sole and though an excellent fish for eating, many of the names under which it is marketed in the United States are merely intended to make it more attractive to the consumer.

flour Finely milled meal of grain, usually meaning wheat. Flour can be steelground in huge industrial machines, which destroys some nutritional value and eliminates the germ, or stone-ground by the old traditional method that preserves the germ and uses less heat. Bolting, or sifting, determines texture. All-purpose flour contains both hard (high-gluten) and soft (low-gluten) wheats; bread flour (high-gluten) is best for yeast breads; cake or pastry flour (fine-textured, low-gluten) is best for cakes and cookies. See also WHEAT, GLUTEN, SELF-RISING FLOUR; nonwheat grains have separate entries.

flummery In British cooking, an oatmeal or custard pudding, thick and sweet; in the United States, it has come to mean a fruit pudding thickened with cornstarch.

flute To make a grooved or furrowed pattern in certain fruits and vegetables, especially mushrooms, or in the edges of a pie crust; also the name of a Champagne glass shaped in a deep slender cone.

focaccia [fō-KAH-chah] A flat, round Italian peasant bread flavored variously but always with olive oil; originally baked on hot stones on the hearth, then in a brick oven. Often eaten as a snack, *focaccia* is similar to pizza, but with more dough, less topping. Each region has its traditional flavorings, shapes, and styles. With its recent American popularity, it is often flavored with garlic and rosemary or sage and pancetta.

foie gras [fwah grah] In French cuisine, the enlarged livers of force-fed geese and ducks, especially the geese of Toulouse and Strasbourg. In the United States, only duck foie gras, from ducks raised for that purpose without being force-fed, is available fresh; goose foie gras is imported, thus already cooked or processed. Foie gras can be prepared many ways, including cooked in a terrine, quickly pan-seared in slices, or made into pâté.

fold To combine a frothy light substance, such as beaten egg whites or cream, with a heavier one by using a gentle circular motion, in order not to lose air and reduce volume and lightness.

Folle Blanche [fōl blanhsh] A French grape variety yielding a pale, light, clean, and acidic wine, productive but vulnerable; also called Picpoul in the Armagnac country, where it produces an excellent brandy but a mediocre table wine.

foncer [fonh-say] In French, to line a cake or pie tin; PÂTE BRISÉE and PÂTE SUCRÉE are types of *pâte à foncer*.

fond, fonds de cuisine [fonh] See STOCK.

fondant [fonh-danh] French for an icing mixture used as a coating in confectionery and pastry.

fond d'artichaut [fonh d'aahr-tee-shō] French for artichoke heart.

fondre, faire [FAYR FONH-dreh] In French, to "melt" vegetables, especially onions, leeks, and garlic, by cooking them very gently until softened.

fondue [fonh-dü] From the French word for melted, fondue has several meanings: in Switzerland, it refers to Swiss cheese, melted with white wine and seasonings in a special earthenware pot over a flame, for dipping bread cubes into. *Fondue bourguignonne* is cubes of raw beef speared and cooked in a pot of oil heated over a flame, then eaten with various sauces. In French cooking, it can refer to minced vegetables, such as tomatoes, cooked in butter or oil until they disintegrate; also a dish of eggs scrambled with melted cheese and butter.

fonduta [fohn-DOO-tah]   An Italian dish of melted FONTINA cheese with eggs, butter, milk, sliced truffles, and white pepper; from the Piedmont region.

Fontal [fohn-TAL]   A pasteurized whole-milk cows' cheese from northern Italy and eastern France, similar to Fontina but without its distinction.

Fontina [fohn-TEE-nah]   Raw whole-milk cows' cheese, semicooked and pressed, originally from the Italian Aosta Valley near the Swiss border; it is pale yellow with a brown crust, about one foot across in wheels, firm but creamy, mild yet nutty; true Fontina is a fine cheese, but there are many inferior imitations, spelled in lowercase.

foo foo   Mashed plantain dumpling, boiled or perhaps fried, served with stews and sauces in the Caribbean; sometimes made from other starchy vegetables; also spelled *fou fou*.

foogath [FOO-gath]   An Indian vegetable dish cooked with coconut.

fool   In British cooking, a purée of fruit, such as rhubarb or gooseberry, mixed with cream; the word apparently does not come from the French *foulé*, meaning crushed, but is akin to the English folly or TRIFLE.

forcemeat   Stuffing.

Forelle [for-EL-leh]   German for trout.

forestière, à la [ah lah for-es-tyayr]   In French cuisine, garnished with sautéed morels or other mushrooms, diced bacon, and diced potatoes sautéed in butter.

formaggio [for-MAJ-jō]   Italian for cheese.

fortified   Refers to wines (such as port, sherry, and Madeira) that have had brandy or another spirit added to them before bottling, thus strengthening their alcohol content.

fouet [foo-ay]   French for whisk; *fouetté* means whisked.

four, au [ō FOOR]   French for baked in the oven.

Fourme d'Ambert [foorm d'amh-bayr]   A tall cylindrical cheese from the French Auvergne, made from raw, partly skimmed cows' milk; it is creamy, with blue veins and a dry rind.

fourrage [foor-rajh]   In French, filling or stuffing, as for pastry.

fragola [FRAH-gō-lah]   Italian for strawberry; *fragoline di bosco* are wild strawberries.

frais, fraîche [fray, fresh]   French for fresh.

fraisage [freh-zajh]   French for a technique for working lumps of butter or other fat into flour by smearing the dough across the work board with the heel of the hand and then regathering it; *fraiser* means to knead.

fraise [frez]   French for strawberry; *fraises des bois* are wild strawberries.

framboise [frahm-bwaz]   French for raspberry.

frambuesa [frahm-BWAY-sah]   Spanish for raspberry.

française, à la [ah lah franh-sez]   In the French style, used very broadly; see also RUSSE, À LA.

Franconia   A wine-producing region of Germany in the upper Main Valley around Würzburg; its white wines, of Sylvaner and Riesling varieties, are bottled in the characteristic squat flat-sided green flagons called *Bocksbeutels*.

frangipane [franh-jhee-pan]   In French cooking, a type of choux pastry, originally Italian; *frangipane* cream is a CRÈME PATISSIÈRE flavored with almonds.

Frankfurter [FRAHNK-foor-ter]   A German sausage from which the hot dog is descended: smoked pork and beet, served poached; called *Bockwurst* in Frankfurt.

frappé [frap-pay]   French for chilled; iced; surrounded by crushed ice.

Frascati, à la [ah lah fra-SKAH-tee]   A classical French garnish of sliced foie gras, truffles, fluted mushroom caps, asparagus, and DUCHESSE potato crescents, with veal stock. Frascati is also a pleasant dry white wine produced in the town of the same name near Rome.

freddo [FRED-dō]   Italian for cold.

free-range   Animals, especially poultry, that theoretically have access to open pasture, as opposed to confinement and battery-feeding.

fresa [FRAY-thah]   Spanish for strawberry.

fresco [FRES-kō, FRETH-kō]   Italian and Spanish for fresh.

Fresno chili   In Mexican cooking, a small cone-shaped chili pepper, fairly hot in flavor.

friandise [free-anh-deez]   French for PETIT FOUR or small confection.

fricassée [free-kas-say]   A French stew of white meat, usually poultry or veal, first sautéed in butter, then braised in a white sauce, as opposed to a BLAN-

QUETTE, which has no initial sauté. In the United States fricasee has come to mean braised chicken with vegetables.

fried rice   See CHĂO FÀN.

Friese [FREE-seh]   A whole or partly skimmed cows' milk cheese from the Netherlands, uncooked and very hard; it is spiced with cloves and cumin, giving it a strong flavor.

frijoles [free-HŌ-lays]   Spanish for beans; in Mexican cooking, *frijoles negros* means black beans; *frijoles refritos*, refried beans—that is, beans that are boiled, mashed, and fried with PIQUÍN chilies for filling tacos and the like.

Frikadellen [freek-ah-DEL-en]   German meatballs of beef, bread crumbs, and egg, often served cold.

frío [FREE-ō]   Spanish for cold.

frire [freer]   In French, to fry; *frit* or *frite* means fried; *friture*, fried food or frying.

frisée   See CHICORY.

frito, frita   Spanish for fried, fried food. In Cuba, *fritas* are little hamburgers in buns topped with shoestring potatoes, a popular fast food.

frittata [free-TAH-tah]   An Italian omelet but more like a tortilla—flat, round, the eggs set but moist, often with other ingredients mixed in with the eggs. *Frittate* are usually eaten for a light evening meal, with many regional variations.

frittèlla [free-TEL-lah]   Italian for fritter.

fritter   Food, either savory or sweet, dipped into batter and deep-fried.

fritto misto [FREE-tō MEES-tō]   Italian for mixed food, deep-fried in batter; can be very elaborate and include a wide variety, such as meat, offal, and vegetables served together.

fritura [free-TOO-rah]   Spanish for fried food or fritter.

frizzante [freet-ZAHN-tay]   An Italian wine term meaning slightly sparkling or effervescent, due to some additional fermentation in the bottle.

frogs' legs   The hind legs of the frog, available fresh and frozen, and cooked lightly to keep their delicate flavor; the size can vary depending on species, but several pairs make one serving; frogs are food in many parts of the world, but the English have long caricatured the French as frog-eaters; see NYMPHES À L'AURORE.

froid [fwah]   French for cold.

fromage [frō-majh]   French for cheese; *fromager* means to add grated cheese, usually Gruyère or Parmesan, to a sauce, dough, or stuffing, or to sprinkle it on top of food for browning in the oven.

fromage de tête de porc   French for HEAD CHEESE, pork brawn.

Frucht [frookht]   German for fruit.

fructose   The form of sugar found in many plants, especially fruits, and also in honey; fructose tastes sweeter than sucrose and contains half as many calories but is not necessarily more healthful or "natural" than other forms of sugar, especially when crystallized.

Frühlingsuppe [FRÜ-ling-zoo-peh]   A German soup of spring vegetables in meat stock.

Frühstück [FRÜ-stük]   German for breakfast.

fruits de mer [FWEE deu MAYR]   French for seafood, usually shellfish.

frumenty [FROO-men-tee]   A porridge of oatmeal or wheat berries and milk with raisins, sugar, and spices—a traditional old English Christmas food; spelled variously.

fruta bomba [FROO-tah BOHM-bah]   Spanish for PAPAYA.

frutta fresca de stagione [FROOT-tah FRES-kah day stah-JŌ-nay]   Italian for fresh seasonal fruit.

frutti di mare [FROOT-tee dee MAH-ray]   Italian for seafood, usually shellfish.

fry   To cook in hot fat, either a large amount (see DEEP-FRY) or a small amount (see SAUTER).

fù gùi jī [foo gway jee]   "Beggar's chicken," a Chinese dish from Peking of a whole chicken stuffed with a savory mixture, enclosed in lotus leaves, encased in clay or dough, and baked; the clay or dough is broken or cut at table.

fuki [foo-kee]   Japanese for coltsfoot, a vegetable similar to celery.

Füllung [FÜ-luhng]   German for stuffing.

ful medames [FOOL meh-DAH-mes]   Brown FAVA beans cooked in olive oil with garlic, lemon, and parsley, and served with hard-boiled eggs; an ancient dish that has become the national dish of Egypt.

fumé [fü-may]   French for smoked.

fumet [fü-may]   In French cuisine, a concentrated liquid that gives flavor and body to stocks and sauces; made by completely reducing stock that may contain wine; see also ESSENCE and EXTRACT.

fungo [FUHN-gō]   Italian for mushroom; the plural is *funghi*.

furai [foo-rī]   In Japanese, to fry.

Furmint   A white wine grape variety grown in Hungary where it is vinified as the main grape in Tokay and also as a good table wine.

fú róng dàn [foo rohng dahn]   Eggs beaten and scrambled with shrimp and garnished with scallions; in Chinese-American cooking, where it may be known as *egg foo young*, it is often more like an omelet with sauce but no shrimp; the Cantonese is *fu yung don.*

fusilli [foo-ZEE-lee]   Thin, spiral-shaped pasta.

fusion cuisine   A style of cooking that combines the traditions of two or more disparate regions, such as French and Chinese (in Cambodian cuisine, for instance), or Polynesian, Chinese, and Spanish (in Philippine). As chefs become familiar with techniques and ingredients from different parts of the world or combine them in their own heritage, this style becomes more popular. The danger, however, is that the culinary distinctions become not fused but confused, the roots neither recognized nor appreciated.

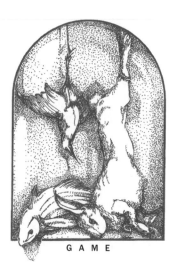

GAME

G

gado-gado [gah-dō-gah-dō]   Indonesian mixed vegetable salad, usually with
BUMBU.

gaeng [gang]   Thai for curry paste; *gaeng ped*, hot curry paste; *gaeng mus-
saman*, a spicy Muslim curry of beef or chicken, with coconut milk and peanuts;
gaeng ped neua, red beef curry, with coconut milk, citrus leaves, and spices.

gai [gī]   Thai for chicken; *gai lae pet*, poultry; *gai tua*, chicken in peanut sauce;
gai yang, marinated grilled chicken in a garlicky piquant sauce.

gai lan   See JIÈ LÁN.

galangal [gah-LAHNG-ahl]   A rhizome of the ginger family used in Southeast
Asian cooking, especially that of Thailand, Malaysia, and Indonesia. Looking
like its cousin ginger, greater galangal (also called Thai ginger, *kha*, *laos*,
lengkuas or *languas*, and *gieng bot*) is used similarly in Thai and Southeast
Asian cooking. Lesser galangal (also called *kencur* and *krachai*), which grows
in long fingers, has a sharper flavor and is used more as a vegetable in stews,
curries, and salads. Galingale is the Old English word for this spice, which
found its way to Europe in the medieval spice trade.

galantine [gal-anh-teen]   In French cuisine, boned poultry, or occasionally fish
or meat, stuffed, rolled or shaped, poached in gelatin stock, and served cold

119

surrounded by its own aspic; often confused with BALLOTINE, which is similar in construction but braised or roasted and served either hot or cold.

galette [gal-et]   A thin broad French cake usually of flaky pastry or *feuilletage*; *galette des Rois* is the Twelfth Night cake, baked with a bean and perhaps other emblems to symbolize good fortune for the finder; its shape and decoration vary according to the traditions of particular French regions.

gallina [gah-LEE-nah]   Spanish for hen.

galumblee [gah-lump-lee]   Thai for cabbage.

Gamay [ga-may]   A red grape variety that produces for Beaujolais, where it is the only grape allowed, an especially light, fruity, and aromatic wine to drink young; also grown in Burgundy and California (as Napa Gamay).

gamba [GAHM-bah]   Spanish for shrimp.

gambero [GAHM-bay-rō]   Italian for crayfish; *gamberetti* are shrimp; *gamberi di fiume* are freshwater crayfish.

game   Wild animals, either furred, feathered, or finned, that are pursued for sport and whose flesh is edible; except for fish, game is often hung and marinated in vinegar or wine and oil to break down tough muscular tissue and develop flavor.

Gammelost [GAM-meh-lohst]   A Norwegian blue cheese made from skimmed cows' milk with interior and exterior molds; apparently the Vikings made this cheese.

gammon   An English term for ham that has changed over time, now usually meaning the upper part of the leg that has been cured but not cooked, often sold for steak or rashers of bacon.

ganache [ga-nash]   A rich chocolate icing or filling for French pastry, made of sweet or semisweet chocolate melted with heavy cream, which sets when cool.

gandules [gahn-DOO-lays]   A Spanish name for the Caribbean staple legume; also called congo, gunga, or pigeon peas.

Gans [gahns]   German for goose; *Gansleber* is goose liver.

ga nuong cam [gah nyoong kahm]   In Vietnamese cooking, chicken in a spicy marinade, grilled or roasted.

garam [GAAHR-um]   In Indian cooking, hot or warm, as for spice. *Garam masala* is a mixture of ground spices—such as cinnamon, cloves, cardamom, cumin, nutmeg, coriander, and black peppercorns—that is sprinkled over a dish just before serving. The spice blend, which can be bought ready-made, may vary widely and is best mixed in small amounts, roasted and ground soon before use.

garbanzo [gar-BAHN-thō, gar-BAHN-sō] Spanish for chickpea.

garbure [gaahr-bür] A thick soup from Béarn in France, varying widely but usually containing cabbage, beans, potatoes, vegetables, and pork, sausage, or ham; usually served with toasted bread.

garde manger [gaahrd manh-jhay] French for a pantry or cold storage area for foodstuffs where the cold buffet in a hotel dining room is prepared; the *chef garde manger* oversees this area and is responsible for pâtés, salads, GALAN-TINES, CHAUD-FROIDS, and so on, and for fancy display garniture.

garganelli [gar-gah-NEL-lee] Homemade Italian macaroni made with egg pasta, rolled with a comblike tool.

gargoulette des émirs [gaahr-goo-let days ay-meer] A Tunisian dish of lamb and seasonings sealed in an amphora-shaped clay pot and slowly baked in a fire; the pot is broken before serving, an old celebratory dish.

gari [GAH-ree] Coarse cassava powder in Nigerian cooking; *gari foto* combines tomatoes, onions, chilies, and egg with *gari* in a kind of risotto; manioc meal.

Garibaldi In classic French cuisine, a demi-glace sauce seasoned with mustard, cayenne, garlic, and anchovy butter.

garlic A plant of the allium or onion family recognizable for its aromatic cloves clustered in a bulb; it is widely used in Asian, Middle Eastern, Mediterranean, and Latin cooking, but disdained by some for its lingering pungency. This odor is released when a clove is cut and strongest when crushed and eaten raw, but the smell dissipates with slow, gentle cooking; burning makes it unpleasantly acrid. Garlic, which has many healthful properties recognized in antiquity, comes in several types: American (from California) is usually white or silvery; Italian tends to be pink or purple, and some consider its flavor finer; and elephant garlic, actually a type of leek, has huge heads with very mild flavor. Garlic is sold in powder, flakes, salt, puréed in tubes, and whole cloves preserved in oil; for flavor and healthful benefits, fresh garlic is far preferable.

garlic chives A member of the allium family, with long flat leaves with garlicky flavor, used as a garnish, and white flowers, also edible.

garnacha See SOPE.

Garnele [GAHR-neh-leh]   German for shrimp, prawn.

garni [gaahr-nee]   French for garnished.

garnish   An edible trimming or embellishment added to a dish, usually enhancing its flavor as well as visual appeal; in classic cuisine the name of the dish, such as *Sole à la florentine* or *Sole florentine*, designates its particular garnish; care must be given to choose appropriate garnishes; see also À LA.

garniture [gaahr-nee-tür]   French for garnish.

garum   A dipping sauce used by the ancient Romans, made of salted, fermented anchovies and spices; very strong, related to the fish sauces of Southeast Asia (see NUOC MAM) and to WORCESTERSHIRE SAUCE.

gasconne, sauce [sos gas-kohn]   In French cuisine, veal velouté with white wine, herbs, and anchovy butter; *gasconne* sometimes means flavored with Armagnac.

gastronomy   The science and art of fine food and drink; the connoisseurship of the culinary arts.

gâteau [ga-tō]   French for cake; the plural is *gâteaux*.

gâteau Saint-Honoré   See SAINT-HONORÉS GÂTEAU.

Gattinara [gat-tee-NAH-rah]   An Italian wine region, near Lake Maggiore in the Piedmont, producing fine red wines (also lesser ones), from the NEBBIOLO grape; big, slow-maturing, and long-lasting.

gaufre [GŌ-fruh]   French for waffle; *pommes gaufrette* are potato chips cut like waffles in a MANDOLINE.

gauloise, à la [ah lah gōl-wahz]   A French garnish for clear soup made of cocks' combs and kidneys.

gayette [gī-yet]   A sausage from Provence of pork liver and bacon wrapped in CAUL and baked.

gazpacho [gahth-PAH-chō, gahs-PAH-chō]   A light, refreshing but thick peasant soup from Andalusia in Spain, made of raw tomatoes, garlic, olive oil, and vinegar, and sometimes bread crumbs, mashed together and thinned with ice water; there is also white gazpacho, with green grapes, garlic, and almonds. Gazpacho's history goes back to the Moors, and there are many regional varieties. Gazpacho is traditionally served with a garnish of diced fresh vegetables, hard-boiled eggs, and croûtons, with many regional variations.

Gebäck [geh-BEK]   German for pastry; *gebacken* means baked.

gebraten [geh-BRAH-ten]   German for roasted.

gebunden [geh-BUHN-den]   German for thickened.

gedämpft [geh-DEMPFT]   German for steamed.

gefilte fish [geh-FIL-teh]   In Jewish cooking, balls of mashed fish, onion, MATZO meal, egg, and spices simmered in broth, reduced, and served in its jellied stock; originally, the fish mixture was stuffed back into the skin of the fish.

Geflügel [geh-FLÜ-gel]   German for poultry.

gefüllt [geh-FÜLT]   German for filled, stuffed.

Geisenheim [GĪS-en-hīm]   A town in the Rheingau region of Germany known for its excellent Rieslings and for its outstanding wine school.

gekocht [geh-KOKHT]   German for cooked.

gelatin, gelatine   A glutinous substance found in animal bones, cartilage, and tendons that, when dissolved in water, heated, and chilled, turns to jelly.

gelato [jeh-LAH-tō]   Italian for ice cream or water ice; a *gelateria* [jeh-lah-teh-REE-ah] is an ice cream parlor.

gelée, en [enh jheh-lay]   French for in aspic.

gemischt [geh-MEESHT]   German for mixed.

Gemüse [geh-MÜ-seh]   German for vegetables.

General Tso's chicken   A favorite dish in Chinese-American restaurants, the original coming from Hunan; chicken cubes cut from the leg, marinated and deep-fried, with a sauce of dried hot chili peppers. There was a General Tso in nineteenth-century Hunan, but his association with the dish is obscure. It has various Cantonese names; the Mandarin is *zuǒ gōng jī* [zō-ah gohng jee].

Gênes, pain de   See PAIN.

genetic modification (GM)   The controversial new technique of biological engineering that transcends conventional crossbreeding and introduces genetic characteristics into plants and animals using laboratory techniques only recently made possible; the controversy arises from questions of responsibility, control, and contamination.

genevoise [jheh-neh-vwahz]   A classic French sauce of salmon stock reduced with red wine and herbs and flavored with anchovy butter.

genièvre [JHEH-NYEV-ruh]   French for juniper berry; also, gin that is flavored with the berry; the Italian is *ginepro*.

génoise [jhay-nwahz]   In French cuisine, a sponge cake made with well-beaten unseparated eggs, the only leavening, to produce a dry, light base with a tight crumb, for buttercream, petit fours, lining for molds, and various other elaborate pastries. *Génoise*, French for "Genoa-style," can also mean with tomato sauce.

genovese, alla [ah-lah jeh-nō-VAY-say]   In the style of Genoa, the northwestern maritime city in Liguria, Italy, whose cuisine features fresh herbs, vegetables, and seafood.

geräuchert [geh-ROY-shayrt]   German for smoked.

German sauce   See ALLEMANDE.

geschabt [geh-SHAHBT]   German for ground, grated, scraped.

geschmort [geh-SHMOHRT]   German for pot-roasted, stewed.

gésier [jhay-zyay]   French for gizzard.

Gevrey Chambertin [jhay-vray shamh-bayr-tinh]   A commune in the CÔTE D'OR producing extraordinary Burgundy wines, including first-growth and GRAND CRU vineyards, most of which carry the name of Chambertin as part of their title.

Gewächs [geh-VEX]   German for growth or cru, usually meaning an estate-bottled wine.

Gewürz [geh-VÜRTS]   German for spice, condiment, seasoning.

Gewürztraminer [geh-VÜRTS-tra-MEE-ner]   A white wine grape variety producing a distinctive spicy, aromatic, refreshing wine ranging to a rich, round, late-harvest *vendange tardive*; planted widely in Alsace, also Germany, Austria, and the Italian Tirol; in the New World, California, Oregon, New Zealand, and South Africa.

ghee [gee]   Clarified butter; in India, *ghee* is usually made of buffalo butter. *Vanaspati ghee*, vegetable ghee—hydrogenated cooking fat, for everyday use; *usli ghee*, pure fat or butter.

gherkin   A small cucumber—the young specimen of certain varieties—used especially for pickling and garnishing.

ghiaccio [GYAH-chō]   Italian for ice; *ghiacciato* means iced.

giardiniera, alla [ah-lah jar-dee-NYAY-rah]   With mixed sliced vegetables, in Italian cooking.

gibier [jhee-byay]   French for game.

giblets   The heart, liver, gizzard, neck, wing tips, feet, leg ends, and sometimes cocks' combs and kidneys of poultry, cooked separately in stocks and stews; goose and duck livers, as special delicacies, are not considered giblets.

gigot [jhee-gō]   French for leg of mutton; *gigot d'agneau,* leg of lamb; *manche à gigot*, a special attachment to the gigot bone that facilitates carving.

gilthead   A type of sea bream from the Mediterranean, with a gold spot on each side of the head; its fine, firm, white flesh is excellent grilled over fennel stalks and in numerous other aromatic preparations.

gingembre [JHINH-JHENH-bruh]   French for ginger.

ginger   The rhizome of a plant native to tropical Asia and used as a spice fresh, preserved, or dried and ground; pervasive in Far and Middle Eastern cooking, important dried in medieval European cooking, it is enjoying a wide popularity used fresh in American cooking.

ginger beer   In Jamaica, a popular and potent drink made from a slurry of grated ginger and lime juice, with yeast for fizz, vastly different from commercial ginger ale or ginger beer; see also SHANDY.

gingerbread   A cake flavored with ginger (and often with other spices) and molasses; also a cookie cut into imaginative shapes and decorated.

ginkgo nut [GINK-ō]   The seed or nut of a tree native to China and considered a delicacy in Asia; eaten raw or cooked, it is high in starch.

ginnan   Japanese for ginkgo nut.

giorno, del [del JOR-nō]   Italian for of the day; *du jour* in French.

gique [jheek]   French for haunch of venison or boar.

giri [gee-ree]   Japanese for a cut, or stroke, of the knife; used with another word, such as *arare-giri*, for dicing or coarsely chopping.

girolle [jhee-rōl]   See CHANTERELLE.

gîte à la noix [jheet ah lah nwah]   SILVERSIDE of beef.

Gjetost [gyeh-TOHST]   A cheese made in Norway from leftover goats' milk whey that is boiled down for some hours; the milk sugar caramelizes and produces a rich brown color and sweet flavor; shaped in a brick, it can be soft or hard and, strictly speaking, is not a cheese.

glaçage [gla-sahjh]   French for browning or glazing; see also GLAZE.

glace [glas]   French for ice cream; cake icing; see EXTRACT; *glacé* means glazed, iced.

125

glacier [gla-syay]   French for ice cream maker—usually a pastry cook in a large kitchen.

glassato [glah-SAH-tō]   Italian for glazed.

glasswort   See SALICORNIA.

glaze   To give a shiny appearance to various preparations both hot and cold in one of several ways: to brown meat in its own stock in the oven or under the SALAMANDER; to brush extract over meat or other food; to coat chilled food with aspic jelly; to cover fish or eggs in a light sauce; to coat hot vegetables with a butter sauce with a little sugar; to coat sweets with sprinkled sugar or strained jam and caramelize them quickly under intense heat; to ice confections.

glögg [gleug]   Swedish hot spiced wine with AKVAVIT or brandy, almonds, and raisins.

Gloucester   See DOUBLE GLOUCESTER and SINGLE GLOUCESTER.

glucose   Natural sugar, found in fruit and other foods, which is easily absorbed by the body.

Glühwein [GLÜ-vīn]   German for mulled wine.

gluten   A substance formed when certain flours, especially hard wheat, are combined with water and yeast into an elastic dough, which rises due to trapped air bubbles produced by the yeast; if dough is put under running water or well chewed, the starch is removed, leaving the viscous gluten behind.

glutinous rice   Sweet or sticky rice with a high starch content and opaque creamy color, easy to eat with chopsticks; in both long- and short-grain varieties.

glycerin, glycerine, glycerol   A sweet, clear, syrupy liquid used to retain moisture in certain kinds of confectionery, such as cake icing, and to sweeten and preserve foods.

gnocchi [NYOHK-kee]   Small Italian dumplings made from choux paste, semolina flour, or puréed potatoes, poached in water, and served covered with cheese or other sauce or in a soup.

goat   The ruminant of the genus *Capra*, closely related to sheep. The goat was domesticated about 10,000 years ago in Southwest Asia, first for its meat, hide, wool, and horn, and then for its milk, which humans learned to make into cheese, chèvre. The goat can tolerate, even thrive, in extreme climates and terrains—mountain and desert—so it is the animal of choice in many challenging or poorer regions. Middle Eastern, Mediterranean, and Latin countries have a tradition of cooking goat, which has never been popular in the United States. Because mature goat meat is tough, kid is likelier to appear on the table. Many chèvres have separate entries.

goats' milk cheese   See CHÈVRE.

gobi [gō-BEE]   Cabbage in Indian cooking; *phul gobi*, cauliflower.

gobō [gō-bō]   Japanese for burdock root.

gochu jang [gō-choo jahng]   Hot fermented chili paste, the staple seasoning in Korean food.

gohan   Japanese for rice.

goi cuon [goy koon]   A Vietnamese salad of varied herbs rolled in rice wrappers and served with bean sauce.

goi-ga [goy-gah]   A Vietnamese salad of poached chicken with shredded cabbage, carrot, and grapefruit, sprinkled with sesame seeds and served with NUOC MAM dipping sauce.

goi tom thit [goy tohm tit]   A Vietnamese salad of pork and shrimp, served with shrimp chips and NUOC MAM dipping sauce.

golden buck   In British cooking, poached eggs on toast with WELSH RAREBIT.

golden oak mushroom   See SHIITAKE.

golden syrup   A British syrup, an invert sugar mixture that, like TREACLE, will not crystallize, used as a sweetener.

goma   Japanese for sesame seeds.

goober   Peanut; the term derives from an African word for the peanut.

goose   A web-footed water bird, similar to a duck but much larger (5 to 18 pounds), with longer neck and legs; the goose has long been appreciated for its meat, fat, liver (and feathers, for arrows and quills); in Europe it takes pride of place on the holiday table; CONFIT and FOIE GRAS are special goose delicacies.

gooseberry   A thorny shrub whose tart fruit, mostly small and green or larger and purple, but sometimes white or yellow, is especially popular in France and England for pies, compotes, or preserves; gooseberry sauce is a traditional accompaniment to mackerel in France.

goosefish   See MONKFISH.

gordita [gor-DEE-tah]   In Mexican cooking, cornmeal and potato dough flavored with cheese, fried in lard, and served with ground pork and GUACAMOLE.

Gorgonzola [gor-gon-ZŌ-lah]   An Italian blue cheese from whole cows' milk, either raw or pasteurized, from the village of the same name near Milan; shaped in 25-pound drums, it has a rough reddish rind and creamy white interior streaked with blue; milder and less salty than ROQUEFORT, it is one of the great blue cheeses, but made from a different mold than most.

Gouda [GOO-dah, HOW-dah]   A round whole-milk cows' cheese from the town of the same name near Amsterdam; creamy yellow and firm, its taste becomes more pronounced with age. Gouda is sometimes flavored with CUMIN or CARAWAY seeds; young cheeses are covered with yellow wax, older cured cheeses with black wax.

gougère [goo-jhayr]   In French cooking, a savory ring of choux pastry flavored with Gruyère cheese, from Burgundy, often eaten as a light meal with red wine. *Gougères* are individual rounds of the same paste, baked into small puffs and served as an hors d'oeuvre.

goujonette [goo-jhoh-net]   In French, fillet of sole cut into strips, floured or breaded, and deep-fried, to resemble little fishes or "gudgeons."

goulash   See GULYÁS.

gourmand [goor-manh]   French for one who appreciates fine food and drink, a gastronome; in English the term has come to mean glutton, but this association is foreign to France.

goût [goo]   French for taste in both senses—flavor and discriminating style.

graham flour   Whole-meal flour made from unbolted wheat; developed in 1840 by the American social reformer Sylvester Graham, who also advocated vegetarianism and sexual abstinence; the crackers sold in supermarkets today under his name, which include among their ingredients sugar, salt, and preservatives, would horrify him.

Grains of paradise   See MELEGUETA

grana [GRAH-nah]   Italian for a hard granular cheese sometimes eaten when young as table cheese but more often aged and used grated on pasta or minestrone or in cooking; dry, crumbly, and long-lasting, several of this type, such as Parmesan, have separate entries.

granada [grah-NAH-dah]   Spanish for pomegranate.

granadilla   See PASSION FRUIT.

granchio [GRAHN-kyō]   Italian for crab.

Grand Cru [granh krü]   For French BURGUNDY WINE, the highest classification, including 30 vineyards in all; their individual appellations usually exclude the name of the commune.

Grand Marnier [granh maahr-nyay]   A French liqueur with a COGNAC base, flavored with bitter orange zest.

grand'mère, à la [ah lah granh-mayr]   In French cuisine, "grandmother's style," garnished with sautéed pearl onions, potatoes cut into olive shapes, parsley, lemon juice, and browned butter.

grand veneur, sauce [sōs granh ven-euhr]   A classic French sauce for game, especially venison, literally "master of the king's hunt," of red wine, currant, cream, and pepper, with game stock.

grandville [granh-vee]   A classic French white wine sauce with truffles, mushrooms, and shrimp.

granita [grah-NEE-tah]   Italian fruit ice or sweetened coffee to which no ITALIAN MERINGUE is added, so that its ice crystals intentionally form a grainy texture, unlike a *sorbetto*. The French word is *granité*.

grape   The berry or fruit, of the genus *Vitis,* that grows in clusters. The grape originated near Mount Ararat, by the Caspian Sea before the advent of man. In antiquity, it provided fruit and wine, also raisins, syrup sweetening, VERJUICE, vinegar, and leaves for wrapping; it also played a part in many ancient religions. Like the Greeks, the Romans particularly liked wine and spread viticulture throughout their empire. In the New World, wild grapes grew profusely, but the American colonists took time learning how to grow wine grapes, *Vitis vinifera*, that could survive in the colder climate. In general, table grapes for eating are sweeter, those for making wine more acid. Grapes for both fall into red (often actually purple or black) and white (pale green or gold) categories; some of these varieties, especially for making wine, have separate entries.

grapefruit   A citrus fruit, first observed in Jamaica in the early nineteenth century, perhaps an accidental cross between the pomelo and citron or orange; it is large, juicy, and relatively bitter and thin-skinned compared to its pomelo parent. Its name, from the French *grappe*, meaning cluster, describes its habit of growing on the tree in bunches, like giant grapes. The two main varieties are Duncan, seedy but flavorful, and Marsh, seedless but blander; growers are developing the deeper red coloring that Americans prefer.

grappa [GRAHP-pah]   Italian MARC.

gratin de, au gratin, gratiné [gra-tinh deu, ō gra-tinh, gra-tee-nay]   In French, topped with a crust of bread crumbs and sometimes grated cheese and browned in the oven or under a grill.

Graves [grav]   A wine region on the left bank of the Garonne River southwest of Bordeaux producing mostly dry white wines; the best reds are sold under their estate names and, except for Château Haut-Brion, were omitted from the 1855 classification; an excellent sweet wine similar to Sauternes, usually named Cérons, is also produced in Graves.

gravlaks, gravlax [GRAHV-lahks]   Scandinavian raw salmon fillets cured for a day or so in sugar and salt and seasoned with dill.

grecque, à la [ah lah GREK]   French for vegetables, particularly Greek ones such as artichokes and mushrooms, stewed in olive oil, lemon juice, water, and seasonings.

green onion   See SCALLION.

green sauce   See under MAYONNAISE.

green tea   See TEA.

gremolada [grem-ō-LAH-dah]   In Italian cooking, a mixture of chopped parsley, garlic, and grated lemon zest sprinkled over OSSO BUCO as an aromatic garnish; sometimes spelled *gremolata*.

Grenache [gre-nash]   A grape variety for both red and white wine, productive and good in quality, usually blended; planted extensively in southern France (both *blanc* and especially *noir* in the southern Rhone's hot climate where it comes into its best), the Rioja region of Spain, California, and Australia; also called Garnacha, Alicante, and Cannonau.

grenadine [gre-na-deen]   Pomegranate syrup; used to color and flavor cocktails.

grenouille [gren-noo-yuh]   French for frog; *cuisses de grenouille*, frog legs.

gribiche [gree-beesh]   A French sauce for chilled fish, based on mayonnaise with capers, chopped gherkins and herbs, and hard-boiled egg whites.

griglia, alla [ah-lah GREE-yah]   Italian for grilled.

grill   To cook over flames or embers or under a broiler in intense direct heat.

grillade [gree-yad]   French for grilled meat; grilling or broiling.

grissino [grees-SEE-nō]   Italian for breadstick.

grits   See HOMINY.

groats   Hulled grain, usually broken up or coarsely ground, as with grits (see HOMINY).

groseille [grō-zay]   French for currant; *groseille à maquereau* means GOOSEBERRY, the traditional French garnish for mackerel.

ground cherry   See CAPE GOOSEBERRY.

groundnut   See PEANUT.

grouper   Several varieties of fish, all members of the sea bass family; the lean, firm, moist meat can be cooked in a wide variety of ways.

grouse   A large family of wild gamebirds, prepared in various ways, depending on age and species; one bird usually serves one person.

gruel   A thin cereal, usually oatmeal, cooked in milk or water.

Grüner Veltliner [GRÜ-ner FELT-lin-er]   A white wine grape variety grown widely in Austria; light, peppery, best drunk young.

grunt   Stewed fruit topped with dumplings; an early American dessert similar to SLUMP.

Gruyère [grü-yayr]   A cows' milk cheese, cooked and pressed, from the valley of the same name in French-speaking Switzerland; originally of skimmed or partially skimmed milk but now made with whole milk. The pale yellow cheese with a golden brown rind is made in rounds of over a hundred pounds and aged; those for the export market are made less salty and with little holes; it is an excellent table or cooking cheese with fine melting properties. Just across the border, the French also make two types of the cheese, Gruyère de Beaufort, with tiny holes, and Gruyère de Comté, with large holes.

guacamole [gwah-kah-MŌ-lay]   In Mexican cooking, mashed avocado, usually served as a dip; may be flavored with onion, garlic, chilies, lime juice, seasonings, and perhaps tomato.

guajillo [gwah-HEE-yō]   A long, thin, dried chili pepper, reddish brown and smooth, very hot, about 4 inches long and 1 inch wide; it is sometimes called CASCABEL because it resembles the tail, rattle, and bite of a rattlesnake, but should not be confused with the cascabel chili.

guajolote [gwah-hō-LŌ-tay]   Mexican for wild turkey.

guanabana   See SOURSOP APPLE.

guarnito [gwahr-NEE-tō]   Italian for garnished.

guava [GWAH-vah] A tropical shrub whose odiferous berrylike fruit is made into pinkish orange jams and jellies; a poor traveler, this delicious fruit is inadequately appreciated outside its native habitat.

güero [GWAYR-ō] A greenish yellow chili pepper, about 4 inches long and 1 inch wide, and pointed; it is fairly hot, with some variation, and is generally used fresh and toasted or canned, but never dried; also called Californian pepper or sweet green pepper.

Gugelhupf [GOO-gel-hupf] Austrian dialect for KUGELHOPF.

guinea fowl A small-crested bird with dark gray plumage flecked white, originally from West Africa, related to the chicken and partridge; the meat is dark, flavorful, and rather dry; a bird weighs ¾ to 4 pounds. The French word is *pintade* or, for young fowl, *pintadeau*; the Spanish, *pintada*; the Italian, *faraona*.

Guinea pepper See MELEGUETA.

guisantes [gwee-SAHN-tays] Spanish for peas.

guiso, guisado [GWEE-thō, gwee-THAH-dō] Spanish for stew, stewed.

gül [guhl] Turkish for rose or rosewater; *gulab* is the Indian word for rose.

gulai [goo-lī] In a spicy coconut sauce, in Indonesian and Malaysian cooking.

gŭ lăo ròu [goo low rō] Sweet-and-sour pork, a favorite in Cantonese-American restaurants. In the classic Chinese version, pork cubes are battered and fried, then served with a sauce of stir-fried scallions, peppers, and other vegetables. The American version includes a sweet-and-sour sauce with pineapple chunks, ketchup, and vegetables overbalanced toward sweet. The Cantonese is *tim suan yuk* [teem swahn yōk].

gulyás [GOO-lahsh] A Hungarian stew of beef or sometimes veal or pork, onions, potatoes, and dumplings, seasoned with plenty of PAPRIKA; it varies widely according to the region and individual, from delicate to hearty. The English spelling is goulash.

gum arabic, gum tragacanth Vegetable gums used as emulsifiers and thickeners in certain processed foods such as ice cream, candy, and commercial sauces.

gumbo A thick Creole soup or dish thickened with OKRA or FILÉ POWDER; the word *gumbo* is derived from an African word for okra.

Gumpoldskirchen [GUM-polts-keer-shen] An Austrian town south of Vienna known for its fine white wine, which is pale, clean, fruity, and pleasing.

Gundel, crêpe à la See PALACSINTA.

gung   Thai for shellfish; *gung foi*, prawns; *gung narng*, shrimp; *gung ta lay*, lobster.

gung   Vietnamese for ginger.

guō tiē   [gwoh tyeh]   Peking ravioli, literally "pot-stickers"; JIǍO ZǏ meat dumplings fried in a pan and served with a dipping sauce; the Cantonese is *wor tip* [woh tip].

Gurke   [GOOR-keh]   German for cucumber.

gwaytio   [gwī-tyō]   Thai soup with large rice noodles; *gwaytio neua nam*, a robust beef noodle soup.

gye tang   [gay tahng]   A Korean spicy crab stew, with onions, chilies, and zucchini, served with rice.

gyro   [YEER-ō]   See KEBAB.

gyuniku   [gyoo-nee-koo]   Japanese for beef.

HARICOT

H

haba [HAH-bah]   Spanish for FAVA or broad bean or, in South America, lima bean; *habas secas* are dried beans.

habanero [hah-bah-NYAYR-ō]   An extremely hot chili pepper, up to 300,000 Scoville units, with aromatic, fruity tones of flavor; lantern-shaped and green, yellow, orange, or red in color; favored in the Caribbean and Yucatán (but not elsewhere in Mexico), also Brazil and Trinidad; the SCOTCH BONNET of Jamaica is closely related.

hachée [ash-ay]   A classic French sauce of chopped shallots and onions reduced in vinegar, mixed with DEMI-GLACE and tomato purée, and flavored with DUXELLES, capers, diced ham, and parsley.

hacher [ash-ay]   To chop or mince, in French; *hachis* means hash; the adjective is *haché(e)*, also the sauce (see HACHÉE entry above).

Hackbraten [HAHK-brah-ten]   German for meat loaf.

haddock   A variety of small COD, usually sold fresh or smoked but not salted.

haggis [HAG-is]   A traditional Scottish specialty of sheep's stomach stuffed with chopped lamb's liver and heart, onions, black pepper, and oatmeal, well steamed like a pudding; celebrated by the Scots poet Robert Burns.

Hahn   German for cock.

hai shen [hī shen]   Chinese for a spineless marine creature, called a sea cucumber or sea slug; a delicacy relished for its gelatinous texture and saved for special occasions.

hake   A small variety of COD.

hakusai [hah-koo-sī]   Japanese for Chinese cabbage.

haldi [HAHL-dee]   TURMERIC, in Indian cooking.

half-mourning   See DEMI-DEUIL, À LA.

halibut   A large flatfish of the FLOUNDER family.

hallacas [ah-YAH-kahs]   Cornmeal mixed with meat, vegetables, and spices, wrapped in banana leaves, and steamed like tamales; from South America.

Hallgarten [HAL-gar-ten]   A village in the German Rheingau producing very good full-bodied white wines.

halvah   A Turkish sweet of flour, butter, nuts or sesame seeds, and sugar or honey, served soft and warm or stiffened into a slab; the name comes from the Arabic word for sweet.

ham   The hind leg of PORK between the hip and hock, cured with salt and aging, sometimes also smoke, so that it keeps well for a length of time at room temperature. There are many variations and traditions, also levels of quality. Among many factors are the breed of pig, feed, age at slaughter, and cut of ham; method of dry-salting, brining, injection-curing, or sweet-curing; smoking temperature and type of wood; length of aging and storage method; and whether a ham is fully cooked, partially cooked, or uncooked. In the United States hams are either mass-marketed in a "city-style" or higher-quality "country-style." Some traditional hams, such as BAYONNE, PROSCIUTTO, SMITH-FIELD, WESTFÄLISCHE SCHINKEN, and YORK have separate entries.

hamaguri [hah-mah-goo-ree]   Japanese for hard-shell clams.

Haman's ears   See HAMANTASCHEN.

Hamantaschen [HAM-un-tahsh-un]   Triangular pastry stuffed with poppy seeds and apple, apricot, or prune filling, traditionally eaten for the Jewish holiday of Purim.

hamburger   Chopped beef formed into a patty, fried or grilled, and served on a bun—the emblem of modern fast-food America.

ham don   See XIÁN YĀ DÀN.

Hammelfleisch [HAM-mel-flīsh]   German for mutton.

hamud [hah-MOOD]   In Egyptian cooking, a lemony chicken soup, sometimes served as a sauce for rice.

Handkäse [HAHNT-kay-zeh]   A pungent acid-curd cheese from Germany made from skimmed cows' milk, in small round or oblong shapes; originally made by hand. In Hesse, the cheese is served "mit Musik"—onion relish—which produces flatulence, hence the name.

Hangtown fry   A dish, apparently from the California Gold Rush, of bread-crumbed oysters, fried bacon, and beaten eggs cooked together like an omelet until set.

háo yóu   See HO YAO.

happy cakes   See BANH XEO.

hard-ball stage   Sugar syrup that has reached a temperature of 250–268°F (121–130°C) and that forms a firm ball between the fingers when immersed in cold water.

hard-crack stage   Sugar syrup that has reached a temperature of 300–320°F (150–160°C) and that, when immersed in cold water, forms brittle threads and sheets that break easily between the fingers.

hard sauce   Butter creamed with sugar and flavored with liquor; served with dessert puddings such as PLUM PUDDING.

hardtack   A hard cracker that was often used for military rations because of its excellent keeping qualities; also known as ship biscuit and pilot biscuit.

hare   A large wild cousin of the rabbit, relished for its dark rich meat with gamy flavor; hare is usually hung, skinned and drawn, marinated, and then roasted or stewed; see also JUGGED HARE.

hareng [a-renh]   French for herring.

haricot [a-ree-kō]   French for bean, either fresh (*frais*) or dried (*sec*); *haricot blanc*, white kidney bean, fresh or dried; *haricot de mouton*, mutton stew with turnips and potatoes but no beans at all; *haricot flageolet*, pale green bean, usually fresh in France and rare in the United States; *haricot rouge*, red kidney bean, fresh or dried; *haricot vert*, green string bean.

harina [hah-REE-nah]   Spanish for flour.

harira [hah-REE-rah]   A rich and spicy Moroccan soup of meat, usually lamb, beef, or chicken; chickpeas; and noodles, rice, or flour; with lemon, tomatoes, and other vegetables. Made in many variations and eaten during Ramadan to break the day-long fast; sometimes spelled *hareera* or *hereera*.

harissa [hah-REE-sah]   A popular North African sauce of dried chili peppers and garlic thinned with olive oil and lemon juice; colored red and extremely hot.

haroset [khah-RŌ-set]   A paste of chopped apples, raisins, nuts, and red wine, traditional in the Passover seder, symbolizing mortar for buildings.

hartgekocht [HART-geh-kokht]   German for hard-boiled.

Hase [HAH-zeh]   German for hare; Hasenpfeffer is a hare stew flavored with pepper and other spices and braised in red wine.

Haselnuss [HAH-zel-noos]   German for hazelnut.

hash   Chopped meat, often with vegetables, usually combining leftovers, seasonings, and gravy; from the French word *hacher*, meaning to chop.

hashi [hash-ee]   Japanese for chopsticks.

hassoo [hah-SOO]   In Tunisia, a thick winter soup filled with little lamb meatballs.

hasty pudding   See INDIAN PUDDING.

Hattenheim [HAT-en-hīm]   A village in the German Rheingau whose vineyards produce excellent white wine.

Hauptgerichte [HOWPT-geh-rish-teh]   German for main course.

Hausfrauen Art [HOWS-frow-en art]   German for housewife's style, meaning with sour cream and pickles.

hausgemacht [HOWS-geh-mahkt]   German for homemade.

Haut-Médoc [ō-may-dohk]   The southern and more elevated half of the French Médoc, north of Bordeaux, including Margaux, Saint-Julien, Pauillac, and Saint-Estèphe; its wines are superior to those from the Bas-Médoc to its north.

Havarti [hah-VAHR-tee]   A Danish cheese made from partially skimmed cows' milk, semihard and containing many small holes; pale and mild, sometimes flavored with herbs, its flavor grows sharper with maturity.

haw mok   A Thai fish dish with green curry paste, coconut milk, chilies, lemongrass, and onions, wrapped in banana leaves and steamed.

hazelnut   The fruit of the hazel tree, native to Europe and the United States; this term usually designates wild nuts, and FILBERT or cob used for cultivated ones, but there is confusion among them. The small, nearly round hazelnut looks like a chickpea when its fuzzy husk and brown skin are removed. Its distinctive flavor turns rich and sweet with ripening, suitable for savory and sweet concoctions. Hazelnut oil, fragrant but perishable, is considered very fine.

head cheese   Meat from a pig's or calf's head and other scraps boiled, molded into a loaf, and served in its own jelly with condiments.

heart   The muscular organ in mammals and birds; tender in young animals, but needs slow moist braising in older ones.

heavy syrup   Two parts sugar to one part water, dissolved; this is a *sirop à trente* with a density of 30 degrees on the Baumé scale. A light syrup has an approximately equal sugar-to-water ratio.

Heilbutt [HĪL-boot]   German for halibut.

heirloom seeds   Seeds from older, open-pollinated vegetables and fruits that are unprofitable to large modern commercial growers, but whose genetic material may produce interesting, tasty, hardy, or otherwise valuable varieties worth saving for posterity; small independent specialty stores and farmers' markets are the best places to find such produce.

heiss [hīs]   German for hot.

helado [heh-LAH-dō]   Spanish for ice cream.

helles Bier [HEL-es BEER]   German light beer.

helva   See HALVAH.

Hendel [HEN-del]   Chicken, in Austrian dialect.

Henne [HEN-neh]   German for hen.

hen of the woods   A fungus with brown leafy "feathers" growing in clumps from 3 pounds on up, sometimes, reportedly, to 100 pounds, in the wild or farmed (in Japan). It is vaguely similar to chicken of the woods but, despite the name, not related. This fungus, after careful cleaning, is best cooked slowly in aromatic braises. In Japan, where it has been cultivated for centuries, its name is *maitake*.

Henry IV [ENH-REE KAT-ruh]   Garnished with artichoke hearts filled with potato balls and BÉARNAISE sauce mixed with meat glaze—a classic French garnish.

hermetical seal   The airtight closure of a casserole or container with bread dough or flour and water paste, designed to keep steam inside during cooking.

Hermitage [ayr-mee-tajh]   A celebrated Rhône wine from a large steep slope south of Lyons; most of this full-bodied, richly colored and flavored wine is red, from the Syrah grape; the white wine is pale gold, dry, and also full-bodied, if not so fine.

herring   A flavorful and nutritious fish, until recently abundant in the Pacific and Atlantic Oceans and very important economically; herring is particularly appreciated in northern Europe and, with its high fat content, lends itself to smoked or pickled preparations. A herring rollmop is a filleted herring rolled around a pickle or onion, marinated, and served as an appetizer.

Herve [ayrv]   A whole-milk cows' cheese, soft, rich, and pungent, made in three-inch cubes with a reddish brown rind; named for the town of Herve, near Liège, Belgium.

hervir [ayr-VEER]   In Spanish, to boil.

Hessia   A region in western Germany delineated on the north and east by the Rhine, on the west by the Nahe, and on the south by the Pfalz, which produces a large quantity of white wine; the best, from the Riesling grape, comes from particular towns along the Rhine, while the rest, from the Sylvaner grape, is quite ordinary.

hé yè bāo [heu yeh bow]   A popular Chinese dim sum of seasoned chicken and sausage with sticky rice, wrapped in a lotus leaf and steamed; also called *nuò mǐ jī*; the Cantonese is *nua mi gai* [now mee gī].

hibachi [hih-bah-chee]   An Americanized word for a Japanese small open charcoal grill; in Japan, this is a heater rarely used for cooking.

hickory   A tree native to North America whose nut was eaten by the Indians and which we still eat, especially the PECAN; the word *hickory* comes from the Algonquian language.

hígado [EE-gah-dō]   Spanish for liver.

hígado a la italiana   A Cuban dish of liver "Italian-style," with onions and peppers, but unknown in Italy.

higo [HEE-gō]   Spanish for fig.

hijiki [hee-jee-kee]   Asian seaweed with a nutty flavor, usually dried, reconstituted, and cooked for garnishes and salads.

Himbeer [HIM-bayr]   German for raspberry.

Himmel und Erde [HIM-mel uhnt AYR-deh]   Apples and potatoes with onions and sausage or bacon (literally "heaven and earth"); a very popular German dish.

hinojo [ee-NŌ-hō]   Spanish for fennel.

hirame [hee-lah-may]   Japanese for flounder.

Hirn [heern]   German for brains.

Hirsch [heersh]   German for stag, venison.

hiyashi [hee-yah-shee]   Japanese for cold, chilled; used with another word.

hochepot [ōsh-pō]   A thick French stew, sometimes more of a soup, made from less desirable cuts of meat and winter vegetables; the English and Scottish hotch-potch, hodge-podge, and hot pot are all derivatives.

Hochheim [HŌHK-hīm]   A town in the northeast corner of the German Rheingau producing distinctive and characteristic Rhine wine even though situated on the Main River; hock, designating Rhine wine to an Englishman, is derived from its name.

hock   See HOCHHEIM.

hodge-podge   See HOCHEPOT.

hoecake   JOHNNY CAKE, originally cooked over an open fire, using the hoe as a griddle, when kitchen equipment was less readily available than now; early American in origin.

hói sìn jiàng [hī shen jung]   In Chinese cooking, hoisin sauce, a thick, rich, dark brown sauce made from fermented soy beans, garlic, sugar, and salt, and used to flavor sauces and marinades; it is a Cantonese version of sweet bean sauce.

hoisin sauce   See HÓI SÌN JIÀNG.

hoja santa [Ō-hah SAHN-tah]   An anise-flavored culinary herb used in southeastern Mexico and around Mexico City.

hollandaise [ō-lanh-dez]   In classic French cuisine, a thick emulsion sauce of reduced vinegar whisked with egg yolks, into which melted butter is gradually beaten. It is then flavored with lemon juice and kept warm in a bain-marie; one of the basic sauces, it is used primarily with fish, eggs, and vegetables; in modern cooking there are many shortcuts in technique and ingredients.

Holsteiner Katenschinken [HŌL-shtī-ner KAHT-en-shink-en]   German for smoked raw ham.

Holsteiner mit Spiegelei; Holstein Schnitzel [HŌL-shtīn-er mit SHPEE-gel-ī]   German for veal chop garnished with a fried egg and smoked salmon.

homard [ō-maahr]   French for lobster.

hominy   Corn kernels with the bran and germ removed either by a lye bath, as for whole kernels in lye hominy, or by crushing and sifting, as for pearl hominy; hominy grits, a southern U.S. favorite, are often served as porridge for breakfast or as starch for dinner seasoned with cheese; the word *hominy* is American Indian in origin.

honey   The sweet viscous liquid produced by honeybees from flower nectar; bees gather the nectar (cross-pollinating at the same time), partially digest it, changing its chemistry, and store it in hexagonal honeycomb cells as sustenance for the hive. The flower nectar determines honey's color and flavor, usually amber but varying widely, darker tasting stronger. In antiquity, before sugarcane production, honey was highly valued for sweetening. Europeans brought the honeybee to the New World. Honey's liquid volume is 1¼ times sweeter than ordinary sugar; in baking, honey's chemistry keeps breads and cakes moist longer than sugar, while adding its distinctive flavor.

honeydew   See WINTER MELON.

hongroise, à l' [ah l'onh-gwaz]   In French cuisine, meat garnished with cauliflower flowerets, glazed with MORNAY sauce, paprika, and sautéed potatoes cut into olive shapes.

hóng shāo [hohng show]   "Red-cooked," in Chinese cuisine; that is, the technique of braising slowly in a soy-based liquid in order to impart the distinctive color and rich favor to the dish; the cooking liquid can be used repeatedly; the Cantonese term is *hong siu.*

Honig [HŌ-nig]   German for honey.

hoogli   See UGLI FRUIT.

Hoppelpoppel [HOHP-el POHP-el]   German for scrambled eggs with potatoes and bacon.

hoppin' John   A dish of rice and beans—usually black-eyed or cowpeas—cooked with bacon; a staple of African-American cooking in the southern United States and Caribbean, traditional for New Year's Day for good luck.

hops   The ripe conical female flowers of the hop vine, used in brewing to impart a bitter flavor to beer, in order to balance the sweetness of the malt; in continental Europe the young male shoots of the hop vine are eaten as a vegetable.

horchata [or-CHAH-tah]   A Spanish cold summer drink, creamy white (but milkless) and without alcohol, made of chufa (tiger) nuts puréed with water, sweetened, with a dash of cinnamon; originally from Valencia.

horehound   A fragrant Old World herb of the mint family used to flavor candy and medicine; also spelled hoarhound.

horenso [hor-en-sō]   Japanese for spinach.

hornear [or-nay-AR]   In Spanish, to bake.

horno [OR-nō]   Spanish for oven; *al horno* means baked.

hors d'oeuvre [OHR-D'EUV-ruh]   Light and stimulating finger food eaten before the main meal (in French, literally "outside the works") as an appetizer; the term is often misspelled: when used as a collective noun it has no final s, but a group of specific appetizers takes the plural s.

horseradish   A vegetable related to mustard, whose pungent root is grated and mixed with vinegar, then folded into a cream or tomato sauce and served as a condiment or sauce; the tender young leaves can be used for salad; native to southeastern Europe.

Hospices de Beaune [hōs-pees deu bōn]   A fifteenth-century charitable hospital in Beaune, France, endowed and maintained with some forty Côte de Beaune vineyards; at the auspicious annual auction the wine, all very good, often sets Burgundy prices for that year.

hotch-potch   See HOCHEPOT and LANCASHIRE HOT POT.

hot cross bun   A British yeast roll, round, slightly sweetened, with spice and dried fruit added, and traditionally cut or iced with a cross; eaten on Good Friday or during Lent.

hot dieu [hop deeyoo]   Vietnamese for ANNATTO seeds, used for their orange color and mild flavor.

hot pot   See HOCHEPOT.

houria [hoo-REE-ah]   A Tunisian carrot salad, puréed or chopped with HARISSA, mint, capers, and vinaigrette.

ho yao [how yow]   In Chinese cooking, the Cantonese term for oyster sauce, consisting of oysters, salt, and seasonings concentrated into a thick paste. The Mandarin is *háo yóu* [how yō]; sometimes it is called *li jiàng* [lee jing], after a brand name.

huachinango [HWA-chih-NANG-ō]   Red snapper in Mexican cooking.

huā jiāo [wha jow]   Hot peppercorns from Sichuan, reddish brown in color; when roasted, crushed, and added to salt as a dipping sauce they become *huā jiāo yén*.

Hubbard squash A family of very large winter squashes varying in appearance and size, with green, gray, blue, or yellow skin, sometimes bumpy, and yellow flesh, and ranging up to 50 pounds.

huckleberry A small black berry, similar to the blueberry but seedier, tarter, and darker in color, lacking the blueberry's silver sheen; the low shrub, which grows wild in North America, was praised by Thoreau and chosen by Mark Twain for the name of his greatest fictional character.

huevo [WAY-võ] Spanish for egg; *huevos a la flamenco*, eggs baked on a bed of peas, peppers, onions, tomatoes, ham, and sausage; *huevos asturian*, scrambled eggs with eggplant, tomatoes, and fava beans; *huevos pasados por agua*, soft-boiled eggs; *huevos rancheros*, tortillas "country style," that is, with eggs and a hot spicy sauce; *huevos revueltos*, scrambled eggs.

Huhn [hoon] German for chicken, hen, fowl.

húi guō ròu [hway gwoh rõ] In Chinese cooking, twice-cooked pork; that is, pork loin boiled and sliced, then fried crisp with green bell peppers and tofu in a sweet and spicy sauce, for contrast of flavors and textures; from Sichuan; the Cantonese is *wei wor yuk*.

huile [weel] French for oil.

huitlacoche [WEET-lah-KŌ-chay] A dark fungus that grows on green corn cobs, making a favorite Mexican stuffing for QUESADILLAS or soup; the fungus makes the kernels grow large, black, and deformed, but tastes delicious.

huître [WEE-truh] French for oyster.

hull To husk or remove the outer covering of a seed or fruit, as of a nut, or the interior pith, as of a strawberry.

Hummer [HOOM-er] German for lobster.

hummus [HOOM-uhs] Chickpeas mashed to a paste with lemon juice and garlic, flavored with TAHINI, and eaten with pita bread; originally an appetizer throughout the Middle East, now widely popular.

hún dùn [whun tun] Chinese for wonton: a pastalike egg dough wrapper, literally "swallowing cloud"; the Cantonese is *hun tun*.

hunkar begendi [hyuhn-KYAHR beh-yen-DEE] "The sultan approved," a Turkish dish of cubed lamb braised with onions and tomatoes, and served on creamed roasted eggplant.

hun yem dou fu See XÌN RÉN DÒU FÙ.

huǒ guō [hoah gwoh]   Hot pot, in Chinese cooking, Mongolian hot pot, a clay vessel or casserole with lid, used for braising over direct heat on the stove; see SĀN XIĀN SHĀ GUŌ MIÀN and SHUÀN YÁNG RÒU.

hush puppies   Deep-fried cornmeal dumplings, sometimes flavored with chopped onions, usually eaten as a savory accompaniment to fried fish; from the southern United States.

hyssop [HIS-up]   A perennial herb of southern Europe and the Middle East, used fresh or dried in savory dishes and liqueurs for its minty and somewhat bitter flavor.

I N D I A N   P U D D I N G

I

ice   See WATER ICE.

iceberg lettuce   A crisphead lettuce, pale green, formed in a densely packed head whose outer leaves can be easily removed; slow to wilt and excellent for shredding but with little flavor.

ice cream   A frozen dessert of cream that is sweetened, flavored variously, and beaten during freezing to keep ice crystals from forming; a custard base is frequently, though not necessarily, used for rich flavor and smooth texture.

icing   A confectionery mixture made of sugar, egg white, butter, flavorings, and so on, used to cover or decorate cakes and other pastries; the various types, both cooked and uncooked, differ according to purpose; see also BUTTER-CREAM and ROYAL ICING.

icing sugar   British for CONFECTIONERS' SUGAR.

Idaho potato   See POTATO.

idli [ID-lee]   Indian steamed rice cake, sweet or spicy, using the same sweet or savory ingredients as for DOSA but a different method; usually eaten with SAMBAL for breakfast, in southern India.

igname [ee-nyam]   French for YAM.

ijja [EU-jah]   An Arab omelet, related to the Spanish tortilla, with many varied ingredients as filling and egg as binder; firm, thick, and cakelike, it is turned out of the pan and cut in wedges to be eaten hot or cold; also spelled *eggah*.

ika [ee-kah]   Japanese for squid.

ikan [ee-kan]   Indonsian for fish; *ikan asam manis*, fish in a piquant sweet and sour sauce; *pepes ikan*, fish marinated and baked with coconut.

Île de France [EEL deu FRANHS]   The region around Paris, the original Frankish kingdom, famous for its fine produce, cheeses, bread, pastry, game, meat, and fish; the Île de France also lays claims to the culinary creations of Paris's many fine restaurants.

île flottante [eel flō-tanht]   A French dessert of a meringue "island" on a sea of custard; also sponge cake sliced, sprinkled with liqueur, spread with jam, nuts, and dried fruit, reshaped and covered with crème CHANTILLY, with custard or fruit purée poured over all.

imam bayıldı [ee-MAHM bī-eul—DEU]   A cold Turkish vegetable dish of eggplant sautéed in olive oil with onions, tomatoes, garlic, and parsley; the name in Turkish means "the priest fainted."

imbottito [eem-boh-TEE-tō]   Italian for stuffed.

impanato [eem-pah-NAH-tō]   Italian for breaded.

impératrice, à l' [ah l'imh-payr-a-trees]   In the style of the empress; for desserts, this means rice pudding with candied fruit and cream.

impériale, à l' [ah l'imh-payr-ryal]   In French cuisine, garnished with truffles, foie gras, cocks' combs and kidneys, sweetbreads, and Madeira sauce.

Indian fig   See PRICKLY PEAR.

Indian pudding   Cornmeal pudding sweetened with molasses and spiced, made by early English settlers with English methods; also called hasty pudding. The word *Indian* indicates corn.

indienne, à l' [ah l'inh-dyen]   In French cooking, served with boiled rice and sauce flavored with curry powder.

infuse   To steep or soak herbs, spices, or vegetables in liquid to extract their flavor and transfer it to the liquid; the solids are then strained out; a tea infuser is a small perforated ball for that purpose.

inhame [een-YAM-ay]   Portuguese for YAM.

injera [IN-jah-rah]   An Ethiopian flatbread made from *teff*, a type of MILLET; the bread is light, spongy, slightly fermented, eaten with WOT.

insalata [een-sah-LAH-tah]   Italian for salad.

interlard   To lard; to thread strips of pork fat or lardons through meat or other flesh in order to baste it during cooking.

invert sugar   Simple sugar changed by heat or the addition of an enzyme or acid, such as lemon juice or cream of tartar, to break down sugar crystals and prevent other sugars from crystallizing; this resulting smoothness is desirable for making icings, candy, ice creams, and sorbets.

involtine [een-vōl-TEE-nay]   Italian for scallops of meat, usually veal, or fish, pounded thin, stuffed, and rolled up; veal birds.

iota   See JOTA.

Irish coffee   Coffee laced with Irish whiskey, usually flavored with sugar, spices, and cream.

Irish Mist   A liqueur made with Irish WHISKEY flavored with heather honey.

Irish moss   See CARRAGEEN.

Irish soda bread   A traditional Irish bread, usually baked in free-form rounds, whose leavening agent is baking soda with buttermilk rather than yeast.

irradiation   The process of subjecting food to doses of ionizing radiation, from accelerated electrons, X-rays, or gamma rays, to kill microorganisms and insects and increase shelf life; the process has been approved by the FDA, but its long-term chemical effects are not yet known, and thus it is controversial.

Ischlertörtchen [EESH-ler-TERT-shen]   In German, a biscuit spread with jam.

isinglass [Ī-zin-glas]   Gelatin, obtained from the air bladder of sturgeon and other fish, that is pure and transparent.

Ismaîl Bayaldi [EES-mīl bī-YAL-dee]   A classic French garnish, originally from Turkey, of sliced fried eggplant, crushed tomatoes, rice pilaf, and sauce POR-TUGAISE; related to IMAM BAYILDI.

Italian meringue   A meringue made by whipping hot sugar syrup into stiffly beaten egg whites; used to frost pastries, to lighten pastry and buttercreams, in soufflés, and in sherbets.

italienne, sauce [sōs ee-tal-yen]   A classic French sauce of finely chopped mushrooms with diced ham and chopped parsley.

ivoire, sauce [sōs ee-vwaahr]   Sauce suprême (see under SUPRÊME DE VOLAILLE) with meat glaze, colored ivory.

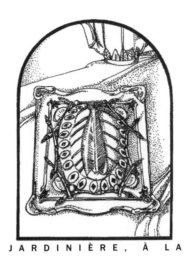

J A R D I N I È R E ,   À   L A

J

jack   See MONTEREY JACK.

jackfruit   The very large oblong fruit of a tree related to BREADFRUIT, probably native to India and grown in Southeast Asia; the starchy bland fruit is similar to pineapple in its complex formation, with yellow flesh and edible seeds; eaten unripe as a vegetable, also pickled or dried; when ripened to sweetness, it is made into custard and other desserts.

Jäger, Jäger Art [YAY-ger]   German for hunter's style—with mushrooms and usually in a wine sauce.

jaggery   See PALM SUGAR.

jah   See ZHÀ.

jaiba [HĪ-bah]   Mexican for crab.

jalapeño [hah-lah-PAY-nyō]   A hot chili pepper from Mexico, a favorite in the United States, about 2 inches long; usually eaten bright green and fresh, often stuffed, also pickled and even candied; when dried and smoked, it becomes a CHIPOTLE.

jalebi [jah-LAY-bee]   An Indian dessert sweet; BESAN batter is pressed through a pastry bag in tubular coils, deep-fried, and dipped in rosewater syrup; also spelled *jellabies*.

jalousie [jha-loo-zee]   In French cooking, a FEUILLETAGE pastry strip with a sweet filling, whose top layer is cut into parallel strips like a Venetian blind (hence its name).

jambalaya [jahm-bah-LĪ-yah]   A dish from CAJUN cuisine of rice with ham, shellfish, sausage, chicken, and beans, seasoned with CREOLE vegetables and spices; the ingredients vary widely.

jambon [jhamh-bonh]   French for HAM.

jamón [hah-MŌN]   Spanish for HAM.

japonaise, à la [ah lah jha-pō-nez]   In French cuisine, garnished with Chinese or Japanese artichokes and potato croquettes.

jardinière, à la [ah lah jhaahr-dee-nyayr]   In French cuisine, "in the style of the gardener's wife": garnished with various fresh vegetables cooked and arranged separately around the main piece of meat or poultry.

Jarlsberg [YAHRLZ-bayrg]   A Norwegian hard cows' milk cheese, made from partially skimmed milk, nutty and sweet, made in large wheels, and similar to EMMENTAL.

jarret [jhaahr-ray]   French for knuckle or hock.

jelabi [jeh-LAH-bee]   In Afghan cooking, lacy fried dough drenched in syrup, served with fish.

Jerez de la Frontera [hayr-ETH day lah frohn-TAY-rah]   A city in southern Spain whose outlying vineyards produce SHERRY; the word "sherry" is an Anglicization of *Jerez*.

jerk seasoning   A combination of seasonings, including chilies, onions, garlic, spices, and herbs, usually rubbed dry onto beef, pork, or chicken or used as a marinade before the meat is barbecued, smoked, or grilled; associated especially with Jamaica; this jerk is a version of JERKY.

jerky   Preserved meat, usually beef and originally sometimes buffalo, that is cut into thin strips and dried in the sun; used by the American Indians and early settlers as a staple for its keeping powers.

jeroboam [jayr-oh-BŌ-um]   A large wine bottle with the capacity of six ordinary bottles (about ⅘ of a gallon); named for the first king of the Hebrews.

Jerusalem artichoke   A tuberous vegetable of the sunflower family, native to North America, whose knotty root is a versatile and nutritious foodstuff; also called sunchoke; "Jerusalem" is a corruption of the Italian *girasole*, meaning "sunflower," because the blossom turns toward the sun.

jeyuk sun [jay-ook sun]   In Korean cooking, pork strips marinated and stir-fried with sliced potatoes, garnished with egg strips, chilies, onions, and sesame seeds.

jhinga [JING-ah]   Shrimp or prawn in Indian cooking; also spelled *ginga*.

jī [jee]   Chinese for chicken; *jī ròu* designates chicken meat.

jiàng [jung]   Chinese for sauce; the word also means ginger.

jiàng yóu [jung yō]   Chinese for soy sauce in light, medium, and dark grades; light soy sauce, saltier and thinner, is used with seafood and chicken; dark soy sauce, thick, rich, and strong, is best with red meat roasts, stews, and barbecues.

jiăo zĭ [jyow zeu]   Meat dumplings, in Chinese cooking, a hearty northern dish of minced pork and cabbage in dumpling skins; these can be boiled, steamed, or fried, when they are GUŌ TIĒ, and are served with a dipping sauce.

jícama [HEE-kah-mah]   A root vegetable, crisp and slightly sweet, that resembles the turnip; used both raw and barely cooked in Mexican and Asian cooking.

jiè lán [jee-eh lahn]   Chinese broccoli, with longer stems and smaller flowerets and slightly more bitter in taste than Western broccoli; the Cantonese is *gai lan* [gi lahn].

jigger   A measure of 1½ ounces for making cocktails.

jing   See ZHĒNG.

jitomate [hee-tō-MAH-tay]   The Mexican word for the ordinary red tomato; not to be confused with the tart green TOMATILLO.

Johannisberg [yō-HAHN-is-bayrg]   A German village in the Rheingau, which produces very good wine and gives its name to Johannisberg Riesling, a fine white grape variety cultivated increasingly in California.

John Dory   A saltwater fish found mainly in European waters, especially the Mediterranean, with a black spot ringed in yellow on each side of the body, said to be the fingerprints of St. Peter (hence its French name, Saint-Pierre); its delicate, flavorful white flesh is valued in many recipes, either in fillets or chunks, as for BOUILLABAISSE.

johnny cake, jonny cake   A hearth- or pancake of cornmeal, sometimes mixed with other grains, cooked in the ashes or in a griddle or pan; the name is often said to be derived from Shawnee and the cake originally from Rhode Island, but what is certain is that early American settlers adapted the native cornmeal to a familiar cooking method.

Joinville, à la [ah lah jhwinh-vee]   Garnished with finely diced shrimp, truffles, and mushrooms, all bound in sauce NORMANDE.

jollof [JOL-uf]   A West African dish of fried beef or chicken pieces with onions, chilies, tomatoes, and rice, in many variations.

jon [jawn]   Korean for pancakes or sometimes fritters; *pa jon*, a scallion pancake, commonly sold as a street snack.

Jonah crab   A variety of crab with a red upper and yellow lower shell, found offshore along the eastern coast of United States, especially from Long Island to Maine.

jook   See ZHŌU.

jota [YŌ-tah]   A robust Italian soup of beans with sauerkraut, potatoes, and bacon cooked slowly; *jota* comes from Trieste, its unusual spelling a holdover from the Austro-Hungarian influence (the Italianized spelling is *iota*).

judía [hoo-DEE-ah]   Spanish for kidney bean, string bean; *judías verdes* are green string beans.

jugged hare   Hare (or other furred game) that is stewed in an earthenware pot or jug to which some of the animal's blood is added, to thicken the sauce just before serving.

jujube [JOO-joob]   The fruit of a tropical Asian plant, sometimes called Chinese date, which is picked ripe, dried, and used to sweeten cough medicines; also the name of a candy.

juk   See ZHŌU.

julienne [jhü-lyen]   Vegetables or other foodstuffs cut into fine matchsticks.

juniper   An evergreen tree whose purple berries flavor gin, marinades, sauerkraut, and game dishes.

junket   Milk curds formed with RENNET and served as a custardlike dessert.

Jurançon [jhür-anh-sonh]   An unusual and renowned wine from the foothills of the Pyrenees in southwestern France, possessing a gold color and a sweet, spicy taste.

jus [jhüs]   French for juice; *au jus* means meat served with its natural juices; *jus de viande* means gravy.

K A L E

K

kabak tatlısı [kah-BAHK TAHT-leu-seu]   A Turkish dessert of pumpkin slices slowly cooked until tender, served in syrup topped with crushed walnuts.

k'ab al-ghzal [kab al-HRAZL]   "Gazelles' horns," crescent pastries filled with almond paste, from Morocco.

Kabeljau [KAH-bel-yow]   German for cod.

Kabinett [kah-bee-NET]   Superior or special reserve unsweetened wine, usually estate-bottled and from the German Rheingau.

kabocha [ka-bō-cha]   Japanese for pumpkin, squash.

kabu [kah-boo]   Japanese for turnip.

kadaif   See KUNAIFA.

kadın budu [kah-DEUN boo-DOO]   "Ladies' thighs," a Turkish dish of lamb and rice meatballs first poached, then battered and fried.

kadın göbeği [kah-DEUN geu-BAY-ee]   "Ladies' navels," a Turkish dish of dimpled balls of batter, deep-fried and soaked in syrup.

Kaffee [KAH-fay]   German for coffee; afternoon coffee in Germany or Austria can include elaborate cakes and sandwiches, a social occasion not unlike English tea.

Kaffir lime [KAF-er]   A member of the citrus family whose fruit has bumpy, nubbly skin; much used in the cooking of Southeast Asia, especially Thailand, its zest, juice, and especially leaves, chopped and added to dishes at the last moment.

kafta [KAHF-tah]   In Arab cooking, ground meat flavored with cinnamon or other spices and shaped into balls; the Turkish is *köfta*, the Indian *kofta*.

Kahlúa [kah-LOO-ah]   A Mexican coffee-flavored liqueur.

kahve [KAH-veh]   Turkish coffee, very strong, aromatic, and foamy on top.

kai [kī]   Thai for egg; *kai kwan* means eggs stuffed with pork and seafood and deep-fried.

kaimaki   See MASTIC.

kakadi [KAH-kah-dee]   Cucumber in Indian cooking.

k'ak bil yuyu [KAHK bil YOO-yoo]   Tunisian doughnuts of orange-flavored egg dough deep-fried and honey dipped; eaten with Arab coffee.

kake [kah-kay]   Japanese for noodles; used in combination with another word, such as *kake-jiru* (noodle broth).

kaki [kah-kee]   Japanese for PERSIMMON; several European languages, including French, have borrowed the word *kaki* for persimmon; it also means oyster in Japanese.

Kalamata   See under OLIVE.

Kalb [kalp]   German for veal; *Kalbschnitzel* means veal cutlet cooked simply in butter; *Kalbshaxe*, veal shanks or knuckles, very popular in Bavaria.

kalbi jim [gal-bee CHIM]   Beef or pork ribs, braised with chestnuts and mushrooms in a spicy sauce; a Korean dish.

kale   A loose, green leafy vegetable of the genus *Brassica* with a stronger taste than its cabbage cousin. At its best in frosty weather, this winter staple supplies vitamins and minerals that can otherwise be scarce in cold regions, explaining its popularity in country dishes such as colcannon and kailkenny that need slow gentle cooking. Of the varieties newly available, often with curly or ruffled edges, Tuscan kale grows in dark elegant plumes on white stalks; ornamental kale has a creamy or fuchsia center that looks like a nosegay; Russian Red's silver-green leaves turn rosy as the weather chills.

kalonji   See NIGELLA.

kalt   German for cold.

kamaboko Japanese fish paste or sausage in many varieties.

kambing Indonesian for lamb.

kampyō Japanese for dried gourd shavings.

kang kung [kahng kuhng] A Laotian soup of melon, dried shrimp, mushrooms, ginger, and chicken stock.

kani [kah-nee] Japanese for crab.

Kaninchen [kah-NEEN-shen] German for rabbit.

kanom [kah-nohm] Thai for cake, cookie; *kanom mo kaeng*, baked custard squares; *kanom klug*, coconut pancakes.

kanten Japanese for AGAR-AGAR seaweed.

kǎo [kow] Barbecuing or roasting in Chinese cooking.

kao [kow] Generic Thai term for rice or grain; *kao nieo* means sticky rice; *kao pad*, fried rice.

Kapaun [kah-POWN] German for capon.

kapee [kap-ee] Thai for shrimp paste.

Kaper [KAH-payr] German for caper.

karashi [kah-rah-shee] Japanese for mustard.

karela [kah-RAY-lah] BITTER MELON, a popular vegetable in Indian cooking.

Karfiol [kar-FYŌL] Cauliflower, in Austrian dialect; see also BLUMENKOHL.

kari [KAH-ree] In Indian cooking, curry, seasoned sauce; also the aromatic leaves of the *kari* plant.

kari-kari [KAH-ree KAH-ree] A Philippine oxtail stew flavored with garlic and onion, the sauce thickened with crushed peanuts and rice flour.

Karotte [kah-ROHT-teh] German for carrot.

Karpfen [KAR-pfen] German for carp—a very popular fish in Germany and traditional for Christmas Eve.

Kartoffel [kar-TOHF-el] German for potato; *Kartoffelbrei* means mashed potatoes, *Kartoffelklösse*, dumplings, and *Kartoffelpuffer*, potato pancakes.

Käse [KAY-zeh] German for cheese; *Käseteller* means cheese plate; *Käsetorte*, cheesecake.

kasha Hulled, crushed, and cooked groats, usually buckwheat, used in Russian cooking.

Kasnudeln [KAHZ-nood-eln]   German noodles stuffed with savory meat and cheese filling or fruit and poppy seed filling for dessert.

Kassler Rippenspeer [KAHS-ler RIP-en-shpayr]   Cured and smoked pork loin served on a bed of sauerkraut, mashed potatoes, and apples or red cabbage and potato dumplings, with a red wine and sour cream gravy; a great favorite in Germany.

Kastanie [kah-STAHN-yeh]   German for chestnut.

Katenschinken [KAT-en-shink-en]   German smoked country ham, originally from Schleswig-Holstein; *Katenwurst* means smoked sausage from the same area; the word *Katen* means a peasant hut or cottage, where these meats were originally cured.

katsuo-bushi [kat-soo-ō-boo-shee]   Japanese dried bonito flakes, essential in making DASHI.

kau muong [kow muong]   Vietnamese for water spinach, with heart-shaped leaves and hollow stems; eaten stir-fried or wilted in salads and soups, its taste is mild yet tangy.

kayısı [KĪ-yeu—seu]   Turkish for apricots.

kaymak [KĪ-mak]   Turkish clotted cream made from buffalo milk, very thick, for spreading on bread or making desserts.

kdra   See QDRA.

kebab [keh-BAHB]   In Turkish cuisine, pieces of seasoned and marinated meat, usually lamb, grilled over or under a fire. In shish kebab, meat cubes are threaded on a skewer or sword (*şiş* or *shish*), often with vegetables; the Russian version, from the Caucasus, is *shashlyk*. For *döner kebab*, long thin strips of meat turn on a spit; the Greek word for this rotating spit is *gyro* [YEER-ō], the Arab *shwarma*.

kedgeree   See KITCHERI.

kéfir [KAY-feer]   Fermented milk, slightly effervescent and alcoholic, widely consumed in the Middle East and Russia; the *kéfir* culture sours the milk (usually cows'), making it thick, frothy, and healthful.

kefta [KEF-tah]   Moroccan for KAFTA.

kejenou [KAY-jay-noo]   Chicken and shrimp braised in an earthenware pot with onions, tomatoes, chilies, spices, and rice and served in individual ramekins; from the Ivory Coast.

Keks [kayks]   German for BISCUIT.

kelapa [keh-lah-pah]   Indonesian and Malaysian for coconut; *kelapa sayur* means vegetables simmered in spicy coconut milk.

Kelerabzug   See ORIGINAL-ABFÜLLUNG.

Kellerabfüllung   See ORIGINAL-ABFÜLLUNG.

kelp   See KONBU.

kesar [KAY-sahr]   Saffron, in Indian cooking.

kesksou [KES-koo]   Algerian for couscous.

ketchup   Historically this word, Chinese in origin, means a savory sauce or condiment, made from diverse foodstuffs, such as mushrooms, anchovies, or oysters, pickled in brine. Today's commercially manufactured tomato ketchup is highly derivative; also spelled catchup, catsup, and katsup.

Key lime pie   A custard pie originally made with a small, very tart variety of lime grown on the Florida Keys (the Key lime has not been commercially cultivated there since the 1926 hurricane, but is still grown in the Caribbean); the pie has a pastry or graham-cracker crust with a lime juice, egg yolk, and condensed milk filling, and sometimes a meringue topping.

kha [kah]   Thai for GALANGAL.

khalia   In Indian cooking, a meat and vegetable style of curry, with thick reddish-brown gravy, soured with raw mango (AM), mango powder, or tamarind pulp.

kheer [keer]   Indian rice pudding made with milk, sweet spices, and almonds; also spelled *khir*.

khira [keer-ah]   Indian for cucumber; also spelled *kheera*.

khoresh [koh-RESH]   Thick sauce, almost like a stew, with small pieces of meat, vegetables, and fruit and mild spices; eaten with rice in Persian cooking.

khorma   See KORMA.

khoshaf [HŌ-shahf]   In Middle Eastern cooking, dried fruit salad, usually of macerated apricots, raisins, almonds, and pistachios.

khoya [KOY-ah]   Fresh milk condensed to a thick paste by boiling and simmering, used for sweet dishes such as KULFI in Indian cooking.

khubz [hoobz]   Arabic for bread.

khudar [HOO-dar]   Arabic for vegetables.

kibbeh [KIH-bee] BULGHUR and ground lamb, onions, and pine nuts, deep-fried or served raw; its origin is Lebanese, and it has many variations.

kid Young GOAT.

kidney A pair of organs embedded in white fat, those from veal or lamb considered best; excellent for various culinary preparations trimmed of exterior membrane and interior gristle, then sautéed or broiled quickly or braised slowly in stews or meat pies.

kielbasa [KEEL-bah-zah] A Polish sausage made of pork, sometimes beef or veal, flavored with garlic, smoked, and cooked; its links are very long and horseshoe-shaped.

Kiev, chicken à la Boned chicken breast rolled up to enclose an herb-flavored butter, egg-and-bread-crumbed, and deep-fried; the delicious butter has been known to squirt out on the unwary diner.

kiku [kee-koo] Japanese edible chrysanthemum.

kikurage [kee-koo-rah-gay] Japanese for cloud ear or wood ear mushroom, usually dried.

kimchee A pungent Korean condiment of pickled shredded vegetables, including Chinese cabbage, radishes, cucumbers, greens, onions, garlic, and chili peppers, seasoned with fermented shellfish and salt; the condiment varies widely in its strength and is especially common in winter, when fresh vegetables are unavailable; also spelled *keem chee* and *kimchi.*

king Thai for ginger.

king crab A large variety of crab living in northern Pacific waters and growing up to twenty pounds; the meat is usually sold cooked and frozen; also called Alaska king crab and Japanese crab.

king salmon See SALMON.

Kipferl [KIP-fayrl] A German crescent-shaped roll, sweeter and more doughy than a CROISSANT.

kippered herring, kipper Herring that has been split, lightly salted, dried, and smoked to preserve it; a favorite breakfast dish in Britain.

Kir [keer] An apéritif of white wine tinged with a little crème de CASSIS, popularized by and named for the Resistance hero and mayor of Dijon, Canon Félix Kir; a *Kir royale* uses Champagne.

Kirsch [keersh] German for cherry.

Kirschwasser [KEERSH-vah-ser]   A German colorless liqueur distilled from the fermented mash of wild cherries, especially those grown in the French Alsace and the German Black Forest; often used as a flavoring in confectionery and pastry; sometimes called simply *Kirsch*.

kissel [KIS-sel]   A Russian and Baltic berry pudding, often made with puréed strawberries, thickened with potato flour or cornstarch; also used as a dessert sauce.

kitcheri [KIH-cher-ee]   Kedgeree: cooked rice, lentils, and spices, of Hindi origin; when the English Anglicized this Indian dish they often served it with leftover fish, hard-boiled eggs, and curry, which is how it survives as a breakfast dish in England today.

kited fillet   Fish cut through along the backbone and filleted but left attached at the belly.

kiwano   A spiky, bright orange fruit that, despite its comic-book looks, is an ancient fruit native to Africa; the green pulp, gelatinous and juicy, with lots of white seeds, tastes bland; also called horned melon.

kiwi   A small tree of Chinese origin whose plum-shaped fruit is covered with a thin layer of brownish fuzz; once peeled, the soft green interior with small black seeds radiating from a pale green center is entirely edible, tasting somewhere between strawberry and melon; also called Chinese gooseberry, but recently marketed as kiwi.

Klopse [KLOHP-seh]   German ground meatballs usually containing two or three kinds of meat. *Königsberger Klopse* are poached meatballs of pork with veal or beef, flavored with anchovies and served with a lemon, sour cream, and caper sauce; from the Slavic northeast.

Klösse [KLEUS-eh]   German dumplings or meatballs; the singular is *Kloss*.

kluay [kloo-ay]   Thai for banana; *kluay tord* means fried bananas.

Knackwurst [KNAHK-voorst]   German sausages similar to hot dogs but thicker.

knädlach [KNED-lakh]   Jewish dumplings of MATZO meal, egg, ground almonds, and chicken fat dropped into chicken broth; spelled variously.

knead   To work dough with the fingers and heels of the hand in order to distribute the ingredients uniformly, develop the GLUTEN, and produce an even texture ready for rising.

knish   Chopped chicken livers or KASHA wrapped in a pastry of mashed potatoes, flour, and chicken fat; a traditional Jewish dish from eastern Europe.

Knoblauch   [KNOB-lowkh]   German for garlic.

Knödel   [KNEU-del]   German for dumpling.

Kobe gyu   [kō-bay gyoo]   Japanese steer raised and pampered to an impeccably high standard for its delectably tender meat, which, in accordance, is exorbitantly expensive.

kofta   See KAFTA.

Kohl   [kōl]   German for cabbage; *Kohlrouden* is cabbage stuffed with ground meats and braised.

kohlrabi   [kōl-RAH-bee]   A vegetable in the cabbage family whose stem swells just above the ground into a bulbous knob; this bulb, the long stems, and the leaves are edible and taste like cabbage and turnip, which together give it its name; favored in central and eastern Europe and Asia.

koi-kuchi shōyu   [koy-koo-chee shō-yoo]   Japanese dark soy sauce, thicker and heavier but less salty than light soy sauce (*usu-kuchi shōyu*).

Kompott   [kohm-POHT]   A German compote of stewed fruit.

konafa   See KUNAIFA.

konbu   [kon-boo]   Japanese dried kelp, essential in making DASHI; sometimes spelled *kombu*; it should be soaked and scored before use and can be reused.

Konditorei   [kohn-dee-tor-ī]   German for a pastry shop, where coffee and hot chocolate are offered.

kong   [kohng]   Thai for snack.

Königenpastete   [KEU-ni-gen-pas-TAY-teh]   German for pastry filled with meat and mushrooms or other savory fillings.

konnyaku   [kon-yah-koo]   Literally, "devil's tongue jelly" in Japanese; a translucent cake made from arum root.

Kopfsalat   [KŌPF-sah-laht]   German for lettuce salad, head of lettuce.

korma   [KOOR-mah]   In northern Indian cooking, meat and vegetables slowly braised with yogurt or cream, usually rich and spicy but not moist or necessarily hot; often misunderstood to be a mild curry. This is a loose term, spelled variously, that appears across the Middle East and western Asia from Turkey to Afghanistan to India and Pakistan.

Korn   German for grain, cereal; the word means the dominant grain in a specific region, whether rye, wheat, or barley—not necessarily corn.

kosher   According to Jewish dietary laws, the kashruth, as set forth in the Talmud.

Kotelett [koh-teh-LET]   German for cutlet, chop.

Krabbe [KRAH-beh]   German for crab, the plural *Krabben* often means shrimp.

Krakauer [KRAHK-ow-er]   German for Polish ham sausage.

Krapfen [KRAH-pfen]   Sweet Bavarian fritters, similar to doughnuts.

Kraut [krowt]   German for plant, herb, greens; on a menu the word usually means cabbage.

kreatopita [kray-ah-TŌ-pee-tah]   A Greek meat pie wrapped in PHYLLO dough.

Krebs [krayps]   German for crab, crayfish.

Kren   German for horseradish; *Krenfleisch* means top round of beef boiled, sliced, and served with bread, gherkins, and horseradish, from Bavaria.

kreplach [KREP-lakh]   A small dough turnover with savory filling, often served in soup, eaten during the Jewish celebration of Succoth.

Kreuznach [KROYTS-nakh]   A German town on the Nahe River, west of the Rhine, that is the center of the valley's wine industry; a good wine school is located there.

Kronsbeere [KRŌNS-bayr-eh]   German for cranberry.

krupnik [KRUHP-nik]   Mushroom barley soup, from eastern Europe.

kuài zi [kwī tseu]   Chinese for chopsticks.

kubecake [KOOB kayk]   Coconut rum ball, sweet and gingery, sold by street vendors in West Africa; potently flavored but not cakelike.

Küche [KÜ-she]   German for kitchen, cooking.

Kuchen [KOO-khen]   German for cake, tart, pastry.

kudamono [koo-dah-mō-nō]   Japanese for fruit.

kugel [KOO-gel]   A baked casserole or pudding, associated especially with the Jewish holiday of Hanukkah.

Kugelhopf [KOO-gel-hohpf]   A German yeast cake, sometimes made from BRIOCHE dough, flavored with currants steeped in brandy and baked in a special fluted mold strewn with almonds; now a specialty of Alsace, it is originally from Austria, where it is called *Gugelhupf*, each region having its traditional molds.

kulfi [KUL-fee] Indian ice cream, made from KHOYA, cream, starch, sugar, nuts, and rosewater; served frozen hard in squares, textured with lumps of cream and nuts.

kulibyaka [koo-lee-BYAH-kah] See COULIBIAC.

kulich [KOO-lish] A tall cylindrical Russian cake in the shape of a priest's hat, flavored with fruit, almonds, and saffron; this is the Russian Orthodox ceremonial dessert for Easter, decorated with the letters XB, signifying "Christ Is Risen," and traditionally served with PASKHA.

kulikuli [KOO-lee-KOO-lee] An African biscuit or ring made of peanut paste, fried and eaten as a snack or RUSK.

Kümmel [KÜ-mel] German for caraway seed, much used with cabbage, stew, and pastry; also the liqueur flavored with caraway.

kumquat A small oval citrus fruit, native to China, eaten whole, either fresh or preserved in syrup, and often used as a garnish; its rind is sweeter than its pulp; the name means "golden orange" in Cantonese.

kunaifa [KNAH-fee] Middle Eastern pastries made from phyllo, similar to BAKLAVA; called *kadaif* in Turkey and Greece.

kuri [koo-ree] Japanese for chestnuts.

Kutteln [KOO-teln] German for tripe.

kuy tieu [kwee tyoo] A traditional Cambodian Khmer soup of noodles, sliced pork, bean sprouts, fried garlic, and cilantro.

kvass [kvahs] A fermented Russian drink similar to beer, made from yeast, rye, and barley; it is used to flavor BORSCHT, CHLODNIK, and other soups; sometimes spelled *kwas*.

kyinkyinga [chin-CHING-ah] West African meatballs skewered with sweet peppers, grilled, and sprinkled with roasted crushed peanuts; often sold on the street.

kyūri [kyoo-ree] Japanese cucumber.

L

laban [LUH-ban]   Arabic for yogurt, especially in Syria and Lebanon; *laban zabadi* in Egypt. In North Africa *laban* means milk.

labna [LUB-nah]   Strained yogurt in the Middle East; also spelled *labni*, *lubni*, or *labneh*; sometimes salted, spiced, shaped into balls, and rolled in olive oil; eaten with flatbread for breakfast, an Arab favorite.

Labskaus [LAHBS-kows]   German "seaman's stew" from Hamburg, of pickled pork or beef cooked with onions and potatoes, sometimes with pickled fish, beets, or gherkins as garnish.

là chăng [lah chahng]   Chinese pork sausage made of pork meat and fat, in Canton sweetened with honey; cured, cooked before serving, and sliced thin; associated with the Lunar New Year festival. The Mandarin term is also *xiāng chăng* [zyahng chahng]; the Cantonese is *lop cheung*.

Lachs [lahks]   German for salmon.

la chuoi [la chooee]   Vietnamese for banana leaves, used for steaming dumplings, coconut rice, fish, and other foods, also for lining steamers.

lacón con grelos [lah-KŌN kōn GRAY-lōth]   Cured pork shoulder with turnip tops—a famous dish from Galicia in Spain.

lactic acid   The acid in milk produced by bacterial starter culture, which turns lactose (milk sugar) into lactic acid, causing the coagulation of the milk and the first step in the cheesemaking process; lactic acid is also present in rested muscle tissue and acts as a natural preservative in slaughtered meat. Many milk products, such as buttermilk, sour cream, *kéfir*, and yogurt, are made by a lactic culture.

lager   Bottom-fermented beer, originally stored up to six months for the yeast to settle, giving a clearer, lighter, weaker brew than top-fermented beer such as porter or stout; most American beers are lager.

lagniappe [lan-yap]   In New Orleans, a CREOLE word meaning a little something extra, a bonus, such as a thirteenth item added to a dozen.

lahm   Arabic for lamb.

lahmejune [lah-meh-JOON]   Armenian pizza; open PITA dough topped with finely chopped lamb, tomatoes, peppers, onions, and herbs; also spelled *lahma bi ajeen* and other ways; the Turkish version is *lahmacun*.

lait [lay]   French for milk; *au lait* means with milk.

laitue [lay-tü]   French for lettuce.

là jiāo jiàng [lah jow jung]   Chinese for hot chili sauce; a condiment made from chili peppers, vinegar, and seasonings; red in color, red hot in taste.

laksa [lahk-sah]   A Malaysian dish of rice noodles in a spicy fish and shrimp soup rich with coconut milk; bean sprouts, shredded cucumber, and greens may be added, and SAMBAL may be served on the side.

lamb   A young domesticated sheep. Baby lamb is 6 to 8 weeks old and milk-fed, with mildly flavored, tender, pale pink flesh; spring lamb is 3 to 5 months of age, also milk-fed and now available year-round; regular lamb (what we usually see at market) is under the age of 1, with pink-red flesh and good flavor; lamb between 1 and 2 years of age is yearling lamb; in the United States, hard-to-find mutton is lamb over the age of 2, with dark red flesh that can be of high quality and fine flavor but is little known or appreciated by Americans. In the West, lamb fat is considered unpalatable, but it is highly valued in the Middle East and Arab countries. Around the Mediterranean, lamb has a long tradition, as for French PRÉ-SALÉ lamb that grazes on salt-meadow grasses, and Italian ABBACCHIO. Many lamb dishes have separate entries.

Lambrusco [lahm-BROO-skō]   A slightly effervescent red wine, fruity, fragrant, and pleasant, made near Modena, Italy, from the Lambrusco grape.

lamb's lettuce   A plant indigenous to Europe, whose dark green, nutty-flavored, whorled leaves are used for winter salads; it is prized by the French; also called *mâche* and corn salad.

lampone [lahm-PŌ-nay]   Italian for raspberry.

lamprey [LAM-pree]   A salt- or freshwater fish similar to the eel; its fatty flesh is eaten in various ways, most often stewed.

Lancashire [LANK-ah-shur]   A creamy white cows' milk cheese from England, cooked and pressed yet still soft and crumbly. True farmhouse Lancashire has a full flavor and excellent melting qualities for WELSH RAREBIT and other dishes, but travels poorly or not at all; the factory-made variety is a pale comparison.

Lancashire hot pot   A traditional English stew of secondary cuts of lamb, especially neck, stewed with layered potatoes and onions, lamb kidneys and oysters often included; a relative of the French HOCHEPOT.

Landjäger [LAHNT-yay-ger]   A smoked sausage from Swabia in Germany.

langouste [lanh-goost]   French for rock or spiny lobster, as it is called in the United States; called saltwater crayfish or crawfish in Britain. Found in the Mediterranean and Pacific, its claws are small, so most of the meat comes from the tail. When cooked, its color is paler than lobster red. The Spanish word for this crustacean is *langosta*.

langoustine [lanh-goo-steen]   French for a small lobster, a saltwater crayfish; also called Dublin Bay prawn (British), Norway lobster, and *scampo* (Italian).

langue [lahng]   French for tongue.

langue-de-chat [LAHNG-deu-SHA]   French for a long, thin cookie shaped like a cat's tongue, hence the name; light and dry, these cookies often accompany simple desserts and sweet wines.

Languedoc [LANH-ge-DŌK]   A region in southern France on the Mediterranean west of the Rhone, a former province, with fine produce and an excellent gastronomic tradition; earlier a Spanish possession, an influence still apparent in the cuisine. Some of its specialties are *cassoulet, confit, brandade de morue,* Roquefort cheese, Bouzigues oysters, and other seafood.

languedocienne, à la [ah lah LANH-ge-DŌ-SYEN]   In French cuisine, meat or poultry garnished with eggplant rounds, cèpes, and tomatoes *concassés*, all sautéed in oil, with chopped parsley.

laos   Indonesian for GALANGAL.

lapin [la-pinh]   French for rabbit; *lapin de garenne* means wild rabbit; *lapin en gibelotte* means rabbit stew with onions, mushrooms, and *lardons*, in white wine sauce.

Lapsang Souchong   A partially fermented Chinese tea with an inimitable smoky aroma and flavor, cured with smoldering pine logs.

lard   Rendered pork fat, excellent for flaky pastry because of its solidity and for deep-frying because of its high smoke point and purity; as a saturated fat high in cholesterol, however, it has become less popular. See also INTERLARD.

lard de poitrine fumé [laahr de pwah-treen fü-may]   Literally "lard from smoked breast," French for smoked and salted pork belly; bacon.

larder [laahr-day]   To lard, to interlard, in French.

lardo [LAR-dō]   Italian for salt pork; *lardo affumicato* is bacon.

lardon [laahr-donh]   French for a thin slice of bacon; also a long thin strip of larding fat threaded through a lean cut of meat with a larding needle, to moisten the meat as it cooks. The term also means a small strip of bacon, blanched and fried, which flavors and moistens braised dishes.

largo   A long, thin chili pepper, pale yellow green in color, fairly hot; often used in Mexican soups and stews.

lasagne [lah-ZAH-nyeh]   Large wide ribbons of pasta, in Italy sometimes squares, baked in layers with sauce, cheese, or other filling; *lasagne* is often made with egg and sometimes puréed spinach as well to color it green. *Lasagna* means a single piece of the pasta.

lassi [LAH-see]   A refreshing Indian yogurt drink, salted or sweet.

lassoon [lah-SOON]   Garlic in Indian cooking.

latkes [LAHT-kez]   Fried potatoes in pancakes, traditionally eaten at the Jewish festival of Hanukkah.

latte [LAHT-tay]   Italian for milk.

lattuga [lah-TOO-gah]   Italian for lettuce.

Lauch [lowkh]   German for leek.

lauro [LOW-rō]   Italian for bay leaf.

lavash [lah-VAHSH]   A thin flat wheat bread from all over the Caucasus, often baked in large sheets; used to scoop up food, or spread and rolled up as a kind of sandwich.

lavender   An evergreen shrub from the Mediterranean whose spiky purple flowers and leaves are used fresh and dried, in washing for their scent (the name comes from the Latin *lavare*, "to wash"), also in cooking, confectionery, and TISANE.

laver [LAY-ver]   A thin, reddish purple highly nutritious seaweed eaten in Japan (where it is called *nori*), China, Ireland (where it is called sloke), and Wales; if dried, it should be soaked first. In Wales, where local people gather it on the coast, it is eaten braised like spinach, pickled, or mixed into oatmeal porridge and fried in flat cakes in bacon fat, called laver bread.

leavening   Any agent that produces gas in dough or batter by means of FERMENTATION, thus raising and lightening it. Yeast, baking powder, and baking soda are all common forms of leavening; beaten egg whites, although they do not involve fermentation, are another kind of leavening.

Leber [LAY-ber]   German for liver.

Leberkäs [LAY-ber-kays]   Meat loaf or pâté of mixed ground meats, from Bavaria.

Leberknödelsuppe [LAY-ber-KNEU-del-zoo-peh]   A soup of clear meat broth with liver dumplings, from Bavaria.

Leberwurst [LAY-ber-voorst]   A German smoked sausage made from ground pork liver and (usually) pork or veal meat.

Lebkuchen [LAYB-koo-khen]   A German spiced honey cake or cookie traditionally eaten at Christmas.

leche [LAY-chay]   Spanish for milk; the word can also mean custard.

lechecillas [lay-chay-THEE-lahth]   Spanish for sweetbreads.

lechón asado [lay-CHŌN ah-THAH-dō]   Spanish for roast suckling pig.

lechuga [lay-CHOO-gah]   Spanish for lettuce.

Leckerli [LEK-er-lee]   A Swiss rectangular biscuit, flavored with cinnamon, honey, dried citrus peel, and almonds; from Basel.

leek   An ancient member of the genus *Allium*, originating in the Mediterranean; its flavor, more subtle than that of other onions, lends itself to soups, stews, and braises. Because the leek lacks a well-defined bulb, dirt gets well down into its leaves, necessitating careful washing.

lees   The sediment that settles in the wine barrel before bottling.

legumbres [lay-GOOM-brayth, lay-GOOM-brays]   Spanish for vegetables; *legumbres secos*, dried vegetables.

legume [lay-GYOOM]   The seed pod of leguminous plants whose peas or beans are eaten fresh (sprouted or not) and dried for their vitamin B, high protein, and carbohydrate value; legumes are an important staple food crop in much of the world, and some of them have separate entries.

légumes [lay-güm]   French for vegetables; the Italian is *legumi* [lay-GOO-mee].

Leicester [LES-ter]   An English whole-milk cows' cheese similar to CHEDDAR. The curd is finely cut, double-milled, pressed, and molded in very large cylinders; it has a hard brownish orange or reddish rind and a yellow, grainy but moist interior. English farmhouse Leicester has a tangy, rich flavor.

lekach [LAY-kakh]   A honey and spice cake, traditional for the Jewish holiday of Rosh Hashanah.

lemon   The fruit of the citrus tree, native probably to India. The Arabs were instrumental in its cultivation and spread east to China and west around the Mediterranean; Columbus took it to the New World. The outer yellow zest concentrates its flavor with the added element of scent; the interior white pith is bitter but rich in pectin. Lemon juice has more vitamin C than other citrus. To the cook it is indispensable, slowing oxidation, whitening food, "cooking" seafood in heatless marinades, gelling low-pectin fruit jams, cleaning hands and equipment. The Meyer lemon is a lemon-orange hybrid, fragrant and sweeter, imported from China by F. N. Meyer in 1908 and now becoming more available in the United States. In Morocco, lemons are preserved in salt, like pickles.

lemon balm   A Mediterranean herb whose leaves, faintly lemon scented, are used in salads, compotes, drinks, tea, and in the making of some liqueurs; also called melissa and bee herb.

lemon curd   Lemon juice, sugar, butter, and egg yolks mixed together and cooked slowly until the yolks thicken (but do not curdle); used for pastries and breads.

lemongrass   A type of grass with long, tapered, fibrous leaves and small tender white bulb; much used in the cooking of Southeast Asia, where lemons do not grow, to impart its subtle but distinct flavor to curries, soups, and other dishes. Lemongrass (sometimes spelled as two words) can flavor indirectly, like bay leaf, when the stalk is removed before eating the dish, or more pungently, when the thicker bulb is finely chopped or ground to a paste before being added to stir-fries, braises, and raw dishes. For storage, lemongrass can be frozen or dried. The Thai word is *takrai*, the Indonesian *sereh*.

lemon thyme   See THYME.

lemon verbena   A fragrant shrub whose lemon-scented leaves flavor teas, fruit drinks, salads, sorbets, and puddings; the fresh leaves are strong in scent, also used dried; native to South America.

lengua de ternere   [LENG-wah day TAYR-nay-ray]   Spanish for calf's tongue.

lenguado   [len-GWAH-dō]   Spanish for sole.

lenticchie   [len-TEEK-kyay]   Italian for lentils.

lentil   A small "lens"-shaped legume that originated in southwest Asia. Rich in nutrients, it has been a high-protein staple in the Middle East and central Asia for millennia and is cultivated in many varieties: the thin-skinned red (or Egyptian, or Masur) lentil, which tends to break up in cooking, may also be yellow, brown, pink, or gray; the small French *verte de Puy* lentil, dark green, has a distinctive earthy flavor from the soil near Puy, in Languedoc. Mung beans and other legumes are sometimes incorrectly called lentils. Unlike other legumes, lentils need no soaking before cooking.

lepre   [LAY-pray]   Italian for hare; *lepre in salmi* is JUGGED HARE.

lesso   [LES-sō]   Italian for boiled, especially boiled meat.

lettuce   The common salad vegetable usually eaten fresh with dressing, occasionally braised; it is related to sharper greens such as chicory, endive, and dandelion. Lettuce falls into four main groups: butterhead, including Boston and Bibb; crisphead, including iceberg; long-leaf, including romaine; and loose-leaf, including oak leaf, salad bowl, and red leaf.

levée, pâte   See PÂTE LEVÉE.

leveret   [lev-ray]   French for young hare.

Leyden   [LĪ-den]   A hard Dutch cheese similar to EDAM, made from partially skimmed cows' milk; the curd is cooked, flavored with cumin, caraway, and spices, molded, and pressed.

liaison   [lyay-sonh]   In French cuisine, the binding or thickening of a soup or sauce by means of egg yolk, blood, or starch such as flour (see BEURRE MANIÉ and ROUX), arrowroot, cornstarch, or tapioca.

lichi, lichee   See LYCHEE.

licorice   [LIK-er-is, LIK-er-ish]   A plant, native to the Middle East, whose name derives from the Greek for "sweet root"; the ancients used the root for medicinal purposes, while today its anise flavoring is used primarily for confectionery; before sugarcane, strips of the raw root were chewed as a kind of candy.

licuado [lee-KWAH-dō]   Spanish for fruit drink, especially citrus.

Liebfraumilch [LEEB-frow-milsh]   A catchall name for Rhine wine, mostly very ordinary; the name means "milk of the Blessed Mother."

Liederkranz   A pasteurized cows' milk cheese invented by a Swiss immigrant in the United States and named after a choral society ("wreath of song"); it is a soft, mild, surface-ripened cheese shaped in rectangles.

liégeoise, à la [ah lah lyejh-waz]   "In the style of Liège," in Belgium; garnished with juniper berries.

lier [lee-ay]   In French, to blend, bind, or connect.

lièvre [LYEV-ruh]   French for hare.

lights   The lungs of an animal, used in the United States for pet food but in other countries combined with other organs and meat in stews, pâtés, and so on, for human consumption.

li jiàng   See HO YAO.

Lillet [lee-lay]   A French apéritif based on red or white wine, fortified with brandy, and flavored with herbs and fruit; Lillet Rouge is sweeter than Lillet Blanc.

lima [LEE-mah]   Spanish for lime; the Mexican *lima agria*, a sour lime from the Yucatán.

lima bean   A legume native to Peru and named for its capitol city, eaten fresh and dried but never raw, as certain varieties are toxic; a staple food in Africa and parts of Asia; popular in the United States as a component of succotash and in the South, where limas are called butter beans.

limande [lee-manhd]   French for lemon sole.

Limburger [LIM-boor-ger]   A pasteurized cows' milk cheese, originally Belgian but now German and American; washed-rind, surface-ripened, creamy yellow, dense, with a very strong and characteristic smell more potent than its taste.

lime   The fruit of the citrus tree, probably native to Malaysia, important for its acidity in tropical regions where the lemon does not grow; in the United States the lime grows only in southernmost Florida and California. The Persian lime (also the Tahiti and California's Bearss lime) is the variety familiar to Americans. The Key lime, named for the Florida islands, and the same as the Mexican or

West Indian lime, also the original Malaysian lime, is smaller and sourer than the Persian. Another variety, sweet and juicy, is eaten in the Middle East and India. Besides the familiar Western uses of lime, the fruit is used fresh and dried in savory Persian and Middle Eastern stews. English sailors were called "limeys" because of their daily ration of Jamaican lime juice in their grog to ward off scurvy.

lime, limette [leem, lee-met]   French for lime.

limon [lee-monh]   French for lime; lemon is *citron*.

limón [lee-MŌN]   Spanish for lemon; but in the Caribbean, *limón* means lime, and *limones franceses* means lemon.

limone [lee-MŌ-nay]   Italian for lemon.

limousine, à la [ah lah lee-moo-seen]   "In the style of Limousin"; in French cuisine, garnished with red cabbage.

limun immallah [lee-MOON ih-MAH-lah]   Moroccan preserved lemons; fresh lemons pickled in salt and their own juice, sometimes flavored with spices and herbs, and ripened for a month to a year; their distinct taste and texture is idiomatic to Moroccan cooking.

lingonberry   A small red tart berry of the cranberry family, made into game and meat sauces, also jellies, preserves, and desserts. The lingonberry is beloved in Scandinavia, also eaten in Russia, Germany, and Canada. Other names are red whortleberry, cowberry, and mountain cranberry.

lingua di bue [LEEN-gwah dee BOO-ay]   Italian for ox tongue.

lingue di passero [LEEN-gway dee pahs-SAY-rō]   Very thin, flat, eggless pasta; in Italian, literally "sparrows' tongues."

linguiça [leen-GWEE-sah]   Portugese pork sausage flavored with garlic; similar to *chouriço* (see under CHORIZO).

linguine [leen-GWEE-nay]   Long, thin, flat eggless pasta in Italian literally "little tongues."

Linse [LIN-seh]   German for lentil; *Linsensuppe* is lentil soup with sausage.

Linzertorte [LIN-tser-tor-teh]   An Austrian tart of ground hazelnut pastry filled with raspberry jam and covered with a latticework crust, named after the city of Linz.

lion's head   See SHĪ ZĬ TÓU.

Liptauer [LIP-tow-er]   A ewes' milk cheese, originally German, now made in Hungary; soft, dense, rindless, and strong, it is made in small blocks.

litchi   See LYCHEE.

littleneck   See QUAHOG.

Livarot [lee-va-rō]   A French cows' milk (lightly skimmed, part whole) cheese from the town of the same name in Normandy, made in discs about 1 pound in size. The cheese is soft, even-textured, and tangy in flavor, with a hard, shiny washed-rind surface; colored rosy reddish gold, each is usually laid on five strips of sedge, "insignia," to give it the nickname "Colonel." Livarot, a fall or winter cheese, one of the oldest and greatest in Normandy, is traditionally accompanied there by Calvados or fine cider.

lobster   The large saltwater crustacean of the North Atlantic, the American lobster (*Homarus americanus*) and its close relative the European lobster (*H. gammarus*), slightly smaller. Its delicate, lean, flavorful meat, concentrated in the large tail and sometimes the claws, tomalley (liver, green when cooked), and roe (orange, turning black when fertilized and about to hatch, when it is called *paquette*) are all prized on the table. The hen lobster is discernible by her wider tail and soft, feathery first pair of swimmerets; on the cock lobster, these are hard and grooved. Hard-shell lobster, though more expensive, is a better buy at market: the meat is firmer than on a recently molted lobster, and it has fully grown into its new shell.

lobster Cantonese   See CHAO LONG XIA.

loc lac [lōk lahk]   Cubed beef in a spicy marinade of garlic, pepper, and soy sauce; a Cambodian dish.

locro [LŌ-crō]   A South American vegetable stew that uses different ingredients in different countries, but is always served hot with rice.

locust bean   See CAROB.

loganberry   A hybrid cultivar of the blackberry, developed by Judge James Logan in California; the fruit is darker, larger, and more prolific than the raspberry and milder in flavor; excellent for cooking.

loin   A cut of beef from the hindquarter, between the rib and round; the full loin contains the tenderest cuts within the sirloin and short loin.

Loire [lwaahr]   The longest river in France, flowing northwest from near Lyons to the Atlantic at Nantes; there are many diverse vineyards in its valley, mostly white and some quite fine, including Pouilly-Fumé, Sancerre, Vouvray, Saumur, and Muscadet.

lok   See LŬ.

lokma [LŌK-mah]   Turkish round fritters in syrup.

lolla rossa   A variety of salad green with frilly edges and splashed pink, with a bitter edge to its flavor; excellent as a garnish and in salad.

lombo, lombata [LOHM-bō, lohm-BAH-tah]   Italian for loin; the Spanish word is *lomo*.

London broil   A cut of beef from the flank—one thin, flat muscle that is usually either braised or broiled and sliced on an angle; other cuts from different sections of beef are sometimes loosely called London broil; unheard of in London, an American term only.

longanzia [lohn-GAHN-thyah]   A large Spanish pork sausage flavored with garlic, marjoram, and pimento.

longe de veau [lonhjh deu vō]   French for loin of veal.

lonza [LOHN-zah]   Italian for loin; the word often means cured loin of pork.

lop cheung   See LÀ CHĂNG.

loquat [LŌ-kwat]   A plum-shaped golden fruit from a small Asian tree, sometimes called the Chinese or Japanese medlar; because it ripens in March, the first fruit to ripen in spring, it was very popular in Europe before air travel; now that fresh fruit is flown from the other side of the globe, the bland but juicy loquat is used mostly in jams and jellies.

lor horn zai   See LUÓ HÀN ZHĀI.

Lorraine [lohr-ren]   A region in northeastern France (a former duchy) bordering on Germany, Luxembourg, and Belgium; its excellent cuisine and wines, like Lorraine's political history, show the influence of Germany, with many distinguished dishes using pork, veal, geese, crayfish, apples, eggs and cream, and pastries.

lorraine, à la [ah lah lohr-ren]   Garnished with braised red cabbage balls and olive-shaped potatoes sautéed in butter, in classic French cuisine.

lotte [loht]   French for MONKFISH.

lotus root   The root of a plant in the water lily family that in cross section has a beautiful starlike pattern; thin slices of the peeled root, crisp but juicy, go well in Asian stir-fries and salads.

loup de mer [loo]   French for sea bass, "wolf of the sea."

lovage [LUV-aj]   An herb once popular but little used today, whose unusual and strong celery flavor seasons meat stews and stocks; its leaves, hollow stems, roots, and seeds can all be used; it is indigenous to the Mediterranean and resembles overgrown celery in appearance; also called love parsley.

lox   Salmon, usually from the Pacific Ocean, cured (but not smoked, as it used to be) with salt, then soaked in water to remove some of the salt; often eaten with cream cheese on bagels; see also NOVA.

lŭ [loo]   Simmering, in Chinese cooking; the Cantonese is *lok* [lahk].

lubina [loo-BEE-nah]   Spanish for sea bass.

luganeaga [loo-gah-nay-AH-gah]   An Italian mild, fresh pork sausage flavored with Parmesan cheese, made in long tubes without links.

lumaca [loo-MAH-kah]   Italian for snail; the plural is *lumache*.

lumpia [lum-PEE-ah]   In Philippine and Southeast Asian cooking, a thin pastry wrapper enclosing a savory filling, either fresh and wrapped in a lettuce leaf or deep-fried like a spring roll.

luó hàn zhāi   "Buddha's delight," in Chinese cooking, a classic mixed vegetable stir-fry; the ingredients vary from one region to another but the dish is very popular throughout China; served at the Lunar New Year and other special occasions; *lor horn zai* [lō hahn tzī] in Cantonese.

lutefisk [LOO-teh-fisk]   In Scandinavian cooking, unsalted dried cod soaked for days in water, then in a lye bath of potash, and soaked in water again, then briefly simmered and served with cream sauce or pork drippings, accompanied by boiled potatoes. This dish is a Christmas tradition and an acquired taste.

lychee [LEE-chee]   The fruit of a small tree, also called the Chinese plum, often used in Asian cuisine. The exterior of the nutlike fruit is a thin red scaly shell; the soft, white, fleshy interior surrounds a stone. The fruit is eaten fresh, dried, canned, or preserved in syrup both as a fruit dessert and as an accompaniment to savory foods; spelled variously.

Lyonerwurst [LEE-ō-ner-voorst]   German ham sausage flavored with garlic.

lyonnaise, à la [ah lah lee-onh-nez]   With onions; *sauce lyonnaise* in classic French cuisine means chopped onions sautéed in butter, reduced with white wine and vinegar, demi-glace added, and strained. The city of Lyons, located near Beaujolais, where the Rhône and Saône Rivers flow together, has a renowned gastronomic tradition. The French spelling is Lyon (no s).

M U S H R O O M

M

maafe [MAH-fee] A West African chicken and peanut stew with chilies, tomatoes, and spices.

ma'amoul [mah-MOOL] Middle Eastern small stuffed pastries, traditional for Easter, with many different fillings.

ma'amrra [MAHM-rah] Moroccan for stuffed.

maasa [MAH-sah] A fritter of MILLET and rice, raised with yeast and lightly sweetened; served as a snack, light meal, or for breakfast with porridge; from Mali.

maatjes herring See MATJES HERRING.

macadamia nut A nut from the tree native to Australia but now cultivated mostly in Hawaii; usually shelled and roasted before purchase, the round nut is white, sweet, and high in fat, making it prized as a dessert nut.

macaroni See MACCHERONI.

macaroon A small, light, round cookie made of almond paste, sugar, and egg whites; in Italy, where they probably originated, these pastries are called *amaretti*.

maccarèllo [mak-kah-REL-lō] Italian for mackerel.

maccheroni   Italian for macaroni, tube-shaped pasta; except in Naples (where it is spelled *macaroni*), Italians spell this type of pasta thus. In eighteenth-century England, young dandies who on their return from Italy affected Continental dress and style were called macaronis; hence the famous line "stuck a feather in his hat and called it macaroni."

mace   The lacy aril covering of the black NUTMEG shell, enclosing the nutmeg kernel; mace dries from bright red to orange brown and is sold in "blade"strips or powdered form. The spice tastes like nutmeg with a hint of cinnamon, at once warmer yet subtler, and is used more widely in savory dishes than is nutmeg.

macédoine [ma-say-dwahn]   French for a mixture of fruits or vegetables served hot or cold; its name refers to the racial diversity of Macedonia.

macerate   To steep food in liquid; usually refers to fresh fruit steeped in liqueur.

mâche [mash]   French for LAMB'S LETTUCE.

machi [mah-CHEE]   Fish or seafood in Indian cuisine.

Mâcon [ma-konh]   A town in southern Burgundy on the Saône River and the center of its wine trade; Mâcon wines are red, white, and rosé, strictly limited according to grape variety; Mâconnais, just north of Beaujolais, is the large wine-producing region encompassing Mâcon.

mad cow disease   See BOVINE SPONGIFORM ENCEPHALOPATHY.

Madeira   A Portuguese island in the Atlantic famous for its fortified wines, which are 18–20 percent alcohol; aged and blended by the SOLERA method like SHERRY, the special character and longevity of Madeira comes from the long and gradual heating process called *estufa*; Madeira wines range from very dry to very sweet, so they are suitable for APÉRITIF and dessert wines as well as for cooking; specific types of Madeira have separate entries.

madeleine [mad-len]   A small French cake made of flour, sugar, butter, and eggs baked in a special shell mold; its origin is uncertain, but the town of Commercy is famous for *madeleines*, Louis XV favored them, and Proust gave them immortality at the beginning of his novel *Remembrance of Things Past*.

madère [ma-dayr]   A classic French sauce of DEMI-GLACE flavored with Madeira.

maderisé [ma-dayr-ee-zay]   French for wine that is partially spoiled by oxidation; an unintentionally maderized wine has acquired a brownish color and the "cooked" aroma of Madeira due to the effects of excessive heat.

madrilène, à la [ah lah ma-dree-len]   "In the style of Madrid"; in French cuisine, flavored with tomato.

mafalde, mafaldine [mah-FAL-day]   Long Italian pasta strips with fluted edges, in medium and narrow widths.

maggiorana [mah-jor-AH-nah]   Italian for MARJORAM.

magnum   A double-sized wine bottle whose volume helps exceptional Bordeaux or Burgundies mature to their fullest, but not advantageous to the development of other wines.

magret, maigret [ma-gray, may-gray]   French for breast of duck, usually cooked rare.

maguey [mah-GAY]   A species of several large succulent plants, misleadingly called cacti; in Mexico, used to wrap food in its leaves, to produce tequila and other alcoholic drinks, and to harbor an insect larva considered a delicacy. It is not available in the United States.

mahammer [mah-HAM-er]   Braised and browned in Moroccan cooking.

mahi mahi   Hawaian name for dolphin (no relation to the porpoise mammal "dolphin," causing confusion); its flesh is usually skinned and cut into steaks or fillets that are versatile in cooking: rich, sweet, moist, firm, with a large flake.

mahleb [MAH-leb]   A Middle Eastern spice from the kernel of the black cherry; golden-brown, aromatic, and ground to flavor rolls and sweet breads.

mah paw dau fu   See MÁ PÓ DÒU FÙ.

mahshi [MAH-shee]   Arab for stuffed.

maiale [mī-YAL-ay]   Italian for pork; suckling pig is *maigletto*.

maigre [MAY-gruh]   A French adjective denoting thin, lean, low-fat; food suitable for fast days, as prescribed by the Roman Catholic Church. Historically, at first only vegetable dishes were allowed during Advent, Lent, and days before important feasts; gradually, butter, milk, eggs, and cold-blooded animals, including fish and eventually waterfowl, were allowed, with many dispensations. The Italian word is *magro*.

maionese [mī-yō-NAY-say]   Italian for MAYONNAISE; the Spanish word is *mahonesa*.

maison [may-sonh]   In French, literally "house"; designates a dish made in a restaurant's own style, such as *pâté maison*.

maître d'hôtel [ME-truh D'Ō-TEL]   French for the person in charge of a restaurant dining room, who must command every aspect of service to patrons; originally, in royal or noble households, it was a position of great importance; the informal *maître d'* is often used today. *Maître d'hôtel* butter is seasoned with chopped parsley and lemon juice.

maize   CORN; the French word *maïs* [mah-ees] actually means sweet corn, while the Spanish word *maíz* signifies dried corn.

makeua taet [MAHK-oo-ah tet]   Thai for tomato.

makhan [mah-KOON]   Butter, in Indian cooking.

makholi [mah-GŌ-lee]   Korean for RICE WINE.

maki [mah-kee]   Japanese for rolled; used with another word.

mak kam [mah kam]   Thai for TAMARIND.

mako   See SHARK.

makrut [mak-rood]   Thai for KAFFIR LIME.

Málaga [MAH-lah-gah]   A sweet, heavy, dark SHERRY from the region north of the southern Spanish city of the same name, where it is blended.

malagueta   See MELEGUETA.

malai [mah-lī]   Cream (all kinds), in Indian cooking.

malakor [MAL-ah-kor]   Thai for papaya.

malanga [mah-LAHN-gah]   A root vegetable from tropical America, similar to (and often confused with) TARO; of many varieties, *malanga amarilla* (yellow) and *blanca* (white) are common; in Puerto Rico, it is called *yautia*.

malassada   An Hawaiian deep-fried yeast doughnut, coated in sugar, traditional for Easter; from the Portuguese word *malasado* meaning "unlucky."

Malbec [mal-bek]   A red wine grape variety grown in southwestern France and Bordeaux that is full of tannin, rich in flavor, faster-maturing than CABERNET, and a principal grape in the Cahors blend (where it is called Cot or Auxerrois). Important in Chile and Argentina, where it makes plush and plummy wines; also grown in California and Australia for wines blended in the Bordeaux style.

Malmsey [MAWLM-see]   The English name for MALVASIA.

malossol   See CAVIAR.

malsouka [mahl-SOO-kah]   In Tunisian cooking, thin pastry leaves used for BRIK, much like WARQA. *Tajin malsouka* is a lamb variation of BASTILLA.

malt   Germinated barley used in brewing and distilling; malt extract, highly nourishing, is used to make food for children and invalids. In malted milk, the malt powder is dissolved in milk, and other flavorings, such as chocolate, may be added. Malt vinegar, popular in Britain, is usually colored brown with caramel; it tends to be robust in flavor rather than fine; used for English pickles, chutneys, mint sauce, and fish and chips.

maltagliati [mal-tah-LYAH-tee]   "Badly cut" flat Italian pasta about ½ inch thick and cut on the bias; used mainly for bean soups.

maltaise [mal-tez]   A classic French sauce of HOLLANDAISE flavored with grated orange zest and blood orange juice; the cold *sauce maltaise* is mayonnaise similarly flavored.

Malvasia [mal-VAY-jha]   A white wine grape variety producing very sweet, heavy, golden Madeira that turns amber with age; this wine, originally Greek, is produced elsewhere, but that of Madeira is the most famous; also vinified as a light, charming table wine, and sometimes used for blending.

Malzbier [MALTS-beer]   Dark, sweet, malty German beer, low in alcohol.

mamé [mah-may]   Japanese for bean.

mammee [ma-MAY]   A tall tropical tree that grows in Central and South America; its round fruit, with smooth orange pulp, is eaten fresh and in ice creams; sometimes spelled *mamey*.

mamuang [mah-MOHNG]   Thai for mango.

manao [mah-now]   Thai for lime.

manche [manhsh]   French for the projecting bone on a chop; a *manchette* is a frill used to cover the bone; for *manche à gigot* see GIGOT.

Manchego [mahn-CHAY-gō]   A pale, golden, dense ewes' milk cheese from Spain; the curd is molded, pressed, salted in brine, and cured; the rind has a greenish black mold that is sometimes brushed off and replaced with a thin smearing of olive oil. *Manchego* also means in the style of La Mancha.

mandarin   The citrus tree whose fruit is generally darker, flatter, and smaller than the orange; its distinctive loose skin, fibrous inside, in some varieties slips off easily. Americans call it tangerine, for its route west through Tangiers, but most countries call it mandarin. Crossbreeding has led to much confusion in this family. The clementine and satsuma are types of mandarin. The tangor is a mandarin-orange hybrid; the Temple is one exemplar. The tangelo is a cross between the mandarin and pomelo; the Minneola, deep orange, luscious, with a nipple protruberance, is one popular tangelo; ugli [OO-glee] fruit from Jamaica is another very different-looking tangelo hybrid, with thick, coarse, yellow-green skin and sweet orange flesh. Mandarins are usually eaten fresh since their distinctive aroma is easily lost in cooking.

Mandel [MAHN-del]   German for almond; the Italian word is *mandorla.*

mandoline [manh-dō-leen]   French for a tool, named after the musical instrument, used to cut vegetables evenly and quickly into thick or thin, furrowed or smooth slices.

mange-tout [manhjh-too]   French for a pea or bean, such as the snow pea or sugar snap, whose pod and seeds are literally "eaten whole."

mango   A tropical evergreen tree, probably of Indian origin, whose fully ripened fruit is considered by some the most luscious of all; varying in size, shape, and color, in the United States it is usually a deep green to orange color and pear shaped, with smooth orange flesh; mangoes are eaten fresh or, still green, cooked in preserves and chutneys. Relatively few varieties are available in the United States, mainly the Tommy Atkins, with mediocre flavor.

manicotti [mah-ni-COHT-tee]   Large tubes, "muffs," of Italian pasta stuffed variously and baked in a sauce.

manié   See BEURRE MANIÉ.

manioc [MAN-ee-ahk]   A plant indigenous to Brazil, its name derived from the native Tupi word *manihot,* which gives the entire genus its botanical name. This staple in tropical and subtropical Latin America, the Philippines, and Asia (especially India and Thailand) is valued for its very high starch content, bland sweet flavor that complements many other foods, and easy digestibility. The leaves are eaten locally and the root boiled and fried; it is also processed into flour, meal, flakes, syrup, and alcoholic drinks. Cassava is the name in the Caribbean, where it is often made into bread; tapioca are the "pearls" from its root that thicken pies and puddings; *yuca* is the Spanish word by which it is increasingly known in the United States. There are some toxic varieties, which are not marketed.

manjar [MAHN-har, MAHN-jhar]   BLANCMANGE; a pudding, custard, or creamed dish in Spanish and Portuguese cooking, sometimes accompanying chicken.

Manteca [mahn-TEK-ah]   A spun-curd cows' milk cheese from southern Italy wrapped around a pat of butter. The word *manteca* means fat, lard, or butter in Italian and Spanish; locally this small cheese is also called Burro, Burrino, or Butirro.

mantecado [mahn-te-KAH-dō]   Spanish for rich vanilla ice cream with whipped cream folded in.

mantequilla [mahn-te-KEE-yah]   Spanish for butter.

manti [MAHN-teu]   A Turkish meat-filled ravioli topped with yogurt and sprinkled with dried mint and SUMAC; the northern Afghan dish *mantu* is essentially the same, sauced with yogurt, split yellow peas, and tomatoes.

manzana [mahn-SAH-nah]   Spanish for apple.

Manzanilla [mahn-sah-NEE-yah]   An extremely dry pale Spanish SHERRY with a special, almost bitter, taste; drunk mostly in Spain, especially in Seville; *manzanilla* also means chamomile or camomile tea in Spanish.

manzo [MAHN-zō]   Italian for beef.

maple syrup   Syrup made from the sap of sugar maples and certain other maple trees in northeastern North America. The trees are tapped with a spigot set into the tree trunk. The sap begins to run in late winter in a natural process not entirely understood by scientists, but recognized by the American Indians; the sap is boiled down into syrup and even further into maple sugar.

má pó dòu fù [mah poh dō foo]   A popular Sichuan dish of bean curd in a fiery contrasting chili paste sauce; the name refers to a pock-marked woman who is said to have created the dish; the Cantonese is *mah paw dau fu.*

maprao [mah-prow]   Thai for coconut.

maquereau [mak-ayr-ō]   French for mackerel.

maraschino [mah-rah-SKEE-nō]   A liqueur made from the sour *marasca* cherry and its crushed stones, originally from Yugoslavia and now from Italy as well. American maraschino cherries are cooked in artificially colored syrup and flavored with imitation liqueur—a far cry from the original.

marbled   A term used to describe meat, especially beef, that has small flecks of fat throughout the muscle tissue. Such meat is generally considered high quality for its juiciness and flavor when cooked. Marbled pastry has light and dark dough swirled together so that it resembles marble stone.

marc [maahrk]   French for pomace: usually grape or sometimes apple skins and seeds remaining after the juice has been pressed; *eau de vie de marc* (often shortened to *marc*) is the strong brandy distilled from these residual grape solids; known in Italy as *grappa.*

marcassin [maahr-kas-sinh]   French for young wild boar.

marchand de vin [maahr-shanh deu vinh]   "In the style of the wine merchant," a classic French sauce for grilled meats, similar to BERCY or BORDELAISE: red wine is flavored with chopped shallots and parsley and greatly reduced; butter is then beaten in.

marcona   A type of almond that is flatter and more oval than pointed, with a distinctive earthy, bittersweet flavor.

maréchale, à la [ah lah maahr-ay-shal]   In French cuisine, "marshal's style": small cuts of meat or poultry, dredged in egg and bread crumbs, fried in butter, and garnished with sliced truffles, asparagus tips, or green peas.

marée [maahr-ay]   French for all saltwater fish and shellfish.

Marengo, à la [ah lah ma-RENG-ō]   Chicken pieces browned in olive oil, braised with tomatoes, garlic, and brandy, and garnished with fried eggs, crayfish, and sometimes croûtons. This famous French dish was devised by Napoléon's chef Dunand after the defeat of the Austrians at Marengo in 1800, when no other food could be found, and was commemorated by Napoléon.

margarine   A butter substitute, originally made from animal fats and now from vegetable fats, developed in 1869 by a French chemist. Similar in cost and calories to butter, but with no cholesterol and less saturated fat, margarine is now questioned by health food purists for its preservatives and hydrogenated oils.

Margaux [maahr-gō]   A wine-producing COMMUNE in the French Haut-Médoc producing some of Bordeaux's very finest red wines.

Marguéry [maahr-gayr-ee]   A classic French sauce of HOLLANDAISE flavored with oyster liquor and garnished with poached oysters.

Maribo [MAR-ee-bō]   A semihard pasteurized cows' milk cheese from the Danish island of Lolland; the large oblong cheese has a yellow wax coating, a white paste with small holes, and a flavor that grows quite strong with age.

Marie Louise [maahr-ee loo-weez]   A classic French garnish of artichoke hearts filled with mushroom purée and SOUBISE; named for Napoléon's second wife.

marignan [maahr-ee-nyanh]   A boat-shaped French pastry made of rich yeast dough soaked in rum-flavored syrup, brushed with apricot jam, and filled with crème CHANTILLY.

marigold   A plant with bright golden flowers used fresh or dried as an herb or a dye.

Marille [mah-RIL-leh]   German for apricot.

marinade A liquid, including seasonings and acid (usually vinegar, wine, or citrus juice), in which food is steeped before cooking in order to flavor, moisten, and soften it.

marinara, alla [ah-lah mar-ee-NAR-ah] Literally "sailor style" in Italian; a loose term often meaning a simple tomato sauce flavored with garlic and herbs, usually served with fettucine or other pasta.

marinière, à la [ah lah maahr-ee-nyayr] Literally "sailor style" in French; seafood cooked in white wine with chopped shallots, parsley, and butter and garnished with mussels; *moules marinière* is the classic example.

marinierter Hering [mar-i-NEER-ter HAYR-ing] German for pickled herring.

mariquita [mar-ee-KEE-tah] Spanish for chip, as in plantain or potato chip.

mariscos [mah-REES-kōs] Spanish for shrimp or scallops; shellfish; seafood; *mariscada* is a shellfish soup.

marjolaine [maahr-jhō-len] A famous French pastry created by Fernand Point of almond and hazelnut DACQUOISE layered with chocolate, praline, and buttercream. *Marjolaine* also means sweet marjoram.

marjoram, sweet marjoram An herb in many varieties, originally Mediterranean, from the mint family; it is used in diverse savory dishes.

marmalade A citrus fruit jam, usually from bitter SEVILLE ORANGES with the rind included, stewed for a long time and reduced to a thick preserve. Marmalade is indispensable to a proper British breakfast. The word derives from the Roman quince and honey preserve, *melimelum* ("honey apple").

marmelade [maahr-muh-lad] French for a thick sweetened purée of fruit (or today, occasionally onion), reduced to a jamlike consistency; not to be confused with MARMALADE.

marmite [maahr-meet] French for a large covered pot, usually earthenware but sometimes metal, for cooking large quantities of food. Marmite is a brand name for a type of yeast extract, very popular in Australia. See also PETITE MARMITE.

Maroilles [maahr-wahl] A soft, uncooked cows' milk cheese, invented a thousand years ago by the monks at the Abbey of Maroilles in Flanders. Square with a reddish rind and pale yellow interior, it is ripened up to six months with regular washings of the rind in brine. The flavor is creamy, rich, and tangy, the aroma attractively strong; also called Marolles.

marqa [MAHR-kah] In Tunisian cooking, with RAGOÛT or sauce.

marquise [maahr-keez]   French for a fruit ice with whipped cream folded in.

marron [maahr-onh]   French for a cultivated chestnut used as a vegetable, for stuffings, and for pastry; *marrons glacés*—whole peeled chestnuts poached for a long time and glazed in a thick syrup—are a choice delicacy. *Châtaigne* is the general French word for chestnut; *marron* is the cultivated species, which contains only a single large nut in a burr.

marrow   A large summer squash similar to zucchini, grown in Britain. See also MULUKHIYA.

marrow bone   A large beef or veal bone cut into short segments and poached or braised to solidify the rich and nutritious interior marrow, which is then scooped out and spread or diced. Marrow is prized in such recipes as OSSO BUCCO and sauce BORDELAISE.

Marsala [mar-SAH-lah]   An Italian FORTIFIED dessert wine, 17 to 19 percent alcohol, from the Sicilian city of the same name. The wine is a deep amber color, usually dry but sometimes sweet, roughly comparable to SHERRY; it is an important ingredient in ZABAGLIONE.

Marsanne [maahr-zan]   A white wine grape variety of the northern Rhone used in Hermitage and other wines, often blended with Roussanne, yielding a full wine that ages well; also planted in Switzerland, California, and Australia.

marshmallow   A confection made from egg whites, sugar, and gelatin, originally flavored with the root of the marshmallow plant.

Marzenbier [MARTS-en-beer]   A strong, medium-colored German beer traditionally brewed in March (hence its name) and drunk in spring and summer; any remaining beer is consumed at festivals such as Oktoberfest.

marzipan   A paste of ground almonds, sugar, and egg white shaped and often colored to resemble fruits, vegetables, animals, and the like; the tradition of these decorative confections is very old, dating at least to the Middle Ages.

masa [MAH-sah]   In Mexican cooking, a dough of dried cornmeal and water, used in making tortillas and other preparations; *masa harina* is cornmeal.

masala [mah-SAH-lah]   Spice or a blend of spices, in Indian cooking, infinitely variable; see also GARAM.

mascarpone [mahs-kar-PŌ-nay]   A soft cows' milk cheese made near Milan; the curd made from the cream is beaten or whipped into a thick, velvety cheese with rich sweet flavor. It is served with fruit and pastries like cream, layered with Gorgonzola to make *torta Gaudenzio*, and used in various other ways, occasionally savory but mostly sweet.

masfouf [mahs-FOOF]   In Tunisia and Algeria, a sweet couscous with raisins, nuts, and butter eaten as a snack; there are also savory *masfouf couscous* dishes of vegetables and perhaps meat, eaten as a meal. Also spelled *mesfouf.*

masitas de puerco fritas [mah-SEE-tas day PWAYR-kō FREE-tas]   Fried pork chunks, a traditional Cuban dish.

mask   To cover food with sauce before serving.

masoor [mah-SOOR]   Red lentils in Indian cooking; also spelled *masur.*

masquer [mas-kay]   In French, to mask.

massa [MAH-sah]   Portuguese for pastry or paste; *massa de pimentao*, a red pepper paste used as a marinade for meat.

massepain [mas-pinh]   French for MARZIPAN.

Mastgeflügel [MAHST-geh-flü-gel]   Specially raised grain-fed poultry from the Vierlande region southeast of Hamburg, Germany, of fine quality.

mastic   A tree in the pistachio family grown on the Greek island of Chios cultivated for its resin, a natural chewing gum; this resin, sweet, aromatic, and licorice-flavored, is also used to flavor bread, confections, puddings, savory dishes, and ice cream called *kaimaki* that is common throughout the Middle East; it also lends it name to the Greek liqueur *masticha* or *mastikha*, similar to OUZO; the Arab word is *mistki.*

matan [MAH-tan]   Goat, in Indian cooking; in the West, lamb is usually substituted.

matelote [mat-lōt]   A French fish stew (usually of freshwater fish) made with red or white wine.

matignon [ma-tee-nyonh]   MIREPOIX cooked in butter, for stuffing or garnish.

Matjes herring [MAHT-yes]   High-quality, lightly salted young "virgin" herring that have not yet spawned; very popular in Germany, the Netherlands, and Scandinavia.

matoutou [mah-too-TOO]   A spicy crab dish from the Caribbean, traditional for Easter.

matsutake [mat-soo-tah-kay]   Japanese "pine" mushrooms.

mattar [mah-TAHR]   Peas, in Indian cooking; *mattar pilau* is a spicy dish of fresh peas and rice.

matzo, matzoh [MAHT-soh]   Flat unleavened bread eaten during Passover to symbolize the Jews' hurried flight from Egypt, when there was no time for the bread to rise; matzo meal is used in other dishes such as KNÄDLACH and GEFILTE FISH.

Maultaschen [MOWL-tahsh-en]   Ground veal, pork, and spinach wrapped in noodle dough and served in gravy or broth for Maunday Thursday; from Swabia, in Germany.

ma uon [mah oowan]   "Fat horses," a Thai snack of chopped pork, chicken, and crab steamed in banana leaf cups; *ma ho*, "galloping horses," is a snack of orange or other fruit topped with a contrasting spicy pork and peanut mixture.

mǎ yǐ shàng shù [mah ee shahng shoo]   In Chinese cooking, "ants climbing a tree," a Sichuan dish of cellophane or other noodles with ground pork in a rich savory sauce; the names comes from the supposed appearance of the bits of pork entwined in the strands; the Cantonese is *mah ngai par seuh*.

mayonnaise [mī-yohn-nez]   The classic French EMULSION of egg yolks seasoned with vinegar and mustard, with oil added very gradually to form a thick sauce. There are many variations of this basic cold sauce and many explanations, none certain, as to the name's derivation. *Mayonnaise verte* is flavored and colored green with finely minced herbs such as spinach, sorrel, watercress, parsley, chervil, and tarragon; the herbs may be blanched first.

May wine   A white-wine spring punch, lightly sweetened and flavored with the herb WOODRUFF and served chilled in a bowl with strawberries; originally German.

mazamorra morada [mah-sah-MOR-rah mor-AH-dah]   "Purple pudding," from Peru and Ecuador, made with purple corn, various fresh and dried fruits, and cornstarch.

mchicha [m'SHEE-kah]   A leafy green vegetable, like spinach, much used in Tanzanian cooking in soups, salads, and stews; *machicha na nazi*, with coconut.

mead   The ancient sweet alcoholic drink of fermented honey, often flavored with herbs.

meat birds   Scallops or slices of meat filled with a savory stuffing, rolled up and secured (usually with string), browned in fat, and braised; also called olives. The French term is *oiseaux sans têtes*, the Italian *olivetti*.

meat loaf   A homey dish of ground mean or poultry, often a mixture such as beef and pork, seasoned, perhaps bound with bread crumbs or egg, and baked; served sliced, often with a sauce. See also PÂTÉ.

mechoui   See MISHWI.

médaillon [may-dī-yonh]   French for a small round "medallion" or scallop of meat, such as beef, lamb, veal, or even a slice of foie gras.

medlar   See LOQUAT.

Médoc [may-dohk]   The French wine-producing region north of Bordeaux bounded on the east by the Gironde River and on the west by the Atlantic Ocean; red wines so labeled come from the northern part, the Bas-Médoc, and are good though generally not as fine as those from the Haut-Médoc in the southern part of the region.

mee   Indonesian for noodles; *mee goreng* means fried noodles; *mah mee*, noodle soup with shrimp, pork, vegetables, and spices; *mee siem*, sautéed rice noodles with spicy minced pork, onions, and bean sprouts, garnished with shredded omelet; also spelled *mie*.

Meerrettich [MAYR-ret-tish]   German for horseradish.

meetha   See MITHAI.

megadarra   Arab lentils and rice with onions, served hot or cold with yogurt; a very old and favorite dish.

Mehlspeise [MAYL-shpī-zeh]   A flour-based German dish, especially popular in Bavaria—DUMPLINGS, pancakes, and STRUDEL are examples; in Austrian dialect this word means pudding.

mejillone [may-hee-YŌ-nay]   Spanish for mussel.

mejorana [may-hor-AH-nah]   Spanish for marjoram.

mela [MEL-ah]   Italian for apple.

melagrana [mel-ah-GRAH-nah]   Italian for pomegranate.

mélanger [may-lanh-jhay]   To mix, in French; the word *mélange* means a mixture or blend.

melanzana [mel-ahn-ZAH-nah]   Italian for eggplant; the Greek word is *melidzanes*.

Melba, pêche   A classic dessert of skinned peaches poached in vanilla-flavored syrup, served on vanilla ice cream with raspberry purée. Auguste Escoffier created this dish for Dame Nellie Melba, the Australian coloratura soprano, also Melba toast, very thin slices of toast.

melegueta [meh-leh-GWAY-tah]   The brown seed of a plant related to CARDAMOM that grows in Guinea and West Africa, where the pulp around the seed is also eaten; the hot, peppery grains are often confused with pepper, but have the aroma of cardamom. Popular in the medieval spice trade, *melegueta* today is part of the Moroccan mix RAS EL HANOUT; also called grains of paradise, Guinea pepper, and malagueta.

melocotón [meh-lō-kō-TŌN]   Spanish for peach.

melokhia   See MULUKHIYA.

melon   This large family of sweet squash or gourds, *Cucumis melo*, crossbreeds so easily that farmers know to plant strains well separated; they divide into three basic categories. The muskmelon, sometimes called netted or nutmeg melon, includes the Persian melon and what Americans know as cantaloupe; muskmelons have orange or occasionally green flesh; the skin may be ridged in segments but always has the raised netted pattern, whether golden beige or green. The true Cantaloupe (*not* the melon that Americans call cantaloupe), named for the town Cantalupo near Tivoli outside Rome, is widely grown in Europe; it is small, round, and very aromatic; the skin is hard, sometimes rough or segmented, but never netted; the French Charentais and Israeli Ogen are true Cantaloupes. All muskmelons and Cantaloupes need to ripen fully on the vine, when a separation layer in the stem pulls away, allowing the fruit to be picked easily and leaving a scar; a cut stem shows that a melon has been picked prematurely. Winter melons, with thicker skins and no separation layer in the stem, ripen slowly for later harvest, even after frost; they never have aroma; Honeydew, Crenshaw, Casaba, and Santa Claus are all winter melons. See also WATERMELON, which is botanically unrelated. Some of these varieties are commonly spelled with lowercase, and muskmelon may be two words.

Melton Mowbray pie   An English pork pie encased in a pastry "coffin" or crust, served cold; an old and traditional convenience food that is easily transportable; named after the Leicestershire town.

membrillo [mem-BREE-yō]   Spanish for quince.

Mendocino [men-dō-CHEE-nō]   A wine-producing county in northern California, near Ukiah, with especially good ZINFANDELS.

Mendoza   An important wine region in Argentina, in the eastern foothills of the Andes, producing many of the country's best wines.

menestra [meh-NETH-trah, meh-NES-trah]   Spanish for stew.

menthe [menht]   French for mint; *crème de menthe*, a mint-flavored liqueur, either green or colorless.

menudo [meh-NOO-dō]   Spanish for TRIPE stew.

mercimek çorbası [mayr-jee-mek CHOR-bah—seu]   Turkish lentil soup, usually red lentils (*suzme*).

merguez   See MIRQAZ.

merienda [mayr-YEN-dah]   Spanish for afternoon tea or snack, to tide the appetite over to late dinner.

meringue   Pastry made of stiffly beaten egg whites with sugar, shaped variously, and baked in a slow oven or poached. In an ITALIAN MERINGUE, hot sugar syrup is beaten into stiffly whipped egg whites, for lightening pastries and buttercreams, soufflés, and sorbets.

Meritage [MAYR-i-tej]   A California wine industry term, coined in the 1980s and trademarked, meaning red or white wine blends of Bordeaux varieties; the reds and Cabernets in particular have caught on.

merlan [mayr-lanh]   French for whiting; the Italian word is *merlango*.

Merlot [mayr-lō]   A red-wine grape variety, productive and early ripening, that yields soft, fruity, and graceful wines; Merlot combines well with the more astringent, later-maturing, and longer-lived CABERNET; widely planted in Bordeaux's Pomerol, St. Emilion, and Médoc, also in California, Switzerland, and northern Italy.

merluza [mayr-LOO-thah]   Spanish for hake; the Italian word *merluzzo* means cod.

mero [MAYR-ō]   Spanish for rock bass.

mesclun [mes-klunh]   A Provençal mixture of young salad greens whose seeds are sown together, traditionally including wild CHICORY, MÂCHE, curly ESCAROLE, DANDELION, rocket, and other tender lettuces; the word *mesclun* comes from the Niçoise dialect word for mixture.

mesquite [mes-KEET]   A scrub tree that grows wild in the southwestern United States and Mexico, whose wood is used for grilling food.

metate [may-TAH-tay]   A sloping slab of porous volcanic rock standing on three legs and used to grind corn and spices in Mexican cooking; similar to a MOLCAJETE. The stone that is rolled over the surface for grinding is called a *mano*.

methi [MAY-thee]   FENUGREEK in Indian cooking.

Methuselah   An oversized bottle of Champagne, holding up to eight regular bottles, named after the biblical patriarch said to have lived 969 years; spelled variously.

Mettwurst [MET-voorst]   German smoked pork sausage with red skin and a coarse texture.

Meunier [meu-nyay]   A fine grape variety, a subvariety of the PINOT Noir; planted extensively in Champagne, Alsace, and California.

meunière, à la [ah lah meu-nyayr]   Lightly dredged with flour, sautéed in butter, and served with melted butter and sliced lemon; in French *meunière* literally means "in the style of the miller's wife."

Meursault [meur-sō]   A village in the French CÔTE D'OR of Burgundy, which produces a large quantity of distinguished white wine.

Mexican saffron   See SAFFLOWER.

Meyer lemon   See LEMON.

mezzani [met-TSAH-nee]   Italian pasta shaped in long narrow tubes.

mezze [MEH-zeh]   Middle Eastern HORS D'OEUVRE, that is, food eaten before or outside the regular meal, such as nuts, cheese, pickled vegetables, smoked meats, and salads; the Turkish word is *meze*, the Greek *mezedes*.

m'hanncha [m'HAHN-shah]   "The snake," a coiled cake of layered WARQA filled with almond paste and aromatic with cinnamon, from Morocco.

miàn [mee-en]   Chinese for wheat noodle; the Cantonese is *mien*. *Miàn jīn* is wheat gluten, spongy-textured and mild-flavored, a versatile and important ingredient in Chinese vegetarian cooking; available canned, dried, or frozen, or made from a dough of wheat flour and yeast, from which the starch is rinsed out.

mi-chèvre [MEE SHEV-ruh]   Half goats' cheese, that is, from mixed goats' and other (usually cows') milk; such cheeses should be at least ¼ goats' milk.

microwave oven   An oven that works on the principle of electromagnetic radiation; these high-frequency waves penetrate the food being cooked to a depth of two inches and heat the water inside very quickly and efficiently but without browning the outside; for this reason some microwave ovens include browning elements.

midollo [mee-DOHL-lō]   Italian for marrow.

midye [MEE-dyay]   Turkish for mussels.

mie [mee]   The crumb or soft interior part of a loaf of bread; *pain de mie* is sandwich bread.

miel [myel]   French for honey; in Italian the word is *miele*.

mien [meen]   Vietnamese for mung bean noodles, cellophane noodles. Also, the Cantonese for MIÀN.

migas [MEE-gahth, MEE-gahs]   Spanish for bread crumbs.

mignonette [mee-nyoh-net]   In French cuisine, coarsely ground white pepper; originally this included various other spices, such as allspice, nutmeg, coriander, cinnamon, ginger, clove, and red pepper. Sometimes *mignonette* means white and black pepper coarsely ground together; finely ground is *poivre gris*. A *mignonette* can also mean a MÉDAILLON of lamb.

mí jiŭ [mee jō]   Chinese RICE WINE, yellow in color.

mijoter [mee-jhō-tay]   To simmer, in French.

Mikado   French for Japanese style.

mikan [mee kahn]   Japanese for tangerine.

milanaise, à la [ah lah mee-lah-nez]   A classic French garnish of julienne of tongue, ham, mushrooms, and truffles with spaghetti, tomato sauce, and Parmesan cheese.

milk   The liquid food mammals provide to their newborns and thus highly nutritious. Cows' milk is the most common type in the kitchen, but milk of goats, sheep, water buffalo, horses, llamas, camels, and reindeer is consumed around the world. In the United States today, raw milk is routinely pasteurized to kill disease-causing organisms and lengthen shelf life; most milk is also homogenized, breaking down and distributing fat molecules throughout, then fortified to replace vitamins A and D. Whole milk contains about 3½ percent milk fat; low-fat 2 percent or 1 percent; nonfat or skim contains less than ½ percent. Because some people, especially those of African or Asian descent, are lactose intolerant, acidolphilus and lactose-reduced milk are easier to digest. Other forms with long shelf life (and altered flavor) are ultra-pasteurized, CONDENSED, EVAPORATED, canned, and powdered skim milk. See also BUTTERMILK, CHEESE, SOUR CREAM, and YOGURT.

mille-feuille [meel foy]   See PÂTE FEUILLETÉE; the Italian term is *mille foglie* or *pasta sfoglia*.

millet   A grain native to Africa and Asia that has been grown in dry, poor soil in hot climates for millennia as an important high-protein staple. Vegetarians value its delicate taste that grows richer when toasted, its fluffy texture, its ability to cook quickly, and its versatility in pilafs, puddings, and other dishes either bland or robust, savory or sweet. Containing no GLUTEN, it is often mixed with other grains and flours.

miloukia See MULUKHIYA.

milt Fish sperm, prepared like roe, and sometimes euphemistically called roe or spleen.

Milzwurst [MILTS-voorst] Veal sausage from Bavaria.

mimosa A garnish of finely chopped hard-boiled egg yolk, sometimes including the white as well, that resembles the mimosa flower; also a drink of Champagne and orange juice, usually served with brunch.

mince British for anything chopped, especially chopped meat.

mincemeat A preserve of chopped mixed foodstuffs much changed over the centuries. In fifteenth-century England it included the meat of small furred and feathered game, spices, and gradually more fruit; in present-day England it consists mainly of fresh and dried fruits, nuts, spices, and rum or brandy, with suet being the only vestige of meat. Mincemeat is cured and baked in a piecrust for a traditional Christmas dessert.

minestra [mee-NES-trah] Italian for soup or sometimes pasta served as the first course; *minestrina* means a thinner soup, while *minestrone* (literally, a "big soup," or meal in itself) means a thick vegetable soup in a meat broth with pasta, Parmesan, and various vegetables, depending on the region and season.

Minneola See MANDARIN.

mint A large family of aromatic herbs that interbreed easily even as they spread in the garden bed. Common garden mint is spearmint, used for sweet and savory dishes, such as roast lamb, mint jelly and mint sauce, mint julep, vegetables, lemon drinks, fruit compotes, and chocolate confections; curiously, the French do not favor mint, except with peas. Peppermint is used to flavor sweet dishes, in particular candies, desserts, and liqueurs. Lemon mint is too strong except in drinks. Pennyroyal is toxic except in small doses, but in the garden keeps away ants. Other kin are apple mint, water mint, and *raripila*. In southern Southeast Asia's hot climate, mint is used extensively. In India, it appears in chutneys and other hot, spicy mixtures, often with coriander, parsley, chives, and chilies, or in a cooling yogurt RAITA. Across the Arab world, mint is used with the same flavor combinations, in TABBOULEH or a simple herb salad, as well as in sweetened tea; in the Middle East dried mint is an important component of many dishes, sometimes along with fresh mint. Mint leaves can be candied to use as dessert garnishes.

mint julep BOURBON and fresh mint cocktail, traditionally served in a silver julep cup; associated with Kentucky.

mint sauce   A British sauce of chopped and lightly sugared fresh mint in vinegar, served with roast lamb; not to be confused with American commercial mint jelly, which is apple jelly flavored with mint and now usually dyed bright green.

Mirabeau [meer-a-bō]   A French garnish of anchovy fillets laid in a crisscross pattern, pitted olives, tarragon, and anchovy butter; for grilled meat. Mirabeau is also a steak garnish of anchovies, tarragon, olives, sometimes watercress and straw potatoes, named after a French politician.

mirabelle [meer-a-bel]   A small golden plum with a highly aromatic perfume, grown almost exclusively in Europe; used in stews, preserves, tarts, and a colorless EAU DE VIE from Alsace.

mirasol   A mild chili pepper from Peru.

mirchi [MEER-shee]   Chili peppers, in Indian cooking; *lal mirchi* means red peppers.

mirepoix [meer-pwah]   In French cooking, a mixture of diced vegetables—usually carrot, onion, celery, and sometimes ham or pork belly—used to flavor sauces and other preparations; see also BRUNOISE.

mirin [meer-in]   Japanese rice wine, syrupy and sweet, used for cooking.

mirliton   See CHAYOTE.

miroton [meer-ō-tonh]   A French stew of meat with onions in brown sauce; the classic sauce *miroton*, a DEMI-GLACE with sautéed onion rings, sometimes flavored with tomato purée and mustard.

mirqaz [mayr-GEZ]   North African sausage; in Algeria a spicy lamb mixture, in Tunisia more often beef; also spelled *merguez*.

mise en place [meez enh plas]   A French term, literally "put in place," meaning that the preparation is ready up to the point of cooking.

mishmishiya [mish-mish-EE-yah]   An Arab stew of lamb and apricots, with almonds, spices, and herbs.

mishwi [MISH-wee]   Arabic for grill and, by extension, food that is grilled or spit-roasted. It often refers to whole lamb spit-roasted over embers and basted with herbed garlic butter, so that the outside is crisp and the inside tender and juicy, traditionally eaten with the fingers. The term can refer to other grilled meats, poultry, or vegetables. Also spelled *mechoui*.

miso [mee-sō]   Japanese fermented bean paste made from soybeans and grain (barley, rice, or soybeans)—a nutritious high-protein staple used extensively as a flavoring and condiment, with regional preferences; *shinshu* is yellow, mellow, thin, salty, and all-purpose; *shiro* is pale, sweetish, used in salad dressings; *sendai* or *inaka* is red, sweet, or salty; and *hatcho* is dark brown, thick, salty, and strong. *Miso-shiru* is a soup thickened with red bean paste, eaten for breakfast and other meals.

mistki   See MASTIC.

misto [MEES-tō]   Italian for mixed.

mithai [mee-TĪ]   Indian sweets or desserts; sweet taste is *meetha*.

mitsuba [mee-ts-bah]   A Japanese green resembling its cousin parsley, sometimes called *trefoil* for its three-part leaves; used fresh in salads and garnishes.

Mittagessen [MIT-tahg-es-en]   German for midday dinner, lunch; traditionally a substantial meal, the main one of the day.

miwa-naurozee [MEE-wah-NOW-roo-zee]   In Afghan cooking, a compote of fruits and nuts served at the new year celebration; originally made with seven fruits, each of whose names includes the letter *sinn*.

mixed grill   Various grilled meats, such as lamb chops, kidneys, bacon, and sausages, served with grilled mushrooms, tomatoes, and fried potatoes; the French *friture mixte* and Italian *fritto misto* are equivalents, including foods appropriate to those countries.

mizuna   A bitter green with spiky leaves, from the mustard family, usually sautéed, steamed, or braised, or mixed into MESCLUN in small amounts.

mocha   Originally, a very fine variety of coffee from the town of Mocha in Yemen, often blended with Java; today this is more likely to be a Mocha-style bean from Africa; mocha often means coffee-flavored and sometimes, more loosely, coffee- and chocolate-flavored.

mochi-gome [mō-chee-gō-may]   Japanese glutinous rice, used for special dishes such as red rice and sweet rice cakes (*mochi*); *mochiko* is the flour made from it.

mochomos [mō-CHŌ-mōs]   In Mexican cuisine, cooked meat, shredded and fried crisp.

mock turtle soup   A clear soup made from a calf's head and often garnished with calf brains, originally intended to spare the expense and trouble of using real turtle. In Tenniel's illustration for *Alice in Wonderland*, the mock turtle is a calf beneath a turtle's shell with mock tears rolling down its cheeks.

mode, à la [ah lah MŌD]   In French cuisine, a large cut of braised beef with vegetables; in the United States, pie or other pastry served with a scoop of ice cream.

moelle [mō-el] French for beef marrow.

moghlai [MŌG-lī] In Indian cuisine, Moghul-style or Muslim, rich and spicy.

Mohn [mōn] German for poppy; *Mohnbeugel, Mohnkipferl,* and *Mohnstrudel* are popular poppy-seed pastries.

Möhre, Mohrrübe [MEUR-eh, MOHR-rü-beh] German for carrot.

Mohr im Hemd A chocolate pudding, from Austria, literally, "moor in a shirt"; *Mohrenkopf* is chocolate meringue with whipped cream.

mojo [MŌ-hō] Spanish for sauce; the Mexican is MOLE, the Portuguese *moljo; mojo crillo,* a pungent CREOLE garlic sauce from Cuba, made with lard, olive oil, citrus, and onion, often served with yuca, pork, and chicken.

moka French for mocha.

molasses The syrup remaining from sugarcane juice after sucrose crystallization, during the manufacture of sugar; the process is repeated three times, each yielding a lower grade of molasses with more impurities and darker color from the high heat; BLACKSTRAP is the third grade, strong in flavor.

molcajete y tejolote [mol-kah-HAY-tay ee tay-hō-LŌ-tay] A Mexican mortar and pestle, made of heavy, porous lava stone, and balanced on three legs; indispensable for grinding spices.

mole [MŌ-lay] In Mexican cooking, a mixture or sauce, from the Aztec word for chili sauce; there are many variations, but it is always a smooth, cooked, complex combination of ingredients including several types of chili. *Mole poblano de guajolate* is a festive Mexican specialty of wild turkey (or pork or chicken) in a rich dark subtle smooth sauce of powdered mulato, ancho, and pasilla chilies simmered with vegetables, seasoning, and a little bitter chocolate for depth of flavor, but not discernible in itself.

molee [MŌ-lee] An Indian curry dish of coconut milk, green chilies, and fresh ginger.

Molinara [mō-lee-NAR-ah] A good Italian red-wine grape variety, used for Valpolicella and Bardolino.

moljo [MŌL-hō] Sauce in Portuguese; the Spanish is *mojo,* the Mexican *mole.*

mollusk, mollusc A class of shellfish: an invertebrate with a soft, unsegmented body, with a single or double shell; includes clams, mussels, octopus, oysters, scallops, squid, whelks, and one land-dweller, the snail.

Monbazillac [monh-ba-zee-yak]   A soft, sweet, golden dessert wine, not unlike SAUTERNES, produced east of Bordeaux in the Dordogne.

Mondeuse [monh-deuz]   A good French red-wine grape variety, extensively grown in the Savoie and Upper Rhône regions and, to a lesser extent, in California.

monégasque, à la [ah lah mō-nay-gask]   In the style of Monaco; a salad of NONATS, tomatoes, and rice; also refers to numerous other preparations.

Monferrato [mon-fayr-AH-tō]   A major Italian wine-growing region south of the Po Valley in Piedmont; none of its many wines bears its name.

Mongolian hot pot   See SHUÀN YÁNG RÒU.

monkey bread   A curious sweet bread, sometimes called bubble bread, made of separate clumps of dough piled and baked in a tube pan; currants are sometimes added; no relation to the monkey "bread" that is the fruit of the BAOBAB tree.

monkfish   A voracious, bottom-feeding, odd-looking fish whose tail contains firm white flesh similar in texture to lobster; the meat can be prepared in numerous ways that show off its sweet delicate flavor; also called goosefish, anglerfish, and *lotte*.

monopole [mō-nō-pōl]   A French wine-label term meaning that the entire vineyard belongs to one proprietor.

monosodium glutamate (MSG)   A type of salt long used in Asian cooking as a taste intensifier and enhancer. MSG was chemically isolated in 1908, but scientists do not fully understand how it works; often found in excessive amounts in Chinese restaurant food and instant and canned soups.

Montasio [mon-TAH-zyō]   A firm, whole-milk cows' cheese from northeastern Italy; this pale yellow cheese with a smooth rind and scattered holes is made in large wheels; it is cooked, pressed, salted, and cured up to two years. When young it makes a mild and nutty table cheese, and when aged it makes a brittle and pungent grating cheese.

Mont Blanc [monh blanhk]   A classic French dessert of chestnut purée sweetened, flavored with vanilla, mounded, and masked with crème CHANTILLY. The Italian version, *Monte Bianco*, includes chocolate and rum and is also named for the Alpine peak.

Montepulciano [mon-tay-pool-CHAHN-nō]   A red wine grape variety grown in eastern Italy (not to be confused with the town of the same name in Tuscany, whose wine is based on the Sangiovese grape), which makes dark, full, flavorful wines—Brunello di Montepulciano, Chianto Classico, and Vino Nobile di Montepulciano among them—which can be exceptional.

monter [monh-tay]   In French, to whip egg whites or cream to give volume; *monter au beurre* means to enrich a sauce with a little butter.

Monterey Jack   A semihard cooked cows' milk cheese first made in Monterey, California, in 1892 and named for its maker, David Jacks. A CHEDDAR-type of cheese, the whole-milk version, aged for three to six weeks, is pale, creamy, bland, a good melting cheese, while the skimmed-milk version, matured for at least six months, is harder and stronger.

Montilla [mohn-TEE-ya]   A Spanish wine from the villages of Montilla and Moriles, very similar to SHERRY and until recently sold as such, but now with its own appellation; Montilla, which is not fortified, makes an excellent apéritif or table wine, chilled.

Montmorency [monh-mohr-enh-see]   A variety of sour cherry, after the town in the Île-de-France, that lends its name to a classic duck dish; also a garnish of artichoke, asparagus, and other vegetables, and Madeira sauce.

montone [mon-TŌ-nay]   Italian for mutton.

Montpensier [mohn-penh-syay]   A classic French garnish of green asparagus tips and sliced truffles, sometimes with artichoke hearts and Madeira sauce.

Montrachet [monh-ra-shay]   A vineyard in the Côte de Beaune of Burgundy, straddling the communes of Puligny and Chassagne, whose celebrated dry Chardonnay white wine lends its name to the fine wines of neighboring vineyards. Montrachet is also the name of a fresh goats' milk cheese, delicate and creamy, best eaten young; shaped in logs, sometimes covered with vegetable ash or herbs, or wrapped in a chestnut or grape leaf. The name for this Burgundian cheese has become the generic term for fresh, mild chèvres of this type.

Montreuil [monh-troy]   In French cooking, with peaches; also fish poached in white wine, served with large potato balls and shrimp sauce.

montrouge [monh-roujh]   In French cooking, with mushrooms in cream.

moo   Thai for pork; *moo daeng* means roasted red pork.

moo goo gai pan   See MUÓ GŪ JĪ PIÀN.

moong dal   See MUNG BEAN.

moo shoo pork   See MÙ XŪ.

moqueca [mō-KAY-kah]   A Brazilian seafood stew, usually from white fish and shellfish, with a rich tomato, green pepper, onion, and herb sauce.

Morbier [mohr-byay]   A hard, uncooked cows' milk cheese with a delicate flavor, from the Franche-Comté of France; it is made in large rounds with a yellowish thin rind and an even paste marked by a traditional horizontal streak of ash between morning and evening milk layers.

morcilla negra [mor-THEE-yah NAY-grah]   A Spanish blood sausage made with pork, garlic, spices, and pig's blood, the best coming from Asturias; *morcilla blanca* is a white sausage containing chicken, bacon, hard-boiled eggs, and parsley.

morcón [mor-KŌN]   A Philippine beef roulade filled with vegetables, sausages, and hard-boiled eggs, braised and sliced into decorative rounds.

morel [mor-EL]   A wild fungus with a spongelike hollow cap, prized for its fine smoky flavor; this mushroom appears in springtime but can be dried successfully for other seasons. Morels are never eaten raw.

morello cherry   A variety of sour cherry, very dark red, with tart flavor excellent for cooking and liqueurs.

morille [MOHR-EE-yuh]   French for morel.

Mornay [mohr-nay]   BÉCHAMEL sauce with butter, grated Parmesan and Gruyère cheeses, possibly with egg yolks beaten in—a classic French sauce.

moros y cristianos [MŌR-ōs ee krees-TYAH-nōs]   "Moors and Christians," a Cuban dish combining black beans and white rice; named for the expulsion of the Moors from Spain in 1492.

mortadella [mor-tah-DEL-lah]   A large Italian sausage of ground pork with white cubes of fat, pistachio nuts, wine, and coriander; the best are from Bologna but should not be confused with American baloney.

morue [mohr-ü]   French for salt cod; see also BRANDADE.

moscada [moh-THKAH-dah, moh-SKAH-dah]   Spanish for nutmeg.

Moscato [moh-SCAH-tō]   Italian for the MUSCAT grape. Moscato wine is fragrant and fruity, and Moscato d'Asti, from Piedmont, is low in alcohol, sweet, lightly sparkling, charmingly delicious; it is best drunk young.

Mosel [mō-ZEL]   A river in western Germany on whose banks, between Trier and Koblenz, where it flows into the Rhine, are many vineyards; Mosel wine, in its characteristic green bottle, comes from the RIESLING grape. Some of these wines, especially those from the Mittel-Mosel or central section, are exceptionally fine, distinguished by their delicacy, fragrance, and spiciness. The river rises in the French Vosges, where it is spelled Moselle.

Most German for fruit juice; cider; MUST.

mostarda di frutta [moh-STAHR-dah dee FROOT-tah] Various fruits preserved in a syrup flavored with mustard; traditionally eaten with bread or cold meat, like chutney; from Cremona in Lombardy.

mouan [mwan] Cambodian for chicken.

moulage [moo-lajh] French for molding, as in molding a dessert; *moule* means a mold or form.

moule [mool] French for mussel.

moulokhia See MULUKHIYA.

mountain oysters The testicles of a bull, pig, or lamb, usually breaded and fried; sometimes called prairie oyster or Rocky Mountain oyster; this American slang term is as much descriptive as euphemistic.

Mourvèdre [MOOR-VEH-druh] A red wine grape variety that produces dark, tannic, full-bodied wines; especially successful in Provence and the sunny south of France, where it is often blended (but not in Bandol); also grown in California (where it is called Mataro), Australia, and now South Africa.

moussaka, mousaka [moo-SAH-kah] A Balkan dish, varying from one region to another, of vegetables layered with minced or ground meat, perhaps with a white sauce or cheese; the Greek version, with eggplant, lamb, tomatoes, and white sauce, is most familiar abroad.

mousse [moos] A sweet or savory French dish, usually cold, lightened with beaten egg whites or cream; from the French word for froth or foam; can also refer to Champagne bubbles.

mousseline [moos-leen] A French dish or sauce with whipped cream or egg whites folded in; it often designates hollandaise or mayonnaise with whipped cream added. The term can also mean a "little mousse" in a small mold or in spoonfuls, especially for seafood preparations. See also MOUSSE.

mousseux [moos-seu] French for sparkling or effervescent wine (literally "foaming"); does not include CHAMPAGNE, which is considered a separate category.

moutarde de Meaux [moo-taahrd deu mō] Mustard from the French town of Meaux made with partly crushed seeds, giving it a pleasantly grainy texture.

mouton [moo-tonh] French for mutton.

moyashi [mō-yah-shee] Japanese for bean sprouts.

Mozzarella [mohts-ah-REL-lah]   An Italian white spun-curd cheese traditionally made from buffalos' milk; the uncooked curd is kneaded into a smooth mass from which small pieces are cut (*mozzare* in Italian) and shaped into single cheeses, which are salted in brine. Mozzarella ripens fast, has a fresh, slightly acidulated flavor, and is sometimes smoked; it is widely imitated with cows' milk for pizza and other uses, spelled with lowercase.

MSG   See MONOSODIUM GLUTAMATE.

mtori [muh-TOR-ee]   A puréed plantain soup with beef stock, onion, and tomato, from the Kilimanjaro region of Tanzania.

muesli [MÜS-lee]   A Swiss breakfast dish of rolled oats with fruit and nuts, devised by the health food advocate Dr. Bircher-Benner.

muffin   A round individual pastry, either flat or raised, often served with butter. An English muffin (unknown in England) is a flat yeast bread baked on a griddle, while a generic muffin is a raised quick bread made of any kind of flour and often including nuts or fruit, baked in a deep mold in the oven.

muhallabia [moo-hah-lah-BEE-yah]   A Middle Eastern pudding similar to BALOUZA but, with rice, milk, and garnish of nuts, more elegant.

muhammara [moo-HAH-mah-rah]   A Middle Eastern *mezze* paste of sweet and hot red peppers, cooked in olive oil with walnuts, SUMAC, POMEGRANATE MOLASSES, ALEPPO PEPPER, cumin, and other spices, garnished with pomegranate seeds.

mu hong fun   See WŬ XIĀNG FĚN.

mujadarra   Arab lentils and rice with onions, served hot or cold with yogurt; a very old and favorite dish.

mukh [mook]   Arabic for brains, very popular in the Middle East.

mulard [mü-laahr]   French for a crossbreed duck bred for its meat and sometimes for its liver; as a hybrid it cannot reproduce.

mulato [moo-LAH-tō]   A dried chili pepper, large, brown, and pungent.

mulberry   A tree originating in China and cultivated for the silkworms that feed upon the leaves of certain varieties; a relative of the fig, it was known in ancient Greece and Rome and is still most appreciated in the Middle East; its berries are white, deep red, or black and are formed like raspberries without the central cone.

Müllerin Art [MÜL-er-in art]   "In the style of the miller's wife"—dredged in flour and fried in butter—the German version of à la MEUNIÈRE.

Müller-Thompson   A white wine grape variety planted widely in parts of Germany and used for Liebfraumilch, but rarely living up to its potential; a cross between SYLVANER and RIESLING.

mullet   The name of several unrelated fish; the Mediterranean red mullet is the most distinguished, and its liver and roe are as prized as its flesh. The American striped and silver mullet, whose roe is used in TARAMOSALATA, are related to the European gray mullet.

mulligatawny   An Anglicized soup of East Indian origin; chicken or lamb poached in broth, flavored with curry and other spices, and served with rice, cream, lemon, and the diced meat.

mulling   A process in which wine, ale, or cider is warmed, sweetened, and spiced for punch.

mulukhiya [moo-loo-KEE-yah]   "Jew's mallow," a mucilaginous vegetable whose green leaves go into an ancient Egyptian soup of the same name, enjoyed throughout the Middle East. The spinachlike leaves are added to meat, duck, rabbit, or poultry broth and served with chopped vegetables, chunks of meat, and rice on the side. Frozen *mulukhiya*, found at Middle Eastern shops, substitutes well for fresh in the United States. Also spelled *melokhia*, *miloukia*, and *moulokhia*.

Münchner   Literally, "from Munich"; used to designate the dark malty beers popular there.

mung bean   A variety of bean usually dried and used for BEAN SPROUTS.

Munster [MUHN-sterh]   A French pasteurized whole-milk cows' cheese first made by Benedictine monks in the Munster Valley of the Vosges mountains. The round cheese has a smooth orange rind and a pale yellow, fairly soft paste with cracks; its delicate salty flavor grows tangy with age. Alsatians eat their favorite cheese with rye or caraway bread, which complements it perfectly. There is also a German Münster cheese (spelled with an umlaut) made after the Alsatian Munster.

muó gū jī piàn [mwah goo jee pyen]   In Chinese cooking, sliced chicken breast stir-fried with mushrooms and other vegetables in a light sauce; a favorite in Chinese-American restaurants, where it is often called *moo goo gai pan* [moo goo gī pyen]; the Cantonese name is *mah gu gai pin*.

Murazzano [moo-rah-TSAH-nō]   A soft uncooked cheese from northwest Italy, made with a mixture of milks, mostly ewes'; the cylindrical cheese has no rind and a dense white paste that grows pale yellow with age.

mûre [mür]   French for mulberry; *mûre de ronce* or *mûre sauvage*, blackberry.

murgh [moorg]   Chicken in Indian cooking; *murgh tandoori* is skinned chicken marinated in yogurt and spices, then roasted in a hot TANDOOR oven; *murgh moghlai*, chicken moghul-style, in a rich saffron sauce.

murol [mü-rōl]   A hard cows' milk cheese, uncooked but pressed, from the Auvergne in France; the wheel-shaped cheese has a pinkish rind with a hole in the center.

Muscadet [mü-ska-day]   A light, dry, fresh white wine from the lower Loire Valley; Muscadet tastes best drunk young and accompanies the seafood of neighboring Brittany exceptionally well.

Muscat   A grape with many varieties that produce white wines—sparkling, dry, and sweet—ranging in color, yield, and quality, but all types have the characteristic musky, grapy, aromatic flavor; planted widely with different names, depending on the location. This variety is also used for table grapes, mostly perfumed and sweet, and raisins.

Muschel, Jakobsmuschel [MOOS-kuhl, YAH-kops-moos-kuhl]   German for scallop, named for St. James, the apostle, whose emblem is this shell.

muscovado sugar [mus-kuh-VAY-dō]   Partially refined cane sugar, soft and sticky, with fine crystals, made in both dark and light brown varieties; also called Barbados sugar and moist sugar.

mush   Cornmeal porridge; an American version of POLENTA, which can be sliced and fried.

mushi [moo-shee]   Japanese for steamed; *mushimono* means steamed food.

mushroom   The fruiting body of a fungus whose spores, if given the proper conditions, sprout up virtually overnight. Gastronomes for millennia have prized edible mushrooms for their delicate flavor and meaty texture, but their cultivation has been understood only since the early eighteenth century. In addition to the common field mushroom, gourmet shops and farmers' markets now sell a variety of wild mushrooms, many of which have separate entries.

Muskatnuss [moos-KAHT-noos]   German for NUTMEG or MACE.

muskmelon   A MELON with netted skin (sometimes called nutmeg melon because of its resemblance to the spice) and orange or pale green flesh; the fruit that Americans call cantaloupe is really a muskmelon, while the true Cantaloupe (not cultivated in the United States) has rough, scaly, or segmented—but never netted—skin. Muskmelons and Cantaloupes have a separation layer in their stems, unlike WINTER MELONS, so that they cannot be harvested into frost. It is sometimes spelled as two words.

müsli   See MUESLI.

musli [MOOS-lee]   A Tunisian dish of lamb braised with potatoes and peppers, garnished with lemon slices.

muslin bag   A cloth bag filled with a BOUQUET GARNI, spices, or other flavorings and tied tightly, used for infusing liquids, then removed without leaving any solids; also used for making jelly.

mussel   A bivalve mollusk with a blue-black shell and beard that attaches to rock or other solid objects (and should be removed before cooking); long popular in Europe in many preparations such as BILLY BI and à la MARINIÈRE, mussels are gaining acceptance in the United States.

must   Grape (or fruit) juice not yet fermented into wine.

mustard   A plant related to cress, radish, horseradish, and turnip and sharing their pungent taste: its name means "burning must." Mustard seeds were eaten by prehistoric man, spread by the Romans, and today are consumed more than any spice but pepper; the black, brown, and yellow varieties are dried, crushed, powdered, moistened, and mixed with many seasonings. Young mustard greens make a refreshing spring vegetable, and mustard oil is important in Indian cooking. See also DIJON.

mutton   See LAMB.

mù xū [moo shü]   In Chinese cooking, shredded pork stir-fried with scallions, cloud ears, and egg, then rolled up in pancakes; in Cantonese this is *mu shu* or *moo shoo* pork.

myrtille [meer-teel]   French for bilberry, whortleberry, blueberry.

Mysost [MÜ-sohst]   A hard uncooked Norwegian cheese made from cows' milk whey; it is dark brown and sweet, usually firm and dense, and is made in several varieties; see also GJETÖST.

N A N T U A   S A U C E

N

naan [nahn]   Indian flatbread baked on the side of a TANDOOR oven until puffed; sometimes flavored with savory or sweet ingredients; from the Punjab; also spelled *nan*, as in Afghanistan, where it can mean food in general as well as generic bread.

nabe [nah-bay]   Pot in Japanese; *nabemono* means one-pot communal cooking.

nacho [NAH-chō]   In Mexican cooking, a small tortilla chip topped with melted cheese and chilies or more elaborate toppings.

Nackenheim [NAHK-en-hīm]   A German wine-producing town overlooking the Rhine south of Mainz; the fruity white wines, from the RIESLING and SYL-VANER grapes, are of high quality.

naeng myon [NAHNG myen]   A cold noodle soup, a popular Korean one-dish summer meal, assembled at table; it includes buckwheat noodles in cool beef broth with vegetables and seasoning on top, finished with hard-boiled egg.

naganegi [nah-gah-nay-gee]   Japanese for a type of long onion, for which the leek can be substituted.

nage, à la [ah lah najh]   In French cuisine, cooked in a COURT BOUILLON of white wine, carrots, onions, shallots, and herbs; *nage* means swimming.

Nahe [NAH-he]   A German river flowing into the Rhine at Bingen; the Nahe Valley wines, from RIESLING and SYLVANER grapes, produce a lot of good white wine.

nam [nahm]   Thai for water; *nam cha* means tea; *nam chuang*, syrup; *nam katee*, coconut milk; *nam prik*, Thai hot sauce, a basic condiment, containing shrimp, garlic, chilies, NAM PLA, and lime juice.

ñame [NYAH-may]   Spanish for YAM; also called *igname*.

naméko [nah-may-kō]   In Japanese cooking, a mushroom appreciated for its slippery texture; usually canned.

nam pla [nahm plah]   Thai fish sauce, salty, fermented, and pungent, used as a condiment and seasoning throughout Southeast Asia; similar to NUOC MAM and PATIS.

Nantua sauce [NANH-tü-ah SŌS]   In classic French cuisine, béchamel sauce reduced with cream, beaten with crayfish butter, and garnished with crayfish tails; *à la Nantua* is a garnish of crayfish tails with Nantua sauce and sliced truffles.

Napa   A valley northeast of San Francisco whose vineyards have always been in the vanguard of the California wine industry, producing some of its best wines; the top varieties planted there now are Cabernet Sauvignon, Merlot, and Bordeaux-style Meritage blends; Pinot Noir, Chardonnay, and Zinfandel; and more recently, Syrah and Sangiovese.

napoleon   A dessert of puff pastry strips spread with CRÈME PATISSIÈRE and stacked in layers, the top often iced; the term sometimes now applies to savory dishes too; this pastry is not French in origin.

napoletana, alla [ah-lah nah-pōl-lay-TAH-nah]   In Italian cooking, a meatless spaghetti sauce made with tomatoes, onion, garlic, and olive oil, in the style of Naples.

napolitain [na-pōl-lee-tinh]   In French cuisine, originally a large ornamental cake—probably created by Carême, who delighted in such constructions—of stiff almond pastry layers spread with different jams, piled high, and elaborately decorated; now it usually means a smaller-scale GÉNOISE filled with jam and spread with ITALIAN MERINGUE and more jam.

napolitaine, à la [ah lah na-pōl-lee-ten]   In French cuisine, "in the style of Naples": veal scallops dipped in beaten eggs and bread crumbs mixed with grated Parmesan, fried, and garnished with spaghetti, tomato sauce, and Parmesan—a classic preparation.

napper [nap-pay]   In French, to coat or mask with sauce.

naranja [nah-RAHN-hah]   Spanish for orange; *naranja agria* is a SEVILLE, or bitter, orange.

nasi   Indonesian for rice; *nasi goreng* is fried rice cooked with various spices and ingredients, usually including chilies, garlic, onions, and shrimp paste and sometimes also meat, chicken, or shellfish; popular throughout Malaysia and Indonesia; when noodles replace the rice it is called *bami goreng* (or *bakmi goreng*); *nasi kuming*, "yellow rice," cooked in coconut milk with turmeric.

nasturtium   A plant whose blossoms, bright orange and peppery tasting, and leaves are eaten in salads; the buds and seeds are pickled like CAPERS.

nasu [nah-s]   Japanese for eggplant.

natillas [nah-TEE-yahth]   A soft runny Spanish custard, made from ewes' milk, sweetened and flavored with lemon and cinnamon; from the Basque country.

nato [na-tō]   A Japanese fermented bean curd product with a mucilaginous texture, an acquired taste.

natural   A term that is used by commercial producers to imply that no pesticides or additives have been used or that there has been no adulteration of any kind; however, the word has no specific legal definition; see also ORGANIC.

nature [na-tür]   French for plain, ungarnished; the Italian is *naturale*, the German *natur*. When used with wine, the term means that nothing—in particular, sugar—has been added.

Naturschnitzel [NA-toor-shnit-sel]   German for an unbreaded veal cutlet.

navarin [na-vaahr-inh]   A French lamb or mutton stew with small onions and potatoes; in spring, when the dish is called *navarin à la printanière*, it is made with young vegetables such as carrots, turnips, new potatoes, and peas.

navarraise [na-vaahr-rez]   French tomato sauce flavored with garlic and chopped herbs.

navel orange   A nearly seedless orange variety with a characteristic protuberance at the blossom end (hence its name), a thick skin, distinct segments, and sweet, flavorful flesh; best for salads and desserts, since its juice, when exposed to the air, turns bitter.

navet [na-vay]   French for turnip; the Spanish word is *nabo*, the Italian *navone*.

navy bean   A variety of common bean legume, small and white, widely used in dried bean dishes such as CASSOULET and BOSTON BAKED BEANS.

Neapolitan ice cream   Ice cream of various flavors, layered in a brick mold; an American term from the late nineteenth century.

Nebbiolo [neb-BYŌ-lō]   A red-wine grape variety that produces Barolo and Barbaresco, some of Italy's finest wines; it grows best in northern Italy and yields robust, tannic, aromatic, full-bodied, long-lived wines; also called Spanna and Chiavennasca.

Nebuchadnezzar [NEB-oo-kad-NEZ-er]   A wine bottle, usually for Champagne, that holds 20 regular bottles; named for the superannuated biblical patriarch.

neck   See CHUCK.

nectarine   See PEACH.

négi [nay-gee]   Japanese for leek, scallion, onion.

négresse, négresse en chemise [nay-gres enh she-meez]   French for chocolate mousse topped with whipped or iced cream; sometimes called by the Spanish term *negrítas*.

negus [NAY-gus]   An English port wine punch flavored with sugar, lemon, and spices, served warm; named after an eighteenth-century captain, Francis Negus.

nem   A spicy Thai sausage.

Nesselrode   A pudding of custard, whipped cream, and chestnut purée mixed with candied fruits, piled in a CHARLOTTE mold, and frozen; apparently invented by Mouy, chef to Count Nesselrode, the nineteenth-century diplomat and chancellor of Russia.

nest   See YÈN WŌ.

nettle   A prickly weed used in northern countries as a green similar to spinach; picked young and cooked, its sting disappears.

neua [NOO-ahr]   Thai for meat.

Neuchâtel [neu-sha-tel]   A region on the northern shore of Lake Neuchâtel in Switzerland that produces pleasant white wine from the Chasselas grape and red from Pinot Noir.

Neufchâtel [neu-sha-tel]   A soft uncooked cheese from the town of the same name in Normandy; made in many shapes from pasteurized cows' milk, either skimmed or whole and sometimes enriched with cream; eaten fresh when delicate or ripe when pungent.

Newburg   A thick cream sauce for lobster meat, enriched with egg yolks and flavored with sherry and cayenne pepper; named after Captain Wenberg, who had the sauce made for him at Delmonico's restaurant in New York.

New England boiled dinner   A Yankee POT-AU-FEU of corned beef and salt pork, possibly a chicken, cabbage, potatoes, carrots, and other vegetables, cooked together in one pot and usually served with mustard or horseradish.

New England clambake   A traditional communal method of cooking seafood learned from the Indians: a pit is dug in the beach, layered with hot rocks, then covered with generous amounts of seaweed, clams, lobsters, chicken, unhusked corn (silk removed), potatoes, and so on; the food cooks by the heat of the steaming seaweed around it.

New Zealand spinach   A creeping perennial with thick green leaves, triangular or arrowhead in shape, that are eaten cooked (not raw) like spinach, but no botanical relation; it deserves to be better known, especially since it is hardy in hot weather and easy to grow; also called tetragonia.

ngo [ngoh]   Vietnamese for coriander.

ngu vi huong [ngoo vee hoong]   Vietnamese for five-spice powder, usually including cloves, cinnamon, fennel seed, licorice, and star anise; see also WǓ XIĀNG FĚN.

ni [nee]   Japanese for braise, simmer; *nimono* means braised or simmered food.

niçoise, à la [ah lah nee-swahz]   A classic French preparation, "in the style of Nice," of tomatoes chopped and sautéed in olive oil with garlic, capers, sliced lemon, anchovies, and black olives; the popular *salade (à la) niçoise* contains, in addition to many of these ingredients, a variety of vegetables (usually including French beans and potatoes), seafood, especially tuna, and herbs.

Nieren [NEER-en]   Kidneys in German.

Nierstein [NEER-shtīn]   An important wine-producing town in the German Rheinhessen, with many good or fine white wines, mostly from the RIESLING grape.

nigella   A plant whose small black angular seeds are used as a spice, whole or crushed, especially in Middle Eastern and Indian cooking, often on breads and pastries or in pickles and vinegars; their flavor is sour and pleasingly bitter, aromatic, and pervasive. Nigella has many confusing names, such as onion seed, black cumin, black sesame, black caraway, devil-in-the-bush, or love-in-the-mist (a close cousin). The Latin name *nigella*, Indian *kalonji*, and Russian *charnushka* all describe accurately the "little black ones."

niku [nee-koo]   Japanese for meat.

nimboo [nim-BOO]   Lemon, lime, in Indian cooking.

ninjin [neen-jeen]   Japanese for carrot.

níspola [NEES-pō-lah]   Spanish for persimmon.

niú ròu [nyō rō]   Chinese for beef.

nivernaise, à la [ah lah nee-vayr-nez]   In French cuisine, "in the style of Nièvre," in Burgundy: garnished with glazed carrots and turnips cut into olive shapes, onions, braised lettuce, and boiled potatoes.

noble rot   A mold, *Botrytis cinerea*, that develops on grapes in certain regions under particular climatic conditions, withering the grapes but concentrating the sugar and flavor; grapes so affected produce very fine—and expensive—wine, such as Château d'Yquem, the great Sauternes; the French term is *pourriture noble*, the German *Edelfäule*.

nocchette [nohk-KET-tay]   Small Italian pasta "bow ties" for soup.

noce [NŌ-chay]   Italian for nut, walnut; *noce moscata* means nutmeg; *nocciòla* means hazelnut.

Nock [nohk]   German for dumpling; in Austrian dialect, the word is *Nockerl*.

Noël, bûche de   See BÛCHE DE NOËL.

nog   See EGGNOG.

nogada [nō-GAH-dah]   In Mexican cooking, walnut sauce; traditionally served with poblano chilies stuffed with shredded pork and garnished with pomegranate seeds—a celebrated dish.

noisette [nwah-zet]   French for hazelnut, or food that is shaped or colored like a nut. The word also means a cut of meat from the rib, usually of lamb, trimmed, rolled, tied in a small round, and served in an individual portion. *Pommes noisette* are potato balls, small, round, and browned in butter; *beurre noisette* is brown butter sauce.

noix [nwah]   French for nut, walnut.

noix muscade [nwah müs-kad]   French for nutmeg.

nok [nohk]   Thai for bird.

Nøkkelost [NEU-kel-ohst]   A Norwegian cheese based on the Dutch LEYDEN and similarly flavored with CUMIN or CARAWAY.

nom krourk [nuhm kroork]   In Cambodia, little pancakes of rice flour and scallions with shrimp and coconut milk.

nonat [nō-na]   French for a very small Mediterranean fish, usually deep-fried or served as an hors d'oeuvre.

nonpareille [nonh-paahr-ay]   French for small pickled capers from Provence—a superior variety "without equal."

nopales [nō-PAH-les]   In Mexican cooking, the fleshy oval paddles of the nopal cactus, eaten with scrambled eggs or in salad; *nopalitos* are cactus leaves eaten in salad.

noques [nōk]   French for the Alsatian version of GNOCCHI; in Austria, *noques* are made into a sweet, light dessert similar to snow eggs.

noquis [NŌ-keeth]   Spanish for GNOCCHI.

nori   In Japanese cooking, thin black sheets of seaweed, used either toasted or untoasted for wrapping SUSHI, rice balls, and crackers, and for coating food to be deep-fried.

normande [nohr-manhd]   In French cuisine, fish VELOUTÉ with mushrooms and oyster liquor, thickened with egg yolks and cream, and enriched with butter—a classic sauce; the garnish *à la normande* consists of oysters, mussels, crayfish, GOUJONETTES, shrimp, mushroom caps, and truffle slices with FLEURONS, in *sauce normande*.

Normande [nohr-manhd]   Normandy, the French province renowned for its butter, cream, cheese, apples, seafood, and salt-meadow sheep; cider is drunk here instead of wine, and CALVADOS is the local brandy.

norvégienne [nohr-vay-jhyen]   "Norwegian style," a classic French sauce of hard-boiled egg yolks mashed and seasoned with vinegar and mustard and beaten with oil for a mayonnaiselike texture; *omelette à la norvégienne* is BAKED ALASKA.

Norway lobster   See DUBLIN BAY PRAWN.

nostrale, nostrano [nō-STRAH-lay]   Italian for native or homegrown.

nougat [noo-gah]   In French cuisine, a confection of roasted nuts (usually almonds or walnuts) with honey or syrup; there are many varieties. *Nougatine*, a vague term, can mean almond brittle or nougat combined with chocolate.

nouilles [noo-yuh]   French for noodles.

nouvelle cuisine [noo-vel kwee-zeen]   Literally "new cooking," a movement starting in the 1970s that features fresher, lighter food in innovative combinations, served in small portions with striking presentations, reduction rather than flour- or egg yolk–thickened sauces, but still cooked by classic French techniques.

nova   Cold-smoked salmon, originally from Nova Scotia and now probably, but not necessarily, from the Pacific; in American-Jewish tradition eaten like lox with cream cheese and BAGELS.

nua mi gai   See HÉ YÈ BĀO.

Nudeln   [NOO-deln]   German for noodles.

nuez   [nwez]   Spanish for nut, walnut; the plural is *nueces*.

Nuits-Saint-Georges   [nwee sinh jhorjh]   A town in the Côte de Nuits whose vineyards produce excellent red Burgundies.

nuoc mam   [nuhk mahm]   Vietnamese fermented fish sauce based on anchovies, salty and pungent, related to NAM PLA and PATIS; an essential ingredient, highly nutritious; *nuoc mam cham* is the dipping sauce.

nuò mǐ jī   See HÉ YÈ BĀO.

Nuss   [noos]   German for nut, walnut.

nutmeg   The oval seed or kernel of the tropical nutmeg tree, native to the Moluccas, which is dried, ground, and used to flavor a wide variety of sweet and savory dishes. Connecticut is known as the Nutmeg State because Yankee peddlers sold wooden "nutmegs" to unsuspecting customers. See also MACE.

nyama   [NYAH-mah]   Beef; *n'dizi ya na nyama*, a plantain and beef stew with co-conut; from Tanzania.

nymphes à l'aurore   [nimhf ah l'ō-rohr]   In French cuisine, "nymphs of the dawn," frog legs poached in white wine and served in a pink CHAUD-FROID sauce with aspic, a favorite dish of Edward VII of England, devised and named by Escoffier.

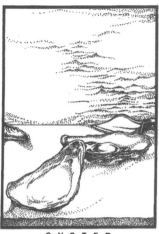

O Y S T E R

O

oats   A cereal traditional to cooler northern climates where many other grains cannot grow and valued there for its high nutritional content. Because oats contain almost no GLUTEN, they are often combined with wheat flour into breads or cooked in oatcakes, PORRIDGE, FLUMMERY, HAGGIS, sausages, and so on. Oat GROATS can be processed coarsely or finely, depending on use. Steel-cut oats, also called Scottish or Irish oats, are whole groats steamed and cut in pieces. Rolled oats are hulled oats ground into meal, steamed to gelatinize some of their starch (reducing spoilage), rolled into flakes, and dried; rolled oats are quicker to prepare as oatmeal than other kinds of oats except instant oats (not a substitute), although they have lost much of their texture.

Obst   [ōbst]   German for fruit; *Obsttorte* is an open mixed fruit tart, glazed, and perhaps garnished with almonds, whipped cream, or meringue; *Obstsuppe nach Hamberger Art* is a soup of puréed fruits, from Hamburg.

oca   [ŌK-ah]   Italian for goose; also a small South American tuber in the wood sorrel family.

ocha   [ō-chah]   Japanese for green TEA.

ocopa   [ō-KŌ-pah]   A South American dish of new potatoes in a sauce of chili peppers, onions, garlic, olive oil, and feta.

octopus A marine mollusk whose flavorful but tough meat is appreciated especially by Asian and Mediterranean cultures, often smoked, marinated, or stewed.

oeil d'anchois [oy d'anh-shwah] Literally "eye of anchovy" in French, this hors d'oeuvre is a raw egg yolk surrounded by anchovies and chopped onions.

oenology [ee-NOL-oh-jee] The science of winemaking.

oeuf [euf] French for egg; *oeufs brouillés* means scrambled eggs; *oeufs en cocotte*, poached in a casserole; *oeufs à la coque*, soft-boiled; *oeufs durs*, hardboiled; *oeufs en gelée*, poached and chilled in aspic; *oeufs mollets*, soft-boiled; *oeufs au plat* or *sur le plat*, fried or baked; *oeufs pochés*, poached; *oeufs pochés bénédictine*, poached and served on a creamed salt-cod base (not eggs Benedict); *oeufs à la poêle*, fried.

oeufs à la neige [euf ah lah nejh] "Eggs on snow," meringue shaped in ovals with spoons, poached in sweetened milk, drained, and served with custard sauce made from the milk; a classic French dessert; see also ÎLE FLOTTANTE.

offal So-called variety meats, consisting of organs or trimmings that the butcher removes from the skeletal meat. Offal includes brains, heart, sweetbreads, liver, kidneys, lungs, pancreas, spleen, tripe, tongue, headmeat, tail, blood, skin, feet, horns, and intestines; some of these have separate entries. Offal can also mean inedible waste or carrion.

oie [wah] French for goose; *oison* is a gosling.

oignon [oy-nyonh] French for onion; *oignon clouté* is an onion studded with cloves.

oil Fat extracted from seeds, nuts, and fruits that is fluid at room temperature, as in hazelnut, canola, olive oil, and so on, also fish oil, which becomes liquid when hot; most of these oils have separate entries. See also FAT.

oiseau [wah-zō] French for bird; *oiseaux sans tête*, MEAT BIRDS, a meat scallop stuffed, rolled up, and cooked.

oja See UJJAH.

okra A tropical plant of the mallow family, native to Africa and brought to the southern United States with the slave trade; its unripe seed pod, star-shaped in cross section, is used as a vegetable and a thickener for soups and GUMBOS because of its mucilaginous texture. Its West African name, *okro*, extends to various soups and stews using okra, especially combining smoked or salted seafood, meat, and vegetables.

Öl [eul]   German for oil.

øl, öl [eul]   Beer or ale in Scandinavian countries.

oleo   See MARGARINE.

olio [Ō-lyō]   Italian for oil; in Italy, *olio* means olive oil—*olio d'oliva.*

olive   A small tree with a gray gnarled trunk, silvery leaves, and deep roots, native to the Mediterranean and of prime importance since ancient times. A tree can grow to great old age still bearing fruit. The fruit, a drupe (the word comes from the Greek word for olive), can be picked at various stages of ripeness, turning green to black. The olive, never eaten raw, can be cured by several methods: in water, brine, oil, lye, or dry-curing in salt. Of many types, Greece produces Kalamata, large, unpitted, richly pungent, purple-black; and Naphlion, black, bitter, dry salt-cured. French Niçoise are brine-cured with stems on, small, brown, and salty; Picholine are larger, briny, and green. Italian Gaeta are dry and wrinkled, Liguria tart. Spain produces the Manzanilla, Gordal, and Hojiblanca. California has Mission olives, ripe, green, and cured in lye; and the bland black, ripe pitted. Olives are often flavored with herbs and spices or stuffed.

olive oil   Olives ripened on the tree are pressed for their oil, which is graded by the amount of refining given and the degree of acidity in the oil, also color, flavor, and aroma. The best, cold-pressed from the first pressing without use of chemicals or heat, has low acidity (under 1 percent). Laws vary from country to country, but extra-virgin is best, followed by virgin, fino, and olive oil (formerly pure). "Light" olive oil, recently marketed in the United States, has little flavor, the same nutritional and caloric profile as other olive oil, and a higher smoke point; its best use is for cooking at high heat. Olive oil is primarily monounsaturated, compared to other vegetable oils. See also OIL.

olives, meat   See MEAT BIRDS.

Olivet [ō-lee-vay]   A French whole- or partially skimmed-milk cows' cheese similar to CAMEMBERT, from Orléans; it is eaten very fresh or matured for a month, when it develops a delicate blue rind and is called Olivet Bleu.

olivette di vitello [ō-lee-VET-tay dee vee-TEL-lō]   Italian veal scallops filled with a savory stuffing, rolled up, and braised; veal birds. See also MEAT BIRDS.

olla podrida [Ō-yah pō-DREE-dah]   A Spanish stew, literally "rotten pot," made from many different meats (mainly pork) and vegetables, including cabbage, chickpeas, and tomatoes; similar to the COCIDO of Madrid; *olla* means stewpot and lends its name to other hearty dishes.

oloroso [ō-lor-Ō-sō]   A type of Spanish SHERRY matured in the SOLERA method like FINO but without FLOR yeast; its color is dark—deep gold to amber—its alcoholic content higher than *fino*, and it has a rich flavor and intense, characteristic bouquet; *olorosos* range from nearly dry to very sweet.

omelette [ōm-let]   French for omelet: eggs beaten and cooked in butter in a special flat pan until set, often filled or flavored with a wide variety of other ingredients.

onion   The underground bulb of the genus *Allium*, essential in the kitchen, usually in a subordinate role; revered by ancient cultures but also disdained because of its characteristic pungency, which makes the eyes tear and the breath fierce. Onions vary widely in size, color, and type. Among varieties are the large white or yellow Bermuda, the rounder Spanish, and red Italian onion; the sweet Vidalia from Georgia, Maui from Hawaii, and Walla Walla from Washington State; the small boiling and pearl onions; the bulbless leek and multilobed shallot, whose subtlety is beloved by the French; the scallion, spring, or green onion, really the juvenile of any variety; and the odiferous chive and garlic; some of these have separate entries.

oolong [oo-long]   A partially fermented, amber-colored tea, mostly from Taiwan—a cross between black fermented tea and green unfermented tea. See also TEA.

Opéra, gâteau   A French GÉNOISE cake with chocolate and coffee flavoring and decoration, named for the opening of the Paris opera house.

Oporto [ō-PORT-ō]   A city in Portugal near the mouth of the Douro River; the fortified wine PORT, whose name comes from that of the city, must by law be shipped from Oporto or the town across the river.

opossum [ō-POS-sum]   A small nocturnal marsupial of the southeastern United States; game that makes a favorite rustic dish braised with peppers and sweet potatoes; known colloquially and in folklore as 'possum.

Oppenheim [OHP-pen-hīm]   A town in the German Rheinhessen whose many vineyards produce good white wines (although not as distinguished as those of its northern neighbor, Nierstein).

orange   The citrus tree that bears flowers and fruit together, offering at once both promise and fulfillment, thus a symbol of fertility. The orange is probably native to China; Arab traders brought it west to the Middle East and Mediterranean, first the sour orange, then the sweet. In 1493 Columbus brought it to the New World, where it has thrived; the bitter and sweet orange remain the two basic types. In the United States today, the thin-skinned, juicy, seedy Valencia is good for eating and juice, grown in Florida and California; its origin is Portuguese, not Spanish. The West Coast navel, named for its distinctive bulge, is early, large, thick-skinned, seedless, with distinct segments, ideal for dessert, but its juice turns bitter with exposure. The blood orange, prized in Italy and the Mediterranean for its luscious raspberry color, is gaining acceptance in the United States. The juice and skin of the bitter orange (Seville, bigarade, and bergamot) flavor many savory dishes and sauces and is essential for orange marmalade. For mandarin and tangerine, see MANDARIN.

orange, sauce [sōs ohr-anhjh]   In French cuisine, demi-glace flavored with orange and perhaps lemon juice and julienne of orange zest.

orange flower water   The aromatic liquid distilled during the extraction of essential oils from bitter orange blossoms and used as a flavoring in cooking and baking; it was the principal flavoring extract before vanilla was discovered and remains so in the Middle East. It flavors various cocktails: a few drops mixed with gin and vermouth makes a Victorian martini.

orange pekoe   A superior grade of black tea from India or Ceylon with leaves slightly larger than pekoe, sometimes called broken orange pekoe; aromatic, delicate, fresh in flavor.

orecchiette [or-ek-KYET-tay]   Eggless pasta in the shape of "little ears"; originally from Apulia, in Italy's heel, and usually made commercially.

oregano [or-AY-gah-nō]   Wild marjoram, an herb especially popular in Italian cooking as well as Greek and Middle Eastern cooking; oregano is very similar to marjoram but more pungent; the Italian word is *origano*, the French *origan*. Mexican oregano usually means *Lippia graveolens*, which is sharp and strong.

Oregon grapes   See BARBERRY.

organic   Food labeled "organic" has generally meant food grown without hormones, antibiotics, synthetic pesticides, irradiated components, genetically modified materials, or reprocessed sewage, but laws have varied from state to state. To avoid inconsistency, "organic" now means food produced and certified in compliance with the National Organic Standards Rule enacted on April 21, 2001 and required since October 21, 2002. There are four categories: (1) products labeled "100 percent organic"; (2) products labeled "organic," meaning 95 percent organic by weight; (3) products labeled "made with organic ingredients" comprising 70 percent or more, and up to three of those ingredients may be listed on the package front; and (4) processed products with less than 70 percent organic, which may list those ingredients on the information panel but not use the term "organic" on the front of the package. Products in the first three categories may show the USDA seal. Detailed information is available on the USDA's web site at www.nal.usda.gov/afsic/ofp.

orgeat [ohr-jha]   French for a syrup or drink originally made from barley and later from almonds, flavored with orange flower water.

orientale, à l' [ah l'or-yenh-tal]   In French cuisine, dishes seasoned with saffron or curry, sometimes in a garnish of tomatoes stuffed with rice.

Original-Abfüllung [or-EE-gee-nal AHB-fül-ung]   German for CHÂTEAU-BOTTLED.

Orloff, veal   A dish from classic French haute cuisine: saddle of veal (or occasionally lamb) braised and carved in slices; each slice is coated with SOUBISE and DUXELLES, the slices are placed back together, then the whole is masked with béchamel and garnished with asparagus tips. Prince Orloff was the Russian ambassador to France under Czar Nicholas I.

ormer   See ABALONE.

ortolan [ohr-tō-lanh]   French for a very small gamebird, the European bunting, prized for its flavor; though once prolific in southern France, it is now nearly extinct and a protected species. It was served plucked and often boned but not DRAWN, since its entrails were considered delicious.

Orvieto [or-VYAY-tō]   A town in Umbria in central Italy whose white wine of the same name is light, pleasant, and popular.

orzo [OR-zō]   Grain-shaped pasta; in Italian the word means barley.

Oscar, veal   Veal cutlets sautéed and garnished with asparagus tips, crab legs or crayfish tails, and sauce béarnaise.

oseille [ō-zay]   French for sorrel.

osetra   See CAVIAR; also spelled *osiotr*.

osso buco, ossobuco alla milanese [OHS-sō BOO-kō ahl-lah mee-lah-NAY-say]   In Italian cooking, veal shanks or shin bones (literally "bone with a hole"), preferably from the hind, slowly braised with onions, garlic, tomatoes (controversial) and other vegetables, stock and white wine, and traditionally garnished with GREMOLADA (sometimes spelled *gremolata*) before serving; the morsels of marrow are removed with a special implement. In Milan, RISOTTO *alla milanese* (with saffron) accompanies the *oss bus*, as it is called in local dialect. The plural form is *ossi buchi*.

ost [ohst]   Cheese in Scandinavian languages.

ostra [OTH-trah]   Spanish for oyster; *ostion* is another kind of oyster, eaten cooked; the Italian word is *òstrica*.

ostrich   A large flightless bird whose dark meat tastes like beef but is low in calories and fat.

ot [eu]   Vietnamese for chili peppers; *ot kho* is dried red Chinese chilies; *tuong ot*, prepared chili sauce.

oursin [oor-zinh]   French for SEA URCHIN.

ouzo [OO-zō]   A clear, sweet Greek liqueur flavored with aniseed, usually served as an apéritif with water, which turns it white and cloudy; also used as a flavoring.

ovos moles [Ō-vōs MŌ-lays]   In Portuguese cooking, egg yolks and syrup cooked together and used as a sauce or filling; in Aveiro, the mixture is molded into fanciful shapes, cooked in rice water, and eaten sprinkled with cinnamon.

Oxford and Cambridge pudding   English apricot tart masked with meringue.

Oxford sauce   Virtually the same as CUMBERLAND SAUCE.

oxidation   In cooking, the process of exposing the food or wine to oxygen in the air, generally causing it to darken and robbing it of its freshness.

oxtail   The tail of beef, excellent for stews and soups because of the gelatin rendered from the high proportion of bones; ox simply means steer.

oyster   A bivalve marine mollusk prized since the Romans; eaten raw on the half shell or cooked in preparations as various as HANGTOWN FRY, ANGELS ON HORSEBACK, and à la NORMANDE. In the nineteenth century overharvesting led to their serious cultivation. Today oysters are usually named for the town where their beds lie, although in modern oyster culture, baby oyster "spat" can be moved. In America, Eastern (Atlantic) oysters are prized, especially those in northerly cold waters, where they mature more slowly: in Eastern Canada (Malpèque, Apalachiacola), Cape Cod (Wellfleet, Cotuit), Long Island (Bluepoint), and Chesapeake (Chincoteague); in the Pacific northwest, Puget Sound's Olympia are very small and fine, also the Kumomoto. The giant Pacific (Japanese) is used mostly for oyster sauce. In Europe, Irish Galway, English Colchester and Whitstable, French Belon and Marennes, and the large Portuguese oysters are other choice varieties.

oyster mushroom   A wild mushroom, pale gray and fan-shaped, often in overlapping clusters; also available cultivated, dried, and canned; its flavor is mild when cooked.

oyster plant   See SALSIFY.

oyster sauce   See HO YAO.

oysters Rockefeller   Oysters on the half shell, resting on a bed of rock salt, each topped with a spoonful of puréed seasoned spinach, quickly browned; originally from Antoine's in New Orleans and named for John D. Rockefeller; apparently first made with absinthe and watercress rather than spinach.

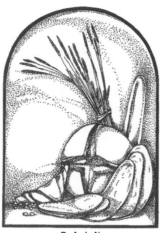

PAIN

P

paan [pahn]   Betel leaves, sometimes stuffed with spices and nuts, and used as a digestive in Indian cooking.

pachadi [PAH-chah-dee]   Vegetables and yogurt with mustard seeds in Indian cooking.

Pacific rim   The cooking style of countries or islands in the Pacific as presented in some restaurants; this style (see FUSION CUISINE) combines traditional techniques with local ingredients and Asian influences.

paella [pah-AY-ah]   A Spanish dish of short-grain rice cooked with a variety of meats and fish (usually chorizo, chicken, rabbit, and shellfish) and an assortment of vegetables, including garlic, scallions, peas, and tomatoes, flavored with saffron, and served in the pan in which it is traditionally made. The exact ingredients vary widely according to region, season, and pocketbook; originally from Valencia and usually made with Valencia rice.

pagello [pah-JEL-lō]   Italian for red snapper.

paglia e fieno [PAH-lyah ay FYAY-nō]   Italian "straw and hay" fettucine, the yellow and green colors coming from egg and spinach pasta dough; usually served in a cream sauce with ham or sausage, peas, and perhaps mushrooms.

paillarde de veau [pī-yaahrd deu vō]   French for grilled veal scallop.

paillettes [pī-yet]   French for pastry straws; *paille* means straw in French.

pain [pinh]   French for bread, loaf; *pain mollet* means soft bread; *pain grillé*, toast; *petit pain*, a roll; *pain perdu*, French toast as made in France, usually sweetened and spiced with cinnamon, so called because the "lost bread" is stale; *pain de mie*, sandwich bread; *pain de Gênes*, Genoa cake, a rich almond pound cake.

pain à l'anglaise   See BREAD SAUCE.

pak [pahk]   Thai for greens, leafy vegetable; *pak chee* is coriander; *pak chee farang*, parsley; *pak kard hom*, lettuce; *pak sod*, a salad of mixed raw vegetables.

pak choy   See BÁI CÀI.

pakora [pah-KOR-ah]   Fritters in Indian cuisine.

palacsinta [pal-ah-SHIN-tah]   Hungarian for crêpe; the celebrated dessert, *palascinta à la Gundel*, with walnuts, chocolate, raisins, and rum, is named for the Hungarian chef Karoly Gundel; the word in Austrian dialect is *Palatschinke*.

palak [PAH-lahk]   Spinach in Indian cooking.

Palatinate   See RHEINPFALZ.

palaver [pah-LAH-ver]   A thick stew from West Africa of spinach with chicken or meat and various vegetables.

pallet knife   A flexible, wide-bladed knife with no sharp edge or point; used for spreading butter, icing, pastes, and other soft mixtures.

palm   A large family of trees and shrubs, usually tropical, many of whose parts are edible: dates are its fruit, coconut its seed or nut, palm hearts (destroying the tree) its new buds or shoots, SAGO a starch from its trunk, and, in addition, palm oil and wine. See also COCONUT.

palmier [pal-myay]   A French pastry made from strips of PÂTE FEUILLETÉE sprinkled with sugar, folded, sliced, and baked, which forms a palm-leaf shape as the pastry puffs out.

palm sugar   A coarse dark sugar made from reducing the sap of certain palm trees, used in the cooking of India and Indonesia; also called jaggery and java sugar.

paloise [pal-wahz]   In French cuisine, "in the style of Pau": classic BÉARNAISE sauce but with mint in place of tarragon.

palombe [pal-omhb]   French for wild pigeon or dove; in Spanish *palombacco* means squab or young pigeon.

palourde [pal-oord]   French for clam.

pamplemousse [pamh-pluh-moos]   French for grapefruit.

pan [pahn]   Spanish for bread; *pan tierno* is fresh bread; *pan duro*, stale bread.

panaché [pa-na-shay]   French for mixed or multicolored; used to describe salad, fruit, or ice cream; also means plumed.

panade [pa-nad]   *Panada*, a French peasant soup of water, stock, or milk thickened with bread; also a thick paste made with flour (see ROUX), bread crumbs, or other starch, possibly thickened with eggs, and used to bind fish and meat mousses and forcemeats.

panais [pan-nay]   French for parsnip.

panato [pah-NAH-tō]   In Italian cooking, fried in bread crumbs.

pancake   A thin batter cake cooked on a griddle or pan and appearing in almost every cuisine the world over. See also CRÊPE.

pancetta [pahn-CHET-tah]   Italian bacon, usually unsmoked, that is sometimes rolled into a solid round; used in BATTUTO.

pancit [pan-seet]   In Philippine cooking, pasta in the form of noodles, often stir-fried with chopped meats, shrimp, and vegetables, or in the form of dough-wrappers stuffed like wontons.

pan de Spagna [pahn day SPAH-nyah]   Italian sponge cake, often soaked in liqueur and filled with jam or cream.

pandorato [pahn-dor-RAH-tō]   In Italian cooking, "gilded bread": bread dipped in an egg and milk batter and deep-fried; sometimes with a savory stuffing.

pandowdy   An early American dessert, probably from New England, of sliced apples mixed with cider, brown sugar or molasses, spices, and butter, covered with biscuit dough, and baked.

pan-dressed   Refers to a whole fish that has been scaled and gutted, with head and fins removed; usually for sautéing or deep-frying.

pane [PAH-nay]   Italian for bread; *panino* is a roll or biscuit; in French *pané* means coated with bread crumbs; see also PAIN, PANADE, and PANURE.

paneer [pah-NEER]   In Indian cooking, fresh milk curds, made from boiled milk curdled with lemon juice, that have been drained and compressed; used like fresh unripened cheese or tofu; also spelled *panir*. Another word for these curds is *chenna*.

panetière [PAN-eh-TYAYR] In French, a cupboard with open latticework for storing bread; it is either suspended from the ceiling to keep away pests or placed on a sideboard. The term can also refer to an edible case, as of pastry, to enclose food.

panettone [pah-net-TŌ-nay] A light Italian yeast cake containing sultana raisins and candied citron peel, baked in a domed shape and eaten for breakfast; originally from Milan, *panettone* is traditional for Christmas.

panforte [pahn-FOR-tay] Italian for fruit cake.

pan-fry To sauté: to cook in a skillet in a small amount of fat, as opposed to DEEP-FRY.

panna [PAHN-nah] Italian for cream; *panna montata* is whipped cream.

pannequet [pan-kay] A small French pancake or CRÊPE filled with a sweet or savory mixture and folded in quarters.

Pannerone [pan-nayr-Ō-nay] An uncooked whole-milk cows' cheese from Lombardy, usually unsalted; the cheese is pale straw colored with many holes, delicate and creamy in taste with a slight tang; it matures quickly; also sometimes called White Gorgonzola and Gorgonzola Dolce, mistakenly.

Pannhas [PAHN-hahs] In German cooking, a kind of mush made from buckwheat flour cooked in broth left over from cooking sausages; this Westphalian specialty, similar to Pennsylvania German SCRAPPLE, is a traditional part of the fall pig slaughter.

panucho [pah-NOO-chō] In Mexican cooking, a small tortilla puffed up, the pocket filled with a savory stuffing, then fried until crisp.

panure [pa-nür] In French, bread crumbs or a golden bread-crumb crust.

panzanella [pahn-zah-NEL-lah] A rustic Italian salad of vegetables and herbs with stale bread soaked in water and squeezed dry, or perhaps fried in olive oil; from Tuscany.

panzarotti [pahn-zah-ROHT-tee] Italian pastry crescents stuffed with cheese and deep-fried.

pào cài [pow tsī] Chinese pickled vegetables eaten as salads all over China and varying from one region to another; the Cantonese name is *pau choy*.

papa [PAH-pah] Spanish for potato; also called *patata*. *Papa seca* is a freeze-dried potato from the Andes, an ancient method of preservation. *Chuno* is another method in which the potatoes are naturally freeze-dried in the high altitude and cold climate.

papa dzules [PAH-pah-TSOO-lays]   Literally "food for the lords," which the Mayans supposedly gave the Spaniards. This Mexican Yucatán specialty consists of tortillas filled with hard-boiled egg yolk, tomato sauce, pumpkin seed sauce, and green pumpkin seed oil.

papain [pah-PAY-in]   An enzyme derived from the PAPAYA and used, diluted in sugar and salt, as a meat tenderizer. South American Indians have for centuries wrapped fresh papaya leaves around meat for the same purpose.

papaw, pawpaw [PAW-paw]   A small tree native to North America whose fruit has yellowish skin and smooth, creamy flesh with sweet, fragrant flavor. American Indians and settlers appreciated it, but today it is ignored. The name is easily confused with the PAPAYA (no relation). Another name for the pawpaw fruit is custard apple, to add further confusion.

papaya [pah-PĪ-yah]   A tall tropical plant native to America; its large pear-shaped fruit has a thin skin that turns yellow when ripe, a smooth yellow or orange flesh, and many black seeds resembling peppercorns. Unripe papaya can be cooked as a vegetable like squash; the sweet ripe fruit is eaten in many ways, like melon, and even the leaves can be boiled like spinach. The plural of papaya is papaya. See also PAPAIN and PAPAW.

papillon [pa-pee-yonh]   A French "butterfly"-shaped pastry cookie made from FEUILLETAGE.

papillote [pa-pee-yōt]   In French cuisine, a paper frill used to garnish the end of the rib bone on chops and crown rib roasts; *en papillote* means an individual portion of fish, poultry, or meat that is wrapped in paper (usually parchment) with seasonings and liquid to moisten it, cooked in the oven, and served while still in the puffed-up paper, slit at table to release the aromatic steam.

papos de anjo [PAH-pōs day AHN-hō]   Literally "angel's breasts" in Portuguese; small yellow egg cakes served with syrup.

pappad [PAH-pahd]   Crisp thin Indian flatbread, roasted, grilled, or fried, made from mung beans or lentils; sometimes called *pappadam*.

pappardelle [pap-par-DEL-lay]   Long flat egg noodles, ⅝ inch broad, cut with a crimped edge; they are the traditional accompaniment to hare cooked in a rich wine sauce; from Tuscany.

paprika   A spice made from a variety of sweet red chili peppers, dried and powdered; widely used in Hungarian cooking and essential to GULYÁS; different types of paprika vary in heat, strength, and flavor.

paprikás csirke [pahp-ree-KAHSH SHEER-kuh]   A Hungarian dish of chicken braised with onions and garlic, with plenty of paprika and sour cream; *paprikás*, a favorite Hungarian dish, is also made with meat and fish.

paquette [pa-ket]   French for fully developed lobster roe about to be laid, turned from bright orange to dark greenish black—considered a great delicacy; *paquette* also means the female lobster carrying such roe.

paratha [PAH-rah-tah]   In Indian cuisine, flaky whole-wheat flatbread fried in GHEE on a griddle, sometimes stuffed with spicy meat or vegetables.

parboil   See BLANCH.

pareve [PAR-uh-vuh]   Food containing no meat or milk and therefore, by Jewish KOSHER law, suitable to be eaten with either.

parfait [paahr-fay]   A French mousselike dessert, originally a coffee cream, but now any fruit, nut, or flavored syrup into which whipped cream is folded, then chilled or frozen; in the United States a parfait is served in a tall narrow glass filled with ice cream, layered with sauce, with whipped cream on top.

parga [PAHR-gah]   Spanish for red snapper.

parihuela salvaje [pahr-ee-WAY-lah sal-VAH-hay]   Mixed fish and shellfish with CHORIZO in a spicy tomato sauce, a Creole dish from South America.

Paris-Brest [paahr-ee brest]   A French pastry ring of PÂTE À CHOUX topped with sliced almonds and filled with *crème praliné* (see PRALINE) or crème CHANTILLY and fresh strawberries.

parisienne, pommes à la [pohm ah lah paahr-ee-zyen]   In French cuisine, potatoes cut into small ovals and sautéed in butter; there are various other *parisienne* preparations, including a white-wine reduction sauce with shallots.

Parker House roll   A yeast-bread roll folded into two halves before baking, named for the Parker House hotel in Boston, where the roll was first created in the nineteenth century.

Parmentier   Any dish with potatoes, after Antoine-Augustin Parmentier, the French agronomist who recognized the potential of the tuber, previously believed poisonous, and championed its acceptance by the French.

Parmesan   See PARMIGIANO REGGIANO.

parmesane, à la [ah lah paahr-meh-zan]   In French cuisine, with grated Parmesan cheese; see also PARMIGIANO REGGIANO.

Parmigiano Reggiano [par-mee-JAH-nō rej-JAH-nō]   A cooked, pressed, partially skimmed cows' milk cheese shaped in large squat cylinders; protected by law, this very old and famous GRANA cheese comes from designated areas in northern Italy. Its rind is smooth and golden, its paste pale straw colored, dense, and grainy, with tiny holes radiating from the center; sweet, mellow, and fragrant, it is eaten young as a table cheese or very old and sharp as a grating cheese.

parrilla [pahr-REE-ah] Spanish for grill; *parrillada di pescado* is mixed seafood grill with lemon.

parsley An herb known to the ancient Greeks and Romans for its medicinal properties but now used for culinary purposes; it grows in several varieties, among them the curly-leaf, most popular in the United States, and the more pungent flat-leaf, popular in Europe, especially the Mediterranean, where it originated. Parsley root is a family member developed for its long thin white root to use in soups and braises.

parsnip A winter and cold-climate vegetable with long thin white root that grows sweeter after frost; excellent streamed, roasted, puréed, and braised, but perceived as unglamorous.

parson's nose See POPE'S NOSE.

partridge A fall game bird with delicate white flesh, cooked in various ways depending largely on age; a single bird serves one.

pasilla [pah-SEE-yah] A very thin chocolate-colored chili pepper, about 6 inches long and very hot.

paskha [PAHS-kah] The traditional cake for Russian Orthodox Easter (*paskha* means Easter) made of cream cheese, dried fruits, and nuts, and shaped in a high four-sided pyramid marked with the letters XB for "Christ is Risen"; usually served with KULICH.

passata [pahs-SAH-tah] Italian for purée.

passatelli in brodo [pahs-sah-TEL-lee een BRŌ-dō] Parmesan, eggs, and bread crumbs mixed to a paste and pressed through a tool to form strands that are cooked and served in meat broth; from Romagna in Italy.

passer [pas-ay] In French, to strain through a sieve or tammy cloth.

passion fruit A climbing vine or shrub, native to Brazil and discovered by Jesuit missionaries, who found the unusual blossom symbolic of Christ's passion. The egg-sized fruit turns deep purple and wrinkled with ripeness; its ocher flesh, perfumed, lemony, and intense, is eaten raw with the seeds or squeezed and bottled for juice. The Spanish word is granadilla.

pasta Italian for dough or paste, as well as the whole family of noodles; *pasta all'uovo* means egg pasta; *pasta asciutta*, "dry" or plain pasta, possibly stuffed or sauced, as opposed to *pasta in brodo*, which is pasta cooked in soup; *pasta frolla*, short pastry; *pasta sfoglia*, puff pastry.

pasta e fagioli [PAHS-tah ay fah-JŌ-lee]   A robust Italian soup of pasta, white beans (some of which are puréed to thicken it), and salt pork.

pastel [PAHTH-tel, PAHS-tel]   Spanish for pie, cake, pastry, pâte; a *pastelería* is a pastry shop.

pastèque [pas-tek]   French for watermelon.

pasteurization   The process of heating food high and long enough to kill microorganisms and prevent or slow fermentation; used especially for milk; named after the French chemist Louis Pasteur.

pasticcio [pahs-TEE-chō]   In Italian cooking, a pie, either savory or sweet, but often of layered pasta with a savory filling; a *pasticcerìa* is a piece of pastry or pastry shop.

pastilla   See BASTILLA.

pastillage [pas-tee-yajh]   French for a mixture of sugar, water, and gum tragacanth that forms a paste that can be molded into fantastic shapes. Though little used today, in centuries past it was used extensively for elaborate table ornamentation; Carême excelled in architectural *pastillage*.

pastina [pahs-TEE-nah]   Small Italian pasta for soup.

pastis [pas-tees]   A potent anise-flavored liqueur popular in southern France; usually mixed with water, which turns its green color cloudy; see also PERNOD.

pastitsio [pas-TEET-syō]   Greek macaroni baked in a dish with ground meat, onion, tomato sauce, and cheese.

pastrami [pas-TRAH-mee]   Beef, usually shoulder, first pickled in spices and then smoked; of Romanian origin and now associated with Jewish cooking.

pastry bag   A cone of paper or cloth with an open point, sometimes fitted with a specially cut tip; soft smooth foods, such as whipped cream, icing, puréed potatoes, and PÂTE À CHOUX, are forced through it to make even and decorative shapes.

pastry blender   A simple kitchen tool—parallel stiff metal wires on a handle—for cutting fat into flour.

pastry comb   A confectioner's tool with serrated edges for making designs on the iced or chocolate tops and sides of cakes and pastries; also called cake comb.

pastry cream See CRÈME PÂTISSIÈRE.

pasty See CORNISH PASTY.

patata [pah-TAH-tah] Italian and Spanish for potato; *patate fritte* are fried potatoes; *patate lesse*, boiled potatoes; *patate stacciate*, mashed potatoes, in Italian.

patate [pa-tat] French for sweet potato.

pâté [pa-tay] French for a rich mixture, usually savory, of meat, poultry, game, seafood, or vegetables cooked in pastry (*pâté en croûte*) or earthenware dish (*pâté en terrine*); *pâté de foie gras*, smooth, rich, and well seasoned, is a typical example; *pâté de compagne* has a coarse, crumbly texture. *Pâté* can also mean pastry, pie, pasty, or patty, but should not be confused with PÂTE.

pâte [pat] French for pastry, paste, pasta, dough, or batter; the word is often confused with PÂTÉ. See following entries.

pâte à choux [pat ah shoo] French for cream puff pastry; a simple paste made by stirring flour into boiling water and butter; eggs are then mixed in; upon cooking, the eggs puff up the dough, making a cavity, so the inside of the pastry is generally filled with flavored cream, as in éclairs, profiteroles, and the like; also spelled *pâte à chou*.

pâte à croissant [pat ah kwah-sanh] CROISSANT pastry dough.

pâte à foncer [pat ah fonh-say] See FONCER.

pâte brisée [pat ah bree-zay] Pie dough, short pastry, literally "broken" pastry in French.

pâte d'amandes [pat d'a-manhd] French for almond paste, MARZIPAN.

pâte feuilletée [pat foy-eh-tay] French for flaky or puff pastry; it is made by enclosing butter within the DÉTREMPE or elastic dough and then folding and turning it many times to produce *mille feuille*, a "thousand leaves" or thin layers; during baking the steam from the melted butter pushes the layers up to make the delicate puff of pastry.

pâte levée [pat leh-vay] French for raised or leavened dough.

pâte sucrée [pat sü-kray] French for sweet pastry for pie dough and pastry shells, very high in fat (butter for best flavor) and low in moisture to form a crumbly base that will not become soggy when filled.

patis [pa-tees] Philippine fermented fish sauce, salty and pungent, related to NUOC MAM.

pâtissier [pa-tees-syay] French for a pastry chef or cook; a *pâtisserie* is a piece of pastry or a pastry shop.

pâtissière, crème See CRÈME PÂTISSIÈRE.

patlıcan [paht-lee-jahn] Turkish for eggplant.

pato, pata [PAH-tō, PAH-tah] Spanish for duck, either drake or hen.

paton [pa-tonh] In French, one recipe or "pad" of PÂTE FEUILLETÉE, of optimal size for handling.

pattie A small pastry with savory stuffing, usually served warm.

pattypan A variety of round summer squash with a scalloped edge, usually white, or yellow; also called scallop, custard squash, or cymling.

Pauillac [pō-yak] A wine-producing town in the Haut-Médoc of Bordeaux, where some of the greatest vineyards lie, including Château Lafite, Latour, and Mouton-Rothschild.

paupiette [pō-pyet] French for a thin slice or scallop of meat filled with savory stuffing, rolled up, and braised; see also MEAT BIRDS and OLIVETTE DI VITELLO.

pavé [pa-vay] A French dish such as a savory mousse or pâté chilled in a square mold and garnished; a square cake, often sponge, spread with buttercream and decorated. The word means paving stone and designates a square or rectangular shape.

Pavlova In Australian cooking, a meringue basket filled with fresh fruit and whipped cream, named for the Russian ballerina.

pavo [PAH-vō] Spanish for turkey.

payasam [PĪ-yah-sahm] An Indian pudding of mung beans, peas, and coconut milk.

paysanne, à la [ah lah pī-zan] "Peasant style": with vegetables—most often carrots, onions, and potatoes—and diced bacon.

pea A leguminous plant known since prehistoric times, of which the common garden pea (English pea, French *petit pois*), an early spring vegetable, is sweet, delectable, and a welcome harbinger; frozen in quantity or older and starchy, it loses its fresh charm. The field pea, a mealy staple, is grown to maturity and dried, for yellow and green split-pea soups and porridges once known as "pease puddings." Peas with edible pods *(mange-touts)*, including sugar snap peas and snow peas, taste sweet, tender, and crisp when lightly cooked. Pea sprouts and shoots with young tendrils are also edible. Other members of the extended

LEGUME family, such as black-eyed peas and chickpeas, have the word *pea* in their name.

peach The orchard tree and its fruit, a drupe related to apricots, cherries, prunes, and almonds. Native to China and named *Prunus persica* for its route west through Persia, it thrives in warmer temperate climates. The peach's yellow-pink skin is prized for its downy softness just as the flesh is for its juicy lusciousness. The fuzzless nectarine is a type of peach, not a plum-peach cross. Peaches divide into two types, cling and free-stone, of which clings are firmer, earlier-ripening, and mostly canned; also into yellow and white varieties, of which the less common whites are later-ripening, perfumed, and delicate. Peaches are also dried and used in various jams and preserves.

peanut The seed of a leguminous bush, not a true nut, indigenous to Brazil and brought to North America by the slave trade; highly nutritious, peanuts are a staple in Africa and an important crop in India and China. The oil, with a high burning point and light flavor, is important for cooking. Peanut butter, a staple of American school lunches, is a paste of nuts and oil. Other names are groundnut and goober, from *nguba*, an African word for peanut.

pear The orchard tree and its fruit, cousin of the apple in the rose family; it is one fruit that needs to be picked mature but unripe, to improve in texture and flavor later. The French preference for the pear over the apple led to their developing many varieties. Of popular American varieties, Bartlett is a summer pear, known as Williams, Bon Chrétien, or Wilhelm in Europe; Anjou, Bosc, Comice, Kieffer, and Packham's Triumph are fine fall or winter pears; the small Seckel is distinguished by its American pedigree and ripening on the tree. The pear's silky or crisp texture make it adaptable for many culinary uses. The ASIAN PEAR, which holds its texture in cooking, is a distant relative.

pearl barley Hulled and polished BARLEY, small and round like pearls, usually eaten in soups or like rice.

pecan [pi-KAN, PEE-kan] The nut of a tall tree native to the Mississippi Valley and a member (with the walnut) of the hickory family; an important dessert nut in the United States but uncommon elsewhere; the name is of American Indian origin.

pêche Melba See MELBA, PÊCHE.

pechuga de pollo [peh-CHOO-gah day PŌ-lō] Spanish for chicken breast.

Pecorino Romano [pek-or-EE-nō rō-MAH-nō] A cooked and pressed whole-milk ewes' cheese, originally made outside Rome but now made mostly in Sardinia.

This ancient GRANA cheese is round, white, or very pale straw colored, and dense, with a yellow-brown rind. Aged at least eight months, its flavor is sharp, salty, and intense. There are other types of *pecorino* (from *pecora*, meaning ewe), but this is the most famous and finest.

Pecorino Siciliano [pek-or-EE-nō see-chee-LYAH-nō]   A hard uncooked Italian cheese made from whole ewes' milk, with a flavor made more pungent by the addition of peppercorns; a GRANA cheese, it is often used for grating.

Pecorino Toscano   TOSCANELLO cheese made with all ewes' milk.

pectin   A jellylike substance found in certain fruits—especially apples, currants, quinces, and citrus—and other plants. Pectin causes fruit to set when it is cooked at a high temperature (220°F or 105°C at sea level) with sugar and acid in jelly making.

ped [pet]   Thai for spicy, hot, peppery, pungent.

Pedro Ximénez [PAY-drō hee-MEN-eth]   A Spanish grape variety, used for Montilla and Málaga wines, also for blending sherries; also planted in South America, California, South Africa, and Australia.

peixe [PAY-shay]   Portuguese for fish, singular and plural.

Peking duck   See BĚI JĪNG KǍO YĀ.

Peking ravioli   See GUŌ TIĒ.

pekoe   See ORANGE PEKOE.

Pélardon [pay-laahr-donh]   A type of chèvre, rustic, disc-shaped, usually fresh but sometimes older, from the French Languedoc; it is often flavored with herbs of the *garrigue* moor and olive oil, baked with bread crumbs or croûte, and served on salad greens.

Pellkartoffeln [PEL-kar-tohf-eln]   German for potatoes boiled in their skins.

pemmican   Preserved meat, often buffalo or venison, dried, pounded, mixed with melted fat and sometimes berries, and pressed into cakes; used by the American Indians and early settlers on expeditions as a high-energy convenience food.

penne [PEN-nay]   Italian for quill-shaped pasta, that is, tubes cut on the diagonal.

penuche   A butterscotch candy with pecans.

pepe nero [PAY-pay NAY-rō]   Italian for black pepper; red pepper is *pepe rosso*.

peperonata [peh-payr-ō-NAH-tah]   Italian for a dish of sweet peppers, tomatoes, onions, and garlic cooked in olive oil and served cold; an Italian PIPÉRADE.

peperoncino [peh-payr-ōn-CHEE-nō]   Italian for a hot red chili pepper, fresh or dried.

peperoni [peh-payr-Ō-nee]   Italian for green or red sweet bell peppers; also an Italian sausage of pork and beef highly seasoned with hot red peppers.

pepino [peh-PEE-nō]   Spanish for cucumber; also a melon from South America with striped purple and yellow skin and delicate flavor.

pepita [peh-PEE-tah]   Spanish for fruit seed; in Mexican cooking this means pumpkin seed.

pepitoria, en [en peh-pee-TOR-ya]   A Spanish sauce, usually for chicken, of almonds, garlic, herbs, saffron, and wine; probably of Arab origin.

pepper (black)   The fruit of a vine, *Piper nigrum*, native to southern India, the table seasoning commonly paired with salt. Black pepper is the berry fermented, dried, and used whole, cracked, or ground to varying degrees, when it begins to lose its aroma. White pepper is the same berry ripened further but with the black outer skin removed before drying, with a milder and slightly different flavor; white pepper is used in pale sauces for aesthetic reasons and is often preferred in Europe. Green peppercorns are berries picked unripe and pickled in brine without being dried in the sun. Cubeb pepper (tailed pepper), long pepper, Alleppey, and Tellicherry are other black pepper relatives from Asia that seldom find their way to the West. Unrelated to the pepper family are *fagara* (Szechuan) and *sansho* (Japanese pepper), as are both pink and red peppercorns. The black pepper is no relation to the red CHILI pepper of the genus *Capsicum*, to which cayenne, paprika, and bell peppers belong. See also MIGNONETTE.

pepper (chili or red)   See CHILI.

pepper (sweet bell)   A mild member of the fiery genus *Capsicum* native to tropical America; the unripe green fruits turn red, yellow, orange, or deep purple when mature and sweeten in flavor.

pepperpot   A soup or stew made from tripe and highly seasoned, originally from Philadelphia and probably derived from the German PFEFFERPOTHAST. The West Indian version of pepperpot contains CASSAREEP (cassava juice), meat, and seafood, as well as vegetables.

pera [PAYR-ah]   Italian and Spanish for pear.

perch   The name given to various fresh- and saltwater fish, many of them unrelated.

perdrix [payr-dree]   French for partridge; *perdreau* is a young partridge; *perdiz* is the Spanish word.

peregrinos [payr-eh-GREE-nōth, payr-eh-GREE-nōs]   Spanish for scallops.

Périgord, périgourdine [payr-ee-gohr]   A French demi-glace sauce with truffle essence and chopped truffles; *à la périgourdine* means garnished with truffles —for which Périgord is famous—and sometimes also foie gras.

Perilla [payr-EE-yah]   A cows' milk cheese from Spain similar to TETILLA; firm in texture, mild in flavor.

perilla leaf   A broad-leafed plant in the mint family, in both red and green varieties, used as a vegetable either whole or shredded, as a wrapper, and as a garnish; also called beefsteak plant, wild sesame, *shiso*, or *tia tô*.

periwinkle   A small sea snail popular along the French and British seashores but largely ignored on the American Atlantic coast.

perlant [payr-lanh]   French for a wine that is slightly and naturally sparkling but not deliberately vinified so literally "in pearls."

Perlwein [PAYRL-vīn]   German for a wine that is slightly sparkling and intentionally vinified so.

pernice [payr-NEE-chay]   Italian for partridge; the Spanish word is *perdiz.*

Pernod [payr-nō]   The brand name of an anise-flavored liqueur, originally AB-SINTHE, now used for PASTIS.

perry   Pear cider.

persil [payr-seel]   French for parsley; *persillade* is chopped parsley—perhaps mixed with chopped garlic—added to a dish before serving; *persillé* means sprinkled with parsley and also designates top-quality beef marbled with fat.

persimmon   The fruit of a tree native to the United States and China, though the Chinese varieties are sweeter and larger through cultivation; the deep orange fruit ripens in mid- to late fall but until then it is unpleasantly astringent. Known as *kaki* to the rest of the world, Americans call it by its Native Indian name. Sharon fruit is a less astringent type of persimmon developed in Israel.

pesca [PES-kah]   Italian for peach (the plural is *pesche*); *pesca noce* means nectarine.

pescado [peth-KAH-dō, pes-KAH-dō]   Spanish for fish; *pescado a la sal* is whole fish baked in rock salt; *pescadilla* is a small fish.

pesce [PAY-shay]   Italian for fish; *pesce persico* means perch; *pesce spada*, swordfish; *pesce San Pietro*, John Dory.

pesto [PES-tō]   A sauce from Genoa of crushed basil, garlic, pine nuts, and Parmesan or Pecorino in olive oil; it is a robust sauce for minestrone and pasta (which in Italy is invariably TRENETTE); PISTOU is the French version.

Petersilie [pay-tayr-ZEEL-yeh]   German for parsley.

pétillant [pay-tee-yanh]   French term for effervescent, slightly sparkling wine; the French equivalent of *frizzante* (Italian) and *Perlwein* (German) and deliberately vinified so (unlike PERLANT).

petite marmite [peu-teet maahr-meet]   In French cuisine, a clear consommé served from the earthenware MARMITE in which it is cooked; lean meat, marrow bones, a whole chicken, and vegetables flavor the broth, which is served with CROÛTES spread with marrow or sprinkled with grated cheese.

petit four [peu-tee foor]   A very small cake or cookie, often elaborately garnished; also a sweetmeat served at the end of a dinner (in French, literally "little oven").

petit pain   See PAIN.

petit salé   See SALÉ.

Petit Sirah   The name used in California for the SYRAH grape.

Petit-Suisse [peu-tee swees]   A French pasteurized cows' milk cheese, sometimes enriched with cream, made into a fresh, mild cheese shaped in small cylinders; it was invented by a Swiss cowherd and a farmer's wife in France in the nineteenth century.

pétrissage [pay-tree-sajh]   French for kneading the dough.

petto [PET-tō]   Italian for breast, chest, brisket; *petti di pollo* are chicken breasts.

pez [payth, pays]   Spanish for fish; the plural is *peces*. The Portuguese is *peixe*.

pez espada [peth eth-PAH-dah, pez es-PAH-dah]   Spanish for swordfish.

pezzo [PET-sō]   Piece, chunk in Italian.

Pfannkuchen [PFAHN-koo-khen]   German for pancake.

Pfeffer [PFEF-fer]   German for pepper.

Pfefferkuchen [PFEF-fer-koo-khen]   A German spice cake, similar to gingerbread, originally from Nuremberg; a traditional Christmas dessert.

Pfefferpothast [PFEF-fer-poht-hahst]   A German stew of beef ribs and onions in gravy, liberally seasoned with pepper and lemon; from Westphalia.

Pfifferling [PFIF-fer-ling]   German for chanterelle.

Pfirsich [PFEER-zish]   German for peach.

Pflaume [PFLOW-meh]   German for plum.

pheasant   A fall game bird with colorful plumage whose flesh, properly hung, is relished at the table; though a bit smaller, hen pheasants are slightly plumper and more succulent than cocks. Plenty of moisture must be provided to prevent the meat from drying out during cooking.

Philadelphia ice cream   A style of ice cream that has no egg or custard base.

pho [feu]   A Vietnamese one-dish meal of noodles in meat broth with bean sprouts, herbs, chicken, pork, or seafood, preserved cabbage, scallions, chilies, and sauces; served in one bowl at breakfast or any other time. *Pho bo*, Hanoi soup, with beef stock, is the favorite; *pho ga*, with ginger and chicken, is another version. The word comes from the French *feu*.

phyllo [FEE-lō]   Very thin sheets of dough, made from flour and water, layered, and filled with savory or sweet foods. In Greek the word means "leaf," and phyllo is, in fact, similar to the French MILLE-FEUILLE; sometimes spelled filo.

piacere, a [ah pyah-CHAYR-eh]   Italian for cooked "to please"; as you like it.

piaz [pee-AHZ]   Onion, in Indian cooking.

pib, pibil [peeb]   In Mexican cooking, a pit used for barbecuing that allows the meat to smoke partially while cooking, from the Yucatán.

picada   See SOPE.

picadilla [pee-kah-DEE-yah]   Spanish for ground, minced, or shredded meat.

picadillo [pee-kah-DEE-yō]   In Spanish cooking, a hash made of ground beef sautéed with chopped vegetables and savory seasonings.

picarones [pee-kah-RŌ-nays]   A Peruvian yeast pastry of puréed squash or sweet potato mixed with dough, deep-fried, and served warm in a spicy sweet syrup.

piccalilli [PIK-ah-lil-ee]   A vegetable pickle, probably Anglo-Indian, prepared with vinegar, mustard, and other spices.

piccante [pee-KAHN-tay]   Italian for piquant, spicy, sharp; the Spanish word *picante* emphasizes hot, spicy flavor.

piccata [pee-KAH-tah]   Italian for veal scallop.

pichón [pee-CHŌN]   Spanish for a squab bred for the table.

pickerel   See PIKE and WALLEYE.

Pickert   [PEE-kayrt]   German for a peasant bread of potato or wheat flour, from Westphalia.

Picón   See CABRALES.

Picpoul   See FOLLE BLANCHE.

pí dàn   [pee dahn]   Chinese thousand-year-old eggs, a delicacy: duck eggs preserved in a clay casing made of ashes, lime, salt, and strong tea, rolled in rice husks, and buried for three months to ferment; the yolks turn greenish brown, the whites deep aubergine, the flavor strong and cheeselike. They are also known as hundred-year-old eggs.

pièce montée   [pee-es monh-tay]   French for an ornamental centerpiece of PASTILLAGE, often inedible and very elaborate, that usually adorned the table at important banquets in the past. Carême's emphasis on *pièces montées* revealed his passion for architecture as well as for display.

piémontaise, à la   [ah lah pyay-monh-tez]   A classic French garnish of RISOTTO timbales mixed with grated white truffles.

pierna de cordero   [PYAYR-nah day kor-DAYR-ō]   Spanish for leg of lamb; *pierna de puerco* is a fresh ham.

Piesport   [PEES-port]   A village in the German Mosel Valley that produces many fine white wines that are fruity and delicate.

pig   See PORK.

pigeonneau   [pee-jhoh-nō]   French for a young squab bred for the table.

pignoli   [pee-NYŌ-lee]   Italian for pine nuts; the French word is *pignons*.

pike   A bony freshwater fish whose sweet white flesh is used in many fine dishes, such as the renowned *quenelles de brochet*. Izaak Walton, seventeenth-century author of *The Compleat Angler*, called the pike "choicely good."

pilau, pilav, pilao   [pee-LAHF, PEE-lahf, pee-LOW, PEE-low]   A Persian dish of long-grain rice sautéed in a little fat and simmered in flavored liquid until the grains are swollen yet separate; pieces of meat, poultry, or vegetables can be added. Pilaf is the Turkish version of the basic technique; many similar rice dishes are related, such as POLO, *pelau* (Provence), *purloo*, and PULAO, using a variety of grains, fats, and flavorings. The emphasis is usually on the first syllable.

pili pili   See PIRI-PIRI.

pilot biscuit   See HARDTACK.

Pilsener LAGER beer; strictly speaking, Pilsener is only the very fine beer brewed in Pilsen, Czechoslovakia, but the term is now used generally for any high-quality lager of the same style. It is pale golden and lower in alcohol and calories than ordinary American beer.

Pilz [peelts]   German for mushroom.

piment doux [pee-menh doo]   French for sweet pepper.

pimienta [pee-MYEN-tah]   Spanish for black pepper; *pimiento* means capsicum red pepper, either sweet (*pimiento dulce*) or hot.

Pimm's Cup No. 1   A prepared cordial mix base for a gin sling, concocted by a bartender at Pimm's restaurant in London in the nineteenth century, to which lemon soda and cucumber garnish were added. It was such a success with customers that it was commercially produced and three more Pimm's cups were added, on whisky (No. 2), rum (No. 3), and brandy (No. 4).

piña [PEE-nyah]   Spanish for pineapple, so named for its visual resemblance to the pine cone; *piña colada* is a cocktail of fresh pineapple juice and light rum, originally from the Caribbean but now made widely and in many variations.

pincha [PEEN-chah]   Spanish for a snack, sometimes served as an appetizer, which "pricks" the palate.

pineapple   This tropical fruit, native to Brazil, took Europe by surprise when Columbus introduced it in 1494; with tufted crown, striking appearance, and intensely sweet-acid flesh, it became a status symbol for those with hothouses in which to grow it. The Spanish called it *piña* for its resemblance to the pine cone, but Portuguese sailors called it *ananas*, from the Brazilian Indian word meaning "excellent fruit"; taking it on their voyages to ward off scurvy, they spread it around the tropical world. A young plant takes two or three years to flower in the spiral formations that later join as a multiple fruit. A fresh pineapple contains bromelin, an enzyme that makes the skin tingle and counteracts gelatin. Once harvested, pineapple cannot ripen further.

Pineau de la Loire   See CHENIN BLANC.

Pineau des Charentes [pee-nō day shaahr-anht]   A French APÉRITIF wine made from new wine with Cognac added, then matured in oak; it is high in alcohol, sweet, and has a distinctive bouquet.

pine nut   The seed of certain pine trees that comes from the pine cone, a multiple fruit, used in savory and sweet dishes, especially in Mediterranean countries.

Pinkel   A German smoked sausage of groats, raw bacon, and onions.

piñón [pee-NYŌN]   Spanish for PINE NUT; the plural is *piñones*.

Pinot [pee-nō]   A family of wine grapes that includes several important varieties. Pinot Blanc, light, fresh, fruity, early-drinking, is increasingly important in Alsace, also in northern Italy as Pinot Bianco; in southern Germany and Austria as Weissburgunder, and further east in Europe; also in California and Oregon. Pinot Gris is a white wine grape with full-bodied, somewhat spicy, acidic flavor, planted widely in Alsace (where it may be called Tokay-Pinot Gris); known as Pinot Grigio in northeastern Italy, where it produces light, crisp, refreshing, occasionally remarkable wine (may be called Tocai, but no relation to Hungarian Tokay); and in eastern Europe; its crispness comes out well in Oregon and California. Pinot Meunier is widely planted in Champagne, where it is blended with Pinot Noir and Chardonnay. Pinot Noir is the variety essential to the wines of Burgundy, especially those of the Côte d'Or, for the grapes' fruitiness maturing to spicy scent and texture; also in Germany, Switzerland, and eastern Europe, but planted with greater success in California, Oregon, and New Zealand; Australia and South Africa are beginning to cultivate it.

Pinotage [pee-nō-tajh]   A South African wine grape variety, a cross between Pinot Noir and Cinsaut, that is becoming increasingly popular in California, New Zealand, South Africa, and elsewhere; it can be densely fruity and long-lived.

pintade [pinh-tad]   French for guinea hen; a young chick is *pintadeau*; the Spanish word is *pintada*.

pinto bean   A variety of common bean, "painted" or splotched red, used in many Latin American stewed dishes.

pinzimonio [peen-zee-MŌ-nyō]   An Italian dipping sauce of oil, salt, and pepper for raw vegetables.

pipérade [pee-payr-ad]   In French cuisine, tomatoes cooked in olive oil with green bell peppers and onions, with lightly beaten eggs and sometimes ham or bacon added; this Basque specialty has many variations.

pipián [pee-pee-AN]   In Mexican cooking, a deep red sauce for chicken made of sesame and pumpkin seeds ground with spices and sometimes peanuts or almonds.

piquante [pee-kanht]   A classic French sauce of chopped shallots reduced with white wine and vinegar, demi-glace added, strained, then garnished with chopped gherkins, parsley, chervil, and tarragon.

piquín [pee-KEEN]   A dark green chili pepper, very small and very hot.

pirão [pee-ROW]   In Brazil, a paste of flour (MANIOC, cornmeal, or another) mixed with coconut milk and DENDÊ.

pırınç [peu-RINCH]   Turkish for raw rice.

piri-piri [PEE-ree-PEE-ree]   A very, very small (¾-inch) and extremely hot chili pepper that is the basis of an incendiary sauce, made with olive oil, onions, and garlic, popular in West Africa and North Africa. The origin is probably *pili pili*, discovered by Portuguese sailors and carried elsewhere on their voyages. The pepper is also available dried and powdered or as a bottled sauce.

piroshki [pee-ROSH-kee]   In Russia, small turnovers or dumplings filled with a savory or sweet stuffing; *pirogi* are large pastries cut into servings; the spellings vary, the fillings are infinite.

Pischingertorte [PISH-ing-er-TOR-teh]   An Austrian torte made of round wafers filled with chocolate hazelnut cream, covered with chocolate icing.

piselli [pee-ZEL-lee]   Italian for peas; *piselli alla romana* are peas cooked with butter, onion, and ham.

pismaniye [pis-MAH-nee-eh]   A Turkish sweet of spun HALVAH.

pissaladière [pees-sa-la-dyayr]   A French pizzalike tart from Nice, made with anchovies, onions, black olives, and perhaps tomatoes arranged in a decorative pattern.

pissenlit [pees-enh-lee]   French for dandelion leaves; the name ("piss in bed") alludes to the plant's diuretic capabilities; see also DANDELION.

pistachio   A deciduous tree, native to Asia, cultivated since ancient times for its nuts; their delicate flavor and green color make them useful in savory and sweet dishes, especially pâtés and stuffings, ice cream, and pastries.

pisto [PEETH-tō]   A Spanish vegetable dish of chopped tomatoes, red or green peppers, zucchini, and onions stewed together, with many variations; this dish is associated with La Mancha.

pistou, soupe au [soop ō pees-too]   A rich Provençal vegetable soup, made with white beans, mange-touts, and vermicelli, garnished with crushed basil and garlic in olive oil; *pistou* is the French version of PESTO.

pita [PEE-tah]   Middle Eastern flat white pocket bread, also spelled *pitta*; the Turkish is *pide*.

Pithiviers [pee-tee-vyay]   A French pastry dessert, named for the town where it originated, consisting of a large round of puff pastry filled with almond paste and traditionally decorated with a pinwheel or rosette pattern.

pizza Literally "pie" in Italian, the word usually denotes an open-faced tart on a yeast dough base spread with all manner of savory foods; originally from southern Italy.

pizzaiola [peets-ī-Ō-lah] Italian fresh tomato sauce with herbs and oregano, like pizza topping, often served with meat dishes; *pizzaiolo* means pizza-maker.

pla [plah] Thai for fish.

plaice A European member of the FLOUNDER family; its fine-textured and delicate white flesh is eaten fresh or sometimes smoked; its many relatives are sometimes called flounder or dab, with much confusion.

plancher [planh-shay] In French, to plank.

plank To bake or broil food, especially fish, on a board of hardwood that seasons the food on it—a technique early settlers learned from the American Indians.

plantain [PLAN-tin, *not* PLAN-tayn] A fruit closely related to the BANANA, but whose higher starch and lower sugar content require that it be cooked for savory or sweet dishes; a staple food in Latin America, the plantain is usually larger than the banana but is sometimes short and fat, with green skin ripening to yellow and black.

plátano [PLAH-tah-nō] Spanish for PLANTAIN, much used in Caribbean cooking; semi-ripe plantains are *plátano pintones*, ripe plantains, *plátano maduros*, and green plantains, *plátano verdes*. *Plátano a la tentación*, very ripe plantains baked with brown sugar, wine or rum, and cinnamon, a rich Cuban dish usually served with savory food.

play cheu [plī cheu] Cambodian for fruit.

pletzlach [PLETS-lahkh] Apricot or plum pastry squares, traditional for Passover.

pleurotte See OYSTER MUSHROOM.

Plinz [pleents] Austrian for pancake, fritter.

plover [PLUH-ver] A shore bird particularly valued in Europe for its delicious eggs; the lapwing and golden plover are favorite species.

pluck The heart, liver, and lungs of an animal.

plum An orchard tree and its fruit, a drupe, cousin of the cherry, peach, and almond; besides varieties native to eastern Europe, there are Japanese and American plums, many of them, crossed to make a complicated family tree. The skin color can be red, blue, deep purple, green, or yellow; the flavor is usually sweet, but some very tart varieties are tamed with cooking and sweetening. Favorite European plums are the yellow perfumed mirabelle of France; Reine Claude, which becomes greengage in England; astringent damson, bullace, and sloe, which make excellent preserves or liqueurs; La Petite d'Agen, from French Armagnac country, which in California became the Italian prune plum, eaten fresh or dried; Santa Rosa, Larosa, and Red Beaut are other California varieties. High-sugar varieties of plums can be dried for prunes.

plum duff   In British cooking, a restrained version of plum pudding made with dried raisins or currants; the word "duff" comes from dough.

plum pudding   A British steamed dessert of various dried fruits (excluding plums) and suet, often flamed with brandy; traditional for Christmas.

plum sauce   See SUÀN MÉI JIÀNG.

pluvier [plü-vyay]   French for plover.

poach   To cook food gently in liquid held below the boiling point.

poblano [pō-BLAH-nō]   A large, dark green chili pepper, mild but varying in flavor; it is about 5 inches long, 3 inches wide, and triangular in shape; sometimes available canned; when ripened and dried it becomes the ANCHO chili.

pocher [pō-shay]   In French, to poach.

pochouse [pō-shooz]   See MATELOTE.

podina [pō-DEE-nah]   Mint, in Indian cooking.

poêler [pwah-lay]   In French cooking, to cook food with a little butter or other fat in a tightly closed pot; *poêle* means both frying pan and stove.

poi [poy]   A native Hawaiian dish, a porridge of cooked TARO root, pounded smooth, thinned with water to the desired thickness, fermented to attain a sour flavor, and eaten with the fingers on its own or as a condiment; an acquired taste.

point, à [ah pwinh]   French for just right or to the perfect point; with reference to steak, *à point* means rare; with reference to fruit and cheese, it means at the peak of ripeness.

poire [pwaahr]   French for pear.

poireau [pwaahr-ō]   French for leek.

pois [pwah]   French for pea; *pois cassés* are split peas; *pois chiches*, chickpeas; *petits pois*, spring peas; *petits pois princesse*, snow peas; *pois à la francaise*, peas braised with lettuce, spring onions, parsley, butter, a pinch of sugar, and a little water.

poisson [pwah-sonh]   French for fish; a *poissonnier* is a fish chef in a large restaurant kitchen or a fishmonger.

poitrine de porc [pwah-treen deu pork]   French for pork belly; *poitrine* can mean chest, breast, or brisket.

poivrade [pwah-vrad]   A French sauce, usually for game, of MIREPOIX cooked in butter with game trimmings, reduced with crushed peppercorns and herbs, moistened with the marinade and vinegar, demi-glace and game essence added, then strained and finished with butter.

poivre [PWAH-vruh]   French for pepper; *grain de poivrade* is peppercorn; *poivré*, pungent or spicy; *poivron* or *poivre de la Jamaïque*, allspice. See also POIVRADE.

Pökel [PEU-kel]   German for pickle.

pokeweed   A leafy plant, usually considered a weed, that grows wild in the eastern United States; only the young leaves and shoots are edible, and they are cooked like spinach and asparagus.

polenta [pō-LEN-tah]   Coarse-ground cornmeal and also an Italian pudding made from the meal, eaten as a peasant porridge or more often cooled, sliced, and fried, grilled, or baked with various other foods. Polenta is a specialty of Venice and northeastern Italy, where natives hold it in special regard; Marcella Hazan has written that "to call polenta a cornmeal mush is a most indelicate use of language."

pollame [pōl-LAH-may]   Italian for poultry.

pollo [PŌL-lō]   Italian and Spanish for chicken; in Italian, *pollo ruspante* means free-range chicken; *pollastrino*, spring chicken. In Spanish, *pollo a la chilindrón*, chicken braised in a sauce of sweet red peppers, tomatoes, onions, and a little garlic and ham.

pollock [POL-ik]   A North Atlantic member of the cod family, usually marketed at 4 to 10 pounds although it grows larger; the flesh is delicate and similar to cod and cooks white, but considered less desirable due to the gray color of its raw flesh, so sometimes marketed as "Boston bluefish"; called saithe or coley in Britain.

polo [PŌ-lō]   In Persian cuisine, rice cooked with other ingredients.

polonaise, à la [ah lah pō-lō-NEZ]   In French cuisine, "Polish style": vegetables, especially cauliflower or asparagus, cooked and sprinkled with chopped hard-boiled egg, bread crumbs, parsley, and melted butter.

polpetta [pōl-PET-tah]   Italian for meat patty, croquette; *polpettone* is meat loaf, *polpetta* is meatball.

polpo, polipo, polipetto [PŌL-pō]   Italian for squid or octopus; in Spanish the word is *pulpo* or *pulpetto*; in French, *poulpe*.

Polsterzipfel [PŌL-ster-zip-fel]   An Austrian jam-filled turnover.

pomace [POH-mus]   The fruit pulp remaining after all of the juice has been pressed out; refers particularly to apple or grape pulp in the making of cider or wine.

pomegranate [POH-meh-gra-nit]   A small tree native to the Middle East with red or gold leather-skinned fruit whose interior chambers hold many edible seeds embedded in white pith, hence its name "seedy apple"; the crimson juice in the seed sacs is refreshingly acid and is used for various savory and sweet dishes, especially in the Middle East, as well as for GRENADINE; the many seeds of the fruit probably account for its part in ancient fertility rites. Pomegranate molasses is a Middle Eastern flavoring of the juice mixed with lemon juice and sugar and reduced to a thick, dark, tangy, aromatic syrup (not to be confused with grenadine).

pomelo [POH-meh-lō]   The largest member of the citrus family, native to Malaysia and similar to the grapefruit, with a thick coarse skin; it is fibrous and sweet, with a dry pulp; also called shaddock, after Captain Shaddock, an English ship commander who is said to have brought the seed from the East Indies to Barbados in 1696. Also spelled pummelo.

Pomerol [poh-mayr-ōl]   A wine-producing area in Bordeaux, just northwest of Saint-Emilion, whose velvety wines have a fullness, warmth, and depth of flavor.

Pommard [poh-maahr]   A commune in Burgundy between Beaune and Volnay, producing a quantity of red wine especially popular in the United States and England, some of them very fine.

pomme [pohm]   French for apple.

pomme de terre [pohm de tayr]   Potato (literally "apple of the earth"); often abbreviated to *pomme*, especially for certain potato preparations, such as *pommes frites*, but not to be confused with apple; *pommes frites* are French fried potatoes (often shortened to *frites*), as are *pommes Pont-Neuf*, originally sold on the Pont Neuf over the River Seine in Paris.

pommes Anna [pohm AN-nah]   A French dish of layered potato slices baked with butter in a special casserole; brown and crisp on the outside, soft on the inside.

pommes château   In French cuisine, potatoes cut into small ovals and sautéed in butter.

pommes paille [pohm pī]   Deep-fried potato "straw."

pomodoro [pō-mō-DOR-ō]   Italian for tomato (literally "golden apple"), so named because the first tomatoes in Europe, in the sixteenth century, were yellow.

pompano [POHM-pah-nō]   A silvery fish found off the southeastern U.S. coastline in the Atlantic Ocean and Gulf of Mexico; its rich white meat is a delicacy that can be cooked in many ways; often *en papillote* with shrimp and crab.

Pont-l'Evêque [ponh-l'eh-vek]   A soft, uncooked, and unpressed cheese made from whole or partially skimmed raw cows' milk, from Normandy; this washed-rind cheese has a rich creamy texture and taste, a full aroma, and a square golden rind.

Pont-Neuf   See POMME DE TERRE.

poo   Thai for crab; *poo cha* means steamed and fried crab cakes.

poor knights of Windsor   Sliced stale bread soaked in sherry, dipped in egg batter, fried in butter, and served with sugar and cinnamon; a British version of French toast.

popcorn   Certain varieties of corn with a high protein content and specific moisture content; with dry heat the corn kernel explodes, and the endosperm swells into the light and crisp American snack known as popcorn.

pope's nose   The tail piece of a bird; also known as "parson's nose."

popone [pō-PŌ-nay]   Italian for melon.

popover   A puffed-up hollow muffin made from an eggy batter like that of YORKSHIRE PUDDING, baked in muffin tins, and served hot with butter; American in origin.

poppy seed   The dried seed of the opium poppy, blue-black, brown, or yellow depending on origin, nutty in flavor with a pleasantly crunchy texture; much used in salads, creamy dishes, breads, pastry, and crackers, as well as in Middle Eastern and Indian cooking. Poppy seed oil is also used for salads.

porchetta [por-KET-tah]   Italian for roast suckling pig; the Spanish is *porcella*.

porcini [por-CHEE-nee]   Italian for the wild bolete mushroom, what the French call *cèpe*; the singular is *porcino*, meaning piglike, referring to its fat shape. *Porcini* are unusual among wild mushrooms in being safe to eat raw; they are prized for their delicious flavor.

porgy   A saltwater fish related to the BREAM; bony but with delicate moist flesh, the porgy is best barbecued or fried.

pork   The flesh of pig used for food. This omnivorous animal, domesticated from the wild boar, efficiently converts what it scavenges into meat, making it of great importance in many regions and climates, with every part used, but taboo to Jews and Muslims. Pork meat should be pale pink (darker in older animals), the fat white; to balance its richness, it is often paired with acid fruits, although it is now bred leaner. Today trichinosis is rare in the United States; meat cooked to 140°F is considered safe (lower than old cookbooks advise). The term pig designates a young animal up to about six months, when it matures into a hog. A porker is a pig bred to be eaten fresh, leaner than bacon pig. The term swine covers the whole tribe. Many pork preparations have separate entries. See also HAM, SAUSAGE, and CHARCUTERIE.

pork buns   See CHĀ SHĀO BĀO.

porridge   A cereal or grain, usually oatmeal, cooked in water or milk to a thick puddinglike consistency; sometimes flavored with salt, sugar, butter, and various other ingredients.

pòrro [POR-rō]   Italian for leek.

port   A sweet fortified dessert wine from Portugal's upper Douro Valley, shipped from Oporto (hence the name); brandy is added to partially fermented grape juice, arresting fermentation and producing a strong, sweet wine that is then matured. Vintage port is wine from exceptional years that is unblended, bottled young, and then aged for at least a dozen years. Tawny port is blended with wine from several years, aged in oak in Oporto to give it a rounder flavor and softer color, then bottled and shipped ready for sale. Ruby port is kept in wood for a shorter time to retain its color and can be blended or not. White port is made similarly but from white grapes. In France, by contrast, *porto* is drunk as an apéritif.

porter   A very dark and strongly flavored British LAGER beer in which the malt is toasted before brewing; porter is usually higher in alcohol than lager beer.

porterhouse   A superior cut of beef from the short loin next to the T-bone, with a large portion of the filet mignon and strip loin.

porto, au [ō POR-tō]   A classic French sauce of demi-glace and PORT; when *à l'anglaise*, it is a reduction of port, orange and lemon juice and zest, shallots, and thyme, strained and mixed with veal stock.

portobello mushroom   A variety of cultivated white field mushroom allowed to develop fully and renamed as a marketing ploy; its large size, earthy flavor, and firm texture work well for grilling and sautéing and as a meat substitute. Also spelled portabella, but portabello or portobella are both incorrect (that is, the a or the o pair needs to agree).

Port-Salut [por-sal-ü]   An uncooked, pressed, pasteurized cows' milk cheese from France, originally made on a small scale by Trappist monks, using unpasteurized milk (this type of cheese is now called Entrammes), but now factory-produced; similar to its cousin SAINT-PAULIN.

portugaise [por-tü-gez]   A classic French sauce of chopped onions cooked in butter or oil, with chopped tomatoes, tomato sauce, meat glaze, garlic, and chopped parsley; the garnish *à la portugaise* is stuffed tomatoes with château potatoes and *portugaise* sauce.

posset [POS-set]   An old-fashioned British punch made of milk, eggs, wine or ale, lemon juice, spices, and sugar, with whipped cream folded in; a remedy for colds as far back as the Middle Ages, posset is akin to SYLLABUB or our latter-day EGGNOG.

possum   See OPOSSUM.

postre [PŌTH-tray, PŌS-tray]   Spanish for dessert.

potage [pō-tajh]   French for soup, especially a thickened vegetable soup, but not as hearty as SOUPE; the Spanish word *potaje* means a thick soup or stew. *Potage Saint-Cloud* is a soup of puréed green peas and lettuce.

potato   A starchy tuber cultivated by the Incas in hundreds of varieties, but accepted slowly in Europe because it was thought to be toxic. Types today tend to be floury (best for boiling) or starchy (best for baking). Of the latter varieties common in the United States, the Russet Burbank, developed by Luther Burbank, is the quintessential Idaho (but rare in Europe). Of newer, mostly small, varieties available in the United States, fingerling, blue, pink, and gold types predominate, but consumers should beware generalizations on the best way to cook them, their flavor, the interior color, and whether they retain their color after cooking (steaming is best). Yukon Gold, an excellent new variety, has butter-yellow flesh, but not a butter flavor. New potatoes are young, freshly dug potatoes of any variety whose sugar has not yet turned to starch; small mature potatoes, though often called new potatoes on menus, are not. The sweet potato and yam are botanically unrelated to the potato. See also PARMENTIER.

potato flour   Flour ground from cooked potatoes, gluten-free, used in thickening gravies and soups and in breads, where it keeps the crumb moister than wheat flour; potato starch.

pot-au-feu [pō-tō-feu]   In French cuisine, meat and vegetables cooked together in water; the resulting broth is served first, followed by the meat and vegetables as the main course; this classic provincial dish can contain several different meats.

pot de crème [pō deu krem]   A small, individual covered cup that holds custard, mousse, and similar desserts; the top keeps a skin from forming on custards.

potée [pō-tay]   Originally any food cooked in an earthenware pot, now usually a thick French soup of pork and vegetables—often potatoes and cabbage.

potiron [pō-teer-onh]   French for pumpkin.

pot liquor, potlikker   The broth remaining after collard greens and vegetables have been cooked; it is nutritious and an essential part of southern African-American cooking, usually served with cornbread or corn pone.

potpie   Meat or poultry and perhaps vegetables, cut up and baked with gravy in a deep dish covered with pie crust; American in origin and ranging in quality from the ridiculous to the sublime.

pot roasting   A method of braising food (usually large cuts of meat) slowly in a tightly covered pot; the food is browned in a little fat and cooked with some stock or other liquid and vegetables over low heat until tender.

pot stickers   See GUŌ TIĒ.

potted shrimps   In British cooking, small shrimps shelled, warmed in clarified butter, seasoned with mace or nutmeg, and preserved in the butter for a few days; served as an hors d'oeuvre with brown bread.

Pouilly-Fuissé [pooy-yee-fwee-say]   A popular French white wine from southern Burgundy, just west of Mâcon, made from the Chardonnay grape; it is dry, clean, fresh, and fruity, with a lovely bouquet.

Pouilly Fumé [pooy-yee fü-may]   A French white wine produced from the Sauvignon Blanc grape in the village of Pouilly-sur-Loire; dry, pale, fresh, with a slightly "smoky" (*fumé*) quality; similar to its neighbor Sancerre but no relation to Pouilly-Fuissé.

poularde [poo-laahrd]   French for a fat hen or chicken—a "roaster"—over four pounds in weight.

poule-au-pot [pool-ō-pō]   POT-AU-FEU including a sausage-stuffed chicken, made famous by Henri IV's perhaps apocryphal remark that he wanted every household in France to have *poule-au-pot* on Sunday; the chicken is a plump hen, even though *poule* means stewing chicken.

poulet [poo-lay]   A young spring chicken—a "fryer" or "broiler"—weighing up to about four pounds; *poule* means a stewing chicken, one that is too old for other treatment; *poulet d'Inde*, a turkey.

Pouligny-Saint-Pierre [poo-lee-nyee-sinh-pyayr]   A French goats' milk cheese, uncooked and unpressed, from Berry; soft, crumbly, and pyramid-shaped.

poultry   All domestic fowl, excluding game birds.

pound cake   A type of cake originally made with one pound each of flour, butter, sugar, and eggs and baked in a loaf pan; there are now many variations of it.

pourriture noble [poor-ee-tür NŌ-bluh]   French for NOBLE ROT.

pousse [poos]   French for rise, as in a first rise for yeast pastry.

pousse café [poos ka-fay]   French for "push the coffee," a postprandial drink to accompany coffee; in the United States the term means an after-dinner drink of several cordials in a narrow glass carefully poured in thin layers, one on top of the other with the heaviest at the bottom, so that with their different specific gravities they remain in layers; a drink popularized in New Orleans in the late nineteenth century.

poussin [poo-sinh]   French for a very young chicken.

Powidl [PŌ-vee-dl]   A special Austrian plum preserve used for pastries and puddings.

pozole [pō-ZŌ-lay]   A thick Mexican soup, almost a stew, made of pork, hominy, and large white dried *cacahuazintle* corn kernels, and served with a hot chili sauce.

praline [pra-leen]   Almonds, or in America often pecans, in a caramel syrup or coating; in French cooking, praline is usually crushed and added to confections; named after the seventeenth-century French maréchal du Plessis-Praslin, duc de Choiseul, whose chef created this preparation; the adjective is *praliné*.

pra ram long song   A Thai dish of sliced beef and greens simmered with onions and spices in coconut milk.

prawn A crustacean similar to the shrimp, strictly speaking, but the term is used loosely for any large shrimp.

Preiselbeer [PRĪ-sel-bayr] German for a red berry similar to the cranberry.

Premier Cru [preu-myay crü] For French Burgundy wine, the next to highest classification of vineyards, usually including the name of the vineyard's commune as well as the name of the vineyard itself. For Premier Cru wines from Bordeaux, see CLASSED GROWTH.

pré-salé [pray-sa-lay] French for lamb and mutton from coastal Normandy that graze on saltmarsh meadows (hence the name), giving their flesh a special salty flavor much prized.

preserved lemons See LIMUN IMMALLAH.

pressure cooker A covered pot that, because it is under pressure, can cook food above the boiling point, saving time and energy. Pressure cookers are suitable for any food cooked by moist heat, such as soup, stock, stew, pudding, and preserves, but generally not for meat. A safety valve keeps the cooker from exploding in case of malfunction.

pretzel A brittle, savory biscuit made from a flour and water paste that is formed into a rope and twisted into a knot, sprinkled with coarse salt, briefly boiled in water, then baked like its relative the bagel. The pretzel is associated with German cooking but goes back to Roman times: the word *pretzel* is derived from the Latin *bracchioli*, meaning arms. The characteristic knot represents folded arms, perhaps originally for prayer or supplication. In Europe, unlike the United States, this association is kept, for the pretzel is always pictured right side up as folded arms.

prezzemolo [PRET-say-MŌ-lō] Italian for parsley, which in Italy is the flat-leafed variety.

prickly pear An edible cactus, native to Mexico, with a spiny exterior and soft interior flesh, brilliant and variously colored, eaten fresh or sometimes cooked; the fruit is shaped like a pear and tastes rather sweet and mild; also called Indian fig; even when debarbed, beware of needles.

prik [pik] Thai chilies of all sorts; *prik thai* means black pepper; *saus prik*, bottled chili sauce.

primavera, alla [ah-lah pree-mah-VAYR-ah] In Italian, literally "spring style"; dishes so garnished, especially pasta, include raw or blanched spring vegetables—the Italian version of à la PRINTANIÈRE.

prime   Top-quality beef graded by the U.S. Department of Agriculture—the top 10 percent of beef cattle, available mostly in restaurants and special outlets, but not generally sold in retail markets.

primeur [pree-meur]   French for early or forced fruit or vegetables; also first or new wine, as in Beaujolais Nouveau.

princesse, à la [ah lah prinh-ses]   A classic French garnish of asparagus tips with sliced truffles in cream sauce; also artichoke bottoms stuffed with asparagus tips, served with NOISETTE potatoes.

pringar [PREEN-gar]   In Spanish, to baste.

printanière, à la [ah lah prinh-ta-nyayr]   In French, literally "spring style"; the classic garnish consists of new carrots, turnips cut into olive shapes, peas, small green beans, and asparagus tips.

prix fixe [pree feeks]   French for the set price for a complete meal, as opposed to *à la carte.*

processed cheese   Cheese produced by a technique developed in the early twentieth century: green and aged cheeses, often of different varieties and qualities, are finely ground and blended. Emulsifiers are mixed in before the cheese is pasteurized to arrest ripening, and it is packaged in plastic while still hot. Certain kinds of acid, salt, preservatives, coloring, spices, water, and other additives may also be used.

profiteroles [prō-fee-tayr-ōl]   In French cuisine, choux pastry puffs with a sweet or savory filling; see also CROQUEMBOUCHE and gâteau SAINT-HONORÉ.

prosciutto [prō-SHOO-tō]   Fresh Italian ham cured by salting and air-drying but not generally by smoking; the name implies that it is *crudo* (uncooked), although *prosciutto cotto* (cooked) is also made; ham from Parma, where pigs are fed the Parmigiano whey, is especially fine and somewhat sweet in flavor.

provençal [prō-venh-sal]   In the style of Provence; the classic sauce consists of chopped tomatoes sautéed in olive oil with garlic, parsley, and a pinch of sugar; the garnish *à la provençale* means small tomatoes with stuffed mushrooms and parsley.

Provence [prō-venhs]   A region in southern France east of the Rhône on the Mediterranean; garlic and olive oil are the basis of its pungent cuisine, and the sunny region abounds with herbs, vegetables, and seafood, not unlike its neighbor Italy.

Provolone [prō-vō-LŌ-nay]   A cooked and kneaded spun-curd cheese made from cows' milk, originally from southern Italy; Provolone is made in many versions, shapes, and sizes, and is matured either briefly or up to two years; when two to three months old, its color and flavor are buttery and pale; when aged and pungent, used for grating.

prugna [PROO-nyah]   Italian for plum; *pruna* and *prugna secca* both mean prune.

prune [prün]   French for plum; *pruneau* means prune.

pub   Short for public house, the British term for a tavern or bar.

puchero [poo-CHAYR-ō]   Spanish for pot; *puchero de gallina* is a special dish of braised stuffed chicken with a sauce of chicken livers; in the Mexican Yucatán, *puchero* is a hot pot including various meats, vegetables, legumes, and even fruit, with the broth served first, followed by the solids.

pudding   A thick, soft dish or preparation containing some kind of thickening, usually sweet; in Britain, a general term for dessert, but sometimes a savory dish, because of its derivation from *boudin*, meaning sausage, where chopped meat and a cereal are stuffed in a casing or mold and boiled.

pudim flan [POO-deem flahn]   The Portuguese version of caramel custard, richer and thicker than the Spanish.

pudina [poo-DEE-nah]   Mint, in Indian cooking.

puerco [PWAYR-kō]   Spanish for pig, pork.

puerro [PWAYR-ō]   Spanish for leek.

puffball   A type of wild mushroom, sometimes very large, that is delicious sliced, sautéed, or diced and cooked in various ways that allow the flesh to absorb flavors.

Puffer [POO-fer]   German for pancake, fritter.

puff pastry   See PÂTE FEUILLETÉE.

puits d'amour [pwee d'a-moor]   In French, a "wishing well": a small round pastry with sweet filling of pastry cream, jelly, or fruit.

pulao [poo-LOW]   An Indian rice dish with vegetables or meat and spices cooked together with water, vegetable, or meat stock; less elaborate than BIRYANI; also spelled *pilau* or *pilao*; see also PILAU.

Puligny-Montrachet [poo-lee-nyee-monh-ra-shay]   A village in the Burgundian Côte de Beaune which, with its neighbor Chassagne-Montrachet, produces excellent dry white wine, almost all from the Chardonnay grape.

pullet   A young hen under one year old.

pulpeta [pool-PAY-tah]   Spanish for meat loaf.

pulse   The edible seeds, usually dried, of leguminous plants such as peas, beans, lentils, and chickpeas; respected by the ancients and virtually all cultures since for their nutritional importance; see also LEGUME.

Pultost [POOL-tohst]   A Norwegian cooked cows' milk cheese, soft and rindless, often flavored with caraway and eaten year-round.

pummelo   See POMELO.

pumpernickel   A dark, coarse-textured, slightly sour bread made from unbolted RYE flour; originally from Westphalia, Germany.

pumpkin   The orange winter squash or gourd, *Cucurbita pepo*, a New World native that ripens in fall in time to give Americans their Halloween jack-o'-lanterns and Thanksgiving pies; unfamiliar varieties are colored white, peach, blue, and aqua. The pumpkin's size can range from petite to huge, like an 816-pound monster grown in Nova Scotia in 1990 (as reported by *National Geographic World*). The best eating pumpkins are small, 2 to 5 pounds, with deep-orange, fine-textured flesh. In other parts of the world, pumpkin's gastronomic tradition is surprisingly wide in sweet, savory, and spicy dishes.

puntarelle [puhn-tah-REL-lay]   A wild chicory whose spears are cut into long thin strips, placed in cold water to curl them, then dressed in a lemony garlicky vinaigrette with anchovies or served tangled with pasta strands; this bitter green vegetable is a specialty of Rome and Latium and heralded early each spring.

Punt e Mes [PUHNT ay MAYS]   An Italian apéritif, amber-colored and orange-flavored.

purée [pü-ray]   French for food that is mashed, very finely chopped, or pushed through a sieve to achieve a smooth consistency.

puri [POO-ree]   An Indian whole-wheat bread deep-fried in GHEE and puffed; also spelled *poori*.

purloo [per-LOO]   Rice cooked with vegetables and seasonings, from the Carolinas and southern United States, derived from pilaf.

purslane   A once-popular herb with small fleshy leaves, now considered a weed except by the French, who eat it fresh in salad and boiled or sautéed like spinach; in its native India it is used more widely.

Puter [POO-ter]   German for turkey.

puttanesca [poo-tah-NES-kah]   Italian pasta sauce "in the style of the prosti-tute," that is, quick, pungent, and satisfying: with garlic, anchovies, black olives, capers, parsley, and tomatoes.

Puy, lentilles de [lenh-teey deu pwee]   Small, dark green LENTILS, from the French town of Puy, considered the best type of lentil because of their earthy flavor; they also hold their shape well in cooking.

pyramide [peer-a-meed]   The generic French term for chèvre, or fresh goats' milk cheese, uncooked and unpressed, shaped in a small truncated pyramid; this type of cheese is very white, soft, crumbly, and delicate in flavor, becom-ing sharper if allowed to mature; it is sometimes covered with vegetable ash to keep it from drying out.

Q

qabili [kah-BEE-lee] In Afghan cooking, a PILAU made with carrots cut into julienne, raisins, almonds, and pistachios, served at weddings and special celebrations.

qarawah bil hummus [KAH-rah-wah bee HUH-mus] In Arab cooking, calves' feet with chickpeas, widely eaten.

qdra [KUH-drah] A Moroccan TAJIN, often with chicken, cooked with SAM-NEH, onions, pepper, saffron, and lemon juice; with many variations.

qrut [kroot] In Afghan cooking, drained yogurt that has dried into firm curds.

quadrucci [kwah-DROO-chee] In Italian cooking, "little squares" of egg pasta for chicken or meat broth.

quaglia [KWAH-lyah] Italian for quail.

quahog [KŌ-hog] A large hard-shelled North Atlantic clam found off the New England coast; firm and meaty, usually eaten raw, like medium-size cherrystones or small littlenecks, or in chowder; the very large ones with heavy shells once used for wampum are particularly good for chowder or stuffed with a bread-crumb mixture.

quail   A small migratory white-meat game bird (two or three per serving) relished for its delicious flavor; there are many varieties the world over, but since wild quail are becoming scarce, those that we eat today are mostly farm-bred; cooked without hanging.

Quark [kvark]   A soft, runny, acid-curd cows' milk cheese from Germany made from skimmed or partially skimmed milk. Quark is a type of cottage cheese and is eaten with fruit or salad or used in cooking; originally central European and also spelled quarg or kvarg. It is known as topfen in Austria and widely used in such pastries as *Topfen Schnitten* and *Topfen Strudel*.

Quartirolo [kwar-teer-Ō-lō]   A soft, uncooked, pressed, whole-milk cow's cheese from Lombardy in Italy; similar to TALEGGIO but cured in caves where it acquires a mushroomy flavor. Quartirolo is square, with a thin washed rind, the paste smooth, pale, and creamy; it is still made by traditional small-scale farmhouse methods.

quasi de veau bourgeoise [ka-zee deu vō boor-jhwahz]   In French cuisine, veal chump or hind end braised in a casserole with pork, calf's foot, and vegetables.

quatre-épices [ka-tr'ay-pees]   A French mixture of "four spices": finely ground ginger, clove, nutmeg, and white pepper; a descendant of the elaborate spice mixtures used to flavor savory and sweet food in the Middle Ages.

quatre-quarts [KA-truh-KAAHR]   A classic French pound cake, made of "four quarters," that is, equal parts of egg, butter, flour, and sugar.

queen of puddings   A British bread-crumb and custard pudding base baked with strawberry or raspberry jam covering, then topped with meringue and lightly browned in the oven.

Queensland nut   See MACADAMIA NUT.

queijo [KAY-hō]   Portuguese for cheese.

quenelle [keh-nel]   A light dumpling made of seafood, chicken, game, or veal forcemeat bound with eggs; although quenelles were once quite large, now they are usually small ovals, like light MOUSSELINES, poached in simmering water or broth and served with a creamy or buttery sauce.

quesadilla [KAY-sah-DEE-yah]   A Mexican tortilla turnover filled with a savory stuffing and toasted or fried.

queso [KAY-thō, KAY-sō]   Spanish for cheese; *queso blanco* is the fresh, smooth, rindless cows' milk cheese made throughout Latin America. It is an acid-curd cheese made from whole or partially skimmed milk, pressed, salted, and eaten fresh with fruit or matured for two or three months.

quetsch [kvech]   A variety of plum made into tarts and other confections but best known for the clear colorless EAU DE VIE or liqueur distilled from it in Alsace.

queue de boeuf [KEU de BEUF]   French for OXTAIL.

quiche [keesh]   A French custard tart, usually savory, from Alsace and Lorraine. In the United States it has come to mean quiche lorraine, which is filled with eggs, cream, bacon, and (more recently) GRUYÈRE, but the variations are infinite; from the German word *Kuchen*.

quick bread   Any bread or muffin made with a quick-acting leavening agent, usually baking powder or baking soda.

quimbombo [keem-BOHM-bō]   OKRA, much used in Cuban and Caribbean cooking and showing its African roots; from the Bantu word *quingombo* for okra.

quince   A tree indigenous to Persia, whose fruit may be the golden apple of antiquity. Popular throughout the temperate world until the last century or so, especially for pies and preserves (because of its high amount of PECTIN), it is now largely ignored except in the Middle East. Long, slow cooking and generous amounts of sugar bring out the quince's mellow flavor and amber color. The plural is quinces.

quinoa [KEEN-wah]   The seed of a South American plant used as a staple, like grain, since the Incas. Light in texture, it is cooked like rice but should be rinsed first to remove any residual soponin covering, a natural bitter substance; when cooked, quinoa's tiny pearls reveal the spiral germ.

Quitte [KVIT-eh]   German for QUINCE; *Quittengelee* is quince marmalade.

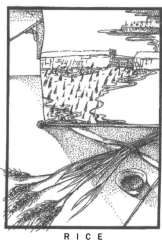

RICE

R

raan Indian roast leg of lamb in a spicy yogurt marinade, Kashmiri-style.

rabadi [RAH-bah-dee] Thickened, reduced milk, in Indian cooking.

rábano [RAH-bah-nō] Spanish for radish.

rabattage [ra-ba-tajh] French for deflating the dough in yeast pastrymaking.

rabbit A small member of the HARE family, both wild and domesticated, whose pale flesh can vary in flavor depending on its age and diet but does not need hanging; leaner and sweeter than chicken, rabbit is cooked in similar ways, especially braised.

rabbit, Welsh See WELSH RAREBIT.

râble de lièvre [RA-bluh deu LYEV-ruh] French for SADDLE of hare.

rabri [RAHB-ree] In Indian cuisine, sweetened milk boiled until condensed and thickened into a cream, flavored with rosewater and sprinkled with pistachios.

Rachel [ra-shel] In French cuisine, garnished with bone marrow and accompanied by BORDELAISE sauce; for TOURNEDOS.

racine [ra-seen] French for root vegetable.

rack A cut of lamb or veal from the rib section, with tender and flavorful meat; can be kept whole, cut into seven rib chops, or made into crown roast.

racking   Drawing off clear wine from one barrel or vat to another, leaving the sediment.

Raclette [ra-klet]   A family of Swiss cheeses whose name comes from the French verb *racler*, to "scrape"; half a large wheel of cows' milk cheese is placed near the fire, melting the rich, buttery cheese, which is scraped onto a plate and eaten with boiled potatoes *en chemise* (in their jackets), pickled onions, and gherkins. It is similar to GRUYÈRE and a specialty of the Valais region of the Swiss Alps; see also WALLISER.

radicchio [rah-DEEK-kyō]   Italian for all members of the chicory family that share a bitter edge of flavor that turns mellow with cooking. In the United States, the Chioggia variety is the most familiar, with round shape, red and white leaves, and crunchy texture; the tapered Treviso and milder, creamy-yellow Castelfranco are less well known. All radicchio is excellent raw in salads and, slow to wilt, for garnishing; braising reveals a subtler, mellower side of its character.

radis [ra-dee]   French for radish.

radish   The root of a plant in the mustard family with crisp flesh and peppery taste. The color, size, and shape of a radish can vary widely, from the familiar small red table radish, to the large turniplike black radish, to the 1½-foot-long white DAIKON of Japan. Americans neglect the radish, usually nibbling it raw, whole, sliced, or shredded, in salads, but in Asian cuisine it is eaten in myriad ways, raw, cooked, and pickled, often the leaves or sprouts too. Some radishes have separate entries.

rafano [rah-FAH-nō]   Italian for horseradish.

raffinade [ra-fee-nad]   French and German for refined sugar.

rafraîchir [ra-fresh-eer]   In French, to "refresh" boiling vegetables by plunging them into cold water to halt cooking and retain color; to chill.

ragoût [ra-goo]   A French stew of meat, poultry, or fish, which may contain vegetables; a ragoût literally "restores the appetite."

Ragoût fin [ra-GOO FINH]   In German cooking, a delicate combination of organ meats such as sweetbreads and brains, cooked with mushrooms in a winy cream sauce; often served in a puff pastry shell.

ragù alla bolognese [rah-GOO ah-lah bō-lō-NYAY-say]   An Italian meat sauce from Bologna and not a stew or ragoût as commonly thought; often used for pasta. Ground beef and sometimes pork and ham are sautéed in butter and oil with chopped vegetables and simmered with milk, white wine, and tomatoes.

Ragusano [rah-goo-ZAH-nō] A spun-curd cows' milk cheese from Sicily, cooked, kneaded, and sometimes smoked, rectangular in shape. This delicate and sliceable table cheese is matured for three months or, for a firm, sharp grating cheese, up to twelve months.

Rahm German for cream.

raidir [ray-deer] To sear, in French.

raie [ray] French for skate.

raifort [ray-for] French for horseradish.

Rainwater A general term for a very pale dry MADEIRA developed by an American in the early nineteenth century.

raisin A dried grape; also French for grape [ray-zinh]; *raisin sec* means raisin. Among types of raisins are currants from Zante, the small black Corinth grape; "golden raisins" and dark raisins from Thompson seedless; Sultanas, Muscatel, Malaga, and others. Old World raisins are usually sun-dried; California raisins are often treated with sulfur dioxide.

raita [RĪ-tah] In Indian cooking, vegetables, raw or cooked, or sometimes fruits mixed with yogurt, to accompany spicy dishes.

rajas [RAH-hahs] Poblano or other chili strips, fried with onions and sometimes potatoes or tomatoes, in Mexican cooking.

rajma [RAHJ-mah] Red kidney beans, in Indian cooking.

rallado [rah-YAH-dō] Spanish for grated.

ramen [rah-men] Japanese soup noodles.

ramequin [ram-kinh] French for a small flameproof dish, a ramekin; also a small cheese tart.

ramp A wild leek with dark green leaves that looks like lily of the valley, with a purple stem and white bulb. Raw ramps taste stronger than leeks and smell stronger still, with an odor that lingers, but gentle cooking tames them somewhat. This Appalachian spring favorite is found in woods from Canada to the Carolinas and west to Minnesota, with West Virginia the center of their celebration.

rampion A plant, cultivated or wild (but rarely eaten today), whose leaves are eaten like spinach and whose roots, also either raw or cooked, taste like SALSIFY.

ranchero [rahn-CHAY-rō] Spanish for country style; *salsa ranchero* combines tomatoes, serrano chilies, garlic, and onion into a hot and spicy sauce known best in *huevos rancheros*, but also served with meat.

rapa [RAH-pah]   Italian for turnip.

rape   A member of the genus *Brassica* (cabbage) whose seeds yield an oil used for salad and frying (mostly in India and increasingly in Europe) and for blending in margarine; it is sometimes confused with its cousin *colza* (see CANOLA OIL). The young leaves and shoots can be braised as a vegetable but are mostly used for fodder. In southern Italy, the tender leaves and stems are savored, especially as a robust accompaniment to ORECCHIETTE. See also BROCCOLI RABE.

rapé [rah-PAY]   Spanish for monkfish, angler.

râper [ra-pay]   In French, to grate, especially cheese; the adjective is *râpé*.

rapeseed oil   See CANOLA OIL.

rapini   See BROCCOLI RABE.

Rapunze [ra-PUHN-tseh]   German for LAMB'S LETTUCE, *mâche*; in Grimm's fairytale of Rapunzel, the pregnant mother's craving as she looks onto the witch's garden outside her window sets the tale in motion.

rarebit   See WELSH RAREBIT.

ras el hanout [RAHS el ha-NOOT]   A celebrated Moroccan spice blend, literally "top of the shop," of 20 or more spices, herbs, and aphrodisiacs, varying from one individual merchant to another; used in meat and other savory and sweet dishes.

ras gulas [rahs GOO-lahs]   Indian cream cheese balls made from PANEER and semolina; they are slowly simmered in cardamom syrup until they puff up and become spongy.

rasher   British for a slice of bacon.

ras malai [ras MAL-ī]   Indian dessert balls similar to RAS GULAS, but served with RABRI.

raspberry   The ruby red berry of the genus *Rubus*, whose geneology is as tangled and thorny as its canes; a composite fruit, each little seed sack surrounds a central core from which the ripe berry slips. The cultivated red raspberry is the best known of this group, which includes the perfumed black raspberry and the sweet yellow raspberry, whose color ranges from gold to amber or blush, an old fruit recently revived. The BLACKBERRY is a raspberry cousin. These berries cross easily, often accidentally; hybrids are the LOGANBERRY, BOYSENBERRY, youngberry, olallieberry, tayberry, tummelberry, and cloudberry. The raspberry's intense sweet and acid flavor makes it a favorite fruit, fresh and cooked, in sweet and savory dishes, and it appears often in French cuisine.

ratafia [rah-TAF-yah]   A liqueur flavored by infusion with the kernels of certain fruits, such as peaches and apricots; a favorite homemade Victorian cordial. In Great Britain, the word also means MACAROON.

ratatouille [ra-ta-TOO-yah]   A vegetable stew from Provence of diced eggplant, tomatoes, zucchini, green peppers, onions, and garlic all cooked in olive oil; there are many variations, and it can be eaten hot or cold.

räuchern [ROY-shayrn]   To smoke, in German; smoked is *geräuchert*.

Rauenthal [ROW-en-tal]   A village in the German Rheingau that produces perhaps the best Rhine wines: fruity, elegant, with a characteristic spiciness.

ravanèllo [rah-vah-NEL-lō]   Italian for radish.

rave [rav]   French for turnip; *petite rave* is a radish.

ravigote [ra-vee-gōt]   A classic French cold sauce of vinaigrette with capers, chopped onions, and herbs; as a classic sauce served hot, it is a reduction of white wine and vinegar with VELOUTÉ, shallot butter, and herbs.

ravioli [rah-VYŌ-lee]   Small pasta squares filled with spinach, ricotta, and herbs rather than meat; see also AGNOLOTTI.

raw   Uncooked, fresh; in reference to milk products, the word means unpasteurized.

ray   See SKATE.

raya [RĪ-yah]   Spanish for skate.

Reblochon [reu-blō-shonh]   An uncooked, lightly pressed cows' milk cheese made in the Haute-Savoie of France and across the Italian border. Originally made with the undeclared second milking (concealed from the owner after his quota had been collected), while the milk was still warm, it is a rich, soft, and delicately fruity cheese shaped in a disc and with a golden rind.

recette [reu-set]   French for recipe, receipt.

rechauffé [reu-shō-fay]   French for food that is reheated or made with leftovers.

récolte [ray-kōlt]   French for harvest, crop, vintage.

red bean buns   See DÒU SHĀ.

red beans and rice   A Louisiana specialty of red beans (sometimes kidney beans) and rice, cooked with ham hock; there are many variations. Louis Armstrong signed his letters, "Red beans and ricely yours."

redeye gravy   Ham gravy made with ice water or sometimes coffee and perhaps a little brown sugar; served in the southern United States for breakfast with grits and biscuits.

red flannel hash   Cooked beets fried with bacon, potatoes, and onions, and often served with corn bread; rustic American fare.

red herring   Herring salted strongly to a deep red color.

red mullet   See MULLET.

red snapper   A saltwater fish from the Gulf of Mexico, usually marketed at about five pounds but sometimes much larger; there are many types of snapper, but the rosy red snapper, with white, succulent, sweet meat, is a choice delicacy cooked in many ways, often stuffed whole.

reduce   To boil down a liquid to thicken its consistency and concentrate its flavor, as in a reduction sauce; Escoffier was the first chef to thicken sauces by reduction rather than with flour or other starch.

réduire [ray-dweer]   In French, to reduce.

Réforme, à la [ah lah ray-form]   Lamb chops coated with bread crumbs, fried, and garnished with julienne of ham, truffles, carrots, and hard-boiled egg whites, with a POIVRADE sauce; created by Alexis Soyer for the Reform Club in London.

refried beans   Cooked pinto beans, mashed and fried with garlic, often for a tortilla filling; of Mexican-American origin. See also FRIJOLES.

régence, à la [ah lah ray-jhenhs]   Garnished with quenelles, truffles, foie gras, and cockscombs, if for sweetbreads or chicken, or with oysters and roe, if for fish—a classic French garnish.

Regensburgerwurst [RAY-gens-boor-ger-voorst]   A short, fat German sausage of pork and beef.

Reh [ray]   German for venison; *Rehrücken* is SADDLE of venison, and also an oblong chocolate cake garnished with almonds.

reiben [RĪ-ben]   In German, to grate or rub; a *Reibschale* is a mortar.

reine, à la [ah lah REN]   French for "queen's style," garnished with chicken in some form; named after Louis XV's queen.

Reis [rīs]   German for rice.

relâcher [reu-lash-ay]   In French, to thin a sauce or purée with liquid; literally, to relax or loosen.

relevé [reu-lev-ay]   French for highly seasoned.

religieuse [reu-lee-jhyeuz]   French for nun because the pastry's shape resembles the hooded habit; a small cream puff tops a large one, each filled with CRÈME PÂTISSIÈRE, glazed, and decorated with buttercream.

relleno [rel-LAY-nyō]   Spanish for stuffing, stuffed.

rémol [RAY-mōl]   Spanish for BRILL.

remolacha [reh-mō-LAH-chah]   Spanish for beet.

rémoulade [ray-moo-lad]   Mayonnaise seasoned with mustard, anchovy essence, chopped gherkins, capers, parsley, chervil, and tarragon—a classic French sauce.

remuage [reu-mü-ajh]   In making Champagne, the daily shaking and turning of the bottles, nearly upside down, to bring the sediment down to the cork before the *dégorgement* (see DÉGORGER).

Renaissance, à la [ah lah reu-nes-sanhs]   Various spring vegetables arranged separately around a large roast—a classic French garnish.

render   To melt fat, thus clarifying the drippings to use in cooking or flavoring.

rennet   The stomach lining of an unweaned calf, kid, or lamb, containing rennin and other enzymes that coagulate milk; in cheesemaking, rennet extracts are used to curdle milk. There are also vegetable rennets with the same property.

renverser [renh-vayr-say]   In French, to unmold or turn out onto a serving dish.

repollo [reh-POHL-lō]   Spanish for cabbage.

repos [reu-pō]   French for repose or rest, as for resting dough in pastrymaking.

res [rays]   Spanish for beef.

reserva [ray-ZAYR-vah]   A designation for Spanish wine that has met specific aging requirements: for red wine, three years, including one in oak; for white and rosé, two years, including six months in oak; *gran reserva* is longer still.

réserve [ray-zayrv]   French for aged wine, but without a legal definition.

resserrer [reu-sayr-ay]   In French, to "tighten" or pull a sauce together by thickening it.

retsina [RET-see-nah, ret-SEE-nah]   A Greek white or rosé wine with a small amount of Aleppo pine resin added at the beginning of fermentation to impart its characteristic turpentine flavor; an acquired taste; served very cold with Greek food; its popularity in Greece is diminishing.

Rettich [RET-ish]   German for radish.

revenir [reu-ven-eer]   In French, to brown, as for meat *(faire revenir)*.

Rheingau [RĪN-gow]   A white-wine district in Germany where the Rhine flows east-west for twenty miles between Mainz and Rüdesheim; the southern-facing slopes produce the finest German wines, mostly RIESLINGS, which have separate entries.

Rheinpfalz [RĪN-pfalts]   A wine-producing region in Germany, also known as the Palatinate, west of the Rhine and northeast of Alsace-Lorraine; the vineyards are on the slopes of the Harz Mountains.

Rhine [rīn]   A major river flowing northwest to the North Sea through western Germany; along the slopes and those of its tributaries, especially the Nahe and the Mosel, most German wine is produced; spelled *Rhein* in German.

Rhône [rōn]   A major river flowing west from Switzerland through Lake Geneva and south through France into the Mediterranean; along the slopes many wine grapes are grown, most notably those in France between Lyons and the sea, for Rhône wines; some of these have separate entries.

rhubarb   Native to southeastern Russia, this leafy vegetable is cultivated for its thick reddish stalks, which are used in pies and compotes and occasionally in savory sauces. The leaves are poisonous because of their oxalic acid, but the astringent stalks are made palatable for "fruit" desserts with sugar and brief cooking.

rib   A section of beef from the top forequarter comprising the most tender steak and roast cuts, including the Delmonico, rib-eye, rib steak, and rib roast.

ribes [REE-bays]   Italian for gooseberry, currant.

rib-eye steak   A cut of beef from the rib section, virtually the same as a Delmonico except that the rib-eye has been further trimmed of fat.

ribollita [ree-bōl-LEE-tah]   A hearty Italian soup of white beans, vegetables, bread, cheese, and olive oil, from Florence; usually served reheated, hence the name.

rib roast   A cut of beef from the forequarter, between the chuck and loin; this seven-rib cut is often divided into three parts, the first cut of which, partially boned, becomes the "prime ribs" of a standing rib roast.

rice   A grain native to India and probably the world's most important food crop, especially in Asia, where it has been cultivated for millennia. The thousands of varieties divide into long-grained rice, which separates into distinct kernels when cooked, and short-grained rice, which is higher in starch, wetter, and stickier when cooked. In the milling process, removal of the hull produces brown rice. Removal of the bran and most of the germ produces unpolished rice. To reduce spoilage, removal of the outer aleurone layer produces polished rice. Converted rice (parboiled) has been steamed and dried before milling for higher nutritional content and easier processing. "Instant" rice grains have been partially cooked and split open, with loss of flavor and nutrition. See also WILD RICE.

rice   Used as a verb, to force cooked fruits or vegetables, especially potatoes, through an instrument with small perforations, so that the food resembles grains of rice; the tool is called a ricer.

rice wine   Distilled from fermented rice and made in many varieties, qualities, and strengths, rice wine is far less common in China than it used to be. Saké, sherry, Scotch whisky, or dry vermouth can be substituted for rice wine in cooking. The Chinese is *mí jiǔ*.

Richelieu, à la   [ah lah REE-she-LYEU]   Garnished with stuffed tomatoes and mushrooms, braised lettuce, château potatoes, and veal stock—a classic French garnish for meat.

ricotta   [ree-KOHT-tah]   Literally "recooked" in Italian, ricotta is strictly speaking not a cheese; ricotta is made from the leftover whey from other cheeses, either ewes' or cows' milk, and is sometimes enriched with milk or cream. As the whey is heated, the cloudy top layer is skimmed off and drained to make the cheese. Bland, slightly sweet, and dry, ricotta is eaten fresh or cooked in pasta and vegetable dishes and sweet desserts.

Riesling   [REES-ling]   A superlative white-wine grape variety probably native to the Rhine Valley, where it has been cultivated since Roman times; it has floral aromas and fruity notes balanced with crisp acidity, can be either dry or sweet, with the ability to mature well and long. Riesling is grown nowhere in France other than Alsace, but it is grown in Germany, Austria, northern Italy, Czechoslovakia, and Switzerland; also in California, the Pacific Northwest, Ontario, New York State, Australia, New Zealand, and South Africa. It is fortunately subject to NOBLE ROT.

rigaglie   [ree-GAL-yay]   Italian for giblets.

rigatoni   [ree-gah-TŌ-nee]   Italian fat-ribbed macaroni, commercially made.

rigodon   [ree-gō-donh]   A brioche custard tart filled with bacon, ham, nuts, or puréed fruit, served either warm or cold; a specialty of Burgundy.

rijsttafel [RĪS-tahf-el]   Literally "rice table," this is the elaborate colonial Dutch version of the Indonesian rice table, with many side dishes. The various offerings in the buffet include meat and seafood dishes, savory fried and steamed foods, SATÉS, sauces, vegetable salads, rice, fruit, and chili dishes—hot and cool, spicy and bland—in profusion.

rillettes [ree-yet]   In French cuisine, pork cubed and cooked with its fat and herbs, then pounded in a mortar and potted; goose, duck, and rabbit are sometimes prepared similarly. *Rillauds* and *rillons* are the same but are not pounded.

Rind [rint]   German for beef; *Rinderbraten* is roast beef, *Rinderbrust,* brisket of beef, *Rindertalg,* beef suet, *Rindswurst,* beef sausage.

riñones [ree-NYŌ-nayth]   Spanish for kidneys.

Rioja [ree-Ō-hah]   A wine region in northern Spain where many dry red and white wines are made, some quite good, others ordinary.

ripièno [ree-PYAY-nō]   Italian for stuffed or filled; stuffing.

Ripp   German for rib; *Rippenbraten* is roast loin, *Rippenspeer,* rib of pork, *Rippenstück,* a chop.

ris de veau [ree deu vō]   French for veal sweetbreads; *ris d'agneau* are lamb sweetbreads.

riserva [ree-ZAYR-vah]   Italian term for wine that is aged longer, usually in barrels, before it is released for sale.

rishta [REESH-tah]   In Arab cooking, fresh egg noodles, like Italian pasta. In Tunisia, *rishta* is a peasant soup of chicken, chickpeas, and thin flat noodles.

riso [REE-zō]   Italian for rice; *risi e bisi* is a very thick soup, almost a risotto, of rice and spring peas cooked in broth with onion, parsley, and Parmesan—a Venetian specialty served at the Doge's banquet on St. Mark's Day.

risotto [ree-ZOHT-tō]   Italian for a dish of starchy short-grain rice cooked in butter and or olive oil with a little chopped onion to which stock is gradually added as it is absorbed; all manner of savory foods—vegetables, mushrooms, seafood, beef marrow, sausage—can be added. Varieties of short-grain rice such as ARBORIO or CARNAROLI give the proper texture, tender and creamy but never sticky. *Risotto milanese* is flavored with SAFFRON, a classic accompaniment to OSSO BUCO; the plural is *risotti.*

rissoler [ree-zō-lay]   In French to brown in hot fat; *rissolé* refers to food, such as potatoes, that has been fried thus; a *rissole* is a puff-pastry turnover or fritter that is stuffed, often with ground meat, and deep-fried.

ristra [REE-strah]   Spanish for chili pods tied together in a festoon for hanging and drying.

riz [reez]   French for rice; *riz à l'impératrice* is rice pudding flavored with vanilla, crystallized fruit soaked in Kirsch, and custard cream.

riz au djon-djon [rees ō jonh-jonh]   A Haitian dish of rice cooked with tiny flavorful black mushrooms.

roast   To cook food by baking it in hot dry air, either in an oven or on or near a fire or hot stones; by extension, the noun roast is a large piece of meat that has been roasted.

Robert [rō-bayr]   A classic French sauce of sautéed onions reduced with white wine and vinegar, demi-glace added, and finished with mustard.

Robiola [rō-BYŌ-lah]   A soft, uncooked, and unpressed cheese from northern Italy; in Lombardy, cows' milk is used and the cheeses are shaped in rectangles, while in Piedmont either ewes' or goats' milk is used, perhaps mixed with cows', and the cheeses are shaped in discs. Robiola is named for its reddish thin rind; the interior paste is smooth and even.

robusta [rō-BOO-stah]   A species of coffee bean, hardy, prolific, and high in caffeine, but with a flavor inferior to that of ARABICA; used mostly for commercial blends and instant coffee.

Rock Cornish game hen   See CHICKEN.

rocket   See ARUGULA.

rockfish   A large family of saltwater fish in the Pacific, sometimes mistakenly called red snapper or rock cod; the firm, lean, delicate flesh is versatile and is especially appreciated by the Chinese.

rodaballo [rō-dah-BAL-lō]   Spanish for turbot.

roe   Fish or shellfish eggs, ranging from the humble cod all the way to beluga caviar; the male milt is sometimes euphemistically called soft roe. Some of these have separate entries; see also CAVIAR.

roebuck   Male roe deer; venison.

Roggenbrot [ROHG-en-brōt]   German for rye bread.

roghan josh [RŌ-gahn JŌSH]   A rich and spicy Muslim lamb dish from northern India, red in color; served with rice.

rognons [rō-nyonh]   French for kidneys; *rognonnade de veau* is saddle of veal with kidneys attached. In Italian the word is *rognoni*.

rognures [rō-nyür] French for trimmings, especially in making PÂTE FEUIL-LETÉE, useful for certain kinds of pastry; also called *demi-feuilletage*.

roh [rō] German for raw; *Rohkost* means raw vegetables or crudités.

rohat lokum [rō-HAHT lō-KOOM] Turkish for "Turkish delight," the luxurious confection flavored with mastic, orange- or rosewater, and almonds or pistachios.

Rohwurst [RŌ-voorst] A German sausage cured and smoked by the butcher, eaten uncooked.

rojak [rō-jak] A Malaysian salad of cucumbers, pineapple, chilies, and shrimp paste.

rolé [rō-LAY] Italian for a slice of meat stuffed and rolled; *rollatini* are small rolls; in Spanish the word is *rollo*.

rollmop See HERRING rollmop.

roly-poly pudding A British nursery pudding of suet or biscuit-dough crust, spread with jam, rolled up, and baked or steamed.

romaine lettuce A variety of lettuce with long, thick central stems and narrow, green leaves; also called cos lettuce.

Romano See PECORINO ROMANO.

Romanoff, strawberries A French dessert of strawberries macerated in orange-flavored liqueur and garnished with crème CHANTILLY.

romarin [rō-maahr-inh] French for rosemary.

romesco, salsa [rō-METH-kō, THAHL-thah] A classic Spanish sauce for fish, from Catalonia, of crushed tomatoes, chilies, garlic, hazelnuts, and almonds, with olive oil and vinegar.

Roncal [rōn-KAL] A ewes' milk cheese from the Navalle Valley in Spain, similar to MANCHEGO but smaller and harder; the texture is close-grained, the flavor pungent.

ropa viejo [RŌ-pah VYAY-hō] "Old clothes," a classic Cuban dish of beef hash in tomato sauce; the beef is first used to make broth, hence the name.

Roquefort [rōk-for] An ancient and celebrated French blue cheese made from the milk of Larzac sheep; the curd from the raw, uncooked milk is molded, salted, and injected with *Penicillium roqueforti*, then matured for three months in limestone caves in the Languedoc town of Roquefort-sur-Soulzon, whose fissures naturally provide the proper humidity and ventilation. The six-pound round cheeses have a thin orange rind, an ivory paste with blue-green veining *(persillage)*, and a salty and sharp but still creamy taste that is unique.

roquette [rō-ket]   French for rocket; see also ARUGULA.

rosbif [rōs-beef]   French for roast beef.

rosé [rō-zay]   French for wine made from black grapes with some of the skins included during fermentation, thus producing its characteristic color; rosé is best drunk young and served chilled. The Italian word for rosé is *rosato*.

rose hips   The fruit of certain roses, which turn red with ripeness. High in vitamin C and pectin, they are used for making syrup and jelly.

rosemary   A shrub native to the Mediterranean, whose needlelike leaves are used fresh and dried as an herb, especially with pork, lamb, veal, and game. Its name means "dew of the sea," although often mistakenly thought to mean "rose of the Virgin Mary." To the ancient Egyptians it symbolized death, to the Greeks and Romans it meant love.

Rosenkohl [RŌZ-en-kōl]   German for Brussels sprouts.

rosewater   An extract distilled from water steeped with rose petals, which impart their essential oil; this extract is used as a flavoring in the Middle East, the Balkans, and India.

Rosine [rō-ZEE-neh]   German for raisin.

rosmarino [rōz-mah-REE-nō]   Italian for rosemary.

Rossini   A classic French garnish of foie gras, sliced truffles, and demi-glace, usually for tournedos; named after the nineteenth-century opera composer and gastronome Gioacchino Rossini.

rossl [ROH-sel]   Fermented beets, traditional for Passover BORSCHT.

Rostbraten [ROST-brah-ten]   In northern Germany, roast beef; in Bavaria and Austria, a thin steak quickly cooked with onions and gravy.

Rostbratwurst [ROST-braht-voorst]   German ham sausage seasoned with caraway and nutmeg, roasted over a wood fire.

Rösti [REU-stee]   Potatoes (sometimes with onions) grated and fried in a pancake, from Switzerland.

roti [RŌ-tee]   The generic word for bread in Indian cooking; also another word for CHAPATI. In Guiana and the Caribbean, *roti* means a wheat pancake with curried meat or fish filling; of Indian origin.

rôti [rō-tee]   French for roasted, a roast; a *rôtisserie* is a broiling device with a motorized spit for roasting large pieces of meat and birds; a *rôtisseur* is the cook responsible for roasting in a large kitchen.

Rotwein [RŌT-vin]   German for red wine.

ròu [rō]   Chinese for meat, generally pork unless otherwise specified; the Cantonese is *yuk.*

rouelle [roo-el]   French for a round slice of meat.

rouennaise [roo-enh-nez]   BORDELAISE sauce with a reduction of red wine and shallots, finished with puréed raw duck livers—a classic French sauce.

rougail [roo-gī]   A spicy chutney of apples, tomatoes, peppers, onions, and other vegetables, ginger, and spices, slowly cooked; a French Creole dish from the Indian Ocean, served with rice and other foods.

rouget [roo-jhay]   French for red mullet.

rouille [roo-eey]   A spicy red pepper and garlic mayonnaise from Provence, served with fish soups.

roulade [roo-lad]   French for a rolled slice of meat or piece of fish filled with a savory stuffing; the term can also mean a sheet of sponge cake or the like spread with a suitable filling, rolled up, and perhaps garnished.

Roulade [roo-LAH-deh]   German for stuffed rolled beef.

rouleau [roo-lō]   French for rolling pin.

round   A cut of beef from the hindquarter, comprising the hind leg; the top and bottom round, eye of round, and top sirloin (sirloin tip) are lean subdivisions that can be further cut into steaks or left whole and braised or roasted.

roux [roo]   French for a mixture of flour and butter or other fat, usually in equal proportions, cooked together slowly and used to thicken sauces and soups. A white roux is heated long enough to cook the flour but not color it and is used for BÉCHAMEL and VELOUTÉ sauces. A blond roux is allowed to color slightly during cooking. A brown roux, which may use a clarified fat other than butter, is cooked slowly for a long time so that it acquires a rich flavor and mellow brown shade to color the sauces it thickens. The word *roux* means reddish or reddish brown.

rowanberry [RŌ-an-bayr-ee]   The fruit of the mountain ash tree, which ripens in the fall. The berries are used to make a bright red, tart jelly often served with lamb, venison, and other game; in Alsace an EAU DE VIE is made from the berries.

royale [rwah-yal]   French for unsweetened custard, possibly flavored, cooked in a mold and then cut into decorative shapes; used to garnish clear soups.

royale, charlotte   See CHARLOTTE.

royal icing   Icing used for pastry-writing, decorating, and glazing Christmas cookies or wedding cakes; made from confectioners' sugar, egg white, and a little lemon juice.

royan [rwah-yanh]   French for fresh sardine.

roz   Moroccan for rice.

Rübe [RÜ-beh]   German for turnip, rape; *Weisserübe* is turnip; *Roterübe*, beet; *Gelberübe*, carrot.

rucchetta [roo-KET-tah]   Italian for rocket; see also ARUGULA.

Rücken [RÜ-ken]   German for saddle.

rucola [ROO-kō-lah]   Italian for rocket; see also ARUGULA.

Rüdesheim [RÜ-des-hīm]   A small town on the western end of the Rheingau, opposite the mouth of the Nahe, on whose steep slopes excellent RIESLING wines are produced.

rue   An herb with bitter flavor used by the ancients for medicinal purposes but now used only as a flavoring for *grappa* and little else.

rugalach [ROO-ge-lukh]   A rich small pastry in a rolled crescent shape, traditionally filled with raisins, nuts, cinnamon, and the like, baked for Hanukkah; also spelled rugelach.

rugola   See ARUGULA.

Rührei [RÜ-rī]   German for scrambled eggs.

rump   A cut of beef from the round, usually braised or roasted; unboned, it is a standing rump roast, while boned, it is a rolled rump roast.

ruote [roo-ō-tay]   Italian wheel-shaped pasta.

rusk   Bread sliced and baked again slowly until crisp and golden brown, such as ZWIEBACK.

russe, à la [ah lah RÜS]   French term for food served sequentially course by course, hot from the kitchen, as opposed to all of the dishes for a service being laid out on the table in a large and elaborate display *(service à la francaise)*. This Russian style of service gradually overtook the older French style in the early nineteenth century and survives today, greatly simplified.

russe, charlotte   See CHARLOTTE.

rustica, alla [ah-lah ROO-stee-kah]   An Italian spaghetti sauce of anchovies, garlic, oregano, and Pecorino cheese.

rutabaga [ROO-tah-BAY-gah]   A yellow or Swedish turnip; the British term is swede.

ruz   Arabic for rice.

rye   A grain native to central Asia and invaluable because of its hardiness in poor soils, in cool climates, and at high altitudes; it has long been the favored flour of northern and eastern Europe. Because it does not form GLUTEN well, rye and wheat flours are often mixed together for bread. In the United States it is also used for making WHISKEY and for fodder. See also PUMPERNICKEL.

ryori [ryō-ree]   Japanese for food, cooking.

SAUCISSE

S

saag [sahg]   Greens or spinach, in Indian cooking.

Saankäse [ZAHN-kay-zeh]   A cooked, pressed, hard Swiss cheese made from cows' milk from two successive milkings; it is made into large orange discs, aged up to five years, and prized as a dessert or grating cheese for its mellow, fragrant flavor.

Saar [zahr]   A German tributary of the Mosel River whose vineyards produce white wine that is legally Mosel but with an austere quality of its own.

saba   Japanese for mackerel.

sabayon [sa-bi-yonh]   The French version of ZABAGLIONE, in which various wines or liqueurs can be substituted for Marsala.

sablé [sa-blay]   French shortbread from Normandy whose high sugar and butter content account for its "sandy" texture; shaped into various forms and thicknesses. *Pâte sablée* is similar to PÂTE SUCRÉE.

sabzi [SAHB-zee]   Mixed vegetables, in Persian cooking, also Afghan.

saccharin   A noncaloric sugar substitute, far sweeter than sugar but with a bitter aftertaste; discovered in the late nineteenth century, reported in the 1980s to be a carcinogenic agent, but in 2000 the FDA dropped the charge.

Sachertorte [ZAKH-er-tor-teh]   A rich chocolate cake containing many eggs, a layer of apricot jam, and chocolate icing; created in 1832 by Franz Sacher, of the Sacher Hotel in Vienna, for Prince Metternich.

sach krourk [sahch kroork]   Cambodian for pork.

sack   The Elizabethan English word for sherry.

sacristain [sa-kree-stinh]   French for a strip of *pâte feuilletée* sprinkled with cheese or chopped almonds and sugar, twisted into a spiral, and baked; so named for its resemblance to a corkscrew (the *sacristain* is responsible for uncorking the Communion wine).

saddle   A cut of meat extending along the hindquarters from the end of the ribs to the legs on both sides.

sadza [SAHD-zah]   A dumpling of maize or red millet flour, served with stews or roasts, fish, or vegetables, the national dish of Zimbabwe; *sadza ndiuraye*, a spicy stew including beef, potatoes, cabbage, tomatoes, and chilies.

safflower   A thistlelike plant, also called Mexican saffron, whose seeds yield oil and whose flowers yield an orange dye; the oil is light in flavor and high in polyunsaturates with a high smoke point.

saffron   The deep orange dried stigmas of a particular crocus, which must be gathered by hand, hence the spice's exorbitant price. Since ancient times and in many cultures, saffron has been used as a medicine, aphrodisiac, dye, and spice; it colors and flavors such classic dishes as RISOTTO MILANESE, PAELLA, BOUILLABAISSE, and KULICH.

Saft [zahft]   German for juice, syrup; gravy, sauce.

sage   A perennial herb with gray-green leaves, used since ancient times for medicinal and culinary purposes; it is used especially, though with discretion, in cooking pork and goose.

Sage Derby [DAR-bee]   DERBY cheese flavored and marbled with sage; aged nine months or more, it is flaky and mild, considered one of England's most distinctive cheeses; also called Derby Sage.

sago [SAY-go]   A starch extracted from the stem of an Asian palm tree and used for thickening puddings and occasionally soups; similar to TAPIOCA, sago is formed into pearly beads.

Sahne [ZAH-neh]   German for cream; *Sahnenkäse* means cream cheese; *Sahnenkuchen* is a cream tart or cake.

saignant [sa-nyanh]   French for rare, as in meat; literally, "bleeding."

saigneux [sa-nyeu]   French for neck of veal or lamb.

Saint-Cloud, potage   See POTAGE.

Sainte-Maure [sinht-mohr]   A French goats' milk cheese, uncooked and un-pressed, from the town of the same name in Touraine, also Poitou; cured for three weeks, the cheese is log-shaped with a white soft smooth paste and a white bloomy rind.

Saint-Emilion [sinht-ay-meel-yonh]   A small town overlooking the Dordogne Valley of Bordeaux celebrated for its many fine red wines, especially the rich full châteaux wines. Saint-Emilion is also the varietal name of the Trebbiano grape in Cognac.

Saint-Estèphe [sinht-es-tef]   A wine commune at the northern tip of the Haut-Médoc producing solid, full-bodied, robust wines, less delicate than that of some of its neighbors; besides its classed growths, its *crus bourgeois* are also excellent.

Saint George's agaric   A wild field mushroom, found in Europe in spring and autumn.

Saint-Germain [sinh-jhayr-minh]   In French cuisine, with fresh peas; *potage Saint-Germain* is a thick purée of fresh peas.

Saint-Honoré, gâteau [ga-to sinh-tohn-ohr-ay]   A French pastry dessert, created by French chef Chiboust: a crown of choux puffs on a base of *pâte brisée* filled with *crème Chiboust*, the whole topped with caramel. Saint Honoré is the pa-tron saint of bakers.

Saint-Jacques   See COQUILLE SAINT-JACQUES.

Saint John's bread   See CAROB.

Saint-Julien [sinh-jhü-lyinh]   A wine commune in the Haut-Médoc of Bor-deaux, just south of Pauillac, overlooking the Gironde River; its red wines are of consistently fine quality, well-balanced and smooth.

Saint-Malo [sinh-ma-lō]   A classic French white sauce for fish, flavored with mustard, shallots, and anchovy essence.

Saint-Marcellin [sinh-maahr-sel-linh]   An uncooked and unpressed French cheese from the Isère Valley, made in farmhouses from goats' milk and in fac-tories from mixed milk; ripened for two weeks, it is disc-shaped with a smooth paste and delicate bloomy rind.

Saint-Nectaire [sinh-nek-tayr]   An unpasteurized cows' milk cheese, uncooked and pressed, from the French Auvergne; the flat rounds are cured up to two months for a dark pinkish rind and creamy smooth interior, with good melting properties.

Saint-Paulin [sinh-pō-linh] A French uncooked, pressed cows' milk cheese made from whole pasteurized milk; it is large and round, with a smooth yellow rind and even mild paste. A descendant of Port-du-Salut and similar to Port-Salut, Saint-Paulin is widely made.

Saint-Pierre [sinh-pyayr] French for John Dory.

saisir [say-zeer] In French, to sear.

sakana [sah-kah-nah] Japanese for fish.

saké [sah-kay] Japanese rice wine, sweet or dry, usually drunk warm in small cups and also used for cooking; sake (without the accent mark) means salmon.

sa lach dia [shah lat dyah] Vietnamese "table salad," a presentation of herbs, sliced fruits, and vegetables in the middle of the table, with rice cakes; an important part of the Vietnamese meal, served with meat and dipping sauce.

salamander A gas oven with a top element for quickly glazing or browning dishes, used in restaurant kitchens.

salambo [sal-amh-bō] A French oval choux pastry filled with kirsch-flavored crème pâtissière and glazed with caramel.

salami An Italian sausage, infinitely variable in ingredients, seasoning, shape, and method, and long made in many countries other than Italy. Salami is usually made of pork meat and fat, sometimes with beef, veal, or other meats, fairly highly seasoned, and cured as long as six months; its name derives from its being salted.

salata khudar mishakal [sah-LAH-tah khoo-DAHR mis-SHAH-kul] In the Middle East, a mixed vegetable salad, with vegetables chopped and dressed with vinaigrette.

Salbei [ZAL-bī] German for sage.

salchicha [sahl-CHEE-chah] Spanish for sausage.

salé [sal-ay] French for salted or pickled; *petit salé* means salt pork; *salaison*, salting. The Italian word for salt is *sale* (no accent mark), the Spanish *sal*.

saleem [sah-lim] A liquid dessert with thin tapioca noodles, from Thailand.

salep [SAH-lep] In Turkey and Greece, a root used to make a sweet, refreshing milk drink of the same name; the Arab word is *sahlab*.

salicornia [sal-i-KOR-nyah]   A plant that grows along the seacoast, also called glasswort and sea bean, among other names; wild and cultivated, it is eaten fresh or lightly cooked; often confused with SAMPHIRE.

Salisbury steak   A patty of lean chopped beef broiled and seasoned; devised by the nineteenth-century dietician Dr. James H. Salisbury to avoid supposedly unhealthy fermentation in the digestive tract.

Sally Lunn   A rich, sweet yeast bun or bread, apochryphally named after the woman who first sold them in Bath, England, in the late eighteenth century.

salmagundi [SAL-mah-GUN-dee]   A British mixed dish, really a salade COM-POSÉE, including greens, chopped meats, hard-boiled eggs, pickles, anchovies, onions, and perhaps other vegetables, all carefully arranged and dressed.

salmi   A French dish made from leftover or partially roasted feathered game, finished in a wine sauce; also spelled *salmis*.

salmon [SA-mun; the L is not pronounced]   A beautiful silvery fish that is spawned in fresh water before migrating to the sea, returning several years later to its original upstream waters to spawn, thus completing its life cycle. Salmon meat ranges from very pale to deep orange red, depending on species and habitat. In the United States, the sockeye turns deep red before spawning and, excellent canned, is commercially important; the king or chinook is largest and its flesh color varies; the smaller coho, or silver salmon, is good for canning; the chum, or dog salmon, is paler and leaner, important in Canada; the humpback swims in the northern Pacific and is important to Asia. The northern Pacific and Atlantic Oceans provide feeding grounds for marine salmon, in addition to landlocked salmon. Because of overfishing, farmed salmon is now common. The firm, rich, flavorful meat—before spawning—lends itself to varied culinary preparations, simple or elaborate; cured salmon is a great delicacy; the specific types have separate entries.

salmonella   Bacteria that cause food poisoning from tainted water or food, especially chicken or eggs; for most people the symptoms—including vomiting, fever, diarrhea, and chills—pass within several hours or a few days, but for the very old, very young, and those with weak immune systems it can be fatal.

salmonete [thahl-moh-NAY-tay]   Spanish for red mullet.

salmon trout   See SEA TROUT.

salpicão [sahl-pee-KOW]   Portuguese for smoked ham roll.

salpicon [sal-pee-konh]   In French cuisine, one or more ingredients cooked separately, cut into fine dice, and bound with a sauce; often used as a filling or garnish, like MIREPOIX. ALLUMETTES cut across into small cubes make *salpicon*.

salpicón [thal-pee-KŌN, sal-pee-KŌN]   In Spanish cooking, a mixed salad of cooked seafood, or possibly meat, with vegetables.

salsa [SAHL-sah, THAAL-thah]   Italian and Spanish for sauce; this is also the general name for hot sauces in Mexican-American cooking; see also SUGO. *Salsa mexicana cruda*, literally "fresh Mexican sauce," is made of tomatoes, onions, and chilies (preferably serranos), chopped and mixed together with water; much used in Mexican cooking, with regional variations.

salsify [SAHL-si-fee]   A plant whose long white tapered root is eaten boiled or sautéed; also called oyster plant, though its resemblance in flavor to oyster requires a vivid imagination. Scorzonera, with its black-skinned root, is very similar.

salt   Sodium chloride, a basic taste, used since before human memory to preserve food. Among various types, table salt is highly refined, sometimes iodized to prevent hypothyroidism. Kosher salt is coarse and irregular in flake, without additives, to meet Jewish laws. Sea salt is seawater evaporated by sometimes ancient methods (called *gros sel* in French; *fleur de sel* is a particular type). Rock salt is less refined salt, used as a bed in baking certain dishes and for freezing ice cream. Pickling salt is fine-grained, without additives, for quick dissolving. *Sanchal* is a black salt used in northern India. See also MONOSODIUM GLUTAMATE.

saltare [sal-TAR-ay]   To sauté, in Italian; literally "to jump."

salt cod   See COD.

salteña [sahl-TAY-nyah]   A Bolivian EMPANADA with cheese fillings.

saltimbocca [sal-teem-BŌK-kah]   An Italian veal scallop with a sage leaf and a thin slice of prosciutto laid on top, braised in butter and Marsala or white wine; this dish, whose name means "jump in the mouth," comes from Rome.

saltpeter, saltpetre   Potassium nitrate; used in small quantities to preserve meat, saltpeter gives flavor and imparts a reddish color.

salt pork   A layer of fat in pork belly that is salted but not smoked; used as a flavoring and generally blanched first, to remove some of the salt, in old-fashioned American dishes such as baked beans.

salty duck eggs   See XIÁN YĀ DÀN.

salumeria [sal-oo-mayr-EE-ah]   An Italian delicatessen.

salvia [SAL-vyah]   Italian for sage.

Salz [zalts]   German for salt; *Salzegebäck* is a salty biscuit or pretzel.

samak [sah-MAK]   Arabic for fish.

samaki wa nazi [sah-MAH-kee wah NAZ-ee]   A Tanzanian fish curry with coconut.

sambal [SAHM-bahl]   A very hot and spicy side dish, often a sauce, several of which accompany the main dish; from Indonesia and Southeast Asia.

sambar [SAHM-bar]   A vegetarian dish from southern India of peas or lentils and vegetables, often with rice; *sambar* spice is a very hot spice mix with mustard oil. Also spelled *sambhar*.

sambuca [sahm-BOO-kah]   An Italian liqueur flavored with elder and anise.

samneh [SAHM-neh]   In Arab cooking, fresh sweet butter that is cooked, clarified, salted, and aged, or sometimes washed and kneaded with spices and herbs and then aged; often, but erroneously, described as rancid. Also called *smen*.

samosa [sah-MŌ-sah]   A triangular savory pastry filled with vegetables or meat spiced with curry or chilies; from India and Pakistan.

samphire [SAM-fīr]   A plant that grows wild along the rocky Mediterranean and European coastline; its crisp leaves are eaten fresh in salads, cooked as a vegetable, and pickled; also called sea fennel and *herbe de Saint Pierre* (its English name is a corruption of the latter). An unrelated plant, SALICORNIA, is sometimes called samphire.

samsa [SAM-sah]   A Tunisian pastry triangle of BRIK leaves stuffed with ground almonds, geranium water or rosewater, and orange zest; then deep-fried, brushed with lemon syrup, and sprinkled with sesame seeds.

Samsø [SAHM-seu]   A whole-milk cows' cheese from the Danish island of Samsø; cooked and pressed, the large, round, firm cheese is golden yellow with scattered holes and a nutty, mild, but not bland taste; widely used in Denmark.

sanbusak [sahn-BOO-zahk]   A Middle Eastern tartlet of minced meat with pine nuts, onions, and cinnamon in a thin yeast dough, popular in Syria, Lebanon, and Egypt.

Sancerre [sanh-sayr]   A town perched on a hill overlooking the Loire Valley in central France; its white wine is agreeably fresh and flinty, not unlike the Pouilly-Fumé produced nearby, also from the Sauvignon Blanc grape; light reds and rosés from the Pinot Noir grape can also be good.

sanchal [SUN-chahl]   A black salt used in the cooking of northern India, with a distinctive flavor; also called *kala namak*.

sanchocho [sahn-CHŌ-chō]   A South American soup of beef or sometimes another meat or seafood with vegetables; a type of boiled dinner.

sandre [sahn-druh]   French for a freshwater fish, a kind of pike, delicate in flavor.

Sangiovese [sahn-jō-VAY-say]   A very good Italian red-wine grape variety planted widely in Tuscany; made in several styles, reaching greatness in Chianti Classico and others.

sangría [thahn-GREE-ah, sahn-GREE-ah]   A Spanish punch, literally "bleeding," of red wine, a little brandy, soda water, sugar, and sliced orange or lemon and other fruit; a cool refreshing drink for warm weather.

sangue, al [ahl SAHN-gway]   Italian for rare, as for steak.

San Pedro [thahn PAY-drō]   Spanish for John Dory.

San Simon [thahn THEE-mon]   A cows' milk cheese from northwest Spain, semihard, rather bland, pear-shaped, and often smoked.

Santa Claus melon   See WINTER MELON.

santen [sahn-ten]   Indonesian for coconut.

sān xiān shā guō miàn [sahn shyen shah gwoh mee-en]   A seafood hot pot or casserole with noodles, a Chinese banquet dish cooked in a traditional earthenware sandy pot.

Saône [sah-ōn]   A tributary of the Rhône River, joining it at Lyons, France, where the Beaujolais is said to be the third river.

sapsago   See SCHABZIEGER.

saracen corn   See BUCKWHEAT FLOUR.

Sarah Bernhardt   In French cuisine, garnished with purée of foie gras, named for the celebrated actress; there are many other dishes named for her.

sardine   A young herring, pilchard, or sprat varying widely in species and treatment; usually brined, cooked, and canned in oil, but excellent cooked fresh.

sarsaparilla [sahr-sah-pah-RIL-ah]   A carbonated drink made from the dried root of smilax, a South American plant in the lily family, a kind of root beer.

sashimi [sah-shee-mee]   Literally "fresh slice," in Japanese this really means raw fish expertly sliced according to the particular variety and served with garnishes, condiments, and sauces.

sassafras   See FILÉ POWDER.

saté [sa-TAY] In Indonesian cooking, pieces of meat or seafood marinated in a spicy sauce, skewered, and grilled; usually served with a peanut sauce; also spelled *satay*.

satsuma See MANDARIN.

sauce From the Latin word meaning salted, sauce includes all liquid seasonings for food and a few that are not liquid. Carême organized the many French sauces into families with four mother sauces: ESPAGNOLE, VELOUTÉ, ALLEMANDE, and BÉCHAMEL, with emulsified sauces, such as MAYONNAISE, forming the fifth group. *Saucier* means the chef responsible for sauces in a large kitchen.

saucisse [sō-sees] French for fresh sausage; *saucisson* is a cured sausage, usually large; see also SALAMI.

Sauerbraten [ZOWR-brah-ten] In German cooking, top round of beef marinated in red wine and vinegar, beer, or buttermilk, then braised, and sometimes served with dried fruit and nuts or other spicy or fruity accompaniments; *sauer* means sour.

sauerkraut [ZOWR-krowt] Shredded white cabbage pickled in brine and flavored with onion and juniper berries—a classic accompaniment to a wide variety of German dishes; the French word is CHOUCROUTE.

sauge [sōjh] French for sage.

saumon [sō-monh] French for salmon.

Saumur [sō-mür] A French town and wine region on the south bank of the Loire River producing a variety of wines, including sparkling wines.

saunf [sownf] Fennel, in Indian cooking.

sausage A general term for chopped meat, often pork, with fat, blood, liver, possibly mixed with other meats or food such as cereal, seasoned, and usually stuffed into a casing; eaten fresh, smoked, or dried. What began as a way of using up scraps from a freshly slaughtered animal has evolved into an art— what the French call *charcuterie*; many sausages have separate entries.

saus prik See PRIK.

sauter [sō-tay] To cook food quickly in butter or other hot fat, stirring to brown it evenly; in French, *sauter* literally means "to jump." A *sauté* is a dish that has been cooked thus; *sauteuse*, a shallow sauté pan with sloping sides; *sautoir*, a shallow pan with straight sides.

Sauternes [sō-tayrn] A French village south of Bordeaux whose five surrounding townships produce the white dessert wine of the same name. Sauternes grapes are late-harvested for their high sugar content and NOBLE ROT, resulting in a very sweet but natural wine: fruity, intense, buttery, golden, and long-lived. Sauterne (without the final s) is altogether unconnected—a meaningless California term for medium sweet white wine.

sauvage [sō-vajh]   French for wild, uncultivated, undomesticated.

Sauvignon Blanc [sō-vee-nyonh blanhk]   An important white-wine grape variety, planted widely in the Loire Valley, especially Sancerre (where it is known as Blanc Fumé), Graves, Sauternes (with the Sémillon grape), and most successfully New Zealand; new plantings everywhere.

savarin [sa-va-rinh]   A ring-shaped BABA filled variously with crème CHANTILLY, CRÈME PÂTISSIÈRE, or fresh fruit; this French pastry is named after the gastronome Brillat-Savarin.

Savoie, biscuit de   See BISCUIT DE SAVOIE.

savory   Food that is not sweet; in Britain, where it is spelled savoury, it is the last dinner course after pudding (dessert), consisting of sharply flavored, salty little dishes intended to cleanse the palate for port—a custom favored by Victorian and Edwardian gentlemen. Savory is also an herb in the mint family known since Roman times and used traditionally with beans, meat, and poultry.

savoyarde, pommes à la [pohm ah lah sav-wah-yaahrd]   In French cuisine, "in the style of Savoie"; potatoes cooked à la DAUPHINOISE, but with bouillon instead of milk; *savoyarde* generally means with cheese and potatoes.

saya-éndō [sah-yah-en-dō]   Japanese for snow pea.

sayur [sah-yoor]   An Indonesian dish of vegetables in broth or stew.

Sbrinz [zbrints]   A whole-milk cows' cheese made immediately after milking, cooked, and pressed; it is an ancient cheese, originally Swiss but now made elsewhere. Hard, grainy, and yellow, Sbrinz is aged six to twelve months or longer and mostly used as a flavorful grating or cooking cheese or slivered into curls to accompany wine.

scald   To heat a liquid, usually milk, to just below the boiling point, when small bubbles form around the edge. For vegetables and fruit, to scald means to blanch.

scallion   A young, undeveloped onion of no particular variety, with long green shoots; sometimes called spring onion or green onion.

scallion pancakes   See CŌNG YÓU BǏNG.

scallop   A bivalve mollusk in a fluted open-fan shell whose large edible adductor muscle quickly opens and closes it for propulsion; in Europe, the pink roe is also eaten. The two types are the scarcer bay scallop (very small, sweet, tender; this includes the fine Nantucket scallop) on the northeast American coast, and the deep-water sea scallop, 1½ inches across, less tender but still excellent. The small Mexican calico scallop, from deep water, is sometimes confused with the bay scallop. Scallops are cream to pink or coral in color, depending on habitat; they should not be soaked in water before sale. See also COQUILLE SAINT-JACQUES. Another meaning of the word scallop is a collop or escalope of meat—a thin slice possibly flattened by pounding.

scaloppina di vitello [scah-lop-PEE-nah dee vee-TEL-lō]   Italian for veal scallop, properly cut across the grain from a single muscle, top round, so that there are no separations.

Scamorza [skah-MOR-zah]   A whole-milk cows' cheese, sometimes mixed with ewes' milk; this spun-curd cheese is similar to MOZZARELLA but firmer, also sometimes smoked. The cheeses are tied near the top in pairs with string or raffia, hence the name, which means "beheaded" in southern Italian dialect.

scampi [SKAHM-pee]   Italian for saltwater crayfish found in the Adriatic and a favorite dish in Venice; pale in color and quite large, similar to the Dublin Bay prawn, *langoustine*, and Norway lobster.

scarola [skah-RŌ-lah]   Italian for escarole.

Schabzieger [SHAHB-tsee-ger]   A Swiss skimmed-milk cows' cheese, uncooked but hard, sometimes called sapsago in the United States; it is flavored with blue melilot clover to give it a pungent flavor and green color and is shaped in truncated cones.

Scharzhofberg [SHAHRTS-hōf-bayrg]   A German vineyard on a steep slope in Wiltingen on the Saar, whose Rieslings yield a very fine white wine with bouquet, depth, freshness, and austerity.

Schaum [showm]   German for froth, foam, mousse; *Schaumrollen* are puff-pastry rolls filled with whipped cream; a *Schaumschlager* is a whisk or beater; *Schaumwein*, sparkling wine or Champagne.

scheena   See TFINA.

Scheibe [SHĪ-beh]   German for slice.

Schiava [SKYAH-vah]   A very fine red-wine grape extensively planted in the northern Italian Adige; also used as an eating grape.

Schinken [SHINK-en]   German for ham.

Schlächter [SHLEK-ter]   German for butcher; a *Schlachtplatte* is a plate of various cold meats and sausages.

Schlag, mit [mit SHLAHG]   In German, with cream; the terms *Schlagobers* and *Schlagsahne* both mean whipped cream.

Schlegel [SHLAY-gel]   German for drumstick.

Schlesisches Himmelreich [SHLEH-see-shes HIM-mel-rīkh]   Salted pork belly and dried fruits stewed together and served with dumplings; in German, literally "Silesian heaven."

Schmalz [shmalts]   German for melted fat, grease, or lard; *Schmaltzgebackenes* is food fried in lard or fat. In Yiddish, the word means rendered chicken fat.

Schmand [shmahnt]   German for sour cream.

Schnapps [shnaps]   A German version of AKVAVIT.

Schnitte [SHNIT-teh]   German for a cut or slice, chop, or steak; *Schnittlauch* means chive.

schnitz, apple   See APPLE SCHNITZ.

Schnitzel [SHNIT-sel]   German for a cutlet, slice, scallop, chop, steak; see also WIENER SCHNITZEL.

Schokolade [shō-kō-LAH-deh]   German for chocolate.

Schrotbrot [SHRŌT-brōt]   German for wholewheat bread.

Schulter [SHOOL-ter]   German for shoulder.

Schwamm [shvahm]   German for bolete mushroom.

schwarma   See KEBAB.

Schwärtelbraten [SHVAYR-tel-brah-ten]   German for roast leg of pork cooked with sauerkraut and dumplings and served with a sour cream sauce; from Silesia.

Schwarzfisch [SHVARTS-fish]   German for carp.

Schwarzsauer [SHVARTS-zowr]   A stew of goose giblets and blood stewed with dried apples, prunes, and pears.

Schwarzwald [SHWARTS-vahlt]   German for Black Forest.

Schwarzwälder Kirschtorte [SHARTS-vel-der KEERSH-tor-teh]   A rich and elaborate chocolate cake made with sour cherries, Kirschwasser, and whipped cream, from the Black Forest.

Schwein [SHVĪN]   German for pork; *Schweinebauch* is pork belly; *Schwein-braten*, roast pork, a very popular dish cooked variously according to region.

scone [skohn, *not* skōn]   A traditional Scottish cake of white flour, sometimes mixed with wholewheat flour, oatmeal, or barley, and combined with butter-milk and baking powder; the dough is usually shaped into a round and quartered or dropped onto a greased girdle (griddle) and turned.

score   To make cuts, usually parallel, in the surface of food to help it cook evenly.

scorzonera   See SALSIFY.

Scotch bonnet   An extremely hot chili pepper, a favorite in Jamaica, colored light green, yellow, or red; very closely related to the HABANERO.

Scotch broth   A Scottish vegetable soup made with lamb and barley.

Scotch whisky   Whisky distilled in Scotland from barley malt dried over peat fires, either blended (malted and unmalted) or single-malt; the latter comes only from malt made by one distillery and has a smokier, richer flavor (and commensurate expense). Whisky means "water of life" in Gaelic. That made outside Scotland and Canada is spelled whiskey (with an e).

Scotch woodcock   A British SAVORY of creamy scrambled eggs on toast with anchovies.

Scoville Heat Unit   See CHILI.

scrapple   Pork scraps, including meat, offal, and fat, boiled together, chopped, seasoned, and thickened with buckwheat and cornmeal to form a brick; slices are then fried. This Pennsylvania German specialty is derived from the West-phalian *Pannhas*.

scrod   A marketing term for young cod under 2½ pounds; schrod (spelled with an h) indicates that the fish is young haddock.

scungilli [skoon-JEEL-lee]   Italian for whelk.

sea bass   See BLACK SEA BASS.

sea bean   See SALICORNIA.

sea cucumber   See HǍI SHĒN.

sea fennel   See SAMPHIRE.

seafood   Edible saltwater fish or shellfish.

sea kale   A perennial vegetable of the mustard family that grows cultivated and wild, especially on the coasts of England, France, and northern Europe; the tender stalks are white and delicate and are cooked like asparagus.

sea moss See DULSE.

sear To cook the surface of food, especially meat, over intense high heat, in order to brown the exterior; searing does not "seal in" the juices, as is commonly thought, but it does affect flavor and texture.

sea slug See HĂI SHĒN.

sea trout A brown trout in its marine cycle, from Atlantic waters; also called the salmon trout (but no relation to seatrout), its succulent pink flesh comes from its diet of crustaceans.

seatrout See WEAKFISH.

sea urchin A spiny marine creature; the French relish it especially cut in half, the pink or orange roe scooped out and eaten raw with a little lemon juice—a delicacy also eaten in Japan, where it is called *uni*.

seaweed Marine vegetation, dried and processed, appreciated for its texture, flavor, and high nutritional value, especially in Asia; sometimes called sea vegetable. Different kinds of seaweed (which have separate entries) are made into gelatin, used in making soup stock and for wrapping sushi, drunk like tea, or simply eaten as a vegetable.

sec [sek] A wine term meaning dry, as opposed to sweet; the exception is in describing Champagne, where *sec* has come to mean sweet; the feminine is *sèche*. The Italian word is *secco*, the Spanish *seco*.

sedano [seh-DAH-nō] Italian for celery.

sediment The solid deposit that a wine naturally leaves in the bottle as it ages. In bottles of red wine, especially big or old ones, the sediment should be allowed to settle and then left behind when the wine is decanted; in white wines, the clear crystals are tasteless and harmless cream of tartar.

seehk kebab [SEEK keh-BAHB] Indian-style shish kebab.

see ji tau See SHĪ ZĬ TÓU.

Seezunge [ZAY-tsung-eh] German for sole.

sekt German for sparkling wine, traditionally all-Riesling for the best quality in Germany.

sel French for salt.

selchen [ZEL-shen] In German, to smoke or cure; *Selchfleisch* is smoked meat, often pork loin.

self-rising flour White flour to which baking powder (and salt) has already been added for convenience; used, especially in Britain, for making cakes, biscuits, and other baked goods; not appropriate for doughs that use yeast or eggs as leavening or that do not rise at all.

selle [sel]   French for SADDLE.

Sellerie [ZEL-eh-ree]   German for celery.

seltzer water   Naturally effervescent mineral water, or water made to resemble it, originally from the German village of Selters near Wiesbaden.

semifreddo [seh-mee-FRED-dō]   Italian for a chilled or frozen mousselike dessert, including cream, custard, cake, and fruit; the Spanish version is *semifrío*.

semilla [theh-MEE-yah, seh-MEE-yah]   Spanish for seed.

Sémillon [seh-mee-yonh]   An exceptional white grape variety extensively planted in southwestern France and Australia, also grown in California. Often combined with Sauvignon Blanc, it is used for Sauternes and Graves. Like the Riesling grape, it is subject, fortunately, to NOBLE ROT. In plantings outside Europe, the grape is spelled Semillon (without the accent mark).

semit [SEH-mit]   In Egyptian cooking, large yeast bread rings covered with sesame seeds, crusty on the outside, soft inside, sold on the street; the Turkish version is *simit*.

Semmel [ZEM-mel]   German for breakfast roll; a *Semmelkloss* is a bread dumpling.

semolina [seh-mō-LEE-nah]   The coarsely milled endosperm of wheat or other flour, from which the bran and germ have been removed; durum semolina, made from a special kind of hard wheat, is excellent for (commercial) pasta because it has few loose starch granules to soften the dough; other types of semolina are good for GNOCCHI and COUSCOUS.

Senf [zenf]   German for mustard.

sen mee   Thai rice vermicelli noodles; *sen mee nam gup* is noodle and pork soup.

Sercial [sayr-syal]   A type of Madeira, pale and dry; an excellent apéritif wine comparable to a *fino* sherry, named after the white grape variety.

Serra [SAYR-rah]   A ewes' milk cheese, sometimes combined with goats' milk, from the mountainous region of Portugal called Serra da Estrela; the disc-shaped cheese is creamy white with a runny center and yellow rind, but with aging it becomes pungent, hard, and crumbly.

serrano [sayr-RAH-nō]   A very hot green chili pepper, about 1½ inches long and torpedo-shaped; used widely in Mexico and the southwestern United States, often cooked fresh but also available pickled and canned.

serrucho [thayr-ROO-chō]   Swordfish, from the Spanish word for saw.

serviette [sayr-vyet]   French for napkin; food served in a folded napkin is *à la serviette.*

sesame   A plant native to Indonesia and East Africa and known to the ancient Egyptians, Greeks, and Romans. In Middle Eastern cooking, sesame seeds are used raw, for oil or tahini, while in Far Eastern cooking they are first roasted, yielding a darker, stronger taste, and used mostly for flavoring rather than frying. Sesame seeds can be white, pale brown, or black, the latter used as a dramatic garnish in China and Japan.

sesos [THAY-thōs]   Spanish for brains.

seun lot tong   See SUĀN LÀ TĀNG.

seviche [say-VEE-shay]   Raw fish or shellfish marinated in citrus juice (usually lime) and seasonings but not cooked by heat; also spelled *cebiche* and often confused with ESCABECHE; from Peru and South America.

Seville orange   A bitter orange whose skin is used widely in making marmalade. Through the Moors, Europeans got to know the bitter orange before the sweet, which explains why a preponderance of their dishes and drinks are flavored with its juice or zest. See also BIGARADE.

sevruga   See CAVIAR.

Seyval Blanc [say-val blankh]   A hybrid white wine grape variety whose disease resistance and hardiness in damp climates has proved itself in England, Canada, New York State, and the eastern United States.

sfogliata [sfō-LYAH-tah]   Italian for puff pastry.

sgombro [S'GOHM-brō]   Italian for mackerel.

shabu-shabu [shah-boo-shah-boo]   In Japanese cuisine, meat and vegetables cooked at table in stock, served with a seasoned sesame sauce; not unlike SUKIYAKI.

shad   A member of the herring family; though there are numerous species, American shad alone is *Alosa sapidissima*—"shad most delicious." This fish migrates from saltwater up rivers on the eastern coast of the United States (now also the Pacific Northwest) for spawning, a welcome harbinger each spring.

Shad flesh has a distinctive, rich, sweet flavor, and removing the rows of tiny bones increases the pleasure of eating it. The roe is a great delicacy, poached, broiled, or sautéed to enhance its nutty flavor.

shaddock   See POMELO.

shahi tukri [SHAH-ee too-KREE]   "Toast of the shah," Indian bread pudding made with cream, *ghee*, saffron, cardamom, pistachios, and rosewater.

shakshouka [shak-SHOO-kah]   In Tunisian cooking, a mixture of sweet peppers, tomatoes, and garlic stewed in olive oil with beaten egg added at the last minute. Also spelled *chouchouka*.

shallot [SHAL-uht; also shah-LOT]   A small member of the onion family whose bulbs form clusters; the French favor its subtle, delicate taste and use it often in their cooking; its use in American kitchens is growing fast.

shandy   In England, beer mixed with lemon soda—a refreshing summer drink; shandygaff is beer with ginger beer.

shāo [show]   Cooked, in Chinese cuisine, especially long-cooked or stewed; the Cantonese name is *siu* [syoo].

shāo mài [show mī]   Open dumplings, steamed wontons, usually filled with a pork mixture; a popular part of the Cantonese dim sum. *Shāo mài pí* [pee] are wonton wrappers or skins made of an egg dough rolled into a thin round (*wonton*) or square (*shāo mài*); the dough is also used for egg noodles and spring roll skins.

sharbat [SHAR-baht]   A fruit punch or flavored drink, from which the word sherbet is derived; the drink appears throughout India and the Arab world.

shark   Although prolific and similar to swordfish in flavor and texture, shark (especially mako and dogfish) is not particularly popular in the United States, probably because of its voracious reputation; its dense, lean, delicate flesh takes well to baking, broiling, and marinating.

shark's fin   See YÚ CHÌ.

sharmoula [shar-MOO-lah]   A Moroccan marinade for fish that combines chopped coriander and parsley leaves, garlic, cumin, lemon juice, paprika, and sometimes hot chili pepper; a Tunisian version is a sweet-and-sour sauce of raisins and onions. Also spelled *charmoula*.

sharon fruit   See PERSIMMON.

shashlyk   See KEBAB.

she-crab soup A springtime soup from South Carolina, made with the meat and roe from female blue crabs, mixed with cream and flavored with Worcestershire sauce and sherry.

shellfish Any kind of seafood with a shell from fresh- or saltwater, including mollusks and crustaceans.

shell steak A cut of beef from the strip loin, a boneless and tender steak.

shepherd's pie Cooked ground meat, usually lamb or beef, in a gravy and covered with a layer of mashed potatoes.

shepherd's purse A wild green in the mustard family, eaten in Europe.

sherbet A frozen mixture much like WATER ICE, made with sweetened fruit juice or purée or another flavoring, such as coffee or liqueur, and sometimes including beaten egg white or Italian meringue to keep ice crystals from forming during freezing; sorbet is the French word for sherbet. American sherbet, especially in the Midwest, sometimes contains milk. See also GRANITA and SPUMA.

sherry A fortified blended wine, strictly speaking from a specified area around the city of Jerez in southern Spain, from whose name the anglicized word *sherry* comes. The young wine, from several grape varieties, is kept in oak casks where it is FORTIFIED, worked on by FLOR yeasts, blended by the SOLERA method, and sometimes sweetened and colored with a dose of reserve sherry. Sherry is made in several different styles such as FINO, AMONTILLADO, and OLOROSO. In California and other countries the term sherry is used more loosely.

shiitake [shee-tah-kay] A Japanese mushroom with a flat round cap, dark brown with an earthy flavor, available both fresh and dried; cultivated widely in Asia and now also in the United States; the woody stem is usually discarded; sometimes called golden oak mushroom in the United States.

shimofuri [shee-mō-foo-ree] In Japanese, to blanch; the name refers to the white color.

shio [shee-ō] Japanese for salt.

ship biscuit See HARDTACK.

shirataki [shee-rah-tah-kee] Japanese translucent noodles made from *konnyaku*.

Shiraz [shi-RAZ] The name used in Australia for the SYRAH grape variety.

shirred eggs Eggs cooked in a shallow dish, either on the stove or in the oven, perhaps with a sauce; the verb is to shirr.

shirumono [shee-roo-mō-nō]   Japanese soup of all kinds, including thick and thin; *suimono* means thin soup.

shish kebab   See KEBAB.

shiso   See PERILLA LEAF.

shī zǐ tóu [sheu tzeu tow]   In Chinese cooking, "lion's head," a Shanghai dish of large pork meatballs with bok choy, thought to resemble a lion's mane; the Cantonese is *see ji tau* [see jee tow].

shōga [shō-gah]   Japanese for fresh ginger.

shoofly pie   A pie with a molasses and brown sugar filling, of Pennsylvania German origin; supposedly so sweet that you have to shoo away the flies.

shortbread   A rich pastry made from butter, flour, and sugar mixed together, shaped in fingers or rounds, and baked until golden; traditional in Scotland for New Year's Day, pastry suns for the winter solstice.

shortening   Any fat, usually butter, lard, or vegetable fat, used in baking; shortening lends its name to rich pastries such as shortbread, shortcake, shortcrust, and shortening bread.

shortening bread   A quick bread from the American South using shortening; often called shortnin' bread.

short loin   A cut of beef from the hindquarter, between the rib and sirloin, comprising the porterhouse, T-bone, and club steak.

shorva   Soup, in Indian cooking; also a versatile style of curry with a soupy consistency.

shōyu [shō-yoo]   Japanese for soy sauce.

shred   To cut, grate, or pull apart into narrow strips.

shrimp   A small decapod crustacean of many species, usually marine—a miniature version of the lobster; the family includes the tiny shrimp from cold northern waters, the rock shrimp off the warmer southeastern American coastlines, and the saltwater crayfish. Commercially marketed shrimp are sorted—and priced—by size and usually flash-frozen on board immediately after they are caught, either peeled or not, raw or cooked; when thawed, shrimp should have a resilient texture and fresh smell. Shrimp are cooked in innumerable ways around the world, from earthy peasant dishes to haute cuisine creations.

shrub   A fruit drink, sometimes alcoholic—a distant relative of the fruit sherbet.

shuàn yáng ròu [sooahn yahng rō]   Mongolian hot pot: pieces of lamb (and sometimes other meats) cooked in a communal pot of simmering stock that is placed in the middle of the table. It is served with sauces, and the rich stock is consumed afterward, a kind of Chinese fondue.

shurba [SHOR-bah]   Arabic for soup; the Turkish is *çorba*, the Persian *shourba*.

shwarma [SHWAHR-mah]   See KEBAB.

sild, sill   Scandinavian for HERRING.

Silvaner   See SYLVANER.

silver dollar cakes   See BANH CAN.

silverside   British term for a cut of beef from the crown of the rump.

simmer   To cook food in liquid just below the boiling point.

singer [sinh-jhay]   In French, to sprinkle or dust, as with flour or sugar.

Single Gloucester   A nearly extinct English cheese made from part skimmed and part whole cows' milk of the rare Gloucester breed (now being revived); half as large as DOUBLE GLOUCESTER and milder in taste.

sippet   A small piece of bread to dip in soup; a piece of toast.

Sirah   See SYRAH.

sirloin   A cut of beef from the hindquarter, between the short loin and round.

sirloin tip   See ROUND.

sirop à trente   See HEAVY SYRUP.

şiş kebab   See KEBAB.

skate   A diamond-shaped relative of the shark, often very large, with edible wings (actually pectoral fins) that are usually skinned and trimmed of cartilage before cooking. Skate is most often poached, fried, or sautéed, and in classic French cuisine, served with *beurre noir*; also called ray.

skim   To remove the top layer from a liquid, as cream from milk or scum from stock.

skim milk, skimmed milk   Milk with nearly all of its cream removed by centrifugal force, leaving .5 percent butterfat; low-fat milk, slightly richer, contains 1 percent butterfat. The skimming also removes vitamins A, D, E, and K, so these nutrients are usually added back later.

skirt steak   A cut of beef, the diaphragm muscle from the flank, long, flat, and thin; flavorful but tough if cooked improperly.

skordalia   A classic Greek sauce of garlic, lemon, and nuts, from the Greek word for garlic; in some versions, bread crumbs or potato purée is added; served with all kinds of savory dishes, especially salted fish.

slivovitz [SLEEV-oh-vits]   Plum brandy from eastern Europe, dry and slightly bitter.

sloe   The fruit of the blackthorn—a wild European plum, small, dark, and astringent; used for flavoring sloe gin and, when touched by frost, for preserves.

slow poke   Nova Scotia name for potted herring.

slump   A dessert of cooked fruit baked with a dumplinglike top, served with cream; popular in eighteenth- and nineteenth-century America. Louisa May Alcott named her home in Concord, Massachusetts, "Apple Slump."

smelt   A small silvery fish, called sparling in Britain, that migrates between fresh- and saltwater unless landlocked; eaten whole or gutted, most often floured and fried.

smen   See SAMNEH.

smetana [SME-tah-nah]   Russian for sour cream.

smitane [smee-tan]   A classic French sauce of chopped onions sautéed in butter, sour cream added, cooked, strained, and flavored with lemon.

Smithfield ham   Ham from hogs fattened in the past on peanuts, today on corn; it is cured, salted, smoked, and aged by traditional methods. To be called a Smithfield ham, it must undergo this lengthy process in the town of Smithfield, Virginia. The ham can be eaten uncooked, like prosciutto, or soaked and cooked by baking or boiling. Richly flavored, salty, and dry, this fine ham should be sliced very thin and served with other food that it accompanies. See also HAM.

smoke   To cure meat over burning wood chips by means of the steady low heat and chemical components in smoke; there are many variations of this prehistoric technique, often used in combination with salt curing.

smörgåsbord [SMEU-yahs-bor]   A profusely varied buffet of open sandwiches, pickled fish, meats, vegetables, eggs, and salads served in Scandinavian countries as hors d'oeuvres or as the meal itself.

smørrebrød [SMEU-breu]   Literally "buttered bread" in Danish, an open-faced sandwich made with all kinds of fish, meat, and vegetable fillings with various sauces, artfully presented.

smothered   Braised; in southern cooking, meat—often chicken—that is cooked in a closed pot with gravy or vegetables to make a sauce.

snail   A land-dwelling gastropod mollusk appreciated by gastronomes since the Romans; usually canned already prepared for the table. *Escargots* (in French) are often served *à la bourguignonne*—fattened on Burgundian grape leaves and bathed in a rich garlic and parsley butter sauce—as well as other ways.

snap bean   String bean.

s'ngao mouan [sngow mwahn]   A Cambodian spicy chicken soup with lemongrass, basil, scallions, and lime.

snow eggs   See OEUFS À LA NEIGE.

snow pea   A variety of pea with a thin, flat, crisp pod; bred to be eaten whole, either raw or blanched, as its French name, *mange-tout* ("eat-all"), implies; much used in Chinese cookery.

Soave [SWAH-vay]   An Italian white wine produced around Verona, dry, pale, fresh, and clean. This wine, which is sold in distinctive tall green bottles, is best drunk young.

soba   A Japanese buckwheat and wheat flour noodle, brownish in color.

socca   A thick pancake from Nice, made of chickpea flour and fried in oil, sold on the street; of Arab origin.

sockeye salmon   See SALMON.

socle [SOHK-uhl]   A bed of starch or vegetables on which a piece of meat or fish is placed; a supportive base for presentation on the buffet table or other display.

soda   See BAKING SODA.

sodium bicarbonate   See BAKING SODA.

soffrito   See BATTUTO and SOFRITO.

sofrito [thō-FREE-tō]   In Spanish cooking, a mixture of chopped vegetables—tomatoes, onions, garlic, and other herbs—cooked together in olive oil, perhaps with diced sweet peppers, ham, and *chorizo*, or other flavorings; the *sofrito*, which can be made ahead, is a base for many sauces and stews. The Italian *soffrito*, made from cooking the BATTUTO, is essentially the same thing.

soft-ball stage   Sugar syrup that has reached a temperature of 234–239°F (113–115°C) and that forms a soft ball between the fingertips when immersed in cold water.

soft-crack stage   Sugar syrup that has reached a temperature of 270–290°F (135–140°C) and that forms brittle threads between the fingertips when immersed in cold water.

soft-shell clam   A steamer clam with a thin, easily breakable shell and siphon (neck) that protrudes, keeping the shell from closing tightly.

soft-shell crab   A blue crab caught while molting, when its new shell is so thin that it is edible; a "buster," a Chesapeake Bay specialty.

sògliola [SŌ-lyō-lah]   Italian for sole.

sole   A flatfish family that includes the flounder and many other varieties (see FLOUNDER); Dover sole is the common sole of European waters, whose white and delicate but firm flesh has inspired many culinary creations. Although there are few true soles in the United States, many types of flounder are called sole to make them more marketable.

solera   The method by which sherry and other fortified wines are blended and matured to achieve consistency: some of the sherry from the oldest barrels of a particular style is bottled and the cask refilled with younger wine of that type, allowing it to acquire the qualities of the older sherry. This progressive method means that sherry is never a vintage wine.

sole Véronique [sōl vayr-on-eek]   In French cuisine, sole poached in white wine and served with velouté sauce, garnished with skinned and seeded white grapes; chicken is prepared similarly.

solyanka [sōl-YAHN-kah]   A Russian stew of freshwater fish with pickled cucumbers, onions, olives, vinegar, sour cream, and dill, also made with meat or game. The name refers to the brined ingredients.

som [sohm]   Thai for the color orange; *som tam* is green papaya and shrimp salad.

somlah kako [sohm-law kah-kō]   A Cambodian Khmer stew of various vegetables and green papaya, with chicken, preserved fish, and lemongrass.

somlah machou [sohm-law mah-choo]   A Cambodian spicy soup of shrimp, tomatoes, and fried garlic.

sommelier [sohm-mel-yay]   French for wine steward, wine waiter.

Sonoma   A California wine-producing county just north of San Francisco and east of the Napa Valley; various wines are grown here, especially reds.

sonth [soonth]   Dried ground ginger in Indian cooking.

sooji [soo-jee]   Semolina, farina in Indian cooking.

sookha dar [SOO-kah dahl]   Coriander seeds in Indian cooking.

sopa [THŌ-pah, SŌ-pah]   Spanish for soup.

sope [SŌ-pay]   In Mexican cooking, a small round of tortilla dough cooked and filled with a savory stuffing; *sopes* can be eaten as a first course or appetizer. Also called *garnacha* or *picada.*

soppressa [sō-PRES-sah]   A large cured salami from the Veneto of coarsely chopped pork meat and fat.

sorbet [sor-bay]   French for SHERBET.

sorghum [SOR-gum]   A grain similar to MILLET and used in Asia and Africa for porridge, flour, beer, and molasses, but in the United States mostly for forage. It is a drought-resistant staple crop in East Africa, where it originated, and in Asia. An African bread called *durra,* flat because sorghum has no gluten, is made from a variety of the grain.

sorrel   A leafy green plant similar to spinach, whose name, derived from the German word for "sour," is appropriate; especially popular in France, this lemony-tasting green is used in salads or cooked for purées, soups, and sauces, often to complement fish. Of the many varieties, wild sorrel is highest in oxalic acid and is sometimes called lemon grass, not to be confused with Asian lemongrass.

Sosse [ZOHS-seh]   German for sauce.

sotanghon [sō-tahn-gōn]   Cellophane noodles in Philippine cooking.

soubise [soo-beez]   Chopped onions sautéed in butter with béchamel and strained; *soubise* can also be a purée of onions and rice finished with butter and cream—a classic French sauce named for the Prince de Soubise, a friend of Louis XV.

Souchong   A black tea with large leaves, from China, India, Sri Lanka, and Indonesia, of which LAPSANG SOUCHONG is one type.

soufflé [soo-flay]   In French cuisine, a sweet or savory pudding made with a white sauce, basic flavoring ingredients, egg yolks, and beaten whites, which cause it to puff up during baking; *soufflé* means blown or puffed up.

soupe   In French cuisine, a hearty and robust peasant soup, usually based on vegetables; not to be confused with CONSOMMÉ or POTAGE.

sour cream   Cream commercially fermented with a lactic culture and usually 18 to 20 percent fat; lower-fat types of sour creams are available.

sourdough   Dough for various baked goods, especially bread, leavened with a fermented starter culture kept from a previous dough rather than with fresh yeast.

sour mash   See BOURBON.

soursop apple   A tropical fruit related to the CHERIMOYA, with thin prickly green flesh ripening to yellow and soft, juicy white flesh that is pleasantly acid; excellent for drinks, purées, and sorbets. Native to the Caribbean, it is now cultivated around the world; also called prickly custard apple and *guanabana*.

sous chef [soo shef]   French for second chef; literally, "under chef."

soused   Pickled in brine or vinegar; usually describes fish.

soutirage [soo-tee-rajh]   French wine term for racking.

souvlakia [soov-LAH-kyah]   In Greek cooking, meat marinated in olive oil, lemon juice, and herbs, then skewered and grilled; Greek shish kebab.

soybean   A bean extremely important to Asia for its nutritive value (very high in minerals and protein) and for its uses in various forms (fresh, dry, sprouted, and processed in innumerable ways). The seeds yield soy milk, flour, and oil (highly unsaturated), all of which can be processed into many useful products. See also TOFU and EDAMAME.

soybean curd   See TOFU.

soy milk   A nutritious vegetable product made from dried soybeans that are soaked in water, crushed, and boiled. Various other products come from soy milk, including soy cheese, made when a coagulant forms curds, and whey from the milk. See also DÒU JIÀNG.

soy sauce   A condiment widely used in Chinese and Japanese cooking (where it is known as *shōyu*), made from naturally fermented soybeans and flour; some commercial brands, however, are chemically fermented and contain additives that attempt to make up for lost color, flavor, and body. Chinese soy sauce (*jiàng yóu*) comes in light, medium, and dark grades, depending on their use. Japanese soy sauce is lighter, sweeter, and less salty than Chinese soy sauce. Some types of soy sauce have separate entries.

spaghettini   Thin spaghetti, "little strings" in Italian.

spaghetti squash   A variety of winter squash whose flesh when cooked and combed separates into long strands, suitable for sauce.

Spam   The brand name of a spiced canned pork product, created by Hormel in 1926, which was widely distributed and eaten in World War II because it was not rationed. In some regions, such as the Philippines, it remains an incongruous staple ingredient in certain traditional Filipino dishes.

spanakopita [SPAH-nah-KŌ-pee-tah]   A Greek spinach pie wrapped in phyllo dough.

Spanferkel [SHPAHN-fayr-kel]   German for suckling pig.

Spanische Windtorte [SHPAH-nish-eh VINT-tor-teh]   An Austrian meringue shell—not unlike the French *vacherin*—elaborately decorated with swirls, filled with berries, and served with whipped cream.

Spanna   A regional Italian name for the red wine grape variety known as NEB-BIOLA.

spareribs   A cut of pork from the breast section, usually grilled or barbecued.

Spargel [SHPAHR-gel]   German for asparagus; the white blanched asparagus are favored in Germany, rather than the green, and in spring much is made of their season.

sparling   See SMELT.

spatchcock   An old English way of cooking small birds, by splitting them down the backbone, spreading them, and flattening them, for quick grilling or sautéing.

spätlese [SHPAYT-lay-zeh]   A German wine term meaning late-picked—after the regular harvest, when these riper grapes yield a bigger, usually sweeter, natural wine (which is also more expensive).

Spätzle [SHPAYTS-leh]   German for a type of noodle or dumpling from Swabia, small and handmade, usually pressed through a colander.

Speck [shpek]   German for bacon or lard. In the Alto Adige of northeastern Italy, *speck* is smoked ham in the style of Austria, across the border, now used for antipasti and cooked dishes throughout Italy.

spelt   A type of wheat native to southern Europe and eaten in ancient times, but in modern centuries neglected. High in protein, excellent in flavor, and tolerated by people with wheat allergies, it is less satisfactory for baking. Like polenta and other rustic peasant grains, spelt is beginning to appear in chic restaurants.

Spencer steak   See DELMONICO.

spèzie [SPET-tsyay]   Italian for spices.

spezzatino [SPET-tsah-TEE-nō]   Italian for stew; literally, "cut into little pieces."

Spickgans [SHPIK-gahns]   German for smoked goose, usually the breast—a great delicacy.

spiedo [SPYAY-dō]   Italian for spit for roasting meat; *spiedino* means skewer or brochette.

Spiegelei [SHPEE-gel-ī]   German for fried egg; literally "mirror egg."

Spiess [shpees]   German for skewer; *Spiessbraten* is meat roasted on a spit.

spinach   A vegetable whose dark green leaves, small or large, flat or crinkled, can be eaten raw or cooked. Native to Persia, spinach cultivation was spread by the Arabs. It is high in iron, calcium, and other nutrients, but the oxalic acid that makes it taste slightly bitter (accentuated by long cooking) may inhibit the absorption of these minerals. Spinach can be prepared in a very wide range of ways, often featuring its green color. In French cuisine, *à la florentine* denotes its presence in a dish.

split pea   A pea of several varieties, generally green or yellow, that is dried and hulled; mostly used for soup and, in Britain, for "pease" pudding or porridge.

sponge   A bread dough mixture based on yeast that is set aside, covered, to develop bubbles and flavor before the remaining ingredients are added and the bread completed. Also the name for an airy gelatin or mousse dessert.

sponge cake   A cake whose texture is lightened with separately beaten egg whites but little or no shortening; it contains some sugar and flour but no leavening other than eggs. See also GÉNOISE.

spoom   See SPUMA.

spoon bread   A moist and unsweetened southern U.S. dish made from cornmeal, milk, butter, and eggs, eaten at various meals; although called "bread," the consistency of spoon bread is more like that of pudding; also called batter bread.

spotted dick, spotted dog   A British steamed suet pudding with raisins or currants—a traditional nursery food.

sprat   See BRISLING.

Springerle [SHPRING-er-leh]   German cookies, ivory-colored and anise-flavored, sometimes molded into very large and elaborate figures; traditional for Christmas and originally from Swabia.

springform pan   A cake pan with a spring or hinge on the side, which detaches it from the bottom, so that the cake is not turned over.

spring onion   See SCALLION.

spring roll   See CHŪN JUǍN.

spritzig [SHPRITS-ish]   German for sparkling, effervescent, as for wine.

sprout   A dried bean that, with proper moisture and warmth has germinated; mung, alfalfa, and soybeans are favorite varieties for sprouting, and they can be eaten raw or lightly cooked.

spuma [SPOO-mah]   In Italian cooking, a fruit or water ice with Italian meringue folded in halfway through the freezing process, as in a sherbet. *Spumone* is a mousselike ice cream lightened with whipped cream or beaten egg whites. In Italian, *spuma* means foam, froth, or mousse.

spumante [spoo-MAHN-tay]   Italian for sparkling, as for wine.

squab   A young pigeon about to leave the nest. Squabs are full-grown at about four weeks but still unfledged; most squabs are domesticated, that is, bred for the table, and their meat is tender, all dark, but not gamy.

squash   The fruit of the prolific *Cucurbita* family whose two main branches are the thin-skinned summer squash (zucchini, pattypan, and the like) and the hard-skinned winter squash (pumpkin, Hubbard, calabaza, and so on). Squash, from an Algonquian word, is the American name for these gourds, many of which have separate entries.

squash blossom   The flower of any member of the large squash family, summer or winter, but most often zucchini. This prolific vegetable produces both male and female flowers, so the male blossoms can be used without sacrificing the fruit or the female flowers used with the baby fruit still attached. The blossom's deep-yellow color, delicate flavor, and natural cuplike form make them versatile and appealing, fresh in salads, lightly sautéed, or stuffed, battered, and deep-fried.

squid   A marine mollusk with a long body and ten arms, highly nutritious and with little waste; most appreciated by Mediterranean and Asian cultures. Squid can be cut into diamonds or rings or stuffed whole to be cooked in various ways, sometimes in sauces flavored and colored with its ink.

Stachelbeere [SHTAHK-el-bayr-eh]   German for gooseberry.

Stampfkartoffeln [SHTAHMPF-kar-tohf-eln]   German for mashed potatoes.

Stange [SHTAHNG-eh]   German for stick; *Stangen* and *Stangerl* are stick-shaped pastries, sweet or savory; *Stangenspargel* means asparagus spears.

star anise   Chinese anise; see BĀ JIĂO.

star apple   A round tropical fruit native to the Caribbean and Central America; it has white or deep purple skin and an interior seed structure such that a cross section looks like a star.

star fruit   See CARAMBOLA.

steak and kidney pudding   A British dish of beef and kidney pieces, flavored with onions, mushrooms, and possibly oysters, steamed in a suet crust (or baked for steak and kidney pie).

steam   To cook by steam heat, thus preserving most of the food's nutrients; food can be steamed over boiling water or, wrapped in leaves, foil, or other protection, directly in hot coals or boiling water.

steep   To soak or infuse in liquid.

Steinbutt [SHTĪN-boot]   German for turbot.

Steinpilz [SHTĪN-peelts]   German for cèpe or bolete mushroom.

stew   To cook food slowly in a small amount of liquid at low heat in a closed container in order to make the food—usually meat—tender and to allow the flavors to mingle; to braise.

Stilton   An uncooked cows' milk cheese (now rarely from pasteurized milk) injected with the *Penicillium roqueforti* mold and aged for about six months to make one of the world's great blue cheeses. Stilton is made in England, in Derbyshire, Nottinghamshire, and Leicestershire, in large cylinders with a brownish crust. The paste is creamy with a variable blue-green veining, moist and slightly crumbly, but not dry or salty. There is also a white Stilton with a flavor unlike the blue.

stir-fry   To cook quickly in a small amount of very hot fat, constantly stirring, to give the food a crisp yet tender texture; a method much used in Chinese and other Asian cooking with the wok.

stock   Broth in which meat, game, poultry, fish, or vegetables have been cooked; stock is usually seasoned, strained, degreased, concentrated, and used as the foundation for soups and sauces—what the French call *fond de cuisine*; meat stock usually contains gelatin, from veal and other bones, and can be white or brown.

Stollen [SHTOHL-len]   German for fruit bread filled with various dried fruits, shaped in a long loaf, and sprinkled with confectioners' sugar; traditional for Christmas and associated with Dresden.

stone crab   A variety of crab found off the southeastern Atlantic and Gulf coastlines, especially Florida, with very fine meat mostly from the claws; sold already cooked.

Stör [shteur]   German for sturgeon.

stout   British ale whose malt has been toasted before brewing to produce darker color, stronger flavor, and higher alcoholic content.

stoved   In Scottish cooking, simmered on top of the stove, as in *étouffer*; stovies is a potato dish cooked thus, possibly with meat drippings and onions.

Stracchino [strahk-KEE-nō]   An uncooked, unpressed cows' milk cheese, originally unpasteurized but now generally pasteurized, from Lombardy; this fresh, rindless cheese is buttery, smooth, and delicate. Stracchino di Gorgonzola is the original name of Gorgonzola. Stracchino cheeses were first made with milk from cows still tired—*stracche* in the Lombardian dialect—from their long descent from the Alps.

stracciatella [strah-chah-TEL-lah]   Italian for light chicken or beef stock thickened with a paste of egg, cheese, and semolina.

stracòtto [strah-KOHT-tō]   Italian for pot roast or braised meat.

strasbourgeoise, à la [ah lah strahz-boor-jhwahz]   Garnished with sauerkraut, small pieces of bacon, and sautéed slices of goose liver—a classic French garnish named for the Alsatian city.

strawberries Romanoff   See ROMANOFF, STRAWBERRIES.

strawberry   The fruit of the *Fragaria* genus, scarlet, fragrant, plump, juicy, unique for having its tiny seeds mounted on the outside. The delectable wild strawberry is native to Europe and America, but the familiar cultivated berry comes from a cross made in the eighteenth century between *F. virginiana*, which Virginia colonists sent back to England, and *F. chiloensis*, discovered in Chile. Little Alpine strawberries, what the French call *fraises des bois*, are choice for their intensity and scent. Strawberries, now available year-round, can be prepared many ways, both simple and fancy.

straw mushroom   A mushroom cultivated in Asia on rice straw and available in the West either canned or dried; it is small with a long thin stem and conical tan cap.

Streusel [SHTROY-zel]   German for a sprinkling, as of sugar or bread crumbs; *Streuselkuchen* is a yeast cake topped with a cinnamon-sugar crumble.

striped bass   A western Atlantic fish that migrates from the sea to spawn in freshwater streams in autumn; its size varies greatly, but smaller fish taste better. The flesh of the striped bass is white, flaky, and firm, with a delicate flavor, making it a popular table fish that is very versatile in cooking.

strip loin   A cut of beef from the top of the short loin, tender and boneless, often cut into steaks.

strudel [SHTROO-del]   Very thin pastry sheets with a sweet or savory filling, rolled up and baked; originally from Bavaria, and in German, as a noun, it is spelled Strudel.

Stück [shtük]   German for piece, portion.

stufa [STOO-fah]   Italian for stove; *stufato* means stew.

sturgeon   A marine fish that spawns in rivers, sometimes growing to great age and size; its flesh is white, rich, firm, and tight in texture—almost like meat—taking well to smoking or pickling; the roe is a great delicacy; see also CAVIAR.

su [soo]   Japanese for rice vinegar.

suān là tāng [swahn lah tahng]   Chinese hot and sour soup, thick and pungent, with shredded meat, tofu, vegetables, mushrooms, and vinegar; very popular in the West; the Cantonese name is *seun lot tong* [swun loht tohng].

suàn méi jiàng [sooahn may jahng]   Duck sauce, a Cantonese dipping sauce (literally "plum sauce") traditionally served with duck or goose and used more widely in American-Chinese cooking; it is a thick sweet-and-sour sauce made of plums, apricots, vinegar, and sugar.

subric [sü-breek]   French for a small ball of vegetable or other food, fried.

succotash   A dish of dried beans and corn derived from the Narragansett Indians' *msickquatash*. Early versions included poultry and meat as well as other vegetables; succotash today need not be reduced to lima beans and corn kernels.

sucker   See BUFFALO FISH.

sucre [SÜK-ruh]   French for sugar; *sucre filé* is spun sugar.

sudado [thoo-DAH-dō, soo-DAH-dō]   Spanish for steamed.

suédoise [sway-dwahz]   Cold "Swedish" sauce of mayonnaise flavored with apple purée and grated horseradish—a classic French sauce.

suet   Solid lumps of fat from around the loins and kidneys of beef, lamb, and other animals, used for making pastry, pudding, and tallow.

sugar   The sweet crystalline substance derived from sugarcane and other plants such as sugar beets, sorghum, and maple, also from honey. Sugar, a basic taste, is used as a flavoring for food, a preservative, and an agent in the fermentation of alcoholic drinks, to name a few uses for this primary ingredient that once was a rare luxury. Raw sugar is refined in many forms—common granulated white sugar, superfine sugar (caster sugar in Britain), confectioners' or powdered sugar (icing sugar in Britain), coarse sugar for decorating; dark and light brown sugar, Demerara, Barbados, muscovado, and turbinado; molasses, treacle, golden syrup—most of which have separate entries. See also CARAMEL, HONEY, MAPLE SUGAR, PALM SUGAR, SACCHARIN, and SUGARCANE.

sugarcane   A tall grass of South Pacific origin from which raw SUGAR was first extracted in India around 500 B.C. To refine the sucrose, the ten-to twelve-month-old stalks are cut, crushed, shredded, and pressed for their juice, which is then clarified, reduced, spun (to separate the sugar crystals from molasses and other impurities), washed, and uniformly crystallized.

sugaring   See CHAPTALIZATION.

sugar snap peas   A cultivated variety of mange-tout with edible pod and peas more developed than snow peas.

sugo [SOO-gō]   Italian for sauce; *sugo de carne* is gravy. When speaking of pasta sauce, *sugo* rather than *salsa* is the correct term. The plural is *sughi*.

suimono [soo-ee-mō-nō]   Japanese for clear soup.

sukiyaki [soo-kee-yah-kee]   Thinly sliced beef and a variety of vegetables, perhaps also noodles and tofu, cooked in a pot with oil at the table, seasoned with dashi and mirin, and served with ceremony; a relatively recent dish in Japanese cuisine.

sukuma wiki [soo-KOO-mah WIK-ee]   A Kenyan stew of leftover meat with onions, tomatoes, sweet peppers, and leafy greens.

sulfite   The salt of sulfurous acid used to preserve food, but banned by the FDA in 1986 for use with fresh fruits and vegetables, to protect people severely allergic to it.

sultana   A large golden RAISIN made from sweet, white, seedless grapes originally grown in Smyrna, Turkey, and named after the Turkish sultan. The Sultana variety (uppercase) is a parent of the Thompson seedless grape.

Sülz [zülts]   German for aspic or meat in aspic, such as head cheese.

sumac   The red berries of the Sicilian sumac shrub whose lemony, fruity flavor is used as a souring agent in Arab and Middle Eastern dishes. The dried seeds are crushed to a brick-red powder that is used to flavor meat, chicken, and fish dishes, also for a drink. This seasoning is not to be confused with American sumac, which is poisonous.

summer pudding   A British dessert of fresh raspberries and red currants stewed together gently, sweetened, pressed in a bread-lined bowl overnight, then turned out and served with cream. The result, though from humble origins, is exquisite and is made with other soft fruit combinations.

sūn [suan]   Chinese for bamboo shoots.

sunchoke   See JERUSALEM ARTICHOKE.

sunflower   A large heliotropic flower whose seeds are roasted and eaten like nuts and whose oil, extracted from the seeds, is light in flavor and mostly polyunsaturated.

sungkaya [SUNG-kī-YAH]   Steamed coconut custard, a popular Thai dessert.

sunomono [soo-nō-mō-nō]   Japanese for vinegared food.

sup [soop]   A thin-textured Vietnamese soup without noodles, served as a first course.

supari [SOO-pah-ree]   Betel nut in Indian cooking.

superfine sugar   Very fine sugar crystals that dissolve quickly in liquid.

supparot [sup-pah-rōd]   Thai for pineapple.

suprême de volaille [sü-prem deu vō-lī]   The breast and wing fillet of a young chicken or other bird, lightly floured and sautéed in butter. *Sauce suprême* is a reduced chicken VELOUTÉ with cream.

surimi [soo-ree-mee]   Japanese for imitation crab meat made from pollock or other inexpensive fish; it is processed in sheets, rolled up, and colored to resemble crab legs; sometimes called seafood legs or other euphemisms.

sushi [soo-shee]   Vinegared rice formed into fingers or rounds, seasoned with WASABI or other condiment, perhaps rolled in seaweed, and garnished with raw seafood or fish and sometimes a vegetable. In Japan, *sushi* is eaten as a meal; in the United States, it is also eaten as an appetizer.

süss [züs]   German for sweet; *süsse Speisen* are sweet dishes or desserts.

Suzette, crêpes   See CRÊPES SUZETTE.

sweat   To cook in a little fat over very low heat in a covered pot, so that the food exudes some of its juice without browning; used especially with vegetables.

swede   In England, a rutabaga or Swedish turnip; the Scottish term is turnip or neep.

sweet-and-sour pork   See GǓ LǍO RÒU.

sweet bean sauce   See TIÁN MIÈN JIÀNG.

sweet bell pepper   See PEPPER (SWEET BELL).

sweetbreads   The thymus or pancreas glands of a calf, sheep, or pig, located in the throat and chest of young animals. Veal sweetbreads are considered the best, pork inferior; the chest or heart sweetbread is larger and therefore the better of the pair. Sweetbreads are highly perishable and should be used soon after purchase. They are soaked in acidulated water to whiten the tissue, blanched and weighted to firm them, and the membranes are trimmed before further cooking.

sweet cicely   See CICELY.

sweet cumin   See ANISE.

sweet marjoram   See MARJORAM.

sweet potato   A root vegetable indigenous to Central America and brought by Columbus to the Old World; high in sugar, nutrients, and calories, it is often confused with the YAM, especially in the United States; the sweet potato has a reddish skin, a texture like the familiar potato, and an affinity for similar preparations.

Swiss chard   A plant in the beet family cultivated for its large green leaves with thick stems. Its three main varieties are distinguished by the color of the stalks and veins: white, red, or multicolored with yellow, pink, orange, red, and white together in a cultivar named Bright Lights (however psychedelic in appearance, it is actually a revival). The origin of the name Swiss is unclear. This nutritious vegetable, with spinachlike leaves and sweet, earthy stems that take slightly longer cooking, is best appreciated by Mediterranean cooks who prepare it with imagination.

Swiss cheese   American-made (or non-Swiss) EMMENTAL.

Swiss roll   British term for jelly roll.

swordfish   A large marine fish with a projecting upper jaw and saillike dorsal fin; its firm white meat, fine-textured and mild-flavored, is sold in steaks or chunks, excellent for baking or broiling.

syllabub [SIL-a-bub]   An old-fashioned British drink made of rich milk or whipped cream with wine, beer, or cider, and flavored with sugar and spices; variously spelled; similar to POSSET and EGGNOG.

Sylvaner [sil-VAH-ner]   A very good white-wine grape, more productive but less distinguished than the Riesling; extensively cultivated in Germany, Austria, Alsace, and also grown in Switzerland, the Italian Tirol, California, and Chile; also spelled Silvaner.

Syrah [see-rah]   An outstanding red-wine grape variety, especially in the French Rhône, yielding a long-lived, deep-red wine; used there for Hermitage,

Châteauneuf-du-Pape, and Côte Rôtie wines; also grown in Australia (where it is called Shiraz), California, and South Africa; sometimes called Petite Sirah.

syrup, heavy   See HEAVY SYRUP.

Szechuan pepper   The red-brown berries of the prickly ash tree, no relation to black pepper, but with a hot tingly flavor used in the spicy cooking of that region; also known as *fagara* and Chinese pepper.

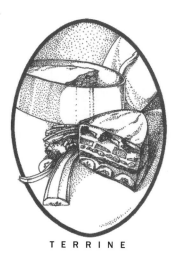

T E R R I N E

T

Tabasco   A fiery hot commercial sauce made of the Tabasco variety of chili pepper, vinegar, and salt, aged in oak barrels and bottled; made since the Civil War in Cajun Louisiana by the McIlhenny Co.

tabbouleh [tah-BOO-lee]   A Lebanese dish of BULGHUR mixed with chopped parsley, tomatoes, mint, onion, olive oil, and lemon juice, proportions varying; eaten as a salad scooped up with lettuce leaves, or perhaps with LAVASH.

table d'hôte [TAB-luh D'ŌT]   French for a full meal at a *prix fixe*.

tacchino [tah-KEE-nō]   Italian for turkey.

taco [TAH-kō]   A tortilla filled with shredded meat and sauce, rolled or folded, and sometimes fried; the Mexican word means "snack."

Tafelspitz [TAH-fel-shpits]   Top round of beef boiled and accompanied with root vegetables, horseradish, and sauces—from Vienna.

taffy   A candy made from sugar or molasses cooked down, usually with butter, nuts, and other flavorings. American taffy, especially saltwater taffy, tends to be soft and chewy, while British toffee is brittle.

tagine   See TAJIN.

tagliatelle [tah-lyah-TEL-lay]   Long thin flat strips of egg pasta; this is the Florentine and northern name for *fettucine*, slightly wider and flatter. RAGÙ BOLOGNESE is the classic sauce for *tagliatelle*.

tagliolini, tagliarini [tah-lyō-LEE-nee, tah-lyah-REE-nee]   Very thin Italian noodles, but not as thin as *capelli d'angelo*; used in soups.

tahini [tah-HEE-nee]   A paste of crushed raw sesame seeds used as the basis of many Arab dishes such as HALVAH, HUMMUS, and BABA GHANOUSH; spelled variously.

tahu [tah-hoo]   Indonesian soft bean curd; *tahu goreng* is fried bean curd, often with spices or sauce.

tajin [TAH-jhin]   In Moroccan cuisine, a braised stew, with infinite variations, named for the earthenware pot with a conical lid in which it is cooked and served; also spelled *tagine*; the plural is *touajin*.

takaw [tah-kaw]   Thai dessert of coconut milk and tapioca flour, with many variations.

takenoko [tah-kay-nō-kō]   Japanese for bamboo shoots.

taklia   An Arab seasoning mixture of crushed coriander seed cooked with garlic in olive oil, much used in the cooking of the eastern and southern Mediterranean, especially Egypt.

takrai [tahk-RĪ]   Thai for lemongrass.

tala [TAH-lah]   Deep-fried, in Indian cooking.

Taleggio [tah-LEJ-jō]   An uncooked, unpressed, raw whole cows' milk cheese, surface-ripened, of the STRACCHINO type. Of the two varieties, traditional Taleggio is made in 8-inch squares with a reddish rind. The delicate, buttery, velvety paste becomes white and dense toward the middle, sometimes ripening to aromatic richness. In Bergamo, near its origin in Lombardy, the traditional accompaniment to Taleggio at the end of the meal is preserves of quince, apricot, and apple. There is also a cooked-curd variety made from pasteurized milk, with a gray rind and less complexity.

Talleyrand [tal-lay-ranh]   A classic French garnish of macaroni mixed with butter and cheese, truffle julienne, and diced foie gras—for sweetbreads and poultry.

tamago [tah-mah-gō]   Japanese for egg.

tamale [tah-MAH-lee]   A Mexican dish of corn dough *(tamal)* made with lard, filled with a savory stuffing, wrapped up in a piece of corn husk, and steamed;

the filling can be savory or sweet. Tamales are traditionally for holidays and special occasions, and their history is ancient. In South America, banana leaves serve as tamale wrappers.

tamari [tah-mah-ree]   A dark, thick, Japanese sauce, similar to soy sauce, also made from soybeans; used primarily as a dipping sauce or in a basting sauce.

tamarillo   A fruit native to Peru that looks like a slender plum tomato in deep red or gold, with dense, smooth flesh and small black seeds. Tasting like an intensely spicy, fruity tomato, it is best cooked with a little acid and sugar and served as a vegetable with meat or in chutney and relish.

tamarind   The pod or fruit of a large tropical tree native to India; when fresh, its pulp is white, crisp, and sweet-sour, but when dried it turns reddish brown and very sour. In Indian cooking it is used both as a souring agent and as a red coloring in curries, chutneys, pickles, sauces, and refreshing drinks. Tamarind is also used in Middle Eastern and Vietnamese cooking.

tamatar [tah-MAH-tar]   Tomato in Indian cooking.

tamis [ta-mee]   French for sieve, sifter, strainer; the Spanish word is *tamiz*. *Tamiser* in French means to strain through a sieve or tammy cloth.

tampon [tamh-ponh]   French for a bed of rice or vegetables.

tan   Thai for palm sugar.

tandoor [tahn-DOOR]   An Indian clay oven, usually recessed in the ground; *tandoori*, the food roasted in it at high temperatures, is first marinated in yogurt and spices.

tandoori chicken   See MURGH.

tang [tahng]   Soup, in Chinese cooking; the Cantonese is *tong*.

tangelo   See MANDARIN.

tangerine   See MANDARIN.

tannin   A chemical compound in the stems and seeds of grapes that imparts a characteristic astringency and puckery quality to wine; tannin is pronounced in young red wines, especially good claret, but gives them longevity.

tansy   An herb with a bitter flavor, whose fresh leaves were once popular in England but now largely ignored; tansy pudding was traditional for Easter; one of the bitter herbs of the Jewish Passover; also called cow bitters and bitter buttons.

tapas [TAH-pahth]   Appetizers served in Spanish bars with cocktails, in great variety and profusion.

tapénade [ta-pay-nad]   French for a mixture of mashed capers, anchovies, black olives, garlic, and perhaps tuna and other foods, thinned to a paste with olive oil; from the Provençal word for caper.

tapioca   A starch extracted from MANIOC root and processed into flour, flakes, and pearls; excellent as a clear glaze for pastry and as a thickener for soups, pies, and puddings. Tapioca keeps its thickening power after freezing, but loses it when overcooked or boiled.

taramosalata [tah-RAH-mō-sah-LAH-tah]   A Greek salad of cured pink fish roe, usually gray mullet, cod, or carp, cured and mashed with bread that has been moistened with a little milk, olive oil, lemon juice, and garlic; served with crusty bread.

tarator [TAHR-rah-tor]   A creamy Turkish sauce of ground nuts and bread crumbs, flavored with garlic and lemon juice or vinegar, usually served with seafood or vegetables; many variations; a similar sauce is made in Syria and Lebanon.

taro [TAAHR-ō]   A tropical and subtropical plant valuable for its spinachlike leaves, asparaguslike stalks, and potatolike root. Its high starch content makes it an important staple in Polynesia, Africa, and Asia. In the Caribbean, its leaves are made into a spicy stew called CALLALOO; dasheen is another word for taro.

tarragon   An herb in the daisy family used widely in French cooking fresh and dried; it is one of the FINES HERBES, essential to the BOUQUET GARNI, and among the *herbes de Provence.* The subtle flavor of true tarragon, hinting of anise, makes it a sophisticated color in the French culinary palate. It appears in preparations such as *sauce béarnaise, poulet à l'estragon,* omelets, and tarragon vinegar; because its flavor quickly disappears, it should be used with care. Russian tarragon is easier to grow, but lacks subtlety.

tart   A sweet or savory pie, usually with no top crust; a flan. A tartlet is a small individual tart.

tartar [TAHR-ter]   Potassium bitartrate, the principal acid of wine, left as a crystal deposit as it ages; also called cream of tartar, it is an ingredient in BAKING POWDER.

tartare [taahr-taahr]   In French cuisine, *sauce tartare* is mayonnaise with hard-boiled egg yolks and garnished with finely chopped onions, chives, and capers; *boeuf à la tartare* is chopped lean raw beef served with capers, chopped onions, and parsley, with a raw egg.

tarte, tartelette [taahrt, taahrt-let]   French for tart, tartlet; *tartine* means a slice of bread spread with butter or jam, also a small tart. The Spanish words are *tarta* and *tartaleta*.

tarte (des demoiselles) Tatin [taahrt day deu-mwah-zel ta-tinh]   A French apple tart, baked upside down, devised by the Tatin sisters in their restaurant near Orléans. The bottom of the pan is buttered and strewn with sugar, covered with sliced apples, then topped with a pastry crust; during baking the sugar on the bottom caramelizes with the apple juices, and the finished tart is inverted and served.

tartufo [tar-TOO-fō]   Italian for truffle.

tasajo [tah-SAH-hō]   Jerked or salt-dried beef, from Cuba.

tasse [tas, TA-seh]   French and German for cup; the Spanish word is *taza*.

tasso [TAS-ō]   A Cajun pork, or occasionally beef, sausage that is highly seasoned with chili and other spices and smoked; used as a flavoring in Cajun dishes.

Tatin, tarte des demoiselles   See TARTE (DES DEMOISELLES) TATIN.

tatlı [TAHT-leu]   Turkish for dessert.

tatsoi   An Asian green with round dark leaves and pale stems; tastes peppery when raw in salads or mellower when steamed or stir-fried; also called rosette bok choy.

tavolo [TAH-vō-lō]   Italian for table.

Tavel [ta-vel]   A rosé wine from the Rhône Valley near Avignon—flavorful, strong, and celebrated.

tavuk göğsü [tah-OOK geu-SÜ]   A Turkish dessert pudding of finely shredded chicken breast, rice flour, milk, and sugar, flavored with cinnamon; akin to medieval BLANCMANGE.

T-bone steak   A cut of beef from the loin, very similar to the porterhouse, but containing less of the fillet.

té [tay]   Italian and Spanish for tea; the German word is *Tee*.

tea   The drink prepared from the dried leaves of a shrub, *Camellia sinensis*, native to China and now cultivated also in India, Ceylon, Kenya, and Taiwan (Formosa). Of the three types, black tea is fermented and dried, making a dark brew; Earl Grey, English Breakfast, Orange Pekoe, Lapsang Souchong, Assam, and Darjeeling are in this category. Oolong tea is made from partially fermented large leaves, between black and green tea; Formosa Oolong is a fine example. Green tea, dried right after picking without fermentation, makes a pale brew with a slightly bitter flavor that is preferred in China and Japan. Gunpowder, with its tightly furled leaves, and *matcha*, the strong, bright green powdered tea used in the Japanese tea ceremony, are different examples of green tea. Many of these teas have separate entries. Herbal tea, or TISANE, is made from plants other than tea. See also CHAI.

tejolate   See MOLCAJETE Y TEJOLOTE.

tel   Oil in Indian cooking.

tempeh [TEM-peh]   An Indonesian staple of fermented soybeans that are pressed into firm blocks, suitable for stir-frying or grilling.

tempered chocolate   Confectionery chocolate that has been stabilized by temperature manipulation—melting and cooling—so that its cocoa butter will not form crystals that appear as gray bloom, but rather as shiny gloss.

Tempranillo [tem-prah-NEE-yō]   A native grape variety for Spanish red wines, especially Rioja, also Portuguese; it ripens early and makes a fruity wine for drinking young, also ages well for mature wine.

tempura [tem-POO-rah]   In Japanese cooking, seafood and vegetables dredged in a light batter and quickly deep-fried in oil; served with a dipping sauce called *tentsuyu*.

tenderloin   A cut of meat, especially beef, from the hindquarter, consisting of one long, slender, and very tender muscle running through the loin section ending at the ribs; it is divided into filet mignon, chateaubriand, and tournedos for roasts or steaks.

tentsuyu   See TEMPURA.

terasi   See BALACHAN.

teriyaki [tayr-ee-yah-kee]   Japanese for poultry, fish, or meat marinated in a sweet soy sauce preparation and grilled over charcoal so that the marinade forms a glaze.

Terlano [tayr-LAH-nō]   A well-known and excellent white wine from the Italian Tirol, in the Alto Adige Valley; dry, fruity, rounded, and soft.

ternera [tayr-NAYR-ah]   Spanish for veal.

terrapin   An edible water turtle that lives in fresh or brackish water; see also TURTLE.

terrine [tayr-reen]   In French cuisine, a mixture of meat, game, poultry, or vegetables and seasonings, cooked in a dish lined with bacon or pork; the dish was originally earthenware, hence its name; see also PÂTÉ.

terroir [tayr-waahr]   French term for earth or soil, meaning the specific climatic conditions that give a wine its individual character and quality.

tête d'aloyau [tet d'al-wah-yō]   French for rump steak.

tête de veau [tet deu vō]   French for calf's head; in Italian, *testa di vitello*.

Tetilla [teh-TEE-yah]   A Spanish cheese usually made from ewes' or goats' milk—soft, creamy, and bland.

tetragonia   See NEW ZEALAND SPINACH.

Tetrazzini   Strips of cooked chicken and spaghetti in a cream sauce flavored with sherry and Parmesan, *gratiné*; named for the Italian coloratura soprano Luisa Tetrazzini.

Tex-Mex   A style of cooking that combines elements of Texan and Mexican food, such as CHILI CON CARNE. This indefinable style is more an American perception of Mexican food as that offered by Mexican restaurants north of the border, as opposed to authentic Mexican food found in Mexico.

tfina [TFEE-nah]   A Moroccan and Algerian stew of beef and chickpeas cooked in the embers on Friday night to be eaten on the Jewish Sabbath.

thé [tay]   French for tea.

thiebou dienne [tyay-BOO dyen]   A rice and fish stew, the national dish of Senegal, traditionally served in a large communal bowl.

Thompson seedless grape   The variety of grape, pale green, thin-skinned, pleasantly sweet if bland, used for table grapes and both dark and sultana raisins; the dominant table grape grown in California.

thon [tonh]   French for tuna.

thousand-year-old eggs   See PÍ DÀN.

thyme   A perennial herb in the mint family, of Mediterranean origin, with small aromatic leaves, an essential part of the BOUQUET GARNI; among its many varieties used fresh and dried are garden, lemon, French, variegated, and caraway thyme. Besides its many culinary applications, it has been used since ancient times for medicinal purposes; in Provence, wild thyme is called *serpolet*.

Tia Maria [TEE-ah mah-REE-ah]   A liqueur of rum flavored with Blue Mountain coffee extract and spices; from Jamaica.

tian [tee-anh]   French for a shallow casserole or, by extension, food baked in it—usually an aromatic gratin of chopped vegetables, perhaps with some leftover meat or seafood; from Provence.

tián mièn jiàng [tyen myen jung]   In Chinese cooking, a thick, sweet, and salty paste made from fermented red beans, flour, salt, and water; used for flavoring sauces and marinades and as a dipping sauce, especially in northern China.

tia tô   See PERILLA LEAF.

tiède [tyed]   French for lukewarm, tepid, at room temperature.

tikki [TIK-ee]   In Indian cuisine, cutlet; also spelled *tikka*.

til [teel]   Sesame seeds in Indian cooking.

tilapia [til-AH-pya]   A fish with mild, white, flaky delicate flesh that responds well to farming and will therefore be increasingly available; related to John Dory but not so fine an eating fish.

tilefish   A western Atlantic deep-water fish with white, lean, firm but delicate flesh with a large flake; it can be eaten whole (marketed at about 6 to 8 pounds), but is usually cut into fillets or steaks. This versatile and delicious fish, brightly colored and spotted yellow, tastes like the lobster and crab that make up its diet, but is underappreciated by Americans.

Tilsit [TIL-sit]   A cooked, unpressed German cheese made from raw or pasteurized cows' milk; oblong or cylindrical, it has a thin yellow rind and straw-colored paste with holes. The acidulated taste becomes more pronounced with age, and the cheese is sometimes flavored with caraway seeds; now made in several central European countries.

timbale [timh-bal]   French for a drum-shaped mold, usually metal, or the food prepared in such a mold, including rice, diced vegetables, or fish *mousseline*; also a high, round, covered pastry case, usually decorated, or the food in such a case.

timo [TEE-mō]   Italian for thyme.

tim suan yuk   See GǓ LǍO RÒU.

tipsy parson or pudding   An old-fashioned English dessert pudding of sponge cake soaked with spirits or fortified wine and covered with custard or whipped cream; not unlike a TRIFLE.

tirage [teer-ajh]   French wine term for "drawing off" wine from the cask.

tiramisù [tee-rah-mee-SOO]   A rich Italian dessert, literally "pick me up," created in the 1960s, that layers sponge cake soaked in brandy and espresso with mascarpone custard cream flavored with chocolate.

tire-bouchon [teer-boo-shonh]   French for corkscrew.

tiropita [TEE-rō-PEE-tah]   A Greek cheese pie wrapped in phyllo dough.

tisane [tee-zan]   French for herbal tea, originally a medicinal brew.

toad-in-the-hole   In British cooking, meat, usually sausage, baked in Yorkshire pudding batter.

tobiko   Flying fish roe, tiny, bright orange, and crunchy, used for garnishes and texture.

Tocai Friuliano [tō-KĪ free-oo-LYAH-nō]   A white wine grape variety grown in northeastern Italy, especially the Collio, Colli Orientali, and the Colli Euganei in the Veneto, producing pleasant dry wines, sometimes with character; no relation to Hungarian Tokay.

tocino [tō-THEE-nō, tō-SEE-nō]   Spanish for bacon; *tocino de cielo*, literally "bacon from heaven," is a thick caramel custard dessert (not made with bacon).

toffee   See TAFFY.

tofu [tō-foo]   Japanese bean curd, white, soft, and easily digestible; in one form or another it is eaten throughout Asia and valued for its healthful properties: high in protein, low in calories, and free of cholesterol. Tofu is made from dried soybeans processed into a "milk" that is coagulated like cheese; the molded tofu curds are kept fresh in water. Of the many types, *momen* ("cotton") is the most common fresh tofu in the United States as well as in Japan; *kinu* ("silk") has a finer texture; *yakidofu* has been lightly broiled. Chinese bean curd (DÒU FÙ) is drier and firmer than Japanese.

togarashi [tō-gah-rah-shee]   Japanese for red hot chili peppers, fresh or dried.

Tokay [tō-KĪ]   A famous wine from the town of the same name in northeastern Hungary, made with some proportion of grapes with the NOBLE ROT in varying grades and ranging in sugar and alcoholic content. The best and rarest Tokay (Aszu and especially Eszencia) has an incomparable rich, buttery, peach-caramel flavor; Tokaji is the proper Hungarian spelling. Tokay is also the name of an Alsatian grape (Tocai in Italy), totally unrelated.

Toma [TŌ-mah]   An uncooked whole or partly skimmed cows' milk cheese, sometimes mixed with ewes' or goats' milk, made in the Italian Alps near the French Haute-Savoie and Swiss borders; shaped in discs, it ripens quickly to a pale supple paste or can be matured to a dense, pungent cheese. See also TOMME DE SAVOIE.

tomalley [toh-MAHL-ee]   The liver of the lobster, colored olive green—a special delicacy.

tomatillo, tomate verde [tō-mah-TEE-yō]   A Mexican fruit, green ripening to yellow, sometimes purple, enclosed within a papery husk—small, firm, fruity, tart, and refreshing; it is not an unripe red tomato (*jitomate*), although it is a distant cousin of the tomato, and often confused with it, and a closer relative to the CAPE GOOSEBERRY. *Tomatillo* is the basis for Mexican *salsa verde*, with serrano peppers, garlic, and cilantro, all chopped together, either fresh or cooked, guacamole, and other savory mixtures.

tomato [tō-MAY-tō, tō-MAH-tō]   A vine in the nightshade family whose fruit is the familiar red vegetable widely enjoyed today, although considered suspicious if not poisonous into the twentieth century. Native to South America, the Aztecs developed the tomato and brought it to Mexico; the Spaniards introduced it to distrustful Europeans. Today the tomato is eaten raw, cooked, dried, commercially prepared as sauce, salsa, paste, ketchup, and combined with an array of savory foods. Because tomatoes ripened on the vine taste best, it is a favorite backyard plant from midsummer to frost. Consumer demand has expanded the types sold; beside the familiar red round tomato, yellow and orange varieties are available; large red beefsteak tomatoes, juicy and meaty; plum tomatoes like the fleshy dry Roma, excellent for cooking; little cherry, grape, yellow pear, and the unusual sweet currant tomatoes; year-round cluster tomatoes, sold on their vine, superior to the hard pink tasteless ones picked green for market. Farmers' markets and better grocers offer "heirloom" varieties in myriad shapes, colors, and flavors.

tomber à glace [tomh-bay ah glas]   In French, to reduce liquid to a glaze.

Tomino [tō-MEE-nō]   An uncooked, unpressed cows' milk cheese, usually pasteurized and sometimes enriched, from the Italian Alps; this rindless cheese ripens quickly to a delicate, fresh flavor and a soft, smooth paste, making it an excellent dessert cheese. See also TOMME DE SAVOIE and TOMA.

tomme au raisin [tohm ō ray-zinh]   French for cheese with grape seeds pressed on the outside.

Tomme de Savoie [tohm deu sa-vwah]   An uncooked, pressed cows' milk cheese from the French Alps, with an Italian version from across the border; made in 8-inch discs with a light brown rind, a pale yellow paste, and a nutty lactic flavor. *Tomme* means cheese in the Savoy dialect, and there are many varieties of it there, made from cows', goats', or ewes' milk. See also TOMA and TOMINO.

Tomme Vaudoise [tohm vō-dwahz]   An uncooked, soft cheese made from whole or sometimes partly skimmed milk in the Swiss Alps; round or oblong, it has a thin, delicately molded white rind and a smooth, buttery, aromatic interior.

tom yam gung   See DOM YAM GUNG.

tonkatsu [ton-kat-soo]   In Japanese cooking, pork marinated in a spicy sauce, dipped in egg and bread crumbs, and fried.

tonno [TOHN-nō]   Italian for tuna.

tooa [TOO-ah]   Thai for peas, beans, peanuts.

Topf [tohpf]   German for pot; stew or casserole.

Topfen   See QUARK.

topinambour [tō-pinh-amh-boor]   French for Jerusalem artichoke; the Italian spelling is *topinambur*.

top round   See ROUND.

top sirloin   See ROUND.

torchon [tor-shonh]   French for a cloth or towel in which food such as foie gras may be rolled, possibly poached, then chilled, and sliced for serving.

tord   Thai for fried; *tord man neua* means spicy fried meat balls.

toriniku [tor-ee-nee-koo]   Japanese for chicken meat.

torrone [tor-RŌ-nay]   Italian for NOUGAT.

torshi [TOOR-shee]   In Afghan cooking, a mix of pickled vegetables, often served with PILAU and always with bread.

torsk   Norwegian and Swedish for cod.

torta [TOR-tah]   In Italian, tart, pie, or cake. In Spanish, cake, loaf, or roll of bread. In Mexican Spanish, the word can also mean a savory pudding of *tortillas* stacked like CHILAQUILES.

Torte [TOR-teh]   German for tart, round cake, flan; *Tortenbäcker* is a pastry cook. In English, torte has come to mean a rich, round cake, often with little or no flour, with eggs, nuts and flavorings.

tortellini [tor-tel-LEE-nee]   Small rounds of egg pasta stuffed, folded, and wrapped around the finger; almost the same as *cappelletti* but round instead of square.

tortière [tor-tyayr]   A French Canadian pork pie, traditional for Christmas Eve.

tortilla [tor-TEE-yah]   In Spain the word means omelet; in Mexico *tortilla* means a thin, flat, unraised pancake made of dried cornmeal flour, salt, and water—from the Aztec cuisine. The Mexican term for omelet is *tortilla de huevos*.

tortoni [tor-TŌ-nee]   Ice cream topped with chopped almonds or macaroons; Italian-American in origin and often called *biscuit tortoni*.

tortue [tor-tü]   French for turtle; *sauce tortue* is demi-glace with tomato purée, herbs, truffle essence, and Madeira; *à la tortue* means calf's head garnished with veal quenelles, mushrooms, olives, gherkins, calf's tongue, and brains, with *sauce tortue.*

Toscanello [tohs-kah-NEL-lō]   A cooked, semihard mixed ewes' and cows' milk cheese from Tuscany and Sardinia, made in 6-pound cylinders; it has a brownish yellow rind and a pale dense paste and is aged three to four months to develop a mild or piquant taste; called Pecorino Toscano when made of all ewes' milk.

toscano [toh-SCAH-nō]   Italian for Tuscan.

tostada [tō-THTAH-dah, tō-STAH-dah]   Spanish for toast; in Mexico this means a tortilla fried flat and then topped with all kinds of garnishes, sometimes stacked high.

tostaditas   See TOTOPOS.

tostones [tos-TŌ-nays]   In Caribbean cooking, thin slices of green plantain fried once, then pounded thinner and fried again; eaten like potato chips as a side dish or with salsa or a garlic dip as a snack.

totopos [tō-TŌ-pos]   Tortillas cut in six to eight smaller triangles, fried crisp, and served with dips or as a garnish.

toulousaine, à la [ah lah too-loo-zen]   Garnished with chicken quenelles, sweetbreads, mushroom caps, cocks' combs and kidneys, and truffle slices arranged separately, with ALLEMANDE sauce—a classic French garnish.

tourage [too-rajh]   French for repeated turns of the dough—rolling and folding—in the making of *pâte feuilletée.*

Touriga Nacional [tour-EE-gah na-syoh-NAL]   An excellent Portuguese red grape variety used for port due to the variety's color, tannin, fruit, and aroma; in the Douro Valley it is also used for table wine.

tourin [too-rinh]   French onion soup made with milk instead of meat stock (as in *soupe à l'oignon*), thickened with egg yolks and cream, and sometimes served with grated cheese; from southwestern France.

tourné [toor-nay]   French for a vegetable that is "turned" or shaped with a knife, as with potatoes and mushrooms; also, food that has gone bad or a sauce that has separated.

tournedos [TOOR-neh-DŌ]   French for thick slices from the middle of the beef fillet, sautéed or grilled.

tourte [toort]   French for tart or pie, usually round and savory; a *tourtière* is a pie dish or flan case.

toute-épice [too-tay-pees]   French for allspice.

tragacanth   See GUM.

Traminer [trah-MEE-ner in German, tra-mee-nay in French]   A white-wine grape family to which the GEWÜRZTRAMINER belongs.

trancher [tranh-shay]   In French, to carve, slice; a *tranche* is a slice, chop, or steak. The Italian word is *trancia*. See also TRONÇON.

Trappiste [trap-peest]   French for a cheese made all over the world by Trappist monks—Port-Salut being the best known of this type—all of them with slight variations. The round cheese is semihard, with a soft rind and a dense, smooth paste with small holes.

trasi [TRAH-see]   A pungent fermented shrimp paste, used in small quantities as a flavoring in Indonesian and Southeast Asian cooking, like Malaysian BAL-ACHAN; sometimes spelled *trassi* or *terasi*.

Traub(e) [trowb, TROW-beh]   German for grape; bunch of grapes.

travailler [tra-vī-yay]   In French, to beat; to stir in order to blend or smooth.

treacle [TREE-kul]   British for a thick syrup similar to molasses but slightly sweeter; used in making puddings, tarts, and other desserts.

Trebbiano [treb-BYAHN-nō]   A white-wine grape much used in Italy (for White Chianti, Soave, and the like) and also grown in southern France and California, where it is called Ugni Blanc.

tree ear   See YÚN ĔR.

tree oyster   See OYSTER MUSHROOM.

trenette [tre-NET-tay]   A flat pasta similar to fettucine, but thicker ("train tracks"); the traditional pasta for PESTO.

trey [tray]   Cambodian for fish; *chien trey* means fried fish; *trey aing*, fish grilled over charcoal, served with raw vegetables, greens, and herbs, with a pungent fish sauce containing roasted ground peanuts.

trid [treed]   In Tunisia, a primitive kind of BASTILLA.

triflach [TREE-flakh]   In Jewish cooking FARFEL lightened with extra eggs.

trifle   A British dessert pudding of sponge cake or biscuits soaked with sherry or other liquor, topped with custard and whipped cream, usually garnished with sliced fruit.

triglia [TREE-lyah]   Italian for red mullet, a Mediterranean fish.

trigo [TREE-gō]   Spanish for wheat.

tripe   The first and second stomachs of ruminants (plain and honeycomb tripe, respectively); *tripe à la mode de Caen* (see CAEN, À LA MODE DE), requiring the laborious preparation of beef tripe, is the classic French dish.

triple sec   French for a type of bitter orange-flavored liqueur, such as Cointreau and Curaçao, made with the zest.

trocken [TROKH-en]   German for dry, as in wine.

Trockenbeerenauslese [TROHK-en-bayr-en-ows-lay-zeh]   A very sweet wine made from raisined (nearly dry) grapes left on the vine and individually chosen from bunches—the most selective and expensive German wine produced and subject to NOBLE ROT.

Troja [TRŌ-yah]   An Italian red-wine grape, productive and widely grown for its deep color and full body; used for blending.

tronçon [tronh-sonh]   French for a thick cut of meat or fish, especially salmon; see also TRANCHER.

trota [TRŌ-tah]   Italian for trout.

trotter   The foot of an animal, especially a pig or sheep.

trout   A game fish, primarily freshwater and related to SALMON, with fine-textured flesh high in fat content, usually white but sometimes pink. With very small scales, a simple bone structure, and succulent flesh, it is adaptable to many culinary uses and is increasingly farmed. Brook, brown, lake, rainbow, sea trout, and char are a few of the many varieties.

trouvillaise, à la [ah lah troo-vee-yez]   Shrimp, mussels, and mushroom caps with shrimp sauce—a classic French garnish.

trucha [TROO-chah]   Spanish for river trout.

truffle   The fruiting body of a black or white fungus that grows underground, unlike other mushrooms. The dense truffle, rough, round, and with interior veining, grows in symbiosis with certain trees, especially oak, and only in particular soils and climates. Trained dogs, goats, and sows can find the scent of truffles, similar to that of boars' saliva in mating season, and sniff them out. Truffles' exquisite aroma makes their exorbitant price worthwhile. The best black truffles, increasingly rare, come from Périgord, France; white truffles come from Alba, in northern Italy. Chocolate truffles are chocolate BUTTER-CREAM balls rolled in cocoa, crushed almonds, or chocolate shavings to resemble real truffles.

truite au bleu   See BLEU, AU.

truss   To tie poultry or game with string in order to hold its shape during cooking, to ensure even cooking, and to improve its appearance; the particular method of trussing depends on the animal, its size, and the cooking method used.

Trut-hahn, Trut-henne [TROOT-hahn, TROOT-hen-neh]   German for tom turkey or hen.

tsukemono [tsoo-kay-mō-nō]   Japanese for pickled food.

tube pan   A ring-shaped cake pan traditionally used for rich cakes, since the hollow center can be filled and the extensive surface coated with syrup or icing.

tubu [DOO-boo]   Korean version of TOFU, thick and soft, not firm like Chinese tofu; *tubu choerim* is fried spiced bean curd.

tuile [tweel]   French for a crisp cookie, sometimes made with crushed almonds, that is placed on a rolling pin immediately after baking so that it curves, when cool, like a "tile" (hence its name).

tukbaege [TOOK-bay-gee]   A Korean round clay pot, an all-purpose cooking container made in various sizes.

tuk trey [tuhk tray]   Cambodian Khmer fish sauce with vinegar, lime juice, sugar, and garlic, used extensively.

tulipe [too-leep]   French for a crisp, thin, cookielike dough ruffled while still warm from the oven into a flower shape to hold dessert berries, ices, and so on.

tuna   A large saltwater fish with rich meat varying in color and oiliness from one species to another and also from one part of a fish to another. Albacore is high-quality tuna with white meat; other species yield darker flesh, bonito being the darkest; tuna is often brined before cooking to lighten the color. Much of the commercial catch is canned, solid ("fancy"), chunks, and flakes being the three styles, packed either in oil or water. Baking, broiling, braising, marinating, and smoking are good cooking methods for fresh tuna; the Japanese hold it in special regard for its use in *sashimi*.

tuna   Mexican word for prickly pear.

Tunke [TUHN-keh]   German for sauce, gravy.

tunny   British term for tuna.

turban   Food, often cooked in a ring mold, served in a circle; used primarily for seafood or poultry dishes.

turbinado sugar   Partially refined sugar, light brown in color, similar to DEMERARA SUGAR.

turbot   An eastern Atlantic flounder with delicate white flesh that rivals the Dover sole in culinary preparations; true turbot is rarely found in the United States.

turkey   A large bird with colorful plumage and wattled neck; native to North America and domesticated by the Aztecs and Mayans long before the arrival of the conquistadors, who took it back to Europe in the sixteenth century. Europeans liked turkey and developed it to proportions early native Mexicans would not have recognized. The turkey Americans traditionally eat for Thanksgiving and Europeans for Christmas has been bred for its huge white-meat breast, sacrificing flavor and making it impossible for turkeys to mate except by artificial insemination; fortunately smaller birds are now more in demand. The English name turkey was first given to guinea fowl, mistakenly thought to have originated in Turkey, then passed to this larger bird; similarly, the French word *dindon* for turkey came from its supposed origin in India (*d'Inde*).

turlu [TOOR-loo]   Turkish for stew.

turmeric [TER-mer-ik]   A spice obtained from the dried and powdered rhizome of an Indian plant of the ginger family, whose bitter flavor and ocher color contribute to curries. In the Middle Ages, its color made it a substitute for saffron, and today turmeric is still used as a dye for cloth and dairy products such as margarine. The word is often misspelled tumeric.

turnip   A vegetable in the genus *Brassica* or mustard family, whose swollen base and tender green leaves are edible; turnips taste best small and young, when they are crisp and sweet; Americans and English tend to eat them over-aged and overcooked. The familiar variety is white with purple tips; there are also all-white varieties. Turnips can be served sliced or shredded raw, lightly sautéed, steamed, boiled, and puréed, or braised and glazed, but care must be taken not to overcook them; in Asia, turnips are often pickled. The large yellow rutabaga, called swede in England, is a close relative.

turnover   A pastry square or round filled with a sweet or savory stuffing, folded in half to enclose the stuffing, and baked; the turnover appears in many cultures.

turrón [toor-RON]   A chewy Spanish candy made of toasted almonds, honey, egg whites, and sometimes other ingredients; from Alicante and traditional for Christmas.

turshi [TOOR-shee]   In Middle Eastern cooking, pickled food.

turtle   Land and water turtles are both edible, but the aquatic green and diamondback are especially valued for their flesh, mainly in soups and braised dishes. The expense and difficulty of preparing turtle meat, as well as conservation measures designed to protect the species' diminishing numbers, have made turtle recipes far less fashionable than in the past. A terrapin is an edible water turtle that lives in fresh or brackish coastal water; tortoise generally means a land turtle.

Tuscany The region around Florence, Italy, producing Chianti and other red table wines. The Tuscan style of cooking is relatively simple, featuring olive oil, herbs, cannelloni and other beans, game, FERRO, and bread, rather than pasta (except for hare with PAPPARDELLE).

tutti-frutti [TOO-tee FROO-tee] Italian for mixed fruits (literally "all fruits") chopped and preserved in syrup, usually with brandy.

Tybo [TÜ-bō] A Danish cooked cows' milk cheese similar to SAMSØ; brick-shaped, supple-textured, with fairly large holes, Tybo is straw-colored on the inside with a yellow rind; its taste is mild and slightly acidulated.

tyrolienne, à la [ah lah tee-rō-lyen] Fried onion rings and tomatoes *concassées*—a classic French garnish.

tyropita [TEE-rō-PEE-tah] A traditional Greek cheese pie made with phyllo and feta, similar to SPANAKOPITA.

tzimmes [TSIM-mes] A casserole of brisket of beef with carrots, prunes or other dried fruit, and syrup, topped with potatoes and dumplings; traditional for Rosh Hashanah and Passover.

U C C È L L O

U

uccèllo [oo-CHEL-lō]   Italian for bird; *uccèlli scappati* (literally "escaped birds") are veal birds skewered with bacon and sage; *uccelletti* or *uccellini* are small birds, usually skewered and roasted whole. See also MEAT BIRDS.

uchepos [oo-CHAY-pōs]   Fresh corn TAMALES from Michoacán.

udang [oo-dahng]   Indonesian for shrimp; *udang goreng* is fried shrimp.

udon [oo-dōn]   Japanese wheat noodle.

ugali [oo-GAH-lee]   Steamed porridge made of maize, or occasionally millet, cassava, or sorghum; a staple food in Tanzania and East Africa, served with meat stews or vegetables, sometimes cooled and fried.

ugli fruit [OO-glee, *not* UG-lee]   A hybrid cross between the tangerine and grapefruit or POMELO, not to be confused with the Minneola tangelo. Grown in Jamaica where it is called *hoogli*, it has a yellowish green, thick, coarse skin and sweet orange flesh. See also MANDARIN.

Ugni Blanc   See TREBBIANO.

ujja [UH-jah]   A Tunisian egg dish with filling, rather like an omelet or tortilla; see also IJJA.

umé [oo-may]   Japanese for plum (actually a kind of apricot); *umeboshi* are pickled plums; *umeshu* is plum wine.

umido, in [een OO-mee-dō]   Italian for stewed.

unagi [oo-nah-gee]   Japanese for eel.

uovo [WŌ-vō]   Italian for egg; *tuorlo d'uovo* is the yolk, *bianco d'uovo* the white; *uovo affogato* is a poached egg, *uovo molletto* is a soft-boiled egg, *uovo al burro* is a fried egg, and *uovo sode* is a hard-boiled egg.

upside-down cake   An American style of cake where the batter is poured over fruit spread in the bottom of a pan, baked, and then inverted so that the fruit is on top, its syrupy juices running down into the crumb; this kind of cake became popular in the 1920s, and pineapple is the most typical.

usu-kuchi shōyu [oo-soo-koo-chee shō-yoo]   Japanese for light SOY SAUCE, clearer, thinner, and saltier than dark soy sauce (KOI-KUCHI SHŌYU).

uva [OO-vah]   Spanish for grape; *uva espina* is gooseberry, *uva passa* or *secca* is raisin.

V A N I L L A

V

vaca frita [VAH-kah FREE-tah] "Fried cow," an informal but popular Cuban dish of beef first simmered for broth, then shredded and stir-fried with chopped onions.

vacherin [vash-rinh] In French cuisine, a meringue shell made of a solid disc of meringue and separate rings stacked on the circumference to form a container; the baked *vacherin* shell is decorated with piped scrolls, then filled with ice cream, crème CHANTILLY, berries, or other fruit.

Vacherin Mont-d'Or [vash-rinh monh d'ohr] A whole-milk cows' cheese, uncooked and unpressed, from the Swiss and French Alps; the disc-shaped cheese has a soft, creamy, rich texture with small holes and a delicate, buttery, sweet flavor. Other types of this winter cheese are Vacherin des Beauges and Vacherin Fribourgeois, all often banded with spruce bark, which imparts its subtly resinous flavor. For legal reasons, the French version of Vacherin Mont-d'Or is now called Le Mont d'Or or Vacherin du Haut-Doubs.

Valdepeñas [val-day-PAY-nyahth] Red and white table wines from La Mancha, south of Madrid, produced in very large quantity; officially called Vino Manchego. The red is especially light, pleasant, best drunk young, and inexpensive.

Valencia [vah-LEN-thyah]   A seaport and region in eastern Spain notable for its short-grain rice and seafood, both of which grace PAELLA *valenciana*. The Valencia orange, sweet and thin-skinned, an excellent juice or dessert orange, actually comes from Portugal.

valenciano [vah-len-SYAH-nō]   A chili pepper similar to the GÜERO.

valencienne, à la [ah lah val-enh-syen]   A classic French garnish of rice pilaf and sweet red peppers with a tomato-flavored sauce.

Valois [val-wah]   A BÉARNAISE sauce with meat glaze; also a classic French garnish of artichokes and sautéed potatoes.

Valpolicella [val-pō-lee-CHEL-lah]   A red wine produced in northern Italy, northwest of Verona, in five townships. The wine is soft, light, dry, and fragrant, best drunk young; it has been called the Beaujolais of Italy.

Valtellina [val-tel-LEE-nah]   A wine-producing region in northern Italy, near Switzerland, where the Nebbiolo grape yields some of the country's best wine: dark, robust, and long-lived.

vanilla   The fruit pod of a climbing orchid indigenous to Central America; the Aztecs used it to flavor their chocolate drink. Vanilla is difficult and expensive to produce; the immature bean is cured in a long slow process. The pod and its seeds flavor sweet and occasionally savory dishes; the pod can be wiped dry and used again, immersed in vodka or sugar, which it permeates with its aroma. The three main types of vanilla bean sold are Bourbon-Madagascar, Mexican, and Tahitian. Vanilla powder, from ground beans, is good for baking. Vanilla extract, pure vanilla extract, and vanilla essence all have natural vanilla flavor, as does natural vanillin. Synthetic or artificial vanillin, sometimes called imitation vanilla, is an inexpensive, inferior substitute. Vanilla flavoring means a combination of pure and imitation vanilla.

vanner [van-nay]   In French, to stir a sauce until cool, ensuring smoothness and preventing a skin from forming.

vapeur [va-peur]   French for steam; to steam is to cook *à la vapeur*.

varietal wine   Wine made from a particular variety of grape, such as Cabernet Sauvignon, Riesling, or Nebbiolo, which in part gives the wine its character. Depending on the location, the wine is not necessarily made entirely from the varietal.

variety meat   Edible meat other than skeletal muscle, especially organs; see OFFAL.

Västerbottenost [VES-ter-BOHT-ten-ohst] A pasteurized cows' milk cheese from Sweden in which the curd is scalded, pressed, and matured for eight months. The rind of this cylindrical cheese is hard, with a wax covering; the paste is firm, with small holes, and the taste is pungent.

vatapa [vah-TAH-pah] A Brazilian paste of ground nuts, dried shrimp, and coconut milk, served as an accompaniment or stuffing for *acarajé* (see AKKRA).

veal The meat of young BEEF; milk-fed veal, lean, and pale pink to white in color, comes from animals under three months of age; grass-fed veal (sometimes called calf or baby beef), rosy pink with cream-colored fat, is under five months of age.

veal Orloff See ORLOFF, VEAL.

veal Oscar See OSCAR, VEAL.

veau [vō] French for VEAL.

vegetable shortening See SHORTENING.

vellutata [vel-loo-TAH-tah] An Italian soup thickened with egg yolk, like French VELOUTÉ.

velouté [veu-loo-tay] "Velvet" white sauce based on a white ROUX with white stock, fish, chicken, veal, or vegetable; this basic classic French sauce is similar to BÉCHAMEL but uses stock rather than milk. A soup *velouté* is a purée combined with *velouté* and finished with cream and egg yolks.

vendange tardive French for late harvest.

venison Deer meat; the word in the past meant any furred game.

vénitienne, à la [ah lah vay-nee-tyen] "Venetian-style" in classic French cuisine: fish fillets poached in white wine, served in a reduction sauce flavored with shallots, tarragon, chervil, and a little vinegar, and garnished with croûtons in the shape of a heart.

ventre [VENH-truh] French for belly, breast.

verbena See LEMON VERBENA.

Verdelho [vayr-DAY-ō] A white-wine grape variety producing a type of MADEIRA, now quite rare, that is fairly dry, not unlike a SERCIAL; the name is from a grape variety. In Australia, Verdelho is a dry white table wine that is soft, fresh, and distinguished.

verdura [vayr-DOO-rah] Italian and Spanish for vegetable; the Italian plural is *verdure*, the Spanish *verduras*. In French, *verdure* means greenery or foliage, not green vegetables.

verjuice   The juice of unripened grapes (or another fruit such as crab apples), that is yeast-free and unfermented. In the Middle Ages sour flavorings such as verjuice and vinegar were used a great deal in cooking, before citrus was commonly available.

Vermentino [vayr-men-TEE-nō]   A white wine grape variety grown in Sardinia, producing a dry, aromatic light wine; also grown in Liguria and Tuscany.

vermicelli [vayr-mee-CHEL-lee]   Very thin pasta—literally "little worms" in Italian—often used for soups and puddings.

vermouth   A white apéritif wine, fortified and flavored with herbs and spices, including WORMWOOD flower (*Wermut* in German, hence its name); French vermouth is dry and pale, Italian vermouth sweet and amber.

Vernaccia [vayr-NAH-chah]   A dry white wine, light and charming, grown from the grape of the same name in Tuscany around San Gemignano.

Véronique, sole   See SOLE VÉRONIQUE.

verte, mayonnaise   See under MAYONNAISE.

vert-pré [vayr-pray]   A French garnish for grilled meats of straw potatoes, watercress, and BEURRE MAÎTRE D'HÔTEL; also, chicken or fish masked with MAYONNAISE VERTE; literally, "green meadow."

vessie [ves-see]   French for pig's bladder; *poularde en vessie* is a famous old dish from Lyons of stuffed chicken poached in a pig's bladder.

Vezzena [vet-SAY-nah]   A hard cows' milk cheese made in the Italian Alps from partially skimmed milk; it is a scalded-curd cheese, aged six months to a year, depending on whether it is to be used as a table or grating cheese.

Vialone [vee-ah-LŌ-nay]   An Italian short-grain rice variety suitable for RISOTTO; shorter than the Arborio and Carnaroli varieties, it can absorb twice its weight in liquid; grown between Lombardy and the Veneto.

viande [vyanhd]   French for meat.

Vichy, carrots à la   See CARROTTES À LA VICHY.

vichyssoise [vee-shee-swahz]   Cream of potato and leek soup, served chilled and garnished with chives; the 1917 creation of Louis Diat, chef of the Ritz-Carlton in New York, and named for his native French city.

Victoria   In French cuisine, lobster sauce with diced lobster and truffles, for fish; also a classic French meat garnish of tomatoes stuffed with duxelles and artichoke quarters sautéed in butter, the pan deglazed with veal stock and port or Madeira; also various cakes and ice cream desserts.

viennoise, à la [ah lah vyen-wahz]   "Viennese style"—coated with egg and bread crumbs, fried, and garnished with sliced lemon, capers, olives, chopped parsley, and hard-boiled egg yolks and whites (separately); a classic French garnish, used especially for veal and chicken cutlets or fish fillets.

Vierlander Poularde [FEER-lahn-der poo-LAAHRD]   German chickens bred in the Vierlande district near Hamburg, known for their fine quality.

vigneron [VEEN-yuh-RONH]   French for winegrower; *à la vigneronne*, "in the style of the vintner's wife," designates a dish with wine, brandy, grapes, or grape leaves.

Villalón [veel-lah-LŌN]   A fresh ewes' milk cheese, originally from the Spanish Old Castile near Portugal; white, even-textured, sharp-flavored, and salty; cylindrical in shape; also called Pata de Mulo.

Villeroi, Villeroy [veel-rwah]   A VELOUTÉ sauce well reduced with truffle and ham essence.

vinaigre [VEE-NAY-gruh]   French for vinegar.

vinaigrette [vee-nay-gret]   A basic French sauce or dressing of oil and vinegar, usually in a proportion of three to one, with salt and pepper and perhaps some chopped herbs or mustard, possibly lemon juice for some of the vinegar.

vindaloo [VIN-dah-loo]   A spicy Indian dish from Goa, highly seasoned with vinegar, chilies, garlic, and curry; usually made with pork or a rich meat; the name is a corruption of *vindalho*, Portuguese for wine-garlic.

vin de pays [vinh deu pay-ee]   French for local wine of a specific region, usually not well known or shipped elsewhere.

vinegar   Literally "sour wine," a weak acetic acid from the secondary fermentation of an alcoholic liquid such as wine, cider, or beer. Vinegar's basic and ancient culinary use is to flavor and preserve food; it also balances rich foods with its tartness; slows oxidation of cut fruits and vegetables; tenderizes meat in marinades; and pickles foods, where at least 5 percent acidity is needed. There are many types of vinegar: cider, malt, rice, wine, balsamic, and so on, many with separate entries.

vine leaves   Young grape leaves blanched and used to wrap small birds and savory mixtures such as *dolmas* (see DOLMASI); the leaves flavor and encase their stuffing and keep it from drying out.

vinho verde [VEE-nyō VAYR-day]   "Green" young wine produced in northern Portugal, often very enjoyable and occasionally sparkling.

vin nature [vinh na-tür]   Unsweetened French wine—a term used loosely.

vin ordinaire [vinh ohr-dee-nayr]   Common French table wine of unknown origin but specific alcoholic content.

Vin Santo [veen SAHN-tō]   Italian "holy wine," a rich, strong, aromatic, usually sweet but occasionally dry wine, from Tuscany and Trentino, also Umbria and the Marches. After harvest, the grapes are spread on mats or hung from rafters to dry for weeks before pressing, then aged in small barrels for several years, bottled, and aged longer. The best, especially from Trentino (where it is called Vino Santo) and Tuscany, can be extremely fine and expensive, with complex, concentrated flavors.

vintage   The grape harvest of a particular year and the wine made from it.

Viognier [vee-ō-nyay]   A white wine grape variety, originally of the Rhône Valley, that produces a full-bodied, complex wine high in alcohol; now grown in California and elsewhere, but tricky to grow and vinify.

violet   A plant whose flowers are crystallized as a dessert garnish; the fresh flowers and leaves can be used in salads.

Virginia ham   See SMITHFIELD HAM.

Viroflay, à la [ah lah vee-rō-flay]   A classic French garnish of spinach balls, quartered artichoke hearts, château potatoes, and veal stock; the term also means with spinach.

vitello [vee-TEL-lō]   Italian for veal; *vitello tonnato* is braised veal marinated in tuna sauce flavored with anchovies and capers with broth and a little cream, or, in the newer version, with mayonnaise; served cold—a classic dish.

vit quay [vit whī]   Vietnamese glazed duck, like Peking duck, but simpler, with a darker glaze, and with more aroma than the Chinese version.

volaille [vō-lī]   French for poultry, fowl, or chicken.

vol-au-vent [vōl-ō-venh]   Puff pastry cases, literally "flight of the wind" in French; either large or small round shells with caps, used to hold savory or sweet fillings; the small shells are sometimes called *bouchées à la reine*.

Volnay [vōl-nay]   A village in the French Côte de Beaune, between Pommard and Meursault, producing excellent and renowned red Burgundy wine; it is soft, delicate, and refined, the best long-lasting.

vongola [VOHN-gō-lah]   Italian for clam.

Vorspeisen [FOR-shpī-zen]   German for appetizers, hors d'oeuvre.

Vosne-Romanée [vōn-rō-ma-nay]   A village and wine-producing commune in the Côte de Nuits of Burgundy with some extraordinarily fine Grand Crus and Premier Crus red wines with exceptional bouquet, balance, and breeding.

Vouvray [voo-vray]   A white wine of the Touraine region of the Loire Valley made from the CHENIN BLANC grape; Vouvray can vary greatly in character from dry, fruity, and tart, to rich, sweet, and golden, also PÉTILLANT and sparkling. For a white wine, it is extraordinarily long-lived.

WATERCRESS

W

Wachau [VAH-khow]   A region in Austria along the Danube producing very good dry white wines, especially Rieslings.

Wachenheim [VAHK-en-hīm]   A wine-producing town in the German Rhein-pfalz; its fine wines are mostly from the SYLVANER and RIESLING grapes.

waffle   A crisp, thin cake made from a pancakelike batter and baked inside a special double-sided and hinged iron, giving a honeycombed surface. Waffles, whose history reaches far back, are eaten with sweet or savory toppings. Belgian waffles have especially large and deep pockets. The French word is *gaufre*.

Wähen [VAY-en]   Large open Swiss tart filled with vegetables, cheese, or fruit.

wakame [wah-kah-mee]   Japanese seaweed of fine flavor and texture, usually bought in dried form for soups or fresh for salads.

Waldmeister [VAHLT-mīs-ter]   German for WOODRUFF.

Waldorf salad   Chopped apples, celery, and walnuts in mayonnaise; created by Oscar Tschirky of the Waldorf-Astoria in New York before the turn of the twentieth century, although the walnuts were added later.

Walewska, à la [ah lah vah-LEF-skah]   Garnished with sliced langoustines and truffles and glazed with Mornay sauce with langoustine butter; a classic French sauce named after the son of Napoléon's Polish mistress.

walleye, walleyed pike   Actually a member of the PERCH family, this excellent freshwater fish, with firm, white, fine-textured flesh, lives in large North American lakes.

walliser [VAL-is-er]   A generic Swiss term for RACLETTE cheese.

Walnuss [VAHL-noos]   German for walnut.

walnut   A tree indigenous to Asia, Europe, and North America, whose nuts have been favored since ancient times. The nut meats are eaten plain or pickled, or are used in sweet and savory dishes; their oil is much esteemed for its distinctive flavor; their husks are even made into a liqueur called *brou*. In several European languages, the word for walnut is also the generic name for nut, showing its dominance. *

warqa [WAHR-kah]   In Moroccan cuisine, a tissue-thin pastry sheet used in BASTILLA, made like the Chinese spring-roll sheet of dough; PHYLLO or STRUDEL are similar and can be substituted.

wasabi [wah-sah-bee]   A plant, often called Japanese horseradish though botanically unrelated, whose root is used as a condiment for raw fish dishes; it comes fresh, powdered, and as a paste, and is very hot in flavor and green in color.

washed-rind cheese   A cheese whose rind is washed with water, brine, beer, wine, or another liquid during ripening. The purpose is to prevent the growth of certain bacterial cultures but encourage that of others and to keep the cheese from drying out.

Washington, à la   A classic French garnish of corn with cream sauce.

wassail [WAH-sul, wah-SAYL]   A spiced punch, traditionally some kind of beer, drunk on festive occasions, very often Christmas; the word, of Scandinavian derivation, means "to your health."

water chestnut   The fruit of a long-stemmed water plant that grows inside irregularly shaped thorns beneath the floating leaves. The starchy fruit has a crisp texture and delicate taste not unlike that of boiled chestnuts and can be used in many ways. It grows all over the world but is little appreciated outside Asia.

watercress   A plant growing in shallow streams, whose crisp, deep green leaves are used fresh as an herb, salad green, and garnish, also cooked in soups, sauces, and savory dishes; a member of the mustard family, its flavor is lightly peppery.

water ice   A frozen dessert of syrup and fruit juice or purée, usually with a little lemon juice or other flavoring such as coffee or liqueur; the ice is frozen smooth but without the addition of egg white, as in a sherbet. See also GRANITA, SHERBET, and SPUMA.

watermelon   A large melon, with green skin and red flesh, 92 percent water, an oasis on a hot summer day; it belongs to a different genus than the cantaloupe, a distant relative. The watermelon, native to Africa, came to the United States with the slave trade; it likes a hot, dry climate and sandy soil. The melon's shape can be small and round or large and oval, weighing anywhere from 5 to 40 pounds or many times more for giants; small ones may be handy, but the larger have a higher proportion of edible flesh. Varieties other than the familiar red have white or yellow flesh; new "seedless" varieties have barely noticeable seeds.

waterzooï   [VAH-ter-zoy]   A traditional Flemish stew, probably originating in Ghent (*à la gantoise*), made with either fish or chicken. The fish version probably came first, with perch, eel, carp, pike, and possibly other varieties of fish, cooked in white wine with herbs; in the other version, chicken is poached in stock with onions, leeks, celery, and carrots, flavored with lemon juice, and finished with egg yolks and cream.

weakfish   Also known as seatrout (but not to be confused with sea trout), this member of the drum family is no trout at all—nor is it weak; this marine fish has lean, sweet, delicate flesh that is versatile in cooking.

Wehlen   [VAY-len]   A small town on the Mosel River whose wines have become the best of the Mittel-Mosel; Sonnenuhr—a sundial painted on a slate outcropping in the steep vineyard slope—is the name given to the best of the fine wines.

Weinbeere   [VĪN-bayr-eh]   German for grape; *Weintraube* means a bunch of grapes.

Weinberg   [VĪN-bayrg]   German for vineyard.

Weissbier   [VĪS-beer]   A light frothy summer beer ("white beer") from Bavaria, served with a slice of lemon.

Weisswurst   [VĪS-voorst]   A small delicate German sausage stuffed with veal, flavored with wine and parsley; a specialty of Munich, it is eaten for breakfast with sweet mustard.

Weizen   [VĪTS-en]   German for WHEAT.

Wellington, beef   See BEEF WELLINGTON.

Welsh rarebit, rabbit [RAYR-bit, RAB-it]   A British SAVORY of Cheddar-type cheese melted with beer or milk and spicy seasonings, poured over toast, and briefly grilled; the dish is Welsh in origin. The rabbit allusion is an obscure joke.

Wensleydale   An English uncooked, pressed cows' milk cheese made in both white and blue styles. The white, made in eight-pound flat discs and aged three to four weeks, is white, flaky, moist, and mellow, properly not yellow or sour. The blue, aged four to six months, is similar to Stilton, but less veined and smoother, sweeter, and nuttier.

Westfälische Schinken [vest-FAY-lish-eh SHINK-en]   Westphalian ham made from acorn-fed pigs, believed by many to be a German rival to PROSCIUTTO, BAYONNE, and SMITHFIELD hams in quality. The meat is lightly smoked, cured, but not cooked, and served in paper-thin slices with pumpernickel bread.

Westphalian ham   See WESTFÄLISCHE SCHINKEN.

wheat   A grain of great importance because of its ability, when combined with yeast and water, to form leavened bread; the GLUTEN thus developed stretches to contain the expanding air bubbles. The higher the proportion of protein to starch in the kernel, the more gluten. There are many types of wheat flour, subject to climate and season as well as variety, but in general soft spring wheat (low in gluten) is good for pastry, cakes, pies, biscuits, and cookies. Hard winter wheat (high in gluten) is good for yeast breads. Durum SEMOLINA (also high in gluten) is good for pasta.

whelk   A gastropod mollusk similar to the PERIWINKLE, appreciated in Europe, especially in Italy as *scungilli*.

whey   The watery liquid that, after coagulation, separates from the curds in the cheesemaking process; whey contains albumin, lactose, and other nutrients and can be used to make RICOTTA or GJETOST.

whiskey   An alcoholic liquor distilled from the fermented mash of grains such as barley, corn, or rye. The alcoholic content is usually 43 to 50 percent, with a minimum of 40 percent (80 proof). The characteristics of whiskey are determined by factors such as the type of grain, yeast, proof, water, barrel, blending, method of distillation, and addition of caramel. The Scottish and Canadian spelling is whisky. See also BOURBON and, for single-malt whisky, SCOTCH WHISKY.

whitebait   Herring and sprat fry, plentiful in the Thames and Garonne Rivers and along the North Sea coast; the tiny fish are usually dipped in batter and deep-fried without being cleaned.

white butter sauce   See BEURRE BLANC.

white chocolate   A mixture of cocoa butter, milk solids, sugar, and perhaps vanilla or another flavoring; because it contains no chocolate liquor, it is technically not chocolate. See also CHOCOLATE.

whitefish   A small freshwater fish, mainly North American, related to TROUT and SALMON, with delicate white meat that tastes best in winter and is often smoked (see CISCO); the roe is used as a CAVIAR substitute.

white sauce   BÉCHAMEL or VELOUTÉ sauce, both made from ROUX, or any of their descendants.

whortleberry   See BILBERRY.

Wiener Schnitzel   [VEE-ner SHNIT-sel]   Literally "Viennese cutlet" in German, veal scallops coated with layers of flour, beaten egg, and bread crumbs, then fried in butter or lard and served without a sauce, usually with a slice of lemon; sometimes spelled as one word.

Wienerwurst   [VEE-ner-voorst]   German for FRANKFURTER sausage.

Wild   [vilt]   German for GAME.

wild boar   The meat of undomesticated male pig (see PORK), eaten in medieval times at ritual feasts; like other game, it is often prepared with acid fruits or in a marinade. The French word for young boar is marcassin, the mature animal sanglier.

Wildgeflügel   [VILT-geh-flü-gel]   German for feathered game.

wild leek   See RAMP.

wild rice   A grass native to the Great Lakes region of North America and a distant cousin of common RICE; now planted and harvested commercially rather than gathered in canoes and grown in the Pacific Northwest, but still expensive. A staple Indian food due to its high protein and carbohydrate value, wild rice is fermented, parched, and hulled before cooking.

Wiltingen   [VIL-ting-en]   A famous town on the Saar River near Trier, Germany, whose steep vineyards planted with RIESLING grapes produce superb wines in good years.

Windbeutel   [VIND-boy-tel]   German for cream puff, literally "wind bag."

winkle   See PERIWINKLE.

wintergreen   A creeping evergreen, native to the American Northeast, with deep green, round leaves and red berries; the aromatic leaves are used as a flavoring in the form of wintergreen extract or flavoring (but *not* wintergreen oil, which is intended for nonculinary uses).

winter melon   A melon with hard, smooth, or furrowed skin and white to pale green or orange flesh. Lacking the perfumed aroma and separation layer in the stem of the MUSKMELON, the winter melon can be harvested into frost and allowed to travel as long as a month on the way to market. Honeydew, Casaba, Cranshaw (or Crenshaw), Santa Claus, and Canary melons fall into this category.

Wirsing   [VEER-sing]   German for savoy cabbage.

witloof   See BELGIAN ENDIVE.

wok   A round-bottomed metal cooking pan, traditionally iron, with sloping sides that provide the large cooking surface suitable for most Chinese methods of cooking: stir-frying, deep-frying, steaming, smoking, and (with the top on) braising and poaching. Special ring trivets or flat-bottomed woks can adapt the utensil to Western electric stoves.

wonton   See HÚN DÙN.

wood ear   See YÚN ĔR.

woodruff   A perennial herb found in forests and sometimes used as a groundcover in shady gardens; its leaves, dried or fresh, are used to flavor teas, drinks, and punches, while its delicate flowers, which bloom in May, impart their scent to MAY WINE.

woon sen   Thai for cellophane noodles.

Worcestershire sauce   [WUHS-ter-sher]   A highly seasoned commercial sauce, made originally by Lea & Perrins of Worcester, England, for 160 years and used widely as a savory condiment; the recipe, of Indian origin, includes soy sauce, vinegar, molasses, anchovies, onion, chilies and other spices, and lime and tamarind juices; the sauce is fermented and cured before bottling.

wormwood   An herb once used as a medicine against intestinal worms, hence its name; the toxic leaf gives ABSINTHE its potency and anise flavor, while the more delicate flower imparts its taste (and its name) to VERMOUTH.

wor tip   See GŪO TIĒ.

wot   Stew in Ethiopian cooking; *yedoro wot* is a spicy minced chicken and onion stew; *yemiser wot,* a spicy lentil stew seasoned with BERBERE; *atakilt wot,* a vegetable stew, also seasoned with *berbere.*

Wurst [voorst]   German for sausage; a *Würstchen* is a little sausage.

Würz [vürts]   German for spice or seasoning; *Würzfleisch* is a special beef stew with sour cream sauce, usually accompanied by dumplings or potatoes.

wŭ xiāng fĕn [oo shyahng fen]   Chinese five-spice powder, now often prepackaged, a medicinal preparation with the number five possessing symbolic potency for health. The variable mixture may contain star anise, fennel seeds, Sichuan peppercorns, clove, cinnamon, or nutmeg, and is used for roasted meat and poultry, especially in southern China and Vietnam; the Cantonese term is *mu hong fun* [moo hahng fahn].

X É R È S

X

xató [shah-TŌ]   A Spanish winter salad from Catalonia of BELGIAN ENDIVE with red chili peppers, almonds, garlic, oil, and vinegar.

xcatic [shah-TEEK]   A long yellow-green chili pepper from Mexico.

xérès [zayr-REZ]   French for sherry.

xiā [shah]   Chinese for shrimp.

xiāng cài [shahng tsī]   Chinese for coriander; the Cantonese is *yim sai*.

xiāng chǎng   See LÀ CHĂNG.

xián yā dàn [shyen yah dahn]   A Chinese delicacy of duck eggs immersed in brine for 30 days, when fermentation gives them a unique texture and taste; the shells turn bluish, the whites opaque, the yolks luminous gold that is accentuated in moon cakes; the Cantonese term is *ham don* [hahm dahn].

xiè [sheh]   Chinese for crab.

ximxim de galinha [SHEEM-sheem day gah-LEE-nyah]   Chicken in a marinade of dried shrimp, chili peppers, ginger, and cashews; a classic dish in the African-Brazilian tradition.

xìn rén dòu fù [sheen ren dō foo]   Almond bean curd, made from jellied almond extract and condensed milk to resemble tofu, served in a fruit salad with syrup; the Cantonese is *hun yem dau fu* [hahn yahm dow foo].

x-ni-pec [shne-PEEK]   A Yucatecan version of *salsa mexicana cruda* (see under SALSA) with juice of the sour orange.

xoconostle [shō-kō-nōst-lay]   Mexican for green PRICKLY PEAR.

xoi vo [soy vah]   Yellow mung beans and coconut rice, a popular breakfast or snack food in Vietnam.

xun [shün]   Smoking, in Chinese cooking; the Cantonese is *yin*.

Y U L E   L O G

Y

yā [yah]   Chinese for duck.

yakhni [YAK-nee]   Indian meat or poultry stock.

yaki [yah-kee]   In Japanese, to grill or broil; *yakimono* means grilled food; *yak-itori* is chicken pieces and vegetables skewered, marinated in a spicy sauce, and grilled.

yam   A tuberous vegetable of African origin whose high starch content has enabled it to serve as a valuable food source for millennia, especially in tropical and subtropical regions. It has white or yellow flesh and brown skin and is often confused with the SWEET POTATO, especially in the United States, where a variety of sweet potato is mistakenly called yam.

yam [yahm]   Thai for salad; *yam gung* is shrimp salad, sharp with citrus and chilies.

yaourt, yahourt [yah-OOR]   French for YOGURT.

yard-long beans   See CHINESE BEANS.

yarrow   A pungent herb, also called *milfoil*, whose fine lacy leaves are used for *tisane*.

yasai [yah-sī]   Japanese for vegetables.

yassa [YAH-sah] A Senegalese marinade of lemon, chili peppers, and onion, for chicken with rice.

yautia See MALANGA.

yeast A microscopic, naturally occurring fungus that induces fermentation, thus initiating the chemical process that makes bread, cheese, wine, and beer. The many types of yeast, mainly fresh, dry, and brewer's, convert starch into gas and alcohol. BAKING POWDER is a comparatively recent chemical alternative for leavening bread.

yedoro wot See WOT.

yemas de San Leandro [YAY-mahth day THAHN lay-AHN-drō] Egg-yolk threads poured into hot syrup and twisted into sweets—a Spanish confection of Moorish origin made by the nuns of San Leandro in Seville.

yemiser wot See WOT.

yemitas de mi bisabuela [YAY-mee-tahs day mee BEE-sah-BWAY-lah] A Mexican sweet of egg yolks, sherry, and syrup formed into balls and rolled in cinnamon sugar.

yèn wō [yen woh] The nest of cliff-dwelling swallows, nutritious and considered a great delicacy in Chinese cuisine. The dried nests, either white or black, are soaked in water to restore their gelatinous texture and used to garnish soups at special occasions; very expensive, especially the white ones, so reserved for banquets. The Cantonese is *yin wor*.

yerba buena Mexican wild spearmint.

yeun bau See YUÈ BÌNG.

yim sai [yim tsī] Cantonese for coriander.

yin wor See YÈN WŌ.

yogurt, yoghurt, yoghourt Milk that has been fermented with a lactic culture, turning it slightly acid and thickening its texture. Although some health claims have been exaggerated, eating yogurt with active cultures is healthful, and it is useful for its cooking and keeping properties. Yogurt originated in the Balkans, where it is still much used in cooking.

York ham A fine English ham, traditionally from the large White Yorkshire pig, cured with dry salt and brown sugar, lightly smoked with oak (supposedly from that used in building the York Minster), and aged for several months before being boiled; this mild ham is eaten hot or cold.

Yorkshire pudding A British savory pudding made from a batter of milk, eggs, and flour, originally baked under a roast beef on an open spit or rack to catch the drippings, puffing up in the process; the pudding is cut into squares for serving. Yorkshire sauce is port wine sauce with red currant jelly, garnished with julienne of orange zest—a classic sauce.

yuca [YOO-kah, *not* YUK-ah] Spanish for yucca; MANIOC. Also, a plant of the agave family with swordlike green leaves and tall white flowers, often confused with the edible yucca of the manioc family.

yú chì [ü cheu] Shark's fin; a nutritious delicacy in Chinese cuisine that, after considerable soaking and preparation, is savored for its gelatinous texture; an expensive specialty reserved for banquets.

yuè bìng [ü-eh bing] Chinese moon cakes, made with sweet or savory fillings; the sweet filling can include dried fruits and nuts; for the moon festival, salty duck egg yolks that resemble harvest moons can be the centers of the sweet lotus nut paste filling. The Cantonese is *yeun bau* [yum bow].

yufka [YOOF-kah] In Turkish cooking, a thin circle of bread dough stretched and used for wrapping much like PHYLLO, but thicker.

Yukon gold A new variety of boiling potato with small size, thin skin, yellow color, and rich (but not buttery) flavor.

yule log See BÛCHE DE NOËL.

yún ěr [yoon er] An irregularly shaped fungus that grows on logs, used in Chinese cooking for its interesting texture; yellow, brown, or black on one side and white on the other, the dried fungus expands greatly with soaking before cooking; also called tree ear, wood ear, and other names.

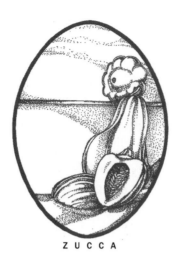

Z U C C A

Z

za'atar [ZAH-tahr]   A thymelike herb that grows in several varieties in the eastern Mediterranean and North Africa, including one rarely imported to the United States that tastes like a combination of oregano, marjoram, and thyme. Confusingly, the word also means a spice blend of the herb with SUMAC and SESAME seeds; this is often eaten for breakfast in the Middle East sprinkled on hot flatbread brushed with olive oil.

zabaglione [zah-bī-YŌ-nay]   An Italian dessert custard in which egg yolks, flavored with MARSALA and sugar, are beaten over simmering water until they foam up into a frothy mass; also spelled *zabaione*; the French version is *sabayon*.

zafferone [zahf-fayr-Ō-nay]   Italian for saffron.

zakuski [zah-KOOS-kee]   Russian hors d'oeuvre starting with caviar and running the whole gamut; traditionally accompanied by vodka. However modest or grand the circumstances, the main meal of the day and any party always begin with *zakuski*, a tradition that goes back a thousand years to Scandinavian influence.

zampone [zahm-PŌ-nay]   A highly seasoned Italian pork sausage encased in the skin of a pig's foot; from Modena.

zanahoria [thah-nah-HOR-yah, sah-nah-HOR-yah]   Spanish for carrot.

zapallo [sah-PAL-lō]   A large deep yellow winter squash used in South American cooking, similar to pumpkin or butternut.

zarda [ZAHR-dah]   A sweet rice PILAO flavored with saffron and other spices, nuts, and raisins, in Indian cooking.

zarzamora [thahr-thah-MOR-ah]   Spanish for blackberry.

zarzuela [thahr-THWAY-lah]   A Spanish seafood stew, varying widely, in a piquant sauce flavored with wine or liqueur, all arranged spectacularly; the word means operetta and implies that the dish is a fantastic mixture.

Zeltingen [TSEL-ting-en]   A wine-producing town in the central Mosel Valley producing a large quantity of fine wine, all estate-bottled Riesling.

zemino [zeh-MEE-nō]   A Middle Eastern sauce of anchovies and garlic with vinegar, sometimes sweetened with sugar, for fish; Sephardic in origin.

zènzero [ZEN-zay-rō]   Italian for ginger.

zest   The outer, colored skin of citrus fruits where the essential oils are concentrated. The French word is *zeste*, not to be confused with *ziste*, the bitter white pith beneath.

zeytin [ZAY-tin]   Turkish for olives; olive oil is *zeytinyaği*. The Arab word used in much of the Middle East is *zeitoun*.

zhà [jah]   Deep-frying, in Chinese cooking; the Cantonese is *jah.*

zhà jiàng miàn [chah jyahng mee-en]   In Chinese cooking, cold spicy egg noodles with diced or ground pork, tofu, sweet bean sauce, and shredded vegetables; from Beijing and the north.

zhēng [juhng]   Steaming, in Chinese cooking; the Cantonese is *jing* [jeen].

zhī má yóu [zeu mah yō]   Chinese sesame oil, which is darker in color and stronger in flavor than Western sesame oil; used more for seasoning sauces than for frying.

zhōu [zho]   *Congee*, Chinese rice porridge, cooked moist and soupy and served hot, topped at table with pickled vegetables, dried fish, roasted nuts, and the like; a common breakfast or snack food, also given to convalescents; also *xī fàn*; in Cantonese, *jook* or *juk* [jōk].

Zigeuner Art [tsi-GOY-ner art]   German for gypsy style; *Zigeunerspies*, an Austrian specialty, is skewered cubes of meat, peppers, and onions grilled over an open fire.

zik de venado [SEEK day veh-NAH-dō]   Venison cooked in a barbecue pit (PIB), then shredded and served with onions, sour oranges, hot chili peppers, and cilantro; from the Yucatán of Mexico.

Zinfandel [ZIN-fahn-del]   A red-wine grape variety of uncertain origin but widely planted in California; its style ranges considerably from light and fruity to deep, strong, berry-flavored, and intense; also vinified in a blush style that is pale indeed.

zingara, à la [ah lah zinh-GAHR-ah]   Gypsy style—a classic French garnish of julienne of ham, tongue, mushrooms, and truffles in a demi-glace flavored with tomato purée, Madeira, and tarragon essence; *zingara* is the Italian word for gypsy woman.

ziti [ZEE-tee]   Large tube pasta cut into segments, in Italian cooking.

Zitrone [tsee-TRŌ-nay]   German for lemon.

zucca [ZOO-kah]   Italian for squash, pumpkin; zucchini means "little squashes."

zùcchero [ZOO-kayr-ō]   Italian for sugar.

zuccotto [zoo-KOHT-tō]   A dome-shaped Italian dessert of cake moistened with liqueur and filled with sweetened whipped cream, chocolate, and nuts; originally from Florence, it supposedly resembles the top of the Duomo: the brown and white segments converge at the top to form a "skullcap."

Zucker [TSOO-ker]   German for sugar; *Zuckerrübe* means sugar beet.

Zunge [TSUNG-eh]   German for tongue.

zuǒ gōng jī   See GENERAL TSO'S CHICKEN.

zuppa [ZOOP-pah]   Italian for soup.

zuppa inglese [ZOOP-pah een-GLAY-say]   Literally "English soup," this is a rich Italian dessert of rum-soaked sponge cake layered with custard and cream—like a trifle.

Zwetschge [TSVECH-geh]   Austrian for damson plum; see also POWIDL.

zwieback   Bread slices baked again (from German "twice baked," like a biscuit); rusks.

Zwiebel [TSVEE-bel]   German for onion; *Zwiebelkuche* is an onion tart from Hesse, made with bacon and cream, perhaps flavored with caraway seeds—not unlike a QUICHE lorraine; *Zwiebelgrün* is a scallion.

SELECTED BIBLIOGRAPHY

Alford, Jeffrey, and Naomi Duguid. *Seductions of Rice*. New York: Artisan, 1998.

Algar, Ayla. *Classical Turkish Cooking*. New York: HarperCollins, 1991.

Anderson, E. N. *The Food of China*. New Haven and London: Yale Univ. Press, 1988.

Arndt, Alice. *Seasoning Savvy: How to Cook with Herbs, Spices, and Other Flavorings*. Haworth Herbal Press: New York, 1999.

Anderson, Jean. *The Food of Portugal*. Rev. ed. New York: Hearst, 1994.

———, and Hedy Würz. *The New German Cookbook*. New York: HarperCollins, 1993.

Andrews, Jean. *Peppers: The Domesticated Capsicums*. Austin: Univ. of Texas Press, 1995.

Androuet, Pierre. *Guide to Cheeses*. Rev. English ed. Nuffield, Henley-on-Thames, England: Aidan Ellis, 1993.

Ayto, John. *A Gourmet's Guide: Food and Drink from A to Z*. Oxford and New York: Oxford Univ. Press, 1994.

Barrett, Judith. *Risotto Risotti*. New York: Macmillan, 1996.

Battistotti, Bruno; Vittorio Bottazzi; Antonio Piccinardi; and Giancarlo Volpati. *Cheese: A Guide to the World of Cheese and Cheesemaking*. New York: Facts on File, 1984.

Bianchini, F., and F. Corbetta. *The Complete Book of Fruits and Vegetables*. New York: Crown, 1976.

Bickel, Walter, ed. *Hering's Dictionary of Classical and Modern Cookery*. London, Dublin, and Coulsdon: Virtue, 1981.

Bloom, Carole. *The International Dictionary of Desserts, Pastries, and Confections*. New York: Hearst, 1995.

Brennan, Jennifer. *The Original Thai Cookbook*. New York: Perigee, 1981.

Browning, Frank. *Apples*. New York: North Point Press, 1998.

Bugialli, Giuliano. *Guiliano Bugialli's Classic Techniques of Italian Cooking*. New York: Simon and Schuster, 1989.

Burros, Marian. "What the Label Can Say, and What It Can't." *The New York Times*, October 16, 2002.

Casas, Penelope. *The Foods and Wines of Spain*. New York: Knopf, 1982.

Chantiles, Vilma Liacouras. *The Food of Greece*. New York: Simon and Schuster, 1992.

Child, Julia. *The Way to Cook*. New York: Knopf, 1989.

Clark, Oz. *Oz Clarke's Pocket Wine Guide*: 2002. New York: Harcourt, 2002.

Cost, Bruce. *Asian Ingredients*. New York: HarperCollins, 2000.

Crewe, Quentin. *The Simon and Schuster International Pocket Food Guide*. New York: Simon and Schuster, 1980.

David, Elizabeth. *French Provincial Cooking*. Harmondsworth, Middlesex, England: Viking Penguin, 1999.

———. *Italian Food*. Harmondsworth, Middlesex, England: Viking Penguin, 1999.

———. *English Bread and Yeast Cookery*. New American ed. Newton, Massachusetts: Biscuit Books, 1994.

Davidson, Alan. *Mediterranean Seafood: A Comprehensive Guide with Recipes*. 3rd ed. Berkeley: Ten Speed Press, 2002.

———. *The Oxford Companion to Food*. Oxford, U.K.: Oxford University Press, 1999.

———, and Charlotte Knox. *Fruit: A Connoisseur's Guide and Cookbook*. London: Mitchell Beazley, 1991.

———. *North Atlantic Seafood*. New York: Viking Penguin, 1980.

———. *Seafood: A Connoisseur's Guide and Cookbook*. New York: Simon and Schuster, 1989.

Del Conte, Anna. *Gastronomy of Italy*. New York, London, Toronto, Sidney, Tokyo: Prentice Hall, 1987.

Duong, Binh, and Marcia Kiesel. *Simple Art of Vietnamese Cooking*. New York: Prentice Hall, 1991.

FitzGibbon, Theodora. *The Food of the Western World*. New York: Quadrangle, 1976.

Grigson, Jane. *Charcuterie and French Pork Cookery*. New York: HarperCollins, 1991.

———, and Charlotte Knox. *Exotic Fruits and Vegetables*. New York: Henry Holt, 1986.

———. *Jane Grigson's Fruit Book*. New York; Atheneum, 1982.

———. *Jane Grigson's Vegetable Book*. Harmondsworth, England: Penguin, 1978.

Grigson, Sophie. *Gourmet Ingredients*. New York: Van Nostrand Reinhold, 1991.

Guillermard, Colette. *Les Mots de la cuisine et de la table*. Paris: Belin, 1990.

Hafner, Dorinda. *A Taste of Africa*. Berkeley, California: Ten Speed Press, 1993.

Harris, Jessica B. *Iron Pots and Wooden Spoons*. New York: Ballantine, 1989.

———. *The Welcome Table*. New York: Simon and Schuster, 1995.

Hazan, Marcella. *Essentials of Classic Italian Cooking*. New York: Knopf, 1995.

Herbst, Sharon Tyler. *The New Food Lover's Companion*. 3rd ed. Hauppauge, New York: Barron's, 2001.

Hess, Karen. *The Carolina Rice Kitchen: The African Connection*. Columbia: Univ. of South Carolina Press, 1992.

Jaffrey, Madhur. *World-of-the East Vegetarian Cooking*. New York: Knopf, 1981.

Jenkins, Steve. *Cheese Primer*. New York: Workman, 1996.

Johnson, Hugh. *Hugh Johnson's Pocket Encyclopedia of Wine*. New York: Simon and Schuster, 2001.

———. *Hugh Johnson's Modern Encyclopedia of Wine*. 4th ed. New York: Simon and Schuster, 1998.

Kennedy, Diana. *The Cuisines of Mexico*. Rev. ed. New York: HarperCollins, 1989.

———. *Mexican Regional Cooking*, New York: Harper Perennial, 1990.

Kochilas, Diane. *The Glorious Foods of Greece*. New York: William Morrow, 2001.

Kummer, Corby. *The Joy of Coffee*. Boston: Houghton Mifflin, 1997.

Lang, Jennifer H., ed. *Larousse Gastronomique: The New American Edition of the World's Greatest Culinary Encyclopedia*. New York: Crown, 1988.

Leach, Helen. "Rehabilitating the 'Stinking Herbe': A Case Study of Culinary Prejudice." *Gastronomica: The Journal of Food and Culture*. Berkeley: University of California Press, Spring 2001.

Levy, Faye. *Faye Levy's International Jewish Cookbook*. New York: Warner 1991.

Lo, Eileen Yin-Fei. *The Chinese Kitchen*. New York: William Morrow, 1999.

Mallos, Tess. *The Complete Middle East Cookbook*. Boston, Rutland, Vermont, and Tokyo: Charles E. Tuttle, 1993.

Manjón, Maite. *The Gastronomy of Spain and Portugal*. New York: Prentice Hall, 1990.

Mariani, John F. *The Dictionary of American Food and Drink*. Rev. ed. New York: William Morrow, 1994.

Marks, Copeland. *The Great Book of Couscous*. New York: Donald I. Fine, 1994.

———. *The Korean Kitchen*. San Francisco: Chronicle, 1993.

Martinez, Zarela. *Food from My Heart*. New York: Macmillan, 1992.

McClane, A. J. *The Encyclopedia of Fish Cookery*. New York: Henry Holt, 1977.

McGee, Harold. *On Food and Cooking: The Science and Lore of the Kitchen*. New York: Scribner's, 1984.

O'Higgins, Maria Josefa Lluriá de. *A Taste of Old Cuba*. New York: HarperCollins, 1994.

Ortiz, Elisabeth Lambert. *The Encyclopedia of Herbs, Spices, and Flavorings*. New York: Dorling Kindersley, 1992.

Owen, Sri. *Indonesian Food and Cookery*. London: Prospect Books, 1986.

Passmore, Jacki. *The Encyclopedia of Asian Food and Cooking*. New York: Hearst, 1991.

Rance, Patrick. *The French Cheese Book*. London: Macmillan, 1989.

———. *The Great British Cheese Book*, London: Macmillan, 1982.

Randelman, Mary Urrutia, and Joan Schwartz. *Memories of a Cuban Kitchen*. New York: Macmillan, 1992.

Reynaldo, Alejandro. *The Philippine Cookbook*. New York: Coward-McCann, 1982.

Riely, Elizabeth. *A Feast of Fruits*. New York: Macmillan, 1993.

Robinson, Jancis, ed. *The Oxford Companion to Wine*. 2nd ed. Oxford and New York: Oxford Univ. Press, 1999.

Robinson, Jancis. *Vines, Grapes and Wines*. New York: Knopf, 2001.

Rojas-Lombardi, Felipe. *The Art of South American Cooking*. New York: HarperCollins, 1991.

Rombauer, Irma, Marion Rombauer Becker, and Ethan Becker. *Joy of Cooking*. New York: Scribner, 1997.

Root, Waverly. *Food*. New York: Simon and Schuster, 1980.

Sahni, Julie. *Classic Indian Cooking*. New York: William Morrow, 1980.

Saulnier, Louis. *Le Repertoire de la Cuisine*. Woodbury, New York: Barron's, 1976.

Schneider, Elizabeth. *Uncommon Fruits and Vegetables*. New York: Harper and Row, 1986.

———. *Vegetables from Amaranth to Zucchini: The Essential Reference*. New York: William Morrow, 2001.

Sharman, Fay and Klaus Boehm. *The Taste of France: A Dictionary of French Food and Wine*. Boston: Houghton Mifflin, 1982.

Simon, André L. *A Concise Encyclopedia of Gastronomy*. Woodstock, New York: Overlook, 1981.

————, and Robin Howe. *Dictionary of Gastronomy*. 2nd ed. Woodstock, New York: Overlook, 1979.

Simonds, Nina. *Classic Chinese Cuisine*. Rev. ed. Boston: Houghton Mifflin, 1999.

Sinclair, Charles G. *International Dictionary of Food and Cooking*. Teddington, Middlesex, U.K.: Peter Collins, 1998.

Solomon, Charmaine. *The Complete Asian Cookbook*. Rutland, Vermont, Boston, and Tokyo: Charles E. Tuttle, 1992.

Stobart, Tom. *The Cook's Encyclopedia*. New York: Harper and Row, 1980.

————, *Herbs, Spices and Flavourings*. New York: Viking Penguin, 1987.

Tropp, Barbara. *The Modern Art of Chinese Cooking*. New York, William Morrow, 1982.

Tsuji, Shizuo. *Japanese Cooking: A Simple Art*. Tokyo, New York and San Francisco: Kodansha International, 1980.

Wheaton, Barbara Ketcham. *Savoring the Past: The French Kitchen and Table from 1300 to 1789*. New York: Simon and Schuster, 1996.

Willan, Anne. *La Varenne Pratique*. New York: Crown, 1989.

Wolfert, Paula. *Mediterranean Cooking*. 2nd rev. ed. New York: HarperCollins, 1999.

————. *The Cooking of the Eastern Mediterranean*. New York: HarperCollins, 1994.

————, *Couscous and Other Good Food from Morocco*. New York: Harper and Row, 1987.

WEIGHTS AND MEASURES CONVERSIONS*

Weight Measures Conversions

U.S.	Metric
¼ ounce	8 grams
½ ounce	15 grams
1 ounce	30 grams
4 ounces	115 grams
8 ounces *(½ pound)*	225 grams
16 ounces *(1 pound)*	450 grams
32 ounces *(2 pounds)*	900 grams
40 ounces *(2½ pounds)*	1 kilogram

Volume Measures Conversions

U.S.	Metric
1 teaspoon	5 milliliters
1 tablespoon	15 milliliters
1 fluid ounce *(2 tablespoons)*	30 milliliters
2 fluid ounces *(¼ cup)*	60 milliliters
8 fluid ounces *(1 cup)*	240 milliliters
16 fluid ounces *(1 pint)*	480 milliliters
32 fluid ounces *(1 quart)*	950 milliliters *(.95 liter)*
128 fluid ounces *(1 gallon)*	3.75 liters

*metric amounts are nearest equivalents

Temperature Conversions

Degrees Fahrenheit (°F.)	Degrees Celcius (°C.)
32	0
40	4
140	60
150	65
160	70
170	75
212	100
275	135
300	150
325	165
350	175
375	190
400	205
425	220
450	230
475	245
500	260

Weights and Measures Equivalencies

dash	less than ⅛ teaspoon
3 teaspoons	1 tablespoon *(½ fluid ounce)*
2 tablespoons	⅛ cup *(1 fluid ounce)*
4 tablespoons	¼ cup *(2 fluid ounces)*
5⅓ tablespoons	⅓ cup *(2⅔ fluid ounces)*
8 tablespoons	½ cup *(4 fluid ounces)*
10⅔ tablespoons	⅔ cup *(5⅓ fluid ounces)*
12 tablespoons	¾ cup *(6 fluid ounces)*
14 tablespoons	⅞ cup *(7 fluid ounces)*
16 tablespoons	1 cup *(8 fluid ounces)*
1 jigger	1½ ounces *(3 tablespoons)*
1 gill	½ cup
1 cup	8 fluid ounces *(240 milliliters)*
2 cups	1 pint *(480 milliliters)*
2 pints	1 quart *(approximately 1 liter)*
4 quarts	1 gallon *(3.75 liters)*
8 quarts	1 peck
4 pecks	1 bushel
1 ounce	28.35 grams *(rounded to 30)*
16 ounces	1 pound *(453.59 grams rounded to 450)*
1 kilogram	2.2 pounds

Liquid Standards

1 milliliter = 0.035 fluid ounces
1 fluid ounce = 30 milliliters
1 US pint = 16 fluid ounces
1 UK pint = 20 fluid ounces
500 milliliters = 16 fluid ounces = 2 cups
1 liter = 1 quart

Solid Weight Standards

1 gram = 0.35 ounces
1 ounce = 30 grams

Length Conversions

1 centimeter = 0.394 inch
1 inch = 2.54 centimeters